Information Exchange Between Competitors in EU Competition Law

International Competition Law Series

VOLUME 88

Editor

In its series editor, Alastair Sutton, Kluwer is fortunate to engage and benefit from the experience and expertise of one of the world's outstanding authorities on European Union and international economic law.

Introduction

In their efforts to regulate competition in an increasingly complex business environment, competition authorities face a daunting task. The European Commission and Courts, as well as national courts and legislatures, policymakers, and regulators, are constantly proposing, enacting, reviewing, and enforcing new legal measures, often addressing novel situations. Every industry and service is affected.

Contents/Subjects

With many titles currently available and new ones appearing regularly, the series' coverage includes detailed analyses of relevant legislation and case law in major global trading jurisdictions, defences used in cases involving the digital network economy, state aid cases, enforcement methodologies and a great deal more.

Objective & Readership

The purpose of Kluwer's International Competition Law Series is to follow the ever-changing contours of this dynamic area of the law, keeping the practice in sharp focus so that practising lawyers (including in-house counsel) and academics can be assured of the most up-to-date guidance and sources, in the widest possible range of applications.

The titles published in this series are listed at the end of this volume.

Information Exchange Between Competitors in EU Competition Law

Martin Gassler

Wolters Kluwer

Published by:
Kluwer Law International B.V.
PO Box 316
2400 AH Alphen aan den Rijn
The Netherlands
E-mail: international-sales@wolterskluwer.com
Website: lrus.wolterskluwer.com

Sold and distributed by:
Wolters Kluwer Legal & Regulatory U.S.
7201 McKinney Circle
Frederick, MD 21704
United States of America
Email: customer.service@wolterskluwer.com

Printed on acid-free paper.

ISBN 978-94-035-3183-0

e-Book: ISBN 978-94-035-3184-7
web-PDF: ISBN 978-94-035-3185-4

Printed in the United Kingdom.

To my parents

Table of Contents

List of Abbreviations

AG	Advocate General
Art.	Article
AEA	Agricultural Engineers Association
APAG	l'Association des Producteurs d'Acides Gras
BER	Block Exemption Regulation
Ch	Chapter
CJ	Court of Justice
e.g.	For Instance
ECHR	European Convention of Human Rights
Eds	Editors
EEA	European Economic Area
et al.	*et alii* (and others)
et seq.	*et sequens* (and in the following)
etc.	*et cetera* (and other similar things)
EU	European Union
EUMR	European Merger Regulation
Fn	Footnote
fns	Footnotes
FX/Forex	Foreign Exchange
GC	General Court
i.e.	*id est*
ibid	*ibidem* (the same place)
IP	Intellectual Property
MIF	Multilateral Interchange Fee
MFN	Most Favoured Nation
OECD	Organisation for Economic Co-operation and Development
p	Page

para.	Paragraph
Paras	Paragraphs
pp.	Pages
R&D	Research and Development
TFEU	Treaty of the Functioning of the European Union
TT	Technology Transfer
UK	United Kingdom
US	United States
vs	Versus

CHAPTER 1

Introduction

The area of information exchange has been perceived by some lawyers as a field of competition law that is highly diverse and complex[1] and that lacks the legal certainty of other areas of competition law.[2] In particular, the preliminary reference judgment of the Court of Justice (CJ) in *T-Mobile*[3] created uncertainty due to its criticised formalistic analytical approach. Critics of the judgment view it as a setback for the generally desired more economic approach in assessing information exchange because it advocates a per se prohibition thinking.[4] While the current 2011 Horizontal Cooperation Guidelines of the European Commission ('Commission') have been seen as a welcomed attempt to codify and clarify the case law and decisional practice on information exchange,[5] the underlying analytical framework is still greatly underdeveloped. The current state of the literature fails to offer a holistic perspective on information exchange, *inter alia*, by bringing together the legal and economic literature in a dogmatically robust and coherent manner.

This book offers a more robust analytical framework for assessing information exchanges under Art. 101 TFEU. Its main argument is that at closer scrutiny, many issues surrounding information exchanges are less complex and more straightforward than one might suggest at first sight. The best example is the long-lasting struggle in the literature on the classification of information exchanges as either restrictions by object or restrictions by effect. A through examination of the relevant case law and decisional practice reveals through common themes on which a robust analytical framework can be built. By identification of these common themes, the case law is surprisingly consistent and coherent.

1. *See* Camesasca, Schmidt and Clancy (2010), p. 417.
2. *See* Seitz (2011), p. 455.
3. *See* Case C-8/08, *T-Mobile.*
4. *See* Meyring (2010), p. 30. The OECD (2011, para. 40) also notes the 'strict view' on information exchanges taken by the Court.
5. *See* Camesasca and Schmidt (2011); Wagner-von Papp (2012).

A robust analytical framework also requires the consideration and discussion of the economic literature. While the economic literature plays a crucial role in constructing plausible theories of harms for those information exchanges that are classified as restrictions by effect, it plays only an insignificant role for those information exchanges that are classified as restrictions by object (such as the type of information exchange in *T-Mobile*). Obviously, the latter observation creates tension with those favouring a more economic approach in assessing information exchange. This book argues that the tension can be resolved at a closer analysis of the relevant conceptual foundation of a restriction by object, which does not lack economic thinking but is greatly shaped by it.

The book is structured as follows. Chapter 2 lays down the *conceptual* framework for assessing information exchanges. This includes an attempt to categorise the various forms of information exchanges based on different perspectives (such as a categorisation based on the ancillarity of the information exchange to other conduct). It also includes a discussion of the various characteristics of information exchange (such as the level of aggregation or age of the information). While the former categorisation aims to generally structure the discussion, the latter discussion is a key ingredient for understanding economic theories of harm for anti-competitive information exchanges, and for developing a robust distinction between information exchange that restricts competition by its object and information exchange that restricts competition (only) by its effect.

Chapter 3 lays down the *economic* framework for assessing information exchanges. This entails a discussion of possible pro-competitive and anti-competitive effects of information exchanges. The primary efficiency of an information exchange is that it enables firms and customers to make decisions on a more informed basis. However, the main concern is that information exchange may also enable firms to engage in collusion more easily and sustain it longer. The discussion focuses on how information exchange can increase the risk of collusive outcomes and what types of information exchanges are particularly harmful (risk classification).

Chapter 4 lays down the *legal* framework necessary for assessing information exchanges under Art. 101 TFEU. It focuses on two of the four conditions for the application of Art. 101 TFEU: (1) the concept of a concerted practice and (2) the concepts of a restriction by object and effect and their distinctions. The discussion on these two conditions lays the foundation for the discussion in the two subsequent sections (Chapters 5 and 6). On the one hand, the discussion of the concept of a concerted practice helps to explain why information exchanges have not become the most potent manifestation of collusion theories in Art. 101 TFEU (Chapter 5). On the other hand, the discussion on the concepts of a restriction by object and effect helps to develop the robust theoretical framework for coherently putting information exchanges either in the 'object box' or 'effect box' (Chapter 6).

As mentioned, Chapter 5 demonstrates the importance of information exchanges for collusion theories under Art. 101 TFEU. On the one hand, the reluctant stance of the European Union (EU) Courts on condemning undertakings for engaging in mere parallel conduct emphasises the importance of evidentiary issues. While parallel conduct can be used only as (weak) circumstantial evidence of possible collusion between undertakings, information exchanges may be used as (strong) documentary evidence. On the other hand, the various Guidelines and Notices of the Commission demonstrate that information exchange is most often used and is thus the most universal theory of harm regarding the risk of collusive outcomes.

Chapter 6 analyses the case law and decisional practice on 'pure' information exchanges, which are information exchanges that are not ancillary to any wider pro- or anti-competitive conduct. In order to identify common themes, cases are categorised according to their classification as restrictions of competition by object or effect (descriptive perspective). This object/effect classification also enables a discussion of whether the current approach of assessing information exchanges is desirable from a competition policy perspective or whether changes should be made (normative perspective). This chapter also discusses the phenomenon of signalling via advance public announcements. Although the phenomenon is not new, its conceptually more nuanced treatment is. The chapter concludes by offering conceptual solutions to some of the perceived issues of the current (often ambiguous and confusing) analytical approach of assessing information exchanges. In particular, it offers clear guidance why certain types of information exchanges are (and should be) classified as restrictions by object, while others are (and should be) classified as restrictions by effect.

CHAPTER 2

The Conceptual Framework

2.1 TYPES OF INFORMATION EXCHANGE

There are essentially four different approaches on how to categorise the different types of information exchange. One can differentiate based on the ancillarity of the information exchange to other wider conduct (*see* section 2.1.1 below), the stage and intensity of the concertation as well as the role of information exchange in each stage (*see* section 2.1.2 below), the anti-competitive subject matter of the information exchange (*see* section 2.1.3 below) and the primary flow of information (*see* section 2.1.4 below).

2.1.1 Based on the Ancillarity to Other Conduct

There are two forms of information exchanges based on the ancillarity of the information exchange to other conduct. Information exchanges either take place as part of another broader conduct (*ancillary* information exchange) or information exchange can be stand-alone (*pure* information exchanges). Although this book focuses mostly on pure information exchanges (*see* particularly Chapter 6), it also discusses those types of ancillary information exchanges that are occasionally mentioned by the Commission in its Guidelines (*see* section 5.2).[6]

6. This approach is in accordance with the literature that regularly discusses only the former category when it refers to 'information exchanges' (*see*, e.g., OECD (2011), para. 5).

2.1.1.a *Ancillary Information Exchanges*

Ancillary information exchanges are information exchanges that occur as part of another wider arrangement and are thus merely ancillary to that broader scheme.[7] This can occur in essentially two different contexts.[8]

First, information exchange can be part of a wider arrangement that mainly has a *pro-competitive* rationale (such as a horizontal cooperation agreement). The important question in this scenario is whether the scope of information sharing goes beyond what is necessary for the realisation of the efficiencies of the horizontal cooperation. If it does, the horizontal cooperation produces negative 'spill-over effects'. These kinds of information exchanges have to be assessed in the legal and economic context of those horizontal cooperation agreements, not on its own.

Second, information exchange can also occur as part of a wider cartel arrangement that has an *anti-competitive* rationale (such as price-fixing or market-sharing).[9] In this scenario, information exchanges are merely one of the means to facilitate the cartel by enabling undertakings *inter alia* to more easily agree on the terms of the collusive outcome, or to monitor their respective conduct and thus detect deviations from the collusive outcome.[10] These kinds of information exchanges will be assessed in the context of the overall cartel arrangement, not on its own.[11]

2.1.1.b *Pure Information Exchanges*

Pure information exchanges (sometimes also referred to as 'stand-alone' information exchanges)[12] occur when the information exchange does *not* occur in the context of another wider arrangement.[13] The information exchange is 'pure' because it is

7. *See*, e.g., Bennet and Collins (2010), p. 328; OECD (2011), p. 4.
8. *See* Horizontal Cooperation Guidelines, paras 56 and 59: 'information exchange can be part of another type of horizontal co-operation agreement (for example, the parties to a production agreement share certain information on costs). The assessment of the latter type of information exchanges should be carried out in the context of the assessment of the *horizontal co-operation* agreement itself. [...] communication of information among competitors may constitute an agreement, a concerted practice, or a decision by an association of undertakings with the object of fixing, in particular, prices or quantities. Those types of information exchanges will normally be considered and fined as *cartels*. Information exchange may also facilitate the implementation of a cartel by enabling companies to monitor whether the participants comply with the agreed terms. Those types of exchanges of information will be assessed as part of the cartel'. (emphasis added)
9. *See*, e.g., Whish (2006), p. 22; Wagner-von Papp (2012), pp. 1-2 who describes the information exchange as the operative part of any cartel agreement.
10. *See* Horizontal Cooperation Guidelines, para. 59.
11. On the related issue of the 'single and continuous infringement', *see*, e.g., Jones (2012); Faull and Nikpay (2014), paras 3.87 et seq. and 8.457 et seq.; Whish and Bailey (2018), pp. 105-110.
12. *See*, e.g., Jones and Sufrin (2016), p. 679.
13. *See*, for this notion, e.g., Robertson (2013); Wijckmans and Tuytschaever (2015), para. 11.07. When the Horizontal Cooperation Guidelines provide guidance in the dedicated section 2 guidance on 'information exchanges', they refer to pure information exchanges.

stand-alone without any ancillarity to other arrangements. The economic function lies in the exchange of information itself.[14]

There are three main forms of pure information exchanges:[15]

(1) *Direct exchange*: the most obvious form of information exchange is the direct exchange of information between competitors.[16]
(2) *Indirect exchange via intermediaries (hub-and-spoke)*: the information exchange between competitors (the spokes) can also occur indirectly through common third-party intermediaries (the hub).[17] These intermediaries include *inter alia* agents,[18] exclusive distributors,[19] category captain,[20] a trade association,[21] independent market research organisation[22] or online platforms to mention the most common ones. One important aspect of the competitive analysis is the nature and the extent of the data distribution from the common intermediary to the competing undertakings (particularly the extent and regularity to which the third party passes on disaggregated information).[23]
(3) *Indirect exchange via public announcements (signalling)*: the information exchange between competitors can also occur indirectly via advance and unilateral public announcements (such as press releases or announcements on website).[24] The concern is that public announcements may be misused to signal future intentions about competitively relevant issues to competing undertakings.[25]

14. *See* Camesasca and Schmidt (2011), pp. 227-228.
15. *See* Horizontal Cooperation Guidelines, para. 55; Stroux (2004), pp. 143 et seq.; OECD (2011), paras 21-30.
16. *See* OECD (2011), para. 20. This also includes the situation when two undertakings are in direct contact during merger negotiations in order to either assess the chances and risks of the acquisition before the deal is signed (pre-merger collusion) or to facilitate the already signed acquisition (gun-jumping) (*see* OECD (2011), fn 5 at para. 5). However, this book will not focus on these two issues.
17. *See* OECD (2011), para. 21; Prewitt and Fails (2015); Wijckmans and Tuytschaever (2015), paras 11.81-11.83; Niels, Jenkins and Kavanagh (2016), para. 5.39.
18. *See* Vertical Guidelines, para. 20.
19. *Ibid.*, para. 154.
20. *Ibid.*, para. 211.
21. *See* Capobianco (2004), p. 1261; Levenstein and Suslow (2006), pp. 59-65; OECD (2011), para. 22.
22. *See* Horizontal Cooperation Guidelines, para. 55. These firms collect, compile and provide industry data and market studies to industry players. If they collect the data independently, they do not fall under Art. 101 TFEU because they do not receive any data from industry players (OECD (2011), paras 23-24).
23. *See* OECD (2011), para. 22.
24. *See*, e.g., Faull and Nikpay (2014), para. 1.111; Rabinovici (2017).
25. *See* OECD (2011), para. 29. *See* section 6.4 for an in-depth discussion on public announcements.

2.1.2 Based on the Stage of the Concertation

Baño Fos argues that information exchanges can also be classified based on the stage and intensity of the concertation and the role of information exchange in each stage.[26] The different stages represent different closenesses to an effectively operating cartel. The idea is that although an information exchange can occur irrespective of the closeness to an effectively operating cartel, the exchange of information has a different function and purpose in each stage:

- *Information exchange as indirect evidence of cartel*: this understanding corresponds with the idea that information exchanges are merely means to effectively execute a cartel (*see* the ancillary information exchange above). From the perspective of an enforcer, information exchanges at this stage can be used as documentary evidence to demonstrate the existence of a cartel.
- *Information exchange as a preliminary step to initiate a cartel*: this understanding relates to the idea that information exchanges may be the first (necessary) step to initiate a full-blown cartel. In accordance with the concept of attempt in criminal law, Baño Fos argues that information exchanges at this stage constitutes an attempt to cartelise and should not be treated differently than information exchanges at the first stage.
- *Information exchange as a facilitating practice outside the 'classic cartel fact pattern'*: this understanding relates to the idea that information exchanges make collusion more likely mainly due to certain structural factors.[27] Baño Fos argues that in such situation information exchanges should only be considered as an infringement if sufficient risk of harm to competition can be proven. Thus, the competitive analysis of information exchanges at this stage seems to rely more on a thorough economic analysis, as opposed to a more legal analysis as with the two former types.

This classification of information exchange deals with the evidentiary issue of how to prove a concertation, which is generally neglected by the literature.[28] It also offers a cross-discipline classification that goes beyond competition law because he also uses ideas from criminal law (the concept of attempt). However, in its third type he falls short of elaborating on how to distinguish between lawful information exchanges and those that constitute unlawful facilitative practices.[29] Still, his categorisation is a useful and original perspective on information exchanges.

---

26. *See* Baño Fos (2015), pp. 207-208.
27. *See* section 3.3.1.d for these structural factors.
28. *See* section 4.2.3.
29. *See* section 6.5.2 for a more sophisticated analytical proposal for using the concept of facilitative practice.

2.1.3 Based on the Anti-competitive Subject Matter of the Information

A different categorisation is offered by Peeperkorn. He focuses on the subject matter of the exchanged information and differentiates according to its anti-competitive objective:

- *Information that helps the colluding undertakings to monitor cheating*: this relates to information exchanges about prices, sales conditions, sales and output.
- *Information that helps colluding undertakings to establish effective punishment mechanisms and identify possible collusion equilibriums*: this relates to information exchanges about current costs, demand and capacity.
- *Information that reduces long-term uncertainties*: this relates to information exchanges about investments and research and development (R&D) as well as about future cost and demand.

He argues that competition policy should focus on the former two categories. Only the two former categories of information enable successful collusion and thus should be at the centre of a competitive analysis.[30] His categorisation follows an economic logic and aligns well with economic literature on collusion theories.[31]

2.1.4 Based on the Primary Flow of Information

One can also differentiate between different types of information exchange based on whether the primary flow of the information is between competitors (horizontal exchanges) or between upstream suppliers and downstream customers (vertical exchanges).

2.1.4.a Horizontal Exchanges

Some types of information exchange have primarily a horizontal setting. This means that the ultimate recipient of the exchanged information is another competing undertaking. In other words, the flow of information should ultimately occur on a horizontal level between competitors. These types of information exchange align well with the three forms of pure information exchanges as discussed below:[32] direct exchanges between competitors, indirect exchanges of information between competitors via common intermediaries and signalling between competitors via advance public announcements.

30. *See* Peeperkorn (1996), p. 7.
31. *See* section 3.3.
32. *See* section 2.1.1.b.

2.1.4.b Vertical Exchanges (With Indirect Horizontal Effects)

The other categorisation consists of those types of information exchange whose primary setting is a vertical one. Although possible anti-competitive effects may occur on a horizontal level, the flow of information mainly occurs on a vertical level, that is, between a supplier and customers/retailers/buyers.[33] The literature mentions three forms:[34]

(1) *English clauses*: these clauses obligate the buyer to disclose to its supplier the existence of competing offers from other suppliers and to inform its supplier about the terms and conditions of such offer. The supplier then has the right to match the competing offer.[35]
(2) *Price matching clauses (also referred to as 'meeting competition clauses' or 'alignment clauses')*: these clauses guarantee the buyer the lowest price that is offered by the supplier's rivals.[36]
(3) *Resale price maintenance practices*: these are practices that have as their direct or indirect object the establishment of a fixed or minimum resale price.[37]

What these three vertical forms have in common with the three horizontal forms are that they also increase market transparency at the suppliers' level. This is because either the buyer has to inform the supplier of competing prices (English clauses and price matching clauses) or because the buyer cannot reduce the price below a certain level (resale price maintenance).[38] This is why theories of harm are partly overlapping.

This book focuses on *horizontal* information exchanges where the primary flow of information occurs at a horizontal level. In the literature, the common understanding is that the issue of information exchanges refers to horizontal information exchanges. However, even though this book focuses on horizontal information exchanges, the scope of issues is still quite broad. It includes exchanges that seem to be mostly vertical at first sight. The horizontal nature is only revealed after closer scrutiny. For instance, as mentioned, even indirect information exchanges via a common third party (such as a supplier or retailer) are ultimately horizontal exchanges between competing undertakings, even though they occur in vertical context. Similarly, if public announcements are employed by firms to signal to other competing undertakings their collusive intentions (such as to raise prices), such announcements are mainly meant for competing undertakings, not for customers.

---

33. *See*, e.g., Niels, Jenkins and Kavanagh (2016), para. 5.39.
34. *See* OECD (2011), para. 20 and fns 40-42.
35. *Ibid.*, para. 20.
36. *Ibid.*, para. 20 on p. 20 and fn 41. Also mentioned by das Nair and Mncube (2013).
37. *See* Vertical Guidelines, para. 48.
38. *See* OECD (2011), para. 20 and fns 40-42.

2.2 CHARACTERISTICS OF THE INFORMATION EXCHANGE

One element of the analytical framework of the Horizontal Cooperation Guidelines refers to the characteristics of the information exchange.[39] It should be noted that the Guidelines merely list seven factors without further categorising them. Conceptually though, these factors can be categorised into two different layers: the 'inner' layer, which concerns the subject matter of the information exchanged itself (*see* section 2.2.1 below), and the 'outer' layer, which concerns the outer circumstances of the information exchange (*see* section 2.2.2 below).

2.2.1 The Inner Layer

The first layer relates to the subject matter of the information exchanged. Four of the factors mentioned in the Horizontal Cooperation Guidelines concern this layer.

2.2.1.a Public Availability (Public vs Private Data)[40]

The Horizontal Cooperation Guidelines consider data as public if it is equally accessible in terms of costs to all market players (including competitors, customers and other market participants). Thus, this test requires an assessment of the level of search and collection costs to access the data.[41]

The case law on the other hand has put forward a different test. The crucial issue is whether those firms that have engaged in the information exchange have gained access more simply, rapidly and directly.[42] The latter test limits the scope of players to competitors and excludes all other market players.[43] Thus, the test put forward by the EU Courts is narrower in scope than the one used by the Commission in the Horizontal Cooperation Guidelines.

Generally speaking, the exchange of public (as opposed to private) data receives a more favourable treatment in competition law since this promotes the interest of unaffiliated parties to the information exchange and thus materialises positive spill-over effects.[44]

39. *See* Horizontal Cooperation Guidelines, paras 86-94. This notion is also used in OECD (2011) section 5.2.
40. *See* for this notion OECD (2011), para. 41. This factor could be also labelled 'target group' (*see* Møllgaard and Overgaard (2006), p. 122).
41. *See* OECD (2011), para. 69.
42. *See* Cases T-202/98, etc., *Tate & Lyle*, para. 60.
43. Wagner-von Papp (2012), p. 30 tries to mediate between both tests by arguing that the crucial test should be whether the acquisition of information is made less costly through the information exchange, regardless of how costly the access is for customers. Thus, his test also only considers the costs of access as the relevant benchmark (like the test in the Horizontal Cooperation Guidelines), but it does limit the scope to competitors (like the test of the GC). This makes sense since the concern of information exchanges is collusion between competitors.
44. *See* Camesasca, Schmidt and Clancy (2010), p. 413.

2.2.1.b *Commercial Sensitivity (Strategic vs Non-strategic Private Data)*[45]

Private data is considered as strategic when it contains commercially sensitive information that is able to reduce strategic uncertainty of other competitors in the market (*inter alia* data about prices or rebates, customer lists, production costs, quantities, turnovers, sales, capacities, qualities, marketing plans, risks, investments technologies or R&D programmes and their results).[46]

However, certain types of private data are considered less strategic (such as market demand or costs) than other types (particularly private data about the very nature of the business, such as prices or quantities).[47] Furthermore, commercially sensitive information may have different weight for the competitive process depending on the specific market. For instance, if the main competitive parameter in a certain market is quantity, the exchange of such private data about quantities has a more detrimental effect on competition than exchanges about other parameters.[48]

2.2.1.c *Level of Detail (Aggregated vs Disaggregated Data)*

Data is considered as 'genuinely' aggregated when the identification of a firm's individualised market conduct is sufficiently difficult to derive.[49] While aggregated data is always anonymous, disaggregated data can be either individualised or anonymous.[50] However, in practice the notions of disaggregation and individualisation are used synonymously.[51] The more disaggregated and individualised the data, the more exposed a firm's individual market performance to competitors.

However, in case of indirect information exchanges, one should draw a distinction between the collection and distribution of data. Even though the collection of data by a third party (such as a trade association) may relate to disaggregated data about firms' performance, *distributed* data can be aggregated.[52] To mitigate competition concern, the role of a third party should be to disaggregate data once it is distributed, which could otherwise not be achieved by direct exchanges between competing firms.

2.2.1.d *Age (Historic Data vs Recent Data vs Future Intentions)*

The Horizontal Cooperation Guidelines are very cautious in providing an abstract threshold under which data becomes historic. Instead, they provide that there is no

45. *See* for this notion OECD (2011), para. 41.
46. *See* Horizontal Cooperation Guidelines, para. 86. *See also* Carle and Johnsson (1998), p. 78 who provide a very similar list of commercially sensitive information.
47. *See* OECD (2011), para. 65. *See also* Niemeyer (1993), p. 151 who distinguishes between information directly related to competitive behaviour (such as prices or rebates) and information that is not directly related to competitive behaviour (such as sales data).
48. *See* Wagner-von Papp (2012), p. 28.
49. *See* Horizontal Cooperation Guidelines, para. 89.
50. *See* Nitsche and von Hinten-Reed (2014), p. 8.
51. *See* Horizontal Cooperation Guidelines, para. 89.
52. *See* OECD (2011), para. 12 point 1 and para. 66.

general threshold under which data is considered historic. This ultimately depends on the specific circumstances (*inter alia* the frequency of the price negotiations or the average length of contracts in a given market).[53]

While historic data has lost its commercial relevance (and thus does not raise any concerns),[54] the exchange of relatively recent data or the exchange of future intentions may be detrimental to competition. Recent data is sometimes referred to as 'hard' information because firms are able to verify the information, while future intentions are referred to as 'soft' information because intentions by their very nature are not verifiable.[55] It is therefore linguistically wise to distinguish between the exchange of 'data', which only refers to past conduct and exchange of 'information', which can also refer to future intentions.

The anti-competitive rationale behind the exchange of individualised recent data may be to monitor rivals' conduct.[56] The anti-competitive rationale behind the exchange of future intentions, particularly on price and quantities, may be to effectively agree on a collusive outcome.[57]

2.2.2 The Outer Layer

The second layer relates to the outer circumstances of the information exchange. Three of the factors mentioned in the Horizontal Cooperation Guidelines can be considered in this layer.

2.2.2.a Frequency

The more frequently an information exchange takes place, the better and more timely firms can adapt their commercial policy on that basis.[58] Whether exchanges are considered 'frequently' depends on the market circumstances, such as the frequency of price changes (e.g., even a yearly exchange of information may be considered as frequent in market with long-term contract durations) and the nature of the product (e.g., markets with heterogeneous products may require more frequent exchanges than markets with homogeneous products due to the complexity).[59]

53. *See* Horizontal Cooperation Guidelines, para. 90. As a rule of thumb data that is more than one year old can be considered as historic in most cases (*see* Carle and Johnsson (1998), pp. 78-79).
54. *See* Kühn (2010), p. 428; Capobianco (2004), p. 1265.
55. *See* Kühn (2001), p. 170; Møllgaard and Overgaard (2006), p. 122; Vives (2006a), p. 84. *See also* the interesting description of the classification by Whish (2006), p. 23: 'pre-notification agreements' relate to exchanges about firms' future conduct, while 'post-notification agreements' relate to the exchange of data of past conduct.
56. *See* section 3.3.4.
57. *See* Carle and Johnsson (1998), p. 79; Kühn (2010), pp. 419-420. *See* section 3.3.5.
58. *See* OECD (2011), para. 68.
59. *See* Horizontal Cooperation Guidelines, para. 91; Levenstein and Suslow (2006), pp. 57-59.

2.2.2.b *Public Availability*

An information exchange takes place in 'public' if the exchanged private[60] data is made equally available to all market players after the exchange (public market transparency).[61] If the exchanged private data is only made accessible to those firms involved in the exchange, the exchange takes place in 'private' (private market transparency).[62]

2.2.2.c *Market Coverage*

The market coverage relates to the scope of relevant market that is affected by the information exchange.[63] This depends on the market positions of the parties involved in the exchange and the products involved. This characteristic can be used to understand the impact of the information on the market. If the market coverage of the exchange is low, its effect on the market will most likely be limited as well. On the other hand, if the information exchange covers a wide share of the market, its impact on the market will be more significant.

60. The public availability factor of the outer layer refers to the conduct *after* private data has been exchanged (i.e., whether private data has been also disclosed to third parties). The public availability factor of the inner layer on the other hand refers to the issue of whether the information *before* the exchange was already accessible or not. Thus, both factors are complementary.
61. *See* OECD (2012a), para. 14.
62. *See* OECD (2011), para. 25.
63. *See* Horizontal Cooperation Guidelines, paras 87-88.

CHAPTER 3
The Economic Framework

3.1 EFFICIENCIES

The primary efficiency of information exchanges is that firms and customers can make decisions on a more informed basis. The economic literature describes this efficiency as an increase in 'market transparency'. It distinguishes between benefits at the level of suppliers (*see* section 3.1.1) and at the level of customers (*see* section 3.1.2).

3.1.1 Benefits for Suppliers (Horizontal Market Transparency)[64]

On the level of suppliers, increased market transparency can help to make markets work better by overcoming inefficiencies (or even market failures) and thus ultimately increase competition:[65]

- *Market knowledge*: market knowledge is essential for the proper functioning of markets.[66] It enables firms to develop more efficient commercial strategies (*inter alia* because they can more easily adapt to new trends or changing demands),[67] improve their investment decisions[68] and better position their products in differentiated markets.[69] Particularly small- and medium-sized

64. For this notion, *see* Wagner-von Papp (2012), pp. 13 et seq.
65. *See* OECD (2011), p. 6.
66. *See* Nitsche and von Hinten-Reed (2014), p. 10 who trace the origin of this back to Adam Smith and his idea of the 'invisible hand' that relies on information exchange.
67. *See* OECD (2011), para. 12 (bullet point 1); Bennet and Collins (2010), p. 318; Vives (2006a), p. 87; Vives (2006b), p. 2 who refers to the 'output adjustment effect' that allows firms to adjust better to demand and cost shocks.
68. *See* Kühn (2010), p. 417; Nitsche and von Hinten-Reed (2014), p. 11; Wijckmans and Tuytschaever (2015), paras 11.51-11.54.
69. *See* OECD (2011), para. 12 (bullet point 2); das Nair and Mncube (2013). The experimental literature has shown that insufficient information induces firms to not maximise consumer welfare (*see* Brown Kruse and Schenk (2000)).

firms benefit from such types of exchange because they lack the financial resources to carry out expensive market research themselves or to pay specialised market research agents to do so.[70] Market knowledge by information exchanges does not only benefit existing market players but also new entrants for whom it becomes easier to enter the market.[71]
- *Benchmarking (productive efficiency)*: information exchanges can also enable firms to compare their market performance with other competitors.[72] Such benchmarking incentivises them to improve their internal efficiency.[73] In the long run, this means that inefficient firms will exit the market and more efficient firms will enter it.[74] The least restrictive means for the competitive process is the collection of individualised data by an independent third party that then anonymises and aggregates the data it distributes.[75]
- *Cost savings (allocative efficiency)*: information exchanges may help firms to save costs (*inter alia* by reducing their inventory, enabling quicker delivery of perishable goods to consumers, and dealing with unstable demand, overproduction and shortages).[76] This efficiency relates to the allocative efficiency because it ensures that scarce resources are allocated to those who require them the most.[77]

In certain markets, information exchanges may even be a necessary condition for their proper functioning:[78]

- *Innovative markets*: information sharing may be essential for the proper functioning of markets where technological changes occur often and where consumer preferences evolve rapidly.[79] This is because uncertainty negatively affects firms' investment decisions which are essential for the technological

70. *See* Niemeyer (1993), p. 151.
71. *See* OECD (2011), para. 12 (bullet point 1).
72. *See* Horizontal Cooperation Guidelines, para. 57; Kühn (2001), p. 191; Vives (2006a), p. 87; Bennet and Collins (2010), p. 318.
73. *See* OECD (2011), para. 12 (bullet point 4). The use of benchmarking studies has received official recognition by the Commission early on in order to boost the competitiveness of European firms (*see* Commission (1996) and (1997)). Carle and Johnsson note though that these benchmarking communications do not fully consider the anti-competitive side effects of possible collusion concerns (*see* Carle and Johnsson (1998, p. 84)). Since they only reflect the underdeveloped economic framework for assessing possible collusion concerns at the time, their today's value for competition law assessment is limited.
74. *See* Nitsche and von Hinten-Reed (2014), p. 17. *See also* Whish and Bailey (2018), p. 6 more generally on the issue of productive efficiency.
75. *See* Wijckmans and Tuytschaever (2015), para. 11.50.
76. *See* Horizontal Cooperation Guidelines, para. 57; Wijckmans and Tuytschaever (2015), paras 11.51-11-52.
77. *See* Bennet and Collins (2010), p. 318; Faull and Nikpay (2014), para. 7.432; Nitsche and von Hinten-Reed (2014), p. 18. Jensen (2007) provides the example with fishermen in Southern India for which the information exchange enables them to increase the allocative efficiencies of where to sell the fish. This led to an average decrease of consumer prices of 4%, while suppliers' profits rose 8%; thus, a win-win for both sides.
78. This is the argument of Capobianco (2004), pp. 1271-1275.
79. *See* Bennet and Collins (2010), p. 318.

development and innovation process.[80] The Commission has recognised the potential for dynamic efficiencies *inter alia* by creating block exemptions for these types of market (the (Technology Transfer-Block Exemption Regulation) TT-BER and R&D-BER).

- *Markets with market failures*: information sharing may also help to overcome market failures that lead to suboptimal market outcomes. On the one hand, market failures can arise when one party has more information than the other party (asymmetric information). This creates the two market failures known as 'adverse selection', where markets fail because firms or consumer cannot distinguish the quality goods from the 'lemons',[81] and 'moral hazard', where the insured person has an incentive to behave riskier than if he would be fully exposed to the risk.[82] Market transparency can overcome information asymmetry and improve the overall welfare (*see* particularly *Asnef-Equifax* on the credit market[83] or the old Insurance BER).[84] On the other hand, in bidding markets the anticipation of the winner's curse – due to the uncertainty of the valuation – can lead to bids below the valuation. More market transparency by good auction design (such as iterative or round-by-round bidding) can result in more aggressive bidding closer to the true valuation.[85]

3.1.2 Benefits for Customers (Vertical Market Transparency)

The benefits of increased market transparency also materialise at the level of customers:

- *Lower search costs*: increased transparency about the various offerings on the market reduces search costs for customers. Stigler identifies search costs as the

80. *See* OECD (2011), para. 12 (bullet point 7). *See also* the discussion comment by Carmen Matutes in Kühn (2001), p. 198. *See* Nitsche and von Hinten-Reed more generally criticise that most of the economic literature on information exchange focuses on static models. Thus, the dynamic benefits derived from information exchanges may be systematically underestimated in the literature.
81. *See* Akerlof (1970). An application is the exchange of information about customer default data and risk characteristics in the bank and insurance sector (*see* Kühn (2001), pp. 191-192).
82. *See* Bennet and Collins (2010), p. 319; Faull and Nikpay (2014), para. 7.435.
83. Discussed in section 6.2.1.g.
84. The Insurance BER has expired as of 31 March 2017. It provided a block exemption for certain aggregated information exchanges within the insurance sector for statistics matters, for joint insurance and for reinsurance of risk pools. The Commission decided that the BER was no longer necessary since the Horizontal Cooperation Guidelines now contain a dedicated section on information exchange (*see* Press Release of 13 December 2016, MEX/16/4369). A useful discussion on the scope of the exemption of the Insurance BER, although relating to the old 2003 Insurance BER, can be found in Capobianco (2004), pp. 1272-1273.
85. *See* Nitsche and von Hinten-Reed (2014), p. 18.

main reason for the emergence of market institutions that improve the exchange of information.[86]

- *More choice*: increased transparency also helps customers to increase the product offering they are able to find on the market. It helps them to find offerings that they would not have found without the increased market transparency.[87]

It should be noted though that these efficiencies on the customer level have a direct effect on the supplier level. First, better-informed customers create a more vigorous upstream competition between suppliers. The (Organisation for Economic Co-operation and Development) OECD 2006 Roundtable of Competition and Regulation in Retail Banking[88] suggests for instance that in order to increase competition between financial institutions, policymakers should take positive actions to increase vertical market transparency.[89] Second, better-informed customers become more sensitive to price differences. It is unlikely that customers that are aware of lower prices will be willing to pay a higher price for the same product. This further intensifies price competition on the supplier level.[90]

However, Bennet and Collins point out that these pro-competitive effects on the supplier level require that customers are not just able to access the information (availability of information) but also able to assess the information (complexity of offerings) and act on that assessment (problem of high transaction costs).[91] The problem is that in differentiated market with complex products (such as telecommunication, financial services or insurance) price transparency alone may not be sufficient to materialise meaningful efficiencies for customers.[92] If customers are not sophisticated enough, the information is only understood by firms but is too complex for customers. In those situations, vertical market transparency fails to create a more vigorous competition on the supplier level.

3.1.3 The Shortcomings of Static Models

Two words of caution on these possible efficiencies caused by market transparency: first, these efficiencies are mostly demonstrated by economists by using static models that are based on assumptions that do not reflect reality (particularly the assumption of fragmented markets with no market barriers).[93] Even if one tries to take these

86. *See* Stigler (1961). The importance of this article in this context is emphasised, e.g., by OECD (2001), p. 21; Nitsche and von Hinten-Reed (2014), p. 17. On the importance of reduced search costs, *see also* early articles such as Bissocoli (2000), p. 82.
87. *See* Horizontal Cooperation Guidelines, para. 57; Whish (2006), p. 20.
88. OECD (2006).
89. *See* OECD (2006), pp. 7-10. This Policy Roundtable was also mentioned in OECD (2011, p. 10) to demonstrate how increased customer transparency helps to promote competition on the supplier level.
90. *See* Møllgaard and Overgaard (2006), p. 109.
91. *See* Bennet and Collins (2010), pp. 315-316.
92. *Ibid.*, p. 316.
93. *See* Møllgaard and Overgaard (2006), p. 104.

theoretical results seriously, Møllgaard and Overgaard argue that they are not immediately useful for competition policy. This is because the welfare effect depends on the specific modelling design (such as the nature of competition or the nature of initially dispersed information).[94] While in some economic models, the overall effect on welfare tends to be positive, in others the effect tends to be negative. It is difficult in practice to identify without error which model a specific market follows. Thus, the application of these models to reality is impracticable. The risk is too high to wrongly model reality and draw false conclusions. Thus, policy implications from these economic models are rather limited and the results from these should be used cautiously.[95]

Second, many of the economic models demonstrating possible efficiencies do not consider the possible effects on collusion. The models are 'non-collusive'. They focus on one side of the competitive coin (the efficiency side) and completely neglect the other side (the anti-competitive side). Since these models are static, they fail to consider the dynamic perspective. Conversely, collusion models consider the dynamic aspect by applying *inter alia* repeated game theory.[96] It is difficult to compare possible efficiencies claimed in static models with possible concerns raised in dynamic models. Since optimal competition policy should consider these difficult trade-offs between the potential for efficiencies and collusion,[97] these models should never be used exclusively but always in conjunction with collusion considerations.

3.1.4 The Stronger Weight of Vertical Transparency for Competition Policy

It is questionable whether both levels of efficiencies are equally important for competition policy. There are valid arguments for allocating different relative weights to horizontal and vertical market transparency.

Wagner-von Papp is one of the scholars who argue that an increase in vertical transparency is always desirable, while an increase in horizontal transparency requires a 'special justification'.[98] Surely, this is reasonable since competition policy gives consumer welfare, as opposed to producer welfare, more weightage in practice. However, this approach may also be sensible in light of the collusive potential of horizontal market transparency which does not exist to the same extent for vertical

94. *Ibid.*, pp. 105-106. *See also* Lenares (1997) for an overview of the economic literature on static welfare models. In game theory models with private information, welfare is only improved in the models with demand uncertainty (as the type of uncertainty) and quantity competition (as the type of competition). Conversely, welfare analysis suggests that in models with demand uncertainty and price competition the scenario without any exchange of information maximised welfare (*see* Lenares (1997), pp. 70-71). On a different question, whether the firms have an incentive to share information in the first place, the answer is even more model-specific (*see* Lenares (1997), pp. 68-70).
95. *See* Vives (2006a), pp. 87-88 for an overview of the literature. This has been also emphasised by Caffarra and Kühn (2006), p. 136.
96. Noted, e.g., by Lévêque (2007), pp. 232-235. For these static models, *see* particularly Kühn and Vives (1995) who pioneered the economics of information exchange in static models. *See* section 3.3 for the collusion concern.
97. For this criticism, *see* Caffarra and Kühn (2006), p. 139.
98. *See* Wagner-von Papp (2012). *See* similarly Vives (2006a), p. 95; González (2012), p. 27; Flores (2017), pp. 63-65.

transparency. He identifies three scenarios where an increase in horizontal transparency is justified:[99]

(1) *Inseparability*: an increase in horizontal transparency may be inextricably linked to the increase in vertical transparency. The announcement of prices is the most prominent example. Public announcements materialise significant efficiencies for customers and inextricably also increase the risk of collusion by making the market more transparent for competitors.
(2) *Ancillarity*: an increase in horizontal transparency may also come with the otherwise pro-competitive horizontal cooperation. The main rationale for the transaction is the efficiency-enhancing cooperation. The increased horizontal transparency is merely a necessary evil that comes with it.
(3) *Stand-Alone*: an increase in horizontal transparency may also be in itself beneficial. This category tries to balance the 'evolutionary view' with the 'intelligent design view'. On the hand, the evolutionary view tends to prefer uncertain but potentially significant long-term benefits from relying on the competitive process. An example of the manifestation of this view can be found in the independence doctrine established by the CJ, which require undertakings to act independently on the market.[100] On the other hand, the intelligent design view tends to prefer more certain short-term benefits for which there is more hard evidence. An example of the manifestation of this view is the application of the individual exemption of Art. 101(3) TFEU on the condition that there is sufficient competition left.[101] Good examples for information exchanges that can be justified stand-alone are those that overcome market failures (such as information asymmetries[102] that ultimately result in a 'market of lemons' that is detrimental for the society overall).[103]

99. *See* Wagner-von Papp (2012), pp. 14-17. In an earlier article (Wagner-von Papp (2007)) he argues that information exchanges can entail two kinds of efficiencies. The first type of efficiency is ancillary to the otherwise pro-competitive transaction. Thus, they are considered under Art. 101(1) TFEU. The second type of efficiency is not ancillary to the transaction and needs to be assessed under Art. 101(3) TFEU (*see* Wagner-von Papp (2007), pp. 264-265). While the former type of efficiency relates most likely to the second scenario, the latter does most likely relate to the third scenario. It should be noted though that in practice, the emphasis of assessing information exchanges is on Art. 101(1) TFEU (*see*, e.g., Whish (2006), pp. 40-41 who notes that Art. 101(3) TFEU does not play a practical role in assessing information exchanges).
100. *See* section 4.2.1.b.2.
101. For this description *see* Wagner-von Papp (2012), p. 16.
102. As described in section 3.1.1.
103. *See* Wagner-von Papp (2012), p. 17. 'To the extent the financial institution cannot distinguish between good and bad borrowers, it has to offer the same credit conditions for all. The borrowers have better information about their status, but often will not be able to signal this credibly to the financial institution. There is an information asymmetry between borrowers and lenders, which can lead to adverse selection – to the extent the good borrowers are unwilling to pay the average risk premium for good and bad borrowers – and ultimately to a "market for lemons". The introduction of the information exchange allows financial institutions to distinguish good from bad borrowers and offer differentiated rates. The avoidance of the market for lemons problem allows for a higher credit volume overall, and for cheaper credit for good

Wagner-von Papp's argument is thought-provoking. It provides a sound analytical approach for understanding the nature of efficiencies caused by market transparency. Particularly the emphasis on the materialisation of vertical transparency finds support in the case law (*see* for instance the *Container Shipping* commitment decision[104] in which the commitments ultimately aimed at materialising vertical efficiencies by limiting the ways in which prices were publicly announced).

3.2 FORECLOSURE: A NEGLIGIBLE CONCERN

There are two theories of harm regarding information exchange: collusion and foreclosure. This section discusses foreclosure, the next section collusion. As a preliminary remark, it should be noted that that foreclosure only plays a negligible role in the literature on information exchange.[105] The vast majority of literature on information exchange is on collusion.

The Horizontal Cooperation Guidelines provide two theories of harm on how information exchange can lead to anti-competitive foreclosure:

(1) *Exclusion by non-participation (horizontal setting)*: the concern is that those competitors that are not part of the information exchange may suffer a 'significant' competitive disadvantage.[106] However, the concern has only a very narrow scope of application. It is not just that the competitive disadvantage has to be significant; the anti-competitive foreclosure only materialises when the exchange entails very strategic information[107] and covers a significant part of the relevant market.[108]
(2) *Exclusion by raising rivals' costs (vertical setting)*: the concern is that an information exchange in an upstream market may enable a vertically integrated firm to increase the price of 'key' components in the downstream market. This could give the vertically integrated firm a competitive advantage and lead to anti-competitive foreclosure of other downstream competitors.[109]

However, neither of these theories of harm is intrinsically linked with information exchanges.[110] The underlying economic issue of the first theory of harm is very

borrowers, but also to more expensive credit – or no credit – for bad borrowers. This effect is independent of any collusion, and in itself does not constitute a restriction of competition in the first place.'

104. Discussed in section 6.4.
105. *See*, e.g., OECD (2011) only briefly mentioning it in one single paragraph.
106. *Ibid.*, p. 12.
107. Wijckmans and Tuytschaever argue that this theory of harm should have a narrow application and only apply to those situations where the access to information is a key factor to operate successfully in the market (*see* Wijckmans and Tuytschaever (2015), para. 11.23).
108. *See* Horizontal Cooperation Guidelines, para. 70.
109. *Ibid.*, para. 71.
110. *See* Wagner-von Papp (2012), p. 12 who argued that foreclosure concerns are not at the heart of information exchange concerns and are not considered particularly specific for information exchanges.

similar to the refusal to supply cases.[111] There is nothing specific about the concern in the context of information exchange. For instance, a firm may also suffer a competitive disadvantage if it does not belong to a trade association, which is economically very similar to not being part of an information exchange system.[112] Thus, this type of foreclosure concern should be dealt with under the analytical framework of refusal to supply.

The second scenario is even more out of place for information exchanges. The underlying economic issue is similar to margin squeezing. Importantly, the anti-competitive concern that directly relates to the information exchange is about the facilitation of collusion. The achievement of foreclosure by margin squeezing may be just one possible objective of a collusion, not even the most common or obvious objective.[113]

Thus, these two foreclosure concerns are better dealt with under the respective analytical frameworks developed in Art. 102 TFEU (refusal to supply and margin squeezing) *inter alia* by using the concept of collective dominance. It is clear from the literature that the primary[114] concern of information exchanges under Art. 101 TFEU is collusion, which is discussed in the following section.

3.3 COLLUSION: THE MAIN CONCERN

The concern is that information exchange enables firms to engage in collusion more easily and to sustain it longer.[115] Conceptually, one can distinguish between the literature on general collusion theories (*see* section 3.3.1) and on the more specific problem of tacit collusion (*see* section 3.3.2). Both strands of literature have influenced the analytical framework for assessing information exchanges. Information exchange is either discussed by the economic literature under the heading of 'facilitative practices' (*see* section 3.3.3), 'market transparency' (*see* section 3.3.4) or 'communication' (*see* section 3.3.5). The difference between the latter two comes down to the temporal dimension of the exchanged information (past data vs future intentions). As shown later,[116] this distinction plays a decisive role in the legal distinction of the by object/effect classification of pure information exchanges.

111. *See* Bennet and Collins (2010), p. 324.
112. *See* Wagner-von Papp (2012), p. 12.
113. *Ibid.*, p. 12.
114. *See* Kühn (2010), pp. 418-419; Bennet and Collins (2010), p. 320; Camesasca and Schmidt (2011), p. 228; OECD (2011), p. 10; Wijckmans and Tuytschaever (2015), para. 11.11.
115. *See*, e.g., Motta (2004), pp. 150-151; OECD (2011), p. 10.
116. *See* Chapter 6.

3.3.1 The Theory of Collusion

3.3.1.a Meaning

In the economic literature, the term 'collusion' refers to any form of coordination among competitors with the objective of raising prices to a level which is higher than the non-collusive/unilateral equilibrium.[117] In other words, it is a strategy of joint profit maximisation where prices may be set close to the monopoly price.[118] However, firms cannot just collude on prices but on all kinds of different variables that are relevant for the competitive process (such as output, product quality, product choice, innovation and so on).[119]

3.3.1.b Forms

The economic literature distinguishes two types of collusion: explicit and tacit collusion. The difference comes down to the *means* in which the collusive outcome is achieved.[120] While explicit collusion (sometimes also referred to as cooperative collusion)[121] refers to a situation where collusion is achieved by any form of direct contact between firms,[122] tacit collusion refers to a situation where the collusive outcome is achieved by independent decision-making.[123]

However, the exact boundaries as defined by the economic literature between the two forms are vague and not necessarily congruent with the legal notions of an 'agreement' and a 'concerted practice' within the meaning of Art. 101 TFEU. This is because economics is only concerned about the *outcome* (higher prices than some competitive benchmark), not with the form or means through which that outcome has

117. *See* OECD (2012a), para. 7. The non-collusive equilibrium in a perfectly competitive market – that is a market with infinite number of firms, homogeneous products and perfect information – is that prices will be set at marginal costs (*ibid.*, para. 9). The Commission has defined collusion in one of the contributions to the OECD as 'coordination (i.e., alignment) of companies' competitive behaviour that result in restrictive effect on competition' (OECD (2012b), fn 1 on p. 179). However, this definition is confusing. If 'competitive' behaviour is aligned, then it is questionable whether one should speak of *competitive* behaviour. It is better to speak of 'conduct on the market' or something similar that does confuse the reader by mixing together competitive conduct and coordinated conduct. A different description could be 'unilateral conduct' vs 'coordinated conduct' (*see* Smith, Ridyard and Petrescu (2015), p. 33).
118. *See* Motta (2004), p. 138.
119. *See* OECD (2012a), para. 7.
120. Motta (2004, p. 138) for instance defines both forms more loosely: 'collusion can occur both when firms act through an organised cartel (explicit collusion), or when they act in a purely non-co-operative way (tacit collusion)'. This description seems to cover only two extremes in a spectrum of possible concertation, but not the 'grey zone' of a more loose form of concertation. A concerted practice does not require an organised cartel to fall in the prohibition of Art. 101 TFEU but also covers a more loose form of concertation (*see* section 4.2).
121. *See* Petit (2013), p. 12.
122. *See* OECD (2012a), para. 21; Niels, Jenkins and Kavanagh (2016), para. 5.28. However, Whish (2006), p. 22 adopts a narrower view and only regards hard-core cartels that concern future conduct as explicit collusion. The mere exchange of past information, even if individualised, should be regarded as tacit collusion. Thus, there is no consensus on where to draw the line.
123. *See* OECD (2012a), para. 22.

been attained.[124] Thus, economics does not feel the need to provide exact demarcations between explicit and tacit collusion which logically leaves a certain degree of blurriness. Whether firms collude tacitly or explicitly, in both scenarios they act in a way that approximates that of a single dominant firm (supra-competitive equilibrium).[125] Put differently, even in markets with merely tacit collusion, firms set their prices 'as if' there had been explicit collusion between them.[126]

This is strikingly different from the legal approach where the *means* are indeed decisive for the application of Art. 101 TFEU. Only conduct that is the result of a concerted practice or an agreement is unlawful, while parallel conduct as a result of independent decision-making is lawful.[127] From an economic perspective, both scenarios are equally detrimental to consumer welfare. In both scenarios the welfare loss is the same.[128]

From an economic perspective, the likelihood of agreeing and sustaining collusion strictly depends on certain structural and behavioural factors.[129] Direct interactions are more effective to find and sustain collusion outcomes because those factors can be changed more effective by means of communication.[130]

3.3.1.c Conditions for Collusion

The economic framework for understanding collusion is heavily influenced by game theory. Game theory is a mix of economics, mathematics and psychology that aims to identify the market conditions that are necessary so that firms can collude successfully.[131] While most benefits occur in static models,[132] collusion arises over repeated episodes of interaction.[133] While the Nash equilibrium in a one-shot game lies in both firms lowering the price irrespectively of the decision of the other firm (i.e., they have a dominant strategy), firms learn to recognise the gained benefits from setting higher prices in *repeated* games.[134] The idea is that through repeated interactions, firms learn to sacrifice short-term profits (profits gained through cheating) over long-term gains (share of a joint profit).[135] Collusion emerges where the long-term incentive to collude is stronger than any short-term gains.[136] However, in order to sustain collusion, the long-term firms need to be able to observe detections and have a punishment

124. *See* Ivaldi et al. (2003), fn 2 on p. 4; Motta (2004), p. 138; OECD (2012a), para. 10.
125. *See* Ivaldi et al. (2003), p. 4.
126. *See* Jones and Sufrin (2016), pp. 650 and 661.
127. *See* section 5.1 for the challenges to derive concertation from parallel conduct alone.
128. *See* Petit (2013), p. 13.
129. *See* OECD (2012a), fn 51. *See* section 3.3.1.d.
130. *Ibid.*, para. 21 (grey box). For instance, direct interactions can help to efficiently structure the cooperation in such a way as to stimulate some of the conditions necessary for the sustainability of the collusion. *See* section 3.3.5 on the importance of communication.
131. *See* Monti (2007), p. 310.
132. *See* already section 3.1.3.
133. *See* González (2012), pp. 20-23 for a good overview of the relevant literature on game theory.
134. *See* Jones and Sufrin (2016), p. 654.
135. *See* Smith, Ridyard and Petrescu (2015), p. 34.
136. Wijckmans and Tuytschaever (2015), para. 11.11.

mechanism for cheaters so that any punishment would outweigh possible benefits from deviations.[137]

More formally, this game theory logic results in four conditions necessary to reach and sustain a collusive outcome:[138]

(1) *Collusive outcome*: firms must be able to reach a 'common understanding' on the terms of the coordination (such as price increases, quality reductions, market-sharing and so on).
(2) *Detection*: firms must be able to monitor to a sufficient degree whether other participating firms deviate from the collusive outcome (more informally described as 'cheating').
(3) *Punishment*: firms must be able to punish those firms that deviate from the collusive outcome in order to deter them from deviating in the first place (also described as 'credible retaliation mechanisms').
(4) *Outsiders*: the collusive outcome must not be threatened by foreseeable reactions from outsiders that are not part of the collusion (such as current or potential competitors or even customers).

The first condition relates to the challenge firms face when trying to move to a collusive outcome. Firms need some kind of focal point to actually achieve this.[139] Habit, past conduct or particular events may provide such focal points.[140] However, firms may also simply communicate their future intentions to overcome those difficulties.[141]

The second and third conditions are crucial ingredients for the *internal* stability of the collusion. Most economic literature focuses on this aspect.[142] Assuming that firms manage to agree on a collusive outcome, firms are always tempted to unilaterally deviate from a collusive outcome because by doing so they increase their profit. From an economic perspective, long-term benefits derived from collusion must outweigh possible short-term benefits from deviating; otherwise collusion is not sustainable in the long run. This constant tension between both types of benefits reflects the dynamic aspect of collusion.[143]

There are four aspects that influence the internal stability of collusion: the discount factor, the probability of detection, the time-lag of detection and the number of punishment periods.[144] The first aspect relates to relative importance of the future

137. *See* González (2012), p. 22; das Nair and Mncube (2013).
138. *See* Horizontal Merger Guidelines, para. 41; OECD (2012a), para. 11; Ezrachi (2018), p. 330. When the economic literature points out that there are merely *three* conditions to achieve and maintain collusion, it combines the first two conditions (collusive outcome and detection) into one condition (*see*, e.g., Stigler (1964); Ivaldi et al. (2003); OECD (2011), pp. 10-11).
139. Schelling (1960) was the first to introduce the notion of focal point (*see*, e.g., Motta (2004), p. 152, fn 35 on this observation).
140. *See* Motta (2004), p. 152.
141. *See* section 3.3.5.
142. *See* Kühn (2001), p. 173.
143. *See* Ivaldi et al. (2003), p. 5.
144. *See* Wagner-von Papp (2007), p. 268.

(discount factor).[145] While retaliation occurs in the future, deviations generate immediate profits. Collusion is only sustainable if firms value *future* profits (i.e., the discount factor is relatively small).[146] The other three aspects relate to the idea that if other participating firms are not able to detect the deviation, cheaters would get away with deviating from the collusive outcome without being punished. The ability to quickly detect and punish deviations is therefore a crucial ingredient to sustain collusion. The quicker the detection, the less pronounced are incentives to deviate in the first place.[147]

The fourth condition relates to the *external* stability of the collusion. If price increases attract new players (potential competition) or if customers are sufficiently powerful to prevent any attempt to increase prices (countervailing buyers' power), collusion cannot be achieved.[148] Therefore the fourth condition requires an assessment of the structural market conditions (particularly market entry and buyer power).

3.3.1.d Factors That Facilitate Collusion

3.3.1.d.1 Introduction

According to modern industrial economics there are certain structural factors that facilitate collusion and thus make reaching and sustaining collusive outcomes more likely. These factors do not actually prove the existence of collusion, but merely provide an analytical framework to analyse if market conditions are *conducive* for collusion.[149] They are on every standard checklist when assessing the structural risk of collusion.[150]

Economic theory is based on the so-called incentive constraint for collusion where each firm compares the immediate gain of a deviation with the profit it gives up in the future due to the punishment. According to this incentive constraint theory collusion is more likely (i) the lower the profit gained through deviating, (ii) the lower the expected profits the firm would make during punishment phase, and (iii) the more weight the firms attaches to the future (i.e., losses through punishment in the long-term are valued more than the short-term gains from deviation).[151]

3.3.1.d.2 Factors Where the Effects on Collusion Is Clear

There are several factors that relax the incentive constraint and thus facilitate collusion.[152] These factors can be categorised into three categories: factors that relate to

145. *See*, e.g., das Nair and Mncube (2013).
146. *See* Ivaldi et al. (2003), pp. 7-8.
147. *See* Motta (2004), p. 139.
148. *See* OECD (2011), p. 11.
149. *See* OECD (2012a), fn 13 in para. 12. The same factors are used in merger control to assess coordinated effects (*see* Wagner-von Papp (2012), p. 19).
150. *See* Smith, Ridyard and Petrescu (2015), p. 34.
151. *See* Motta (2004), p. 142.
152. *See*, e.g., Horizontal Merger Guidelines, paras 44-48; Stroux (2000), pp. 7-13; Ivaldi et al. (2003), pp. 11-57; Motta (2004), pp. 142-149; OECD (2011), paras 57-62; OECD (2012a), para. 12.

characteristics of the structure of market, the demand side of the market and the supply side of the market.[153]

Factors that relate to the structure of the market are:

- *Market concentration*: collusion is more likely when there are fewer firms on the market..[154] This factor is certainly one of the most important factors in practice.[155] The more concentrated the market, the easier it is to agree to the terms of collusion and the easier it is to monitor each other.[156] The latter means that cheating is more easily detectable as even small changes in the collusive outcome can be attributed to price-cutting.[157] However, even if measures of concentration are high, the effect on collusion might be ambiguous when assets are asymmetrically distributed. This is because higher concentration and higher asymmetry affect each other in opposite ways.[158]
- *Market entry*: collusion is more likely when the entry barriers are higher (which are determined by fixed entry costs that new firms would have to sink into the market in order to enter it).[159] The level of entry barriers determines the competitive constrained by potential (as opposed to actual) competition.[160] However, even if entry barriers are low potential entrants might be deterred from entering the market if incumbents are able to pose credible threat to react aggressively in case of an entrance.[161]
- *Frequent interaction*: collusion is more likely when the orders are made more regular and frequent. This is because firms are then able to react more quickly to deviations.[162] Conversely, unusually large orders would give firms a strong temptation to deviate. Infrequency of orders would prevent other firms from punishing cheaters timely.[163]
- *Lack of network effects*: network effects create a winner-takes-all effect and thus tilt the market in favour of one firm. In those markets, collusion is

153. *See* Ivaldi et al. (2003), p. 11.
154. *See* Horizontal Merger Guidelines, para. 45; Ivaldi et al. (2003), pp. 12-14; Stroux (2004), pp. 17-19; OECD (2012a), para. 12 first bullet point. *See also* Kühn and Vives (1995), pp. 82-83 in the context of information exchanges.
155. *See* Whish (2006), pp. 29-31 who mostly discusses the level of concentration when discussing the importance of the market structure in dealing with information exchanges.
156. *See* OECD (2011), para. 59.
157. *See* Stroux (2004), p. 18.
158. *See* Motta (2004), p. 143. In the example where there are many firms in the market, a small firm would get only a small profit share of the collusive outcome while it may be able to get all the market if it deviates from the collusive outcome (*ibid.*, p. 142).
159. *See* Ivaldi et al. (2003), pp. 16-19; OECD (2012a), para. 12 third bullet point. *See also* the Horizontal Merger Guidelines, paras 68-75, which explain that potential market entry must be likely, timely and sufficient to deter any potential anti-competitive effect of a merger.
160. *See* Stroux (2004), p. 22. In perfectly contestable market (i.e., where entry and exit are costless and immediate) economic theory suggests that prices will be set at competitive level. Such markets are also referred to as 'hit-and-run entry' markets. However, they are very rare in practice.
161. *See* Motta (2004), p. 144.
162. *See* Ivaldi et al. (2003), pp. 19-22.
163. *See* Motta (2004), p. 145; Stroux (2004), pp. 26-27.

unlikely because the incentives for cheating are enormous (up to the entire market).[164]

- *Longer-lasting market*: game theory provides that in a market with only a limited number of contracts to be won (i.e., in the game theory language a game with only a limited number of periods), collusion is unlikely to occur.[165] These may be markets with products that have a short life cycle or where in the foreseeable future only a limited number of contracts can be won (such as certain large projects).[166]

Factors that relate to the demand side of the market are:

- *Demand growth*: collusion is easier to sustain in growing markets where today's profits are small compared to tomorrow's. Conversely, when demand is declining tomorrow's profits are small and incentives for deviations are high.[167] This conclusion assumes though that the number of market participants remains the same. If one gives up that assumption and assumes that market entry will occur in growing markets (particularly if market entries are low), market growth is actually detrimental to collusion.[168]
- *Demand stability*: collusion is less likely in markets with demand fluctuations (such as seasonal cycles). This is because when market demand is at the peak, short-term profits from deviations are significant, while potential costs are low because subsequent retaliation occurs during times of lower demand.[169]
- *Lack of buying power*: collusion is more likely when the buyers are weaker. Conversely, a sufficiently strong buyer may have sufficient countervailing buying power to break up the collusive outcome (e.g., by grouping small orders together in large and infrequent orders or by vertical integration).[170]

Factors that relate to the supply side of the market are:

- *Structural links among competitors*: collusion is more likely when there are structural links between competitors (either directly or indirectly via joint ventures).[171] The first concern is that the acquiring firm may obtain access to

164. *See* Ivaldi et al. (2003), p. 57.
165. Game theory solves this by 'backward induction' which is explained by Peeperkorn (1996), p. 2: 'In a one period prisoners dilemma type non-cooperative game the best strategy for each player will be not to cooperate. This means that in a multi-period game it is rational for both players not to cooperate in the last period. Given the certainty that both will not cooperate in the last period it is also not rational to cooperate in the pre-last period, as there can be no reward in terms of cooperation in the last period etc.'
166. *See* Peeperkorn (1996), p. 3.
167. *See* Ivaldi et al. (2003), pp. 26-27; Motta (2004), pp. 145-146; Stroux (2004), p. 26.
168. *See* Ivaldi et al. (2003), p. 28.
169. *Ibid.*, pp. 29-32.
170. *See* Snyder (1996); Stroux (2004), p. 24; OECD (2012a), para. 12 fourth bullet point, which describes buyer power as 'number and strength of the outsiders'. *See also* the Horizontal Merger Guidelines, paras 64-67, which list buyer power as one of the countervailing powers.
171. *See* Horizontal Merger Guidelines, para. 48.

privileged information about the acquired firm.[172] The second concern is that the incentives of the acquiring firm to compete in markets where the acquired firm operates as well may be reduced.[173]

- *Symmetry*: collusion is more likely when the firms are more symmetrical ('collusion is easier among equals').[174,175] Conversely, asymmetric structures hinder collusion because, on the one hand, it is harder to agree on a focal point and, on the other hand, more efficient firms always have a higher incentive to deviate.[176] This logic helps to explain why mavericks are normally unwilling to participate in collusion. A maverick is a disrupter because it simply has a drastically different cost structure.[177] Symmetry is not just limited to the cost structure. It can also relate *inter alia* to market shares,[178] number of product varieties, technological knowledge, capacity level[179] or level of vertical integration.[180]
- *Lack of innovation*: innovation is an important competing factor and may give firms substantial advantages over competitors.[181] Thus, in markets where innovation is not an important competitive factor, collusion is more likely.[182]
- *Multi-market contacts*: multi-market contacts can facilitate collusion in several ways. First, they can smooth out asymmetries between firms in specific

172. *See* Gabrielsen et al. (2011), pp. 840-841 (passive minority shareholdings), p. 842 (active minority shareholdings) and pp. 843-844 (interlocking directorships); Commission (2013), paras 47-48; Levy (2013), p. 734. This might be true: (i) in case of active minority shareholdings, where the acquiring firm has some influence over the commercial policy of the acquired firm (e.g., through the appointment of one of the board directors), or (ii) even in case of passive minority shareholdings when national law grant access to sensitive information to protect the right of minority shareholders (*see* Gassler (2018), pp. 25-26).
173. There are two effects that have to be considered in determining whether passive minority shareholdings will increase the likelihood of collusion; the collusion-enhancing and the destabilising effect. The collusion-enhancing effect means that the likelihood of collusion decreases because the acquirer and the target now share losses when cheating (*see*, e.g., Gilo, Moshe and Spiegel (2006), p. 82). The destabilising effect means that the acquisition might lead to negative unilateral effects which reduce the incentive to engage in the collusion in the first place (*see*, e.g., Paha and de Haas (2016), p. 11). The industrial economic literature suggests that it depends on the market conditions which effect outweighs the other (*see* Gassler (2018), pp. 27-28 who suggests that the concern is with markets that follow the Bertrand model with homogeneous or heterogeneous products).
174. For this, *see* Ivaldi et al. (2003), p. 55.
175. Stroux refers to this as the 'homogeneity of suppliers' (*see* Stroux (2004), p. 20). However, this is misleading since homogeneity mainly refers to products and not firms. Thus, in this book 'homogeneity' is only used for products while 'symmetry' is used for firms.
176. *See* Ivaldi et al. (2003), pp. 35-40. However, firms can share profits unevenly and grant larger proportions of the profits to the more efficient firms.
177. *Ibid.*, pp. 40 and 55-56.
178. Ivaldi et al. explicitly note that market shares are merely an indication for a more profound asymmetry between firms. In other words, asymmetry is the cause, market shares are merely a more obvious indicia for that (*see* Ivaldi et al. (2003), pp. 14-16).
179. *See* more in-depth discussion on this aspect by Ivaldi et al. (2003), pp. 41-45.
180. *See* Horizontal Merger Guidelines, para. 48; Motta (2004), p. 147; Stroux (2004), p. 20.
181. *See* OECD (2011), para. 57.
182. *See* Ivaldi et al. (2003), pp. 32-35.

markets so that when all markets are taken together firms are more symmetric.[183] Second, they can also increase the frequency of the interaction between firms.[184]

3.3.1.d.3 Factors Where the Effects on Collusion Is More Ambiguous

There are also factors for which the effect on the incentive constraint and thus the effect on the facilitation of collusion is more ambiguous:[185]

- *Product homogeneity*: the Commission points out that it is easier to reach a collusive outcome if products are homogeneous.[186] The intuitive logic is that it is easier for firms to collude on prices for a single and homogeneous product than for many differentiated products.[187] However, the fact that collusion is easier to reach does not mean that collusion is easier to *sustain*.[188] This is because product homogeneity is a double-edged sword. Although it makes collusion easier to agree on, it does also make deviations more likely (i.e., even small price cuts may be sufficient to attract a substantial part of demand). Thus, product homogeneity needs to be combined with other factors (such as the speed of detecting deviations) to make a robust statement about the likelihood of collusion.
- *Product heterogeneity*: the level of heterogeneity of products (as referred to as vertical differentiation)[189] is also an ambiguous factor for the likelihood of collusion. If products are heterogeneous it becomes more difficult to punish deviators. The deviator would be still left with some demand even after a significant price war. This makes punishment less effective and thus collusion *less* likely.[190] However, heterogeneous products make any deviation also costlier. This is because the deviator has to offer a significant price cut in order to gain market shares. This makes deviation less likely and thus collusion *more* likely.[191]
- *Demand elasticity*: demand elasticity of the market has an ambiguous effect on the likelihood of collusion. For instance, a very elastic demand means that although cheating will result in significant short-term profits, it will also result in significant losses during the punishment period. However, the elasticity will

183. *See* Motta (2004), p. 149.
184. *See* Ivaldi et al. (2003), p. 48.
185. *See* Motta (2004), pp. 146-149. For a slightly different view, *see* Ivaldi et al. (2003), pp. 45 et seq.
186. Horizontal Merger Guidelines, para. 45; Horizontal Cooperation Guidelines, para. 82. *See also* Stroux (2004), pp. 24-25; Whish (2006), p. 22.
187. *See* OECD (2011), para. 61.
188. *See*, e.g., Niemeyer (1993), p. 156 who fails both to consider the sustainability of the collusion and to merely focus on the easiness of finding a collusion outcome; Camesasca, Schmidt and Clancy (2010), p. 412.
189. *See*, for this notion, Ivaldi et al. (2003), p. 45.
190. *See* Ivaldi et al. (2003), pp. 45-46.
191. *See* Motta (2004), p. 146; OECD (2011), paras 61-62.

affect the *level* of the collusive price: the lower the elasticity the higher the collusive price.[192]

- *Excess capacities*: the effect of large excess capacities is also ambiguous on the likelihood of collusion. On the one hand, large excess capacities give firms an incentive to deviate. On the other hand, it enables other firms to punish deviators more quickly.[193]

3.3.1.d.4 The Desirable Analytical Approach

One should avoid a formalistic, isolated and abstract analytical treatment of these factors. Instead, these factors should be assessed in a holistic manner under consideration of the specific economic context and market characteristics.

A *formalistic* approach should be avoided because all these factors are factors of scale. There is no clear abstract threshold for each of the factors which marks the 'tipping point'. Instead, one has to consider the specific market characteristics.[194] For instance, a low frequency of the information exchange may be less problematic in a market with short-term contracts (where price negotiation occurs more often), while it may be problematic in a market with long-term contracts.[195]

An *isolated* assessment of these factors should also be avoided. Instead, these factors should be assessed as a moveable system that aims to offer a holistic picture of the effect on competition.[196] While some factors may raise competition concern, others may produce significant efficiencies. Therefore, one has to come to an overall conclusion after considering all factors. This multifactor analysis makes it difficult to provide any kind of safe harbour.[197]

An *abstract* analysis without considering the specific economic context of the information exchange should be avoided as well. The relevance of some of these factors for collusion is not as clear-cut and may depend on the specific context. For instance, the exchange of commercially sensitive data about deliveries to customers may be relevant if collusion relates to market and customer sharing, but may be irrelevant if it relates to the level of discounts.[198] Also, the exchange of technology data may be more strategic in markets where firms compete regarding R&D efforts.[199] Thus, the specific context plays a crucial part in the substantive conclusion of the concrete assessment of the case.

192. *See* Ivaldi et al. (2003), pp. 50-52; Motta (2004), p. 145.
193. *See* Motta (2004), p. 149.
194. This has been emphasised, e.g., by Carle and Johnsson (1998), p. 75; Wijckmans and Tuytschaever (2015), para. 11.01.
195. *See* Horizontal Cooperation Guidelines, para. 91; Wijckmans and Tuytschaever (2015), para. 11.68.
196. *See* similarly Wagner-von Papp (2012), pp. 4 and 20-21.
197. *See* Wagner-von Papp (2012), p. 21. *See* section 6.2.3 for a discussion about the usefulness of safe harbours for pure information exchanges.
198. *See* OECD (2011), para. 65.
199. *See* Wijckmans and Tuytschaever (2015), para. 11.65 for this example.

3.3.2 The Theory of Tacit Collusion

3.3.2.a Meaning

The notion of 'tacit collusion' discussed in the economic literature refers to a situation where firms tend to conform to conducts of other competing firms because they act in response to or in anticipation of the market behaviour of these firms.[200] The greater the ability of a firm to anticipate the behaviour of other firms due to high levels of interdependence, the more likely uniform conduct will occur.[201] In other words, parallel conduct of a firm in such a scenario is the expression of an independent, conscious and intelligent reaction on the market, but not the result of a concertation.[202]

3.3.2.b Terminology

Unfortunately, there is a lack of semantic homogeneity in the economic literature on the issue of 'tacit collusion'. Tacit collusion[203] has been described *inter alia* as conscious parallelism,[204] mere parallelism,[205] tacit coordination,[206] implicit collusion[207] or consciously parallel action.[208] All these notions refer to the same issue.[209]

Petit argues that linguistically the word 'parallelism' should be avoided because this is also a feature of perfectly competitive markets. He prefers the notions of 'tacit/implicit/non-cooperative collusion' or 'tacit/implicit/non-cooperative coordination' because the former words clearly symbolise the lack of explicit collusion.[210] However, Whish and Bailey argue that the expression of 'collusion' should be avoided altogether because it is bizarre for lawyers that a concept that contains the word 'collusion' should be perfectly lawful under competition law rules. Therefore, they propose to use the expression 'tacit coordination' because it eliminated the word 'collusion' while still retaining the notion referring to parallel conduct.[211]

200. *See* Ray Pfeiffer (1974), p. 114. He further notes: 'The term "conscious parallelism" can be understood as a form of over-competition in which actively competing enterprises learn so much about each other that by sophisticated, rational, independent decision-making, based on carefully calculated probabilities, they are able to neutralize each other's pricing behavior, producing an ostensibly noncompetitive relationship.' (*ibid.*, p. 115)
201. *Ibid.*, p. 127; Jones and Sufrin (2016), p. 660.
202. *See* Cucu (2013), p. 225.
203. The US terminology (*see* Filippelli (2013), p. 76).
204. *See* Posner (1969), p. 1578; Ray Pfeiffer (1974), p. 114; Heimler (2010), p. 402; Wagner-von Papp (2012), p. 18; Ezrachi (2018), pp. 345 et seq.
205. *See* Filippelli (2013).
206. *See* Ivaldi et al. (2003), fn 2 on p. 4.
207. *See* OECD (2012a), para. 21; Petit (2013), p. 24.
208. *See* Page (2007), p. 429.
209. Sometimes 'oligopolistic tacit collusion' is used synonymously (*see*, e.g., Petersen (2016), p. 22). However, tacit collusion in oligopolistic markets is merely one of the situations where tacit collusion may occur (*see* section 2.2.3).
210. *See* Petit (2013), pp. 23-24.
211. *See* Whish and Bailey (2018), p. 573. *See also* Jones and Sufrin (2016), p. 660 recognising this issue, although they are fine with using tacit collusion.

Since this book focuses on the assessment of information exchanges under Art. 101 TFEU, the long-lasting struggle to deal with parallel conduct under Art. 101 TFEU is explored later in order to understand the importance of information exchanges for collusion theories.[212] There is also a conceptual overlap between certain cases that at the time were considered in light of the tacit collusion literature and are now partly reconsidered under the idea of signalling with advance and unilateral public announcements.[213]

3.3.2.c Situations in Which Tacit Collusion Can Occur

Cucu identifies three scenarios in which it is rational for firms to respond and anticipate market behaviour of competing firms.[214] In other words, these are situations where one should expect tacit collusion to occur:

(1) *Transparent markets*: on transparent markets, where each firm is able to observe the prices of its competitors, prices will be equal or roughly equal for similar goods simply because price competition forces them to do so.
(2) *Price leadership*: on certain markets other firms will simply follow the perceived price leader. This may occur in form of either a 'dominant firm' price leadership, a 'barometric' price leadership or 'collusive' price leaders, although only the latter form is caught by Art. 101 TFEU.[215]
(3) *Oligopolistic markets*: in oligopolistic markets,[216] firms have an increased ability to correctly anticipate actions of their competitors because of the

212. *See* section 5.1.
213. *See* section 6.4.
214. *See* Cucu (2013), p. 225.
215. Price leadership may occur in the form of: (i) a *dominant firm* price leadership which involves a market with a firm that is more powerful or larger than other firms in the market (smaller firms will simply follow the prices of the perceived market leader), or (ii) a *barometric* price leadership which involves a market where some firms are better informed than other firms and the less informed firms simply delay their decision until the better-informed firms move first (*see* OECD (2012a), para. 68; Petersen (2016), pp. 28-29 in the context of interlocks).
Both types fall outside the scope of competition law. In the dominant firm price leadership scenario, the industry has simply accepted that there is a price leadership of the dominant firm. In the barometric price leadership scenario, the better-informed firm simply provides a useful signal about the changing market conditions. The concerns lie with the third scenario, the collusive price leadership.
216. An oligopolistic market is a market with few buyers. Economists have been reluctant to concretise how few players in a market should have to be regarded as an oligopoly (*see* Petit (2013), fn 1). Selten famously stated that 'four are few and six are many' (*see* Selten (1973)). Whatever the exact number is, in oligopolistic markets, firms are more interdependent in their pricing and output decisions than in competitive markets. Each decision of one firm has an impact on, and result in, a counter response from other firms (*see* OECD (2012a), para. 21).
An excellent and easily understandable overview of the different models used in the economic literature to assess oligopolies can be found in Stroux (2004), Chapter 0. His classification of the different models distinguishes between static models of oligopoly (Cournot, Bertrand, Stackelberg and Edgeworth) and game theory models (*one-shot games vs repeated games*; cooperative and non-cooperative models). She also explains the different schools of thought in the US on how to deal with the oligopoly problem (*structuralists or Harvard school vs behaviouralists or Chicago school*).

simplification of economic calculations caused by the low number of market players (the so-called oligopoly problem that is caused by the oligopolistic interdependency).[217]

As one can see from this list, the issue of tacit collusion is mostly a *structural* problem.[218] Parallel conduct has to be expected in markets that are transparent, concentrated or have an incumbent. The problem is that Art. 101 TFEU prohibition is *conduct*-related. In these three scenarios firms can engage in parallel conduct and still act independently in the sense that there is no joint decision-making or concertation between them.[219] In other words, concertation may not be the only explanation for parallel conduct. Other explanations may offer a plausible alternative for why firms act in parallel. This is at the heart of the case law on parallel conduct, where EU Courts have been reluctant to derive concertation from mere parallel conduct without any further proof from some kind of documentary evidence of concertation.[220]

3.3.3 The Concept of 'Facilitative Practices'

3.3.3.a Meaning

The concept of a facilitative practice is not as clear-cut as one might think. Proposed definitions not only vary quite a lot but are also quite vague. The OECD for instance has defined the concept of a facilitative practice as a 'conduct by firms, typically in an oligopolistic market, that falls somewhere between an explicit, "hardcore" cartel agreement and pure and simple oligopolistic interdependence and helps firms to reduce uncertainty in the market and coordinate their conduct more effectively'.[221] This definition is rather vague and may only be used to categorise the concept conceptually (i.e., it is something between parallel conduct and hard-core cartels).

217. *See* Ray Pfeiffer (1974), p. 114. *See also* the description by the OECD (2012a, paras 21-23): 'In oligopolistic markets, firms tend to be interdependent in their pricing and output decisions so that the actions of each firm impact on, and result in, a counter response from the other firms. In such circumstances, oligopolistic firms may take their rivals' actions into account and co-ordinate their actions as if they were a cartel, but without an explicit agreement. [...] In contrast to explicit collusion, in a tacitly collusive context, the non-competitive outcome is achieved by each participant deciding on its own profit maximizing strategy independently of its competitors. [...] No profit-maximising firm wants to make zero profits forever and each firm knows that it could earn supra-competitive profits by collectively charging a non-competitive price. The indefinitely repeated interaction makes the threat of punishment credible so that each firm knows that any deviation from the non-competitive equilibrium would trigger a price war pushing prices towards the competitive equilibrium. Therefore, such oligopolistic interaction renders individual strategies conducive to an equilibrium at noncompetitive prices/output rational, without actually communicating or agreeing explicitly.'
218. *See* Jones and Sufrin (2016), p. 661.
219. *See* Kühn and Vives (1995), p. 76.
220. *See* section 5.1.2 on the issue of parallel conduct and section 4.2.3 on this evidentiary issue of hard/soft evidence.
221. OECD (2007a), p. 9.

A different definition is given by Petit who describes facilitating practices as ways to 'artificially' increase the chances of successful collusion.[222] This definition necessarily makes reference to economic theories about collusion. In this sense, facilitative practices try to either limit the influence of those factors that destabilise collusion (e.g., reduce buying power) or enhance the influence of those factors that support collusion (e.g., make the market more concentrated).[223]

Game theory argues in a similar direction. According to game theory facilitative practices can affect the pay-off matrix and thus alter the incentives to collude.[224] This is done by changing the firms' environment in such a way that each firm has the incentive to choose an action that belongs to a joint profit-maximising strategy.[225] In other words, facilitating practices may alter the *structural conditions* in markets so that even tacit collusion is sufficient to achieve supra-competitive outcomes (such as making the market more concentrated, making market entry more difficult, making firms more symmetrical and so on).[226] More trenchant, they may be the last straw that breaks the camel's back.

3.3.3.b Forms

There seems to be no consensus in the literature on which conduct falls within the scope of the concept. However, there is one exception to general observation: the exchange of information is always mentioned as one example of a facilitative practice.

The following facilitative practices have been identified for instance by Stroux:[227]

- *Information exchange*: may increase collusion because of the increased market transparency.
- *Price leadership*: the prices set by the perceived price leader in the industry act as powerful focal points for other firms in the market.
- *Product standardisation*: may increase the risk of collusion because of the increased market transparency.

222. *See* Petit (2013), pp. 30-31. *See also* Grillo (2002), pp. 160-161 and Petersen (2016), p. 22. Similarly, the Horizontal Cooperation Guidelines provide in the context of information exchange that by '*artificially* increasing transparency in the market, the exchange of strategic information can facilitate coordination (that is to say, alignment) of the companies' competitive behaviour and result in restrictive effects on competition'. (emphasis added) (Horizontal Cooperation Guidelines, para. 65).
223. *See* Peeperkorn (1996), p. 5.
224. *See* Stroux (2004), p. 27.
225. *See* Grillo (2002), p. 161.
226. *See* Monti (2007), p. 335.
227. *See* Stroux (2004), pp. 27-34. For a narrower list, *see*, e.g., Monti (2007), pp. 339-340: information exchange, resale price maintenance and English clauses. For a wider list, *see*, e.g., Petit (2013), pp. 31-33: horizontal cooperation agreements, vertical agreements, structural links and technology transfer agreements. While the former list has been suggested by an economist, the latter list was provided by a lawyer. Thus, the difference can be explained by the framing of the issue.

- *Geographical pricing system* (such as basing point pricing): may facilitate the calculation of prices because they will mainly remove the price discretion on shipping charges.
- *Contingency clauses* (such as Most Favoured Nation (MFN) clauses or meeting competition clauses): even though they occur in a vertical setting, they may entail horizontal coordinated effects.

3.3.3.c *Information Exchange as a Facilitative Practice*

In reality, it might be often difficult to reach mutually acceptable terms of collusion and to ensure that each firm does not deviate from it. As one of the OECD paper puts it 'there can be a considerable gap between the intention to co-operate and the ability to so successfully'.[228] Therefore firms need ways to overcome the practical challenges faced by firms willing to collude.

From an economic perspective, there are broadly speaking two ways in which collusion can be facilitated: either practices that facilitate the process of *finding* of a collusive outcome[229] or practices that facilitate the process of *sustaining* collusion.[230]

Information exchange can constitute a facilitative practice because it may 'artificially' increase the chances of successful collusion in these two ways. Regarding the first way, the exchange of intended future conduct can be an effective means to overcome the equilibrium selection problem.[231] Regarding the second way, information exchange can make it easier for competitors to sustain collusive outcomes *inter alia* because it makes monitoring collusive outcomes easier or because it enables more targeted punishments.[232]

3.3.3.d *Current Shortcomings*

The concept at its current stage offers little *substantive* guidance. It is not always clear that when the literature uses the notion of 'artificial' in the context of information exchanges, it is not merely used as a substitute for 'anti-competitive'.[233] The concept of a facilitative practice would then simply refer to the legal distinction between lawful and unlawful practices without providing any substantive guidance. Similarly, it is not clear how to distinguish between 'artificial' and 'natural' market transparency.[234] However, the difference is decisive since only the former category should be caught by the Art. 101 TFEU prohibition. Thus, the concept has currently merely *descriptive* value

228. OECD (2012a), para. 24.
229. *See* the first condition for collusion as explained in section 3.3.1.c.
230. *See* the second and third conditions for collusion as explained in section 3.3.1.c.
231. *See* Wijckmans and Tuytschaever (2015), para. 11.15. *See also* section 3.3.5.b.
232. These two examples are mentioned by Peeperkorn (1996), p. 5 in this context.
233. *See*, e.g., Capobianco (2004), p. 1256 who fails to refer to the concept of a facilitative practice more generally and fails to provide any substantive guidance on the notion of 'artificial'. *See also* section 3.3.4.b.
234. *See* in this context Wagner-von Papp (2012), p. 18.

to distinguish lawful information exchanges (natural market transparency) from unlawful information exchanges (artificial market transparency).

The concept of a facilitative practice could though be an important analytical concept for implementing economic theories into the legal framework. In other words, the concept could be used to 'translate' collusion concerns raised by lawyers into concrete guidance for lawyers to assess information exchanges. This way, the concept could develop its full analytical potential for assessing information exchanges. This book does exactly that and proposes a more elaborated analytical framework for assessing pure information exchanges.[235]

3.3.4 The Role of Market Transparency for Collusion: It Is Mainly About Past Data

3.3.4.a The Notion of Market Transparency

A vast amount of the economic literature on information exchange relates to the issue of market transparency. In its simplest form, the idea is that because information exchange increases the transparency of the market, it makes collusion easier. However, before discussing the ways in which the market transparency can facilitate collusion,[236] the notion itself should be explored further. Market transparency can relate to all variables relevant to the competitive process (particularly though prices and quantities). It entails three different aspects relevant to collusion.

First, the level of market transparency depends on the *costs* required to discover transaction prices.[237] This entails an assessment of the resources necessary to access the information. Even if the information as such is free, the access of that information may still entail some costs (such as the time to find that information). Even free information may not be without costs.

Second, the level of market transparency also depends on the *speed* with which firms can reliably inform themselves of competitors' actions.[238] This aspect plays a role in how easily and reliably cheating can be detected and subsequently punished. The quicker the detection, the more credible the punishment mechanism and possible smaller gains from deviations.

Third, the level of market transparency also depends on the *scope of players* which have access to that information. Transparency can be achieved mainly through private exchanges between competitors (private market transparency) or advance public announcements (public market transparency).[239] Since customers only benefit from public market transparency, private market transparency is generally seen as

235. *See* section 6.5.2.
236. *See* next section 3.3.4.b.
237. *See* OECD (2001), p. 21.
238. *See* OECD (2012a), para. 13.
239. *Ibid.*, para. 13. For a different definition, *see* discussion comment by Benny Moldovanu in Kühn (2001), p. 200: public communication relates to announcements that have some commitment effect.

more problematic. As a rule of thumb, public transparency is more likely to intensify competition, while private transparency is more likely to restrict it.[240]

3.3.4.b *The Ways in Which Market Transparency Facilitates Collusion*

As mentioned, information exchange improves market transparency. The effect of increased market transparency is that it increases the observability of firms' actions on the market.[241] This holds true for private and public market transparency since the extent of observability from the perspective of firms that have access to that information is the same. Although the private/public market transparency distinction matters to customers, their access to exchanged information does not matter for collusion risk between firms.

Increased market transparency entails essentially three consequences for collusion. First, market transparency increases the *internal stability* of the collusion. Market transparency of past conduct enables firms to monitor each other and detect deviations, particularly if the data is highly disaggregated.[242] This increases internal stability of the collusion due to the greater precision in detecting and punishing deviations (targeted punishments).[243] The more likely and quickly the deviations are detected, the cheaper is any punishment for the punisher and the more effective the punishment to deter cheaters. Targeted punishments make the threat of punishment more credible and therefore lower the incentives to deviate in the first place (sometimes referred to as the 'threat of credible punishment').[244] This helps to explain why the

240. *See* OECD (2012a), para. 14. This aligns with the position of the Commission in its Horizontal Cooperation Guidelines: 'In general, exchanges of genuinely public information are unlikely to constitute an infringement of Article 101. Genuinely public information is information that is generally equally accessible (in terms of costs of access) to all competitors and customers. For information to be genuinely public, obtaining it should not be more costly for customers and companies unaffiliated to the exchange system than for the companies exchanging the information. [...] An *information exchange* is genuinely public if it makes the exchanged data equally accessible (in terms of costs of access) to all competitors and customers. The fact that information is exchanged in public may decrease the likelihood of a collusive outcome on the market to the extent that non-coordinating companies, potential competitors, as well as costumers may be able to constrain potential restrictive effect on competition.' (Horizontal Cooperation Guidelines, paras 93-94)

241. *See* Motta (2004), p. 150.

242. *See*, e.g., Peeperkorn (1996), p. 6; Bissocoli (2000), pp. 83-84; Vives (2006a), p. 91; González (2012), pp. 28-30.

243. *See* Kühn and Vives (1995), p. 77; Kühn (2001), pp. 173 and 187-188; OECD (2001), p. 24; Ivaldi et al. (2003), pp. 22-26; Møllgaard and Overgaard (2006), pp. 106-108; Vives (2006a), p. 89; Bennet and Collins (2010), p. 322; OECD (2011), p. 11 (bullet point 2 in para. 16); Wagner-von Papp (2012), pp. 10-11; Nitsche and von Hinten-Reed (2014), pp. 25-26. *See also* Wagner-von Papp (2007), pp. 265-266 and 267-268 who suggests that the identification of individual competitors is in any case possible with just two firms in the markets, but may also be possible when there are more players if there are other items of information available that enable the identification (such as press announcements with individual data).

244. *See* Wagner-von Papp (2007), pp. 267-269. *See also* Motta (2004), pp. 139-140 and 151; das Nair and Mncube (2013); Nitsche and von Hinten-Reed (2014), p. 27. However, even long reaction lags and infrequent communication may be sufficient to sustain collusion is some markets (*see* Vives (2006a), p. 92).

frequency of an information exchange matters for the stability of collusion: the more exchanges the quicker subsequent punishments.[245]

Furthermore, market transparency is also existential for the internal stability of collusion when demand shocks occur. Without market transparency firms do not know whether the lower-than-expected demand is caused by a demand shock or by deviations of other firms from the collusive outcome (and thus redirecting demand to them). Without the observability of individual market conduct there is a high risk that punishment will be triggered by such demand changes. Market transparency prevents such 'misinterpretations' of demand shocks and thus contributes to the internal stability of collusion.[246]

Second, increased market transparency also increases the *external stability* of collusion.[247] For collusion to sustain, it is also necessary to have external stability. Market transparency allows participating firms to better identify possible opportunities for new market entrants and coordinate possible responses.[248]

However, the concern mostly materialises in case of private market transparency. Conversely, improved public market transparency enables new entrants to better estimate market conditions and thus establish themselves more successfully on the market.[249] Furthermore, customers may be tempted to switch to other suppliers that are not participating in the collusion.[250]

Third, increased market transparency also *enables tacit collusion*. If markets become more transparent firms can simply follow each other's pricing without any form of direct communication between them.[251] In other words, market transparency opens the Pandora's Box of legal challenges to condemn parallel conduct under Art. 101 TFEU.[252]

However, it should be stressed out that although market transparency improves the conditions necessary to sustain collusion, this does not imply that market transparency will necessarily result in collusion. From an economic perspective, the *likelihood* of successful collusion strictly depends on a holistic assessment of all the

245. *See* Capobianco (2004), p. 1266. The issue is also emphasised by the Horizontal Merger Guidelines, para. 53: 'Retaliation that manifests itself after some significant time lag, or is not certain to be activated, is less likely to be sufficient to offset the benefits from deviating. For example, if a market is characterised by infrequent, large-volume orders, it may be difficult to establish a sufficiently severe deterrent mechanism, since the gain from deviating at the right time may be large, certain and immediate, whereas the losses from being punished may be small and uncertain and only materialise after some time. The speed with which deterrent mechanisms can be implemented is related to the issue of transparency. If firms are only able to observe their competitors' actions after a substantial delay, then retaliation will be similarly delayed and this may influence whether it is sufficient to deter deviation.'
246. *See* Motta (2004), pp. 150-151.
247. *See* OECD (2011), p. 12 (bullet point 3 in para. 16).
248. *See* Bennet and Collins (2010), p. 323; Wagner-von Papp (2012), p. 10; Wijckmans and Tuytschaever (2015), para. 11.21.
249. *See* OECD (2001), p. 24.
250. *See* González (2012), p. 30. *See* already section 3.1.2 for this competitive-enhancing effect on the upstream level.
251. *See* Cucu (2013), p. 225.
252. *See* section 5.1.

structural and behavioural factors that facilitate collusion.[253] These three ways merely explain how market transparency can facilitate collusion. On the one hand, increased market transparency caused by information exchange may provide the crucial 'tipping point' for some market so that even tacit collusion is sufficient to achieve supra-competitive outcomes. Conversely, even if information exchange has made the market more transparent (and thus monitoring and detecting easier), collusion might still not be achieved due to the lack of external stability (*inter alia* because market entries are low or buying power is high).

3.3.4.c The Requirement of Causal Attribution

Caffarra and Kühn argue that what should matter for the condemnation of information exchange that increases market transparency under Art. 101 TFEU is the *contribution* of the information exchange to collusion concerns.[254] Wijckmans and Tuytschaever similarly argue that what should matter for the economic analysis is not only whether collusion in the market is likely but also whether the exchange is a necessary ingredient to it.[255]

The literature essentially argues that only those information exchanges 'artificially' increase market transparency: (i) that do so in markets that are structurally prone to tacit collusion, or (ii) that change the structure of the market so that even tacit collusion may be sufficient to achieve supra-competitive outcomes. This idea is the expression of a *preventive* approach that does not only prohibit actual collusion but also preparatory forms of conduct that facilitate tacit collusion. This is why the idea can be described as the 'causal attribution' of the information exchange to the increased market transparency and the increased likelihood of collusion.

The idea is certainly valuable for the analytical approach. It emphasises the counterfactual analysis in determining the contribution of the information exchange to possible anti-competitive effect. One has to assess the situation before and after the information exchange and assess the changed conditions caused by the information exchange (the delta).[256] This requires a robust economic theory on how the information exchange in question facilitates collusion.[257]

However, this idea may well be misused as a formalistic argument that only those information exchanges should be considered as anti-competitive that exceed a certain threshold of market transparency increase. The danger is the establishment of an absolute level. However, it has been already emphasised that it is analytically important to consider the specific market circumstances. Under certain market conditions even minor changes may be sufficient to 'tip' the market towards collusion. What

253. *See* Capobianco (2004), p. 1259; OECD (2012a), fn 51. *See* already section 3.3.1.d.
254. *See* Caffarra and Kühn (2006), p. 146.
255. *See* Wijckmans and Tuytschaever (2015), para. 11.61.
256. *Ibid.*, para. 11.61.
257. *See* das Nair and Mncube (2013).

should matter is the relative or marginal[258] impact on the 'collusiveness' of the market in light of the specific market circumstances.

Support for the importance of the relative impact also comes from Wagner-von Papp.[259] He argues that even truly aggregated information can facilitate collusion if: (i) market conditions are such that even an untargeted deterrent mechanism (such as a general price war, as opposed to a targeted punishment of the cheater) is sufficient to sustain collusion; and (ii) the exchanged aggregated information shows at least *that* a cheat has occurred. His argument is that even though the individual cheater cannot be identified, the market has been made sufficiently transparent to enable firms to observe deviations.[260] Thus, the level of aggregation necessary for making collusion more likely is highly market-specific. While in some markets even highly disaggregated information does not make collusion more likely, in others a slight increase of market transparency, even if it merely concerns truly aggregated information, may be problematic.

The concept of causal attribution helps to explain the lack of enforcement activity regarding the dissemination of market data by independent third parties (such as Nielsen or Dataquest). Although those third parties are often commissioned by firms, the market data is largely based on public information or on market research conducted by the third party itself. Even though the market has become more transparent firms' conduct on the market has not contributed to its transparency (i.e., there was no exchange of information between competitors). However, concerns arise when the third party is *jointly* commissioned by several firms. In such situation there is potential scope for a hub-and-spoke collusion.[261]

3.3.4.d The Balancing of Pro- and Anti-competitive Effect: Circumstances Matter

The fact that information exchange increases market transparency is per se neither pro-competitive nor anti-competitive. Instead, market transparency is a double-edged sword. On the one hand, horizontal and vertical market transparency can bring many efficiencies that ultimately make the market work better and thus increase competition.[262] For instance, if undertakings know what other competitors are charging for their products, they may have a strong incentive to undercut their prices (in the short term) and to become more competitive to be able to offer better prices (in the long term).[263] On the other hand, market transparency can facilitate collusion if certain structural factors are present in the market that increase the likelihood of collusion. This creates an inherent tension between the materialisation of the efficiency and the

258. For this word, *see* Caffarra and Kühn (2006), p. 135.
259. *See* Wagner-von Papp (2007).
260. *Ibid.*, pp. 268-269.
261. *See* Capobianco (2004), pp. 1261-1262.
262. *See* already section 3.1.
263. *See* Niels, Jenkins and Kavanagh (2016), para. 5.36.

increased risk of collusion.[264] In other words, market transparency is an ambiguous factor for competition which can entail pro-competitive as well as anti-competitive effects.

The ambiguous nature of market transparency on competition disfavours a general and abstract assessment. This is why any competition law assessment has to consider the specific circumstances of the market in order to carefully balance potential efficiencies against potential anti-competitive effects (contextual approach).

A useful example for the balancing of the collusion concern with *horizontal* efficiencies would be the comparison between oligopolistic and competitive markets. Increased transparency in oligopolistic markets makes the anticipation and prediction of the behaviour of other competitors easier, while it may increase competition in more competitive markets.[265] Thus, an increase in market transparency by undertakings in a concentrated market should raise more concerns than in a more competitive market simply because the collusion concern has more weight.

A useful example of the balancing of collusion concern with *vertical* efficiencies would be the prevailing level of searching costs on a given market. Information exchange that enhances customer transparency may be more problematic when search costs are already low (*inter alia* because products are homogeneous, offerings are simple and customers are experienced buyers). This is because the vertical efficiency argument has little weight against the significant anti-competitive collusion concern.[266]

The disadvantage of such contextual approach is that it entails the risk that competition authorities drift off into a somewhat arbitrary case-by-case decision-making, over-emphasising certain factors and neglecting others. This would be detrimental to legal certainty and the rule of law.[267] However, it would be wrong to conclude that a one-size-fits-all approach is the appropriate analytical approach for assessing information exchanges. Instead, one should always be aware that due to the ambiguous nature of market transparency on competition *in abstracto*, the specific facts of the case are crucial for the substantive assessment and conclusion *in concreto*.

3.3.5 The Role of Communication for Collusion: It Is Mainly About Future Intentions

3.3.5.a The Notion of Communication

When the literature refers to 'communication' instead of 'market transparency' it usually assumes a different temporal dimension. While communication through any

264. *See*, for this balance act, e.g., Vives (2006a), p. 94; OECD (2011), paras 7-9.
265. *See* OECD (2007a), p. 10.
266. *See* Faull and Nikpay (2014), para. 7.431.
267. *See* Wagner-von Papp (2012), p. 17.

sort of information exchange usually relates to future intentions, market transparency by information exchange relates to current or past data.[268]

This classification may help to explain why the frequency of exchange matters for market transparency (i.e., effective monitoring requires frequent exchanges of current data), but not for communication (i.e., one single communication of future intentions may be sufficient to tip the market to collusion).[269] The importance of this classification for the assessment of pure information exchange is discussed later.[270]

3.3.5.b The Ways in Which Communication Facilitates Collusion

There are two main ways in which communication about future intentions can facilitate collusion. It can either help to overcome challenges in finding a collusive outcome that works for all firms (i.e., improve the equilibrium selection) or it can help to sustain collusion (i.e., reduce possible misinterpretation).

The first way starts with the idea that signals to collude are costly.[271] For instance, actual price changes (that are executed in the hope that other firms would eventually follow) might result in significant losses of sales to competitors not understanding the signal or not willing to follow.[272] Furthermore, such signals may not be as effective in choosing a collusive outcome because there are simply too many possible combinations[273] (referred to as the 'equilibrium selection problem').[274] This multiplicity of equilibria is the main issue to overcome even if structural factors are present that facilitate collusion.[275]

While it is not impossible to achieve a collusive outcome without communication, it is certainly very difficult. For instance, firms could have different cost structures or different conceptions about demand. Consequently, their individual equilibrium will

268. This is the main argument of Lévêque (2007) and González (2012). However, most use the notion of 'information exchange' to describe both (*see*, e.g., Kyprianides (2012), p. 408 when distinguishing between future intentions and current data).
269. Noted by Lévêque (2007), p. 355.
270. *See* sections 6.3.2.d and 6.5.1.
271. Such as focal points, public announcements or simply trying to set different prices (*see* on this list of signals Levenstein and Suslow (2006), pp. 44-46; Vives (2006a), p. 86).
272. *See* Smith, Ridyard and Petrescu (2015), p. 39.
273. Motta (2004, p. 141) explains the underlying economic logic quite well: 'If firms cannot communicate, they make mistakes, and select a price (or a quantity) which is not jointly optimal for the firms, and might be difficult to change. Using the market to signal intentions to coordinate on a different price might be very costly. If a firm believes the "right" price for the industry is higher and increases its own price to signal it, it will lose market share in the adjustment period. If a firm decreases its own price to try to coordinate on a lower equilibrium price, this move might be understood as a deviation and trigger a costly price war. Therefore, experimenting with price changes to coordinate on another collusive equilibrium might be too costly.'
274. *See* Wagner-von Papp (2012), pp. 8-9 for a more formal explanation. He argues that there might be some situation where the mere exchange of information is sufficient to signal the equilibrium, while in other situations unilateral signalling may not be enough.
275. *See* Smith, Ridyard and Petrescu (2015), p. 34.

differ.[276] It is then very likely that they make mistakes in selecting the price that suits most firms.[277]

Still, there may be situations where the selection of a possible equilibrium is possible. One solution for overcoming the ambiguous literature about the effect on collusion regarding the homogeneity of products[278] is to differentiate between the finding and sustaining of collusion. Although homogeneous products may not make it easier to *sustain* a possible collusion outcome (because even small price cuts may be sufficient to attract a substantial part of demand),[279] they may make it easier to *find* a collusive outcome (because homogeneity narrows down the scope of possible equilibriums).

Communication of indented conduct is an effective means of overcoming the equilibrium selection problem.[280] It is costless and avoids the expensive market experiments that signals entail.[281] Firms do not bear the same risk of losing market shares because the focal point lies in the future.[282] Niemeyer for instance argues that any competitive behaviour of firms always refers to future transactions and decisions. The exchange of information of past conduct does not offer the same competitive value as the exchange of future intentions.[283]

The fact that empirically most successful cartels use sophisticated, direct and repeated communication emphasises the importance of communication.[284] Although such kind of communication is neither binding nor verifiable (the 'cheap talk critique'),[285] there is empirical evidence that communication is still an effective means to achieve collusion mainly because it creates trust and strengthens personal relationships.[286] In the real world, this effect might be even stronger than in experimental settings. The people working for firms build social interactions which are even more

276. *See* González (2012), p. 24.
277. *See* Wijckmans and Tuytschaever (2015), para. 11.13.
278. *See* section 3.3.1.d.3.
279. *See* Motta (2004), pp. 146-147.
280. *See* Wijckmans and Tuytschaever (2015), para. 11.15.
281. *See* Smith, Ridyard and Petrescu (2015), p. 40.
282. *See* Wijckmans and Tuytschaever (2015), para. 11.29.
283. *See* Niemeyer (1993), p. 155.
284. *See* Levenstein and Suslow (2006), pp. 44 and 49-53. They conclude that '[s]ome of the most systematic information exchanges, such as regular face-to-face meetings and written exchanges of individual firm data are undertaken at considerable risk, given the current legal environment. These risks are accepted in part because each firm believes that heightened communication will move the industry to a collusive agreement that favours the interests of their firm. [...] The fact that multilateral face-to-face cartel meetings were regularly supplemented by bilateral meetings, as well as phone conversations and memos, shows how much communication was generally necessary to sustain these collusive conspiracies'. (Levenstein and Suslow (2006), pp. 65-66)
285. The cheap talk critique argues that the communication between firms has little value in facilitating coordination unless the information is verifiable (*see* Bennet and Collins (2010), pp. 323-324).
286. *See* Kühn (2001), pp. 182-183; Kühn (2010), p. 419. *See also* Levenstein and Suslow (2006), pp. 48 and 53-54 on the importance of trust; Nitsche and von Hinten-Reed (2014), pp. 23-24 who point out that such communication necessarily relates to future plans, not to past conduct.

long term than interactions in laboratories.[287] This has led to strong criticism of the cheap talk critique because it underestimates the importance of communication.[288]

The second way of how communication about future intentions can improve collusion is by reducing the scope for misinterpretations. Without communication external shocks might be misinterpreted by other parties as deviations from the collusive outcome. Such misinterpretation would then trigger costly punishment mechanisms.

Conversely, communication makes it is easier to adjust the collusive outcome caused by changed market conditions without triggering punishment mechanisms.[289] In other words, communication reduces the 'noise in the system' as to the interpretation of possible deviations from the collusive outcome which strengthens the internal stability of the collusion. Communication is intended to reduce the incentives to deviate and thus tackle the dynamic challenges faced by collusion.[290]

3.3.5.c The Importance of Communication for Competition Policy

Communication plays only a minor role in the (vast) economic literature that focuses on the various punishment mechanisms, which are at the heart of economic theory for the likelihood of the internal sustainability of collusion.[291]

Kühn is one of the prominent scholars who argues that competition policy should focus on the communication between firms when fighting collusion.[292] He argues that there are too many practical problems in applying econometric evidence to fight collusive outcomes. The data is either not available or not observable in which case one has to rely on assumptions about the unobservable.[293] It is then the decision of economists on the design of the model that would decide the substantive outcome of the case, not the actual observable conduct of firms.[294] Such misspecification in modelling is difficult to control in a systematic manner.[295]

He therefore argues that competition policy should focus on communication as a 'secondary activity' that is not just highly correlated with actual collusion but also has a relatively low probability of occurring in absence of collusion.[296] There is no need then to apply modern econometric tools to try to detect collusion from firms' market

287. *See* Wijckmans and Tuytschaever (2015), para. 11.20.
288. *See* Møllgaard and Overgaard (2006), pp. 108-109; Vives (2006a), p. 89; Bennet and Collins (2010), p. 324. For a more sceptical view, *see* Caffarra and Kühn (2006), pp. 137-138.
289. *See* Motta (2004), p. 141; Vives (2006a), p. 91.
290. *See* Levenstein and Suslow (2006), pp. 47-48 and 54-65.
291. *See* Kühn (2001), p. 173.
292. *Ibid.*
293. *Ibid.*, pp. 176 and 190. On the issue of assumption in economic models, *see also* Stroux (2004), p. 35: 'One should, nevertheless, bear in mind that economic theories are necessarily based on simplifying assumptions often obtained in the context of stylized economic models that cannot take into account all the complexities of real life cases.'
294. *See* Kühn (2001), pp. 177-179.
295. *Ibid.*, pp. 176-177.
296. *Ibid.*, p. 180.

conduct (such as parallel conduct).[297] Unlike market conduct, communication is more easily observable and verifiable.[298]

In a similar direction goes the argument by Peeperkorn in his article on the role of game theory for competition policy on information exchanges.[299] He observes that communication does only play a minor role in the literature on game theory.[300] According to game theory, collusion does only arise in games with unknown or infinite number of periods played. However, communication does not change the choice of each player's best strategy (collude or compete) because any promise to compete is merely 'cheap talk'. What is relevant for a collusion outcome is exclusively determined by the pay-off matrix that is based on the assessment of the best strategies of competitors (collude or compete), not by communication.[301] Only once collusion is everyone's best strategy, communication may help to overcome the equilibrium selection problem.[302]

He argues that the theoretical literature on game theory – although very influential for the conceptualising the economic framework on collusion – systematically *underestimates* collusion. For instance, these models have rather unrealistic assumptions (such the assumption that a firm that slightly undercuts other firms gets the whole market) and ignore the influence of structural factors on collusion (such as the level of concentration or the symmetry of firms). Also, as mentioned, the experimental literature suggests that communication and its social and personal implications between natural persons are more powerful in practice than what game theory predicts. Communication may even be crucial for preventing firms from acting rationally as assumed by game theories. He therefore suggests that the theoretical literature on game theory should be only used cautiously. In particular, the distinction between merely 'cheap talk' and 'committed future conduct' should not be followed for competition policy.[303]

Both influential authors emphasise the importance of communication for collusion. A narrow focus on merely increased market transparency might neglect one important facet of successful collusion: the ability to talk about future intentions in order to avoid costly signals to collude. Both authors also admit that economic theory should be used only very cautiously to derive collusion from market conduct alone. Essentially, they argue that circumstantial evidence may only be used as a first indication to suspect collusion; further investigation to discover documentary evidence is necessary to actually be able to prove collusion.[304]

---

297. *Ibid.*, p. 197. While econometric evidence may be of little use for detecting collusion *ex ante*, it could be helpful for assessing damages *ex post* (*see* Kühn (2001), p. 202).
298. *See* Kühn (2001), p. 171.
299. *See* Peeperkorn (1996).
300. This has been also observed by Stroux (2004), p. 17.
301. Only binding commitment changes the pay-off matrix, such as investment, but not cheap talk (*see* Stroux (2004), p. 16).
302. *See* Peeperkorn (1996), pp. 2-4 and 6.
303. *Ibid.*, pp. 9-10 and 19.
304. *See* section 4.2.3 on these evidentiary issues.

3.3.6 The Risk Classification of Information Exchanges

3.3.6.a The Theoretical Level: The Effect of Each Factor on Collusion

The manifestation of each of these factors shaping the specific characteristics of an information exchange has a specific effect on collusion.[305] The exchange of information is seen by the Horizontal Cooperation Guidelines as more problematic:

- the more strategic the information exchanged (commercial sensibility);
- the more individualised the information exchange (aggregation);
- the more recent the information exchange (age);
- the more frequent the exchange occurs;
- the more private the exchange occurs; and
- the wider the market coverage of the information exchange.[306]

3.3.6.b The Practical Level: Identifying the Most Harmful Factors for Collusion

On a more practical level, the economic literature attempts to classify the different types of information exchange on the basis of the expected level of harm for competition. While some authors admit that the anti-competitive effect is a continuum,[307] others try to offer a simpler three-tier classification: high-risk, medium-risk and low-risk.[308] This latter three-tier classification is useful as it aligns well with the legal framework: object box, effect box and safe harbours.[309]

The high-risk category consists of information exchange that is most harmful to the process of rivalry and thus most effective to achieve collusion:

- *Information about future prices and production plans (only if private)*: the private exchange of prices and quantities normally does not entail any efficiencies.[310] Such exchange is particularly problematic because it is the most

305. *See* already section 2.2 for these factors.
306. *See* Horizontal Cooperation Guidelines, paras 86-94.
307. *See* Bennet and Collins (2010), particularly p. 333.
308. *See* Kühn (2010), pp. 422-428 (an economist that uses for the three-tier classification the legal notions: object box, effect box, safe harbours) and Baño Fos (2015), pp. 104-111 (an lawyer that uses for the three-tier classification the notions that would seem to be more intuitive for economists: high-risk, medium-risk and low-risk). Padilla (2010) is however sceptical to employ such classification and align it with the legal framework. He argues that even private exchanges of future intentions and data about prices that are highly individualised should not fall within the object category (*see* Padilla (2010), pp. 437-440). However, one gets the impression that main reason for his hostility against the object box is his personal experience with trying to show that the conduct, even though in falls within the object box, does not restrict competition or should be individually exempted (*see* Padilla (2010), pp. 440-444).
309. *See* section 4.3 on the distinction between restrictions of competition by object and effect.
310. *See* Bissocoli (2000), p. 83.

useful information to achieve and sustain a collusive outcome.[311] The exchange of future intentions on other not-as-key competition parameters (particularly costs and demand) normally does not enable firms to predict firms' future conduct as reliably. Therefore the exchange of such information is not as problematic for the competitive process.[312] The exchange of future intentions of prices and output reduces the independence of firms' decision-making and thus eliminates the essence of the competitive process: uncertainty of competitors' conduct on the market.[313] If the exchange is private, it excludes actual and potential competitors that are not part of the exchange and thus increases the external stability of the collusion.[314] However, once future intentions are expressed publicly, the materialisation of significant vertical efficiencies justifies a more favourable classification (*see* medium-risk below).[315]

- *Information about past prices or quantities that is individualised*: the more disaggregated and individualised past data about prices and quantities, the more exposed a firm's performance becomes to its competitors. This makes it easier to detect deviators and punish them effectively.[316] As with the first category, prices and quantities are the most important variables for the competitive process and thus deserve a stricter treatment.[317] However, once exchanged information about past prices or output is sufficiently aggregated, significant horizontal efficiencies (such as benchmarking) justify a more favourable classification (*see* low-risk below).[318]

The medium-risk category consists of types of information exchange where the materialisation of anti-competitive effects depends on specific circumstances[319] and where significant efficiencies are normally materialised. These considerations justify a more cautious treatment and a more favourable risk classification:

311. *See* Horizontal Cooperation Guidelines, para. 73; Kühn (2001), p. 196; Caffarra and Kühn (2006), p. 140; Møllgaard and Overgaard (2006), p. 124; Bennet and Collins (2010), p. 321; Kühn (2010), pp. 422-423; OECD (2011), para. 67; das Nair and Mncube (2013). For a different view *see* Vives (2006a), p. 93; Padilla (2010), pp. 437-439.
312. *See* Bissocoli (2000), p. 83; González (2012), p. 26.
313. *See* Ghezzi and Maggioline (2014), p. 657. *See* section 4.2.1.b.2 for the independence doctrine.
314. *See* Horizontal Cooperation Guidelines, para. 94; Smith, Ridyard and Petrescu (2015), p. 40.
315. *See*, e.g., Kühn (2001), pp. 171 and 183 and 196; Heimler (2010), p. 403; Smith, Ridyard and Petrescu (2015), p. 40. Käis argues that the private exchange of future prices is more problematic than future output because there is no good justification for the former. There may be instances where the private exchange of future output-setting is justified (*see* Käis (2013), p. 355).
316. *See* Kühn and Vives (1995), p. 81; Kühn (2001), p. 196; OECD (2001), p. 30; Vives (2006a), p. 93; Bennet and Collins (2010), p. 323; Kühn (2010), pp. 428-429; Baño Fos (2015), p. 106. For a different view, *see* Møllgaard and Overgaard (2006), p. 124; Padilla (2010), pp. 439-440; Smith, Ridyard and Petrescu (2015), p. 44.
317. *See* González (2012), pp. 31 and 33.
318. *See* Kühn (2001), p. 196.
319. *See*, for this word of caution, OECD (2010), para. 65.

- *Information about future prices and production plans (if public):*[320] public announcements materialise significant vertical efficiencies for customers (such as reduced search costs or more choice). This is why a more lenient approach is justified.[321] Furthermore, public attempts to collude are more difficult to hide since potential competitors and customers can more easily undermine any collusive outcome.[322] However, the exchange of intentions of future price-setting and output-setting still remains the most useful information for collusion which is why it is 'only' in the medium-risk category. Concerns remain particularly in a situation where firms do not implement their own announcements, but instead make the implementation contingent on the responses of competitors.[323]
- *Information about future investment plans*: investment decisions are long-planned decisions that have a greater degree of irreversibility.[324] Although this reduces the scope for collusion, it does not completely eliminate it.[325] The concern lies particularly with those investment decisions that are reversible since they are more similar to price announcements.[326] At the same time, such exchange of information enables significant efficiencies (such as the acceleration of investments on the market, the avoidance of duplication of investments and the probability of successful innovation).[327]
- *Information about costs that is individualised*: the exchange of costs data normally generates efficiencies (such as the pressure to become more competitive).[328] In general, information about costs, even if individualised, does not entail the same anti-competitive risk as the exchange of past prices or quantities. This is because data about costs is generally irrelevant for monitoring rivals' conduct.[329] The main way how cost data can facilitate collusion is by helping to allocate market shares according to their cost structures in order to prevent deviations.[330] Furthermore, cost data may also enable the better evaluation and predication of firms' future conduct since costs are necessarily the basis for future pricing strategies.[331]

320. It is noted though that some authors are more sceptical regarding the distinction between private and public exchange for the classification (*see* Kühn (2010), p. 428; Padilla (2010), p. 439).
321. *See* Kühn and Vives (1995), pp. 78-79; discussion comment by Carmen Matutes in Kühn (2001), pp. 197-198; Lévêque (2007), p. 236; Bennet and Collins (2010), pp. 324-327; Baño Fos (2015), pp. 107-108.
322. *See* Peeperkorn (1996), p. 6; Jones and Sufrin (2016), p. 685.
323. *See* Kühn (2001), p. 183; Wijckmans and Tuytschaever (2015), paras 11.37 and 11.32. *See* section 6.4 on the issue of advance public announcements.
324. *See* Ivaldi et al. (2003), pp. 60-61 in the context of tacit collusion.
325. *See* Kühn (2010), p. 423; OECD (2010), para. 65.
326. *See* Wijckmans and Tuytschaever (2015), paras 11.53-11.54.
327. *See* Padilla (2010), p. 438; OECD (2010), para. 65.
328. *See* Bissocoli (2000), p. 83.
329. *See* Kühn (2010), pp. 425-426. *See* similarly Caffarra and Kühn (2006), p. 143; Lévêque (2007), p. 237; Nitsche and von Hinten-Reed (2014), p. 24.
330. *See* Kühn (2010), p. 426.
331. *See* Niemeyer (1993), p. 154.

- *Information about demand that is individualised*: information about current demand reduces demand uncertainties. This makes it easier to predict the conduct of other firms, although to a lesser extent than the exchange of current and individualised quantities.[332] However, the exchange of demand data, even if individualised, can entail significant efficiencies (such as investment planning) which justifies a more lenient approach.[333]
- *Information about deliveries that is individualised*: while the impact of data about deliveries on the ability to monitor firms' conduct is negligible, the potential for efficiencies is significant (particularly in the vertical context such as reduced storage costs).[334] Therefore a lenient approach is justified.

The low-risk category covers types of information exchange that only exceptionally entails anti-competitive harm. This is why the most favourable risk classification is justified. Importantly, it only covers information exchanges that relate to exchange of past data, not future intentions:

- *Information that is sufficiently aggregated*: aggregated data does only exceptionally[335] enable firms to detect deviation and punish deviators accordingly. Thus, such exchanges normally fail to fulfil the second and third conditions for collusion and are thus considered unproblematic.[336]
- *Information that is genuinely public (except for prices and production plans):* the exchange of such data is not just unproblematic regarding collusion concerns,[337] it is also unlikely that firms would choose to exchange such information because it is collectable with ease from the market.[338]

However, one should keep in mind that this risk classification may not be appropriate for all markets. While, the exchange of prices and quantities may be generally the most problematic competitive parameter, the importance of other factors may vary across industries. Levenstein and Suslow, for instance, have found that the information exchange among those cartels they have analysed was shaped rather individualistically, i.e., by what allowed the members of the cartel to detect and deter

332. *See* Caffarra and Kühn (2006), p. 142.
333. *See* Vives (2006a), pp. 92-93; Lévêque (2007), p. 237.
334. *See* Caffarra and Kühn (2006), pp. 143-145.
335. *See* section 3.3.4.c for that exceptional circumstance.
336. *See* Vives (2006a), pp. 93 and 97; Bennett and Collins (2010), p. 331; OECD (2011), para. 66; Baño Fos (2015), pp. 108-110.
337. *See* however the exception in para. 93 of the Horizontal Cooperation Guidelines (para. 93): 'Even if there is public availability of data (for example, information published by regulators), the existence of an additional information exchange by competitors may give rise to restrictive effects on competition if it further reduces strategic uncertainty in the market. In that case, it is the incremental information that could be critical to tip the market balance towards a collusive outcome.' However, in *TACA*, a case pursued under the concept of collective dominance under Art. 102 TFEU, the GC stated that the exchange of public information does not infringe competition law (*see* Case T-191/98, *TACA*, para. 1154).
338. *See* Horizontal Cooperation Guidelines, para. 92.

cheating most effectively.[339] As seen in *Thyssen Stahl*,[340] even the exchange of delivery data may be sufficient in certain markets to achieve collusive outcomes.

Thus, this risk classification should be a merely first starting point for analysing the specific information exchange in question in its legal and economic context. A robust theory of harm needs to go beyond general economic theory. Such abstract risk classification is too inflexible in light of the desirable context-specific analytical approach of assessing information exchanges.[341] A robust theory of harm has to show how the information exchange in question causally contributes to the collusion concern and thus increases the risk of collusion.[342] Such approach would also be consistent with the nature of any risk analysis. It is not about the materialisation of the actual damage that the risk analysis aims to prevent (i.e., collusion), but about the prevention of the likely emerge of such damage.

3.3.6.c The Policy Level: The Principle of Indispensability

It is finally worth emphasising that the classification of the two types of information exchange in the high-risk category is based on the consideration that other less restrictive means are available in order to achieve very similar efficiencies.[343] If firms want to materialise possible efficiencies that come with the exchange of future intentions on prices and production plans, the *public* exchange is the less restrictive means to do so.[344] Public exchange of future pricing or production plans materialises significant vertical efficiencies that have positive effects on upstream competition.[345] The same is true for the exchange of past price and quantities. If firms want to materialise possible efficiencies that come with the exchange of past prices and

339. *See* Levenstein and Suslow (2006), p. 56.
340. *See* section 6.2.1.e.
341. *See* already section 3.3.1.d.4.
342. *See* already section 3.3.4.c.
343. *See* explicitly Kühn (2001), pp. 172 and 195. On the principle of indispensability of certain types of information exchanges under Art. 101(3) TFEU, *see* Kyprianides (2012).
344. Motta for instances argues that 'it is unlikely that firms need to exchange individual and disaggregate data in order to achieve whatever efficiency there might be' (Motta (2004), p. 152). Similarly, Kühn argues that 'it is very difficult to justify information exchange of individualized data in theory and in individual cases. It is very hard to construct hypothetical situations in which very disaggregated data on past actions is really necessary to achieve substantial efficiency gains' (Kühn (2001), p. 196). In other words, the obvious lack of any meaningful efficiency justifies that the exchange of individualised information compared to the exchange of aggregated information should generally raise serious concerns irrespective of the specific circumstances.

However, this harsh treatment should be limited to situations where individualised data is *accessible* to the other firms. If a third party collects the individualised data with the aim of aggregating the data and with mechanisms ensuring that the collected individualised data is not shared with the firms participating in the information exchange, then this should justify the exception to the exception, i.e., such regime would fall back in the general rule and requires an assessment of the specific circumstances (*see* for instance *Asnef-Equifax* discussed in section 6.2.1.g).
345. *See* already section 3.1.1.

quantities such as benchmarking,[346] they can do so by exchanging *sufficiently aggregated* information.[347]

The common theme of both types of information exchange in the high-risk category is the concept of indispensability.[348] The emphasis is not so much on the search for possible efficiencies (or the almost impossible balancing between potential efficiencies and anti-competitive risks of collusion),[349] but instead on indispensability of the *means* of achieving the same or very similar efficiencies.[350] Thus, the classification entails a normative value judgment that recognises the scope for efficiencies, but condemns the selection of the most anti-competitive means to achieve these efficiencies.[351]

346. *See* already section 3.1.2.
347. *See* Bissocoli (2000), p. 104; Bennett and Collins (2010), p. 330. But *see also* Nitsche and von Hinten-Reed (2014), pp. 20, 24 and 26 who cite economic literature where the exchange of individualised information is necessary to achieve the efficiencies. However, this does not make the exchange of individualised data less problematic from a collusion perspective. If the exchange of individualised data is the only way to materialise the claimed efficiencies this still has to be balanced with the increased risk of collusion.
348. *See* Wagner-von Papp (2012), pp. 17-18 and 21-22.
349. *Ibid.*, p. 21.
350. *See* similarly Caffarra and Kühn (2006), p. 142; das Nair and Mncube (2013).
351. Caffarra and Kühn describe this competition policy approach as 'preventive' because it focuses on the prohibition of certain means of information exchange (*see* Caffarra and Kühn (2006), p. 146).

CHAPTER 4

The Legal Framework of Art. 101 TFEU

4.1 THE STRUCTURE OF ART. 101 TFEU

4.1.1 Prohibition

There are five cumulative conditions for the application of Art. 101(1) TFEU:[352]

(1) *Entity:* the conduct must be carried out by an 'undertaking' or an 'association of undertakings'.
(2) *Conduct*: the collusive conduct must manifest itself either as an 'agreement' or 'concerted practice'[353] between two or more undertakings or as a 'decision' by an association of undertakings.
(3) *Restriction of competition*: the conduct must either restrict competition 'by object' or 'by effect'.[354]
(4) *Effect on inter-state trade*: the conduct must have an appreciable effect on inter-state trade (jurisdictional scope of EU competition law).
(5) *Effect on competition*: the conduct must have an appreciable effect on competition (*de minimis* doctrine).

A word of caution when applying these conditions to information exchanges: a too formalistic application of these rather open-texted conditions is doomed to fail. Such an approach does not offer a dogmatically convincingly analytical framework to

352. For a good overview, *see*, e.g., Faull and Nikpay (2014), pp. 183 et seq.; Jones and Sufrin (2016), pp. 113 et seq. Whish and Bailey (2018), pp. 82 et seq.
353. *See* section 4.2.
354. *See* section 4.3.

tackle the challenges arising from information exchanges.[355] As seen from the discussion of the case law on those two elements that are relevant for the exchange of information[356] neither of these conditions is dogmatically clear-cut.

4.1.2 Exemption

There are two ways in which a conduct that falls within the scope of Art. 101(1) TFEU may still be lawful and therefore escape the legal consequences that come with an infringement of Art. 101 TFEU. It can either fulfil the conditions set out in one of the regulations that exempt certain categories of conduct (block exemption) or fulfil the four conditions set out in Art. 101(3) TFEU (individual exemption).

Most block exemptions are adopted by the Commission, which acts under the powers conferred to it by the regulations of the Council.[357] The regulations that are relevant for this book are:[358]

- *Vertical BER* (for vertical agreements): the Commission provides extensive guidance on this BER and on vertical agreements generally in its Vertical Guidelines.
- *Specialisation BER* (for production agreements): the Commission provides some guidance on this BER in the Horizontal Cooperation Guidelines.
- *R&D-BER* (for R&D agreements): the Commission provides some guidance on this BER in the Horizontal Cooperation Guidelines.
- *TT-BER* (for agreements that concern the licensing of technology rights in order to produce a good or service): the Commission provides extensive guidance in the TT-Guidelines.

For an individual exemption of restrictive conduct under Art. 101(3) TFEU four cumulative conditions have to be fulfilled (two positive and two negative):[359]

(1) *Efficiency gains*: the restrictive conduct must improve the production or distribution of goods or promote the technical or economic progress.
(2) *Indispensability of the restriction*: the restrictive conduct must not impose restrictions that are not indispensable to the attainment of the efficiencies created by the conduct.[360]

355. *See* Baño Fos (2015), pp. 119-120: 'this method of interpretation is very flawed, when applying Article 101 TFEU as a sanctioning provision, as it forces the interpreter of Article 101 TFEU, to extract from a dispersed system of sources (mostly soft law) a body of clear rules which it has to incorporate, afterwards, into the supposed categories of Article 101 TFEU, which is nothing more than a carefully open provision'.
356. *See* sections 4.2 and 4.3.
357. *See* Whish and Bailey (2018), pp. 177-178 for a list of Council Regulations.
358. *See* section 5.2.
359. *See* Art. 101(3) Guidelines, particularly paras 38 et seq.
360. The Commission examines this condition before the second condition (*see* Art. 101(3) Guidelines, para. 39).

(3) *Fair share for consumers*: consumers must receive a fair share of the efficiencies that are generated by the restrictive conduct.
(4) *No elimination of competition*: the restrictive conduct must not result in the elimination of competition with respect to a substantial part of the products concerned.

4.1.3 Consequences of an Infringement

If a restrictive conduct cannot be exempted, the conduct infringes Art. 101 TFEU. The consequences of such infringement materialise on essentially three levels:[361]

(1) *Civil level*: relates to the consequences for the private relations between the parties. This includes the voidness of affected clause or entire agreement[362] (explicitly set out in Art. 101(2) TFEU) and possible liabilities for damages.
(2) *Administrative level*: relates to the measures and sanctions that can be imposed by authorities and courts. At EU level, the powers of the Commission to impose such measure or sanctions are laid down in Regulation 1/2003, particularly in Art. 7 (imposing of behavioural and structural remedies), Art. 9 (making commitments of undertakings legally binding) and Art. 23 (imposing fines).
(3) *Criminal level*: relates to the sanctions that can be imposed on individuals by a national criminal court. Although criminal sanctions exist in some Member States pursuant to their respective criminal code,[363] there are no criminal sanctions at EU level.

4.2 THE CONCEPT OF A 'CONCERTED PRACTICE'

The concept of a concerted practice is an important part of understanding information exchanges. As Baño Fos notes 'information exchanges cannot be interpreted without recourse to the [CJ]'s case law on concerted practices, to such an extent that both terms have ultimately become almost synonyms'.[364] This is why this section aims to explore the concept of a concerted practice from a jurisprudential perspective (*see* section 4.2.1) as well as from an academic perspective (*see* section 4.2.2).

361. *See* Baño Fos (2015), pp. 44 et seq.
362. If the clause cannot be separated from the agreement (*see* Case C-319/82, *Société de Vente de Ciments et Betons de l'Est*, paras 11-12).
363. *See*, e.g., Whish and Bailey (2018), pp. 437 et seq., for the cartel offence in UK law.
364. *See* Baño Fos (2015), p. 204.

4.2.1 Guidance by the EU Courts

This section explores the rich case law on the meaning of a concerted practice. Although the concept of a 'concerted practice' is different from the concept of an 'agreement', they both aim to prohibit collusive conduct (*see* section 4.2.1.a). Since the concept is not defined in the TFEU it has required the interpretation by the EU Courts.[365] The EU Courts have derived from the literal interpretation[366] that there are three conditions of the concept of a concerted practice: (1) there must be a concertation between undertakings; (2) that is followed by market conduct; and (3) there must be a relationship of cause and effect between the concertation and the market conduct.[367] The former condition relates to the first word of a '*concerted* practice' (*see* section 4.2.1.b), the latter two conditions relate to the latter word of 'concerted *practice*' (*see* section 4.2.1.c).

4.2.1.a Demarcation from the Concept of an 'Agreement'

4.2.1.a.1 The Concept of 'Agreement'

In many of the controversial cases before *Bayer* (which is now the leading case on the concept of an agreement) the CJ derived the existence of an agreement from the fact that the supplier had formally communicated its intention to dealers, even though the existence of an agreement was clearly not in the interest of the (according to the CJ tacitly accepting) dealers.[368] In *AEG*,[369] for instance, the supplier had refused to accept those dealers to be part of the selective distribution network that did not want to comply with the high-price policy of AEG. In *Ford*,[370] the supplier had informed the German dealers by circular letters that it would cease to accept orders for its right-hand cars. In *Sandoz*,[371] the invoices sent out by the supplier explicitly stated 'exports prohibited'. In all these cases the CJ concluded the existence of an agreement, despite

365. The advantage of this approach is that it gives EU Courts more flexibility to tackle the specific issues of a case. A further advantage is that such flexibility may overcome the limitations that come with the binary legal distinction (*unlawful vs lawful conduct*) (*see* Black (2005a), pp. 184-185). However, the disadvantage is that such flexibility reduces the unity of the conceptional meaning; particularly with the number and diversity of cases under Art. 101 TFEU but also in other contexts that try to tackle the same oligopoly problem (Art. 102 TFEU and EUMR) (*see* Black (2005a), p. 141).
366. *See* Case C-199/92 P, *Hüls*, para. 166.
367. *See* Case C-49/92 P, *Anic*, para. 118; Case C-8/08, *T-Mobile*, para. 51; Case T-588/08, *Dole*, para. 57. *See also*, for these three elements, Bellamy & Child (2018), para. 2.069 and Ezrachi (2018), p. 79. The OECD background paper on facilitative practices summarises the case law on a concerted practice that there are the following three elements of a concerted practice: (i) direct or indirect interaction between competitors which is likely to affect their independence of judgment; (ii) some form of manifested consensus to replace competition with forms of collusion between the firms; and (iii) a causal link between the concertation and the market conduct (*see* OECD (2012a), para. 44).
368. *See* Broberg and Jakobsen (2002), p. 136.
369. Case C-107/82, *AEG*.
370. Cases C-25/84, etc., *Ford*.
371. Case C-277/87, *Sandoz*.

the fact that dealers either protested against (*AEG* and *Ford*) or simply ignored (*Sandoz*) the unilateral expression of will by the manufacturer.

However, *Bayer* is different from these cases. In this case, the supplier (Bayer) had not formally communicated the reason why orders from the Spanish dealer of Bayer's pharmaceutical product Adalat were not fulfilled entirely. The General Court (GC) concluded that no agreement within the meaning of Art. 101 TFEU has been concluded. Thus, to establish an agreement within the meaning of Art. 101 TFEU, there must be a *formal manifestation* of the intention on side of the supplier.[372] Without an expression of wills the EU Courts are not willing to conclude the existence of an agreement. The commonality with the strict stance of the EU Courts on mere parallel conduct[373] is that in both situations the EU Courts are reluctant to derive subjective elements (i.e., the anti-competitive objective of the conduct) from evidentiary evidence alone.

4.2.1.a.2 The Concept of a 'Concerted Practice' as a Residual Clause

The concept of a concerted practice in Art. 101 TFEU aims to capture those forms of collusion between undertakings that are not captured by the concept of 'agreement' because the intensity and form in which the collusion manifests itself is different.[374] In *Del Monte*, for instance, the GC clarified that it is not necessary to show a 'meeting of minds' (as required for the concept of an agreement).[375] The concept is a residual clause for more loose forms of collusions.[376] Thus, the important function of the concept of a concerted practice is that it sets out the *lowest* threshold for conduct to be regarded as unlawful[377] and thus demarks the outer boundaries of the scope of Art. 101(1) TFEU.[378]

4.2.1.a.3 The Fluid Boundaries Between Both Concepts

The exact demarcations between both concepts are fluid though. Under the broad definition of an agreement – in *Bayer*, the GC stated that the concept of an agreement 'centres around a concurrence of wills between at least two parties, the form in which it is manifested being unimportant so long as it constitutes the faithful expression of the parties' intentions'[379] – also loosely formalised forms of cooperation fall under that definition. Thus, the broad definition given by EU Courts on the concept of an agreement blurs the line between an agreement and a concerted practice.[380]

372. *See also* Albors-Llorens (2006), pp. 848-849.
373. *See* section 5.1.
374. *See* Case C-49/92 P, *Anic*, paras 112 and 131 and more recently Case C-8/08, *T-Mobile*, para. 23.
375. *See* Case T-587/08, *Del Monte*, para. 300.
376. *See* Black (2005a), p. 141; Albors-Llorens (2006), p. 840; Rivas and Van De Walle De Ghelcke (2012); Faull and Nikpay (2014), para. 3.126.
377. *See* Franzosi (1988), p. 387.
378. *See* Bellamy & Child (2018), para. 2.067.
379. Case T-41/96, *Bayer*, para. 69.
380. *See* Albors-Llorens (2006), pp. 842-843.

However, the exact determination of the boundaries between both concepts does not matter that much in practice. In cases with complex infringements it is often difficult to determine where an agreement ends and when a concerted practice begins. For instance, an infringement may begin as a concerted practice and progressively transform into a more intensive form of collusion that may be more appropriately classified as an anti-competitive agreement.[381] In such circumstances it may be artificial and burdensome to distinguish between both concepts. Both concepts 'are intended to catch forms of collusion having the same nature'.[382] Therefore, the EU Courts have established that it is legally not necessary to distinguish between agreements and concerted practices for the purpose of applying Art. 101 TFEU ('dual or joint classification') as long as proof of collusion is found.[383] This joint classification already indicates that the practical emphasis lies on the proof of the subjective element of collusion.[384] Put differently, the important distinction for applying the prohibition of Art. 101(1) TFEU is between collusive and non-collusive behaviour, not its form of manifestation.[385]

4.2.1.b The Element of a 'Concertation'

4.2.1.b.1 Dyestuffs (First Definition)

In *Dyestuffs*, the CJ was given the first opportunity to define the notion of a concerted practice. AG Mayras noted that at this point only the French competition law has expressly included the concept of a concerted practice, while the German competition law has not.[386]

The CJ defined the concept of concerted practice as 'a form of coordination between undertakings which, without having reached the stage where an agreement properly so-called has been concluded, knowingly substitutes practical cooperation between them for the risks of competition'.[387] This statement makes clear that a concerted practice requires some form of concertation. It already vaguely indicated that

381. *See* Faull and Nikpay (2014), para. 3.150.
382. Case C-49/92 P, *Anic*, para. 131.
383. *See* Cases T-305/94, etc., *PVC II*, paras 695-699, particularly the explanation given in para. 698: 'the dual classification must be understood not as requiring simultaneous and cumulative proof that every one of those factual elements reveals the factors constituting an agreement and a concerted practice, but rather as designating a complex whole that includes factual elements of which some have been classified as an agreement and others as a concerted practice within the meaning on Article [101(1) TFEU], which does not provide for any specific classification in respect of that type of complex infringement'. *See also* Case T-1/89, *Rhône-Poulenc*, para. 127 and Case C-199/92 P, *Hüls*, para. 299.
384. *See* section 4.2.2.a.1 below for this argument.
385. *See* Whish and Bailey (2018), p. 104.
386. *See* opinion of AG Mayras in Case C-48/69, *Dyestuffs*, p. 670.
387. Case C-48/69, *Dyestuffs*, para. 64. This definition has been repeated by the EU Courts in subsequent case law (*see*, e.g., Cases C-40/73, etc., *Suiker Unie*, para. 26; Cases C-114/85, etc., *Woodpulp II*, para. 63; Case C-8/08, *T-Mobile*, para. 26; Case T-588/08, *Dole*, para. 56).

mere parallel conduct does not infringe Art. 101 TFEU. Instead, parallel conduct must result from a concertation whereby the former may be an indication of the latter.[388]

4.2.1.b.2 Suiker Unie (Independence Doctrine)

In *Suiker Unie*, the CJ was faced with the question whether a concerted practice required proof of an actual plan. On the facts of the case, the Commission had not shown that there was an actual plan to affect the competitive conditions of the internal market. The CJ stated that the concertation does not go so far as to require the demonstration of the existence of an actual plan between undertakings.[389]

It then stated 'that each economic operator must determine independently the policy which he intends to adopt on the [internal] market including the choice of the persons and undertakings to which he makes offers or sells'.[390] The CJ went on to explain that this does not deprive undertakings of their right 'to adapt themselves intelligently to the existing and anticipated conduct of their competitors'.[391]

In these statements the CJ developed the so-called independent economic policy doctrine[392] (or simply 'independence doctrine') that aims to demarcate prohibited conduct ('practical cooperation') from permitted conduct ('intelligent adoption').[393] The doctrine requires that each undertaking has to determine its conduct on the market independently in order to fall outside the scope of Art. 101 TFEU. A conduct that aims to reduce the uncertainty of each other's conduct that is inherent to the competitive process is caught by Art. 101 TFEU.

Although it is commonly understood that it is not required to completely remove all uncertainty – one can never be entirely sure about future conduct[394] – it is neither clear from this statement to what types of uncertainties the CJ refers to nor what amount of decrease in uncertainties the CJ had in mind.

The CJ then went on and provided an immensely important example of the kind of conduct the CJ had in mind that would be covered by the independence doctrine. It stated that the requirement of independence does 'strictly preclude any direct or indirect *contact* between such operators, the object or effect whereof is either to influence the conduct on the market of an actual or potential competitor or to disclose to such a competitor the course of conduct which they themselves have decided to adopt or contemplate adopting on the market'.[395] The concern with contacts between competing undertakings is that they necessarily reduce the inherent uncertainty of

388. *See* Ghezzi and Maggioline (2014), p. 653.
389. *See* Cases C-40/73, etc., *Suiker Unie*, para. 173.
390. *Ibid.*, para. 173. *See also* Case C-8/08, *T-Mobile*, para. 32.
391. Cases C-40/73, etc., *Suiker Unie*, para. 174.
392. *See* Baño Fos (2015), p. 143.
393. Later cases confirmed this doctrine (*see*, e.g., Case C-172/80, *Züchner*, para. 13; Cases C-114/85, etc., *Woodpulp II*, para. 63; Case T-35/92, *John Deere*, para. 60; Case C-8/08, *T-Mobile*, para. 56).
394. *See* Osti (1994), pp. 177-180.
395. Cases C-40/73, etc., *Suiker Unie*, para. 174 (emphasis added). This formula has been repeated many times subsequently (*see*, e.g., Case C-172/80, *Züchner*, para. 14; Case T-35/92, *John Deere*, para. 87; Case C-8/08, *T-Mobile*, para. 33; Case T-588/08, *Dole*, para. 61).

competitors' actions on the market.[396] Uncertainty is one central characteristic of the competitive process, and any action that aims to undermine this has the potential risk of making competition ultimately less effective.[397]

The independence doctrine with its clear focus on direct or indirect contacts between competing undertakings is the cornerstone for understanding the current importance of information exchanges under Art. 101 TFEU. It explains why the EU Courts are so reluctant to condemn undertakings for engaging in mere parallel conduct.[398]

However, the concern has been raised that a formal understanding of the independence doctrine with a focus on prohibiting *any* form of contacts is short-sighted and not desirable.[399] There may be occasions[400] or even industries[401] where contacts between competitors pursue a legitimate efficiency-enhancing goal. Those contacts that generate significant efficiencies should be treated differently from those that do not. In essence, this criticism exposes the blurred line between the concept of a concerted practice and the restriction of competition when assessing any conduct between undertakings. The concept of concerted practice already linguistically implies an anti-competitive rational of the conduct. Thus, the independence doctrine blends over into the object/effect classification and requires a more holistic analytical framework.

From an economic perspective the independence doctrine helps to explain why certain conduct that is perfectly lawful in competitive markets, may be problematic in concentrated markets. In the latter markets, oligopolists already have an increased ability to correctly anticipate the actions of their competitors because of the simplification of economic calculations caused by fewer players on the market.[402] The degree of uncertainty is already weakened due to the concentrated market structure. Consequently, the relative threshold for information exchanges to further reduce uncertainty should be lower in concentrated market than in competitive markets. This idea means that the doctrine is context sensitive and is thus able to adapt to the specific circumstances of the case.

396. *See* Case C-48/69, *Dyestuffs*, para. 118. *See also* Horizontal Cooperation Guidelines, fn 61: 'Strategic uncertainty in the market arises as there is a variety of possible collusive outcomes available and because companies cannot perfectly observe past and current actions of their competitors and entrants.' In *Solvay*, the GC clarified that a possible lack of trust between competitors does not rule out that a concerted practice cannot be established (*see* Case T-186/06, *Solvay*, para. 152).
397. *See* Bellamy & Child (2018), para. 2.068.
398. *See* section 5.1.
399. *See* Zampa and Carli (2015), p. 80.
400. *See* section 5.2.1 on horizontal cooperations.
401. Zampa and Carli for instance explain that in the financial/commodity market some form of contact between traders may be necessary to materialise efficiencies for specific transaction (*see* Zampa and Carli (2015), pp. 80-81).
402. *See* already section 3.3.2.c.

4.2.1.b.3 Cimenteries and Subsequent Case Law (Element of Reciprocity)

In *Cimenteries,* the GC built on the independence doctrine but clarified that the concept of a concerted practice does imply the element of reciprocity: 'That condition is met where one competitor discloses its future intentions or conduct on the market to another when the latter requests it or, at very least accepts it.'[403] One the one hand, the GC seems to clarify that unilateral conduct (as opposed to unilateral disclosure of strategic information that is tacitly accepted by another party)[404] is not covered by the concept of concerted practice. On the other hand, this statement lays the foundation for covering unilateral information disclosure under Art. 101 TFEU.[405]

The threshold for satisfying this condition is quite low when there is evidence of a participation in a meeting or an exchange of information with anti-competitive purpose. In *Tate & Lyle,* for instance, the GC concluded that even if the participation of an undertaking in a meeting with anti-competitive purpose is limited to the *mere receipt* of information concerning the future conduct of competitors, the condition of reciprocity is satisfied.[406] However, one should keep in mind that the obvious anti-competitive objective of the meeting in question was a significant factor for the low threshold of reciprocity in this case. The language (i.e., the threshold for reciprocity) might have been different when the exchange involved other competitive parameters.[407]

In *Aalborg* (the appeal of the GC's judgment in *Cimenteries*), the CJ clarified that the only[408] way for undertakings, which participates in such meetings with anti-competitive rationale, to escape the infringement of Art. 101(1) TFEU is to publicly distance themselves from what was discussed at the meeting (or even go so far as to inform the authorities about it).[409] In other words, passive modes of participation are indications of collusion. An undertaking then tacitly approves the anti-competitive content, encourages its continuation and compromises its discovery.[410] The clear rule of manifest opposition also helps to provide legal certainty for undertakings and saves resources for public enforcement authorities.[411]

403. *See* Cases T-25/95, etc., *Cimenteries,* para. 1849.
404. *See* Stroux (2004), pp. 157-158; Monti (2007), p. 329; Rabinovici (2017), p. 154. In other words, information can be shared reciprocally but also unilaterally and constitutes a concerted practice as long as the recipient has at least tacitly accepted the information (*see* Zampa and Carli (2015), p. 75).
405. *See* Baño Fos (2015), p. 153.
406. *See* Cases T-202/98, etc., *Tate & Lyle,* para. 58. *See* the case comment by Albors-Llorens (2006), p. 859: 'Such a sweeping definition of reciprocal communication has allowed the category of concerted practices to cast a very wide net over contacts between market players. In this context, exchanges of information, participation in meetings of market players and discussion between competitors, or even discussion with third parties, may amount to sailing into very perilous waters.'
407. This is the argument of Wagner-von Papp (2012), pp. 26-27.
408. *See* Ghezzi and Maggioline (2014), pp. 659-651. They note that '[p]ublicly distrusting the potential anticompetitive arrangement is, indeed, the only safe course of action for firms intended to disassociate themselves from strategic information received unwillingly'. (*ibid.*, p. 661)
409. *See* Cases C-204/00, etc., *Aalborg,* paras 82 and 84.
410. *See* Case C-74/14, *Eturas,* para. 28.
411. *See* Ghezzi and Maggioline (2014), p. 667.

The element of reciprocity also helps to explain why the EU Courts are so reluctant to derive from mere parallel conduct the existence of some form of 'joint intention'[412] to conduct themselves on a specific way. Conversely, information exchange does not face the same evidentiary challenge of this mental element. If there is hard evidence of direct or indirect exchange of information, the element of reciprocity is easily satisfied. There is no need to formally accept the information received.[413]

4.2.1.b.4 Eturas (Importance of Evidentiary Issues)

Eturas[414] is an interesting preliminary reference judgment given to a Lithuanian court. The national court asked whether the mere dispatch of a message with an anti-competitive content (namely to cap the discount to no more than 3%) by the administrator of online travel booking system to the account inboxes of the various travel agencies constituted sufficient evidence to establish that the travel agencies were aware or ought to have been aware of the content of that message.

The case is often cited by the literature when discussing the concept of concerted practice.[415] However, the core issue of this case is not a substantive one, but a procedural one. The issue was not about the exact boundaries of the concept of a concerted practice (substantive issue), but about various evidentiary issues (burden of proof, standard of proof, presumption of innocence, etc.). It demonstrates that at the lower threshold of unlawful collusive conduct, evidentiary issues become more important in deciding the substantive outcome of a case.[416]

The CJ started by stating that it is for the national court to assess whether it was convinced according to national evidentiary rules (limited by the EU law's principles of equivalence and effectiveness) that the dispatch of the message in light of the overall assessment of facts had proven a concertation.[417] The CJ then stated though that the national court is precluded from inferring from the mere dispatch of a message (or the mere existence of a technical restriction implemented in the system which made the

412. *See* Jones and Sufrin (2016), p. 153 for this expression of the 'mental consensus' that the concept of a concerted practice requires.
413. *See also* Ghezzi and Maggioline (2014), pp. 659-660.
414. Case C-74/14, *Eturas*. *See also* the case comment of Rusu (2016) and Havu and Zupančič (2016).
415. *See*, e.g., Jones and Sufrin (2016), p. 158.
416. *See* Havu and Zupančič (2016), pp. 259 et seq. They are pessimistic that the judgment provides much clarity to national courts since 'but the entire conundrum of evaluating evidence and facts in the light of EU law remains an intricate task for the national court, both in this case and future cases of similar nature. [...] The Court underlines the difference between issues of EU competition law and evaluating evidence on the basis of national rules of procedure. The presumption of innocence is highlighted as affecting evaluation of evidence, not the core of competition law interpretation. Regardless of underlining the difference between evidentiary standards (a matter of national law within the limits set by EU law) and interpreting Article 101 (a matter of EU law), the judgment in its entirety shows that the border between the *concept of concerted practices in EU competition law* and *practical matters pertaining to finding or showing* such practices is hazy'. (*ibid.*, p. 263)
417. *See* Case C-74/14, *Eturas*, paras 32 and 34-35.

granting of a 3 % discount more difficult but still possible)[418] that travel agencies ought to have been aware of the content of the message (presumption of innocence).[419] However, this does not preclude the national court from inferring concertation 'in light of other objective and consistent indicia'.[420]

The judgment is an excellent example for the increasing importance of evidentiary challenges faced by enforcers when trying to prove a concerted practice.[421] While the weight of evidentiary issues may have not been clearly emphasised by the EU Courts in appeals of Commission decisions, it has been made clear in this preliminary reference. The case demonstrates that the CJ is reluctant to derive from mere circumstantial evidence the proof of the mental element (concentration).[422] In that sense, the judgment is perfectly consistent with the strict case law on mere parallel conduct.[423]

4.2.1.c The Element of 'Practice'

4.2.1.c.1 Dyestuffs (First Vague Indication of a Second Element)

Already in *Dyestuffs*, the CJ explained that by its very nature 'a concerted practice does not have all the elements of a contract but may *inter alia* arise out of coordination which becomes apparent from the *behaviour* of the participants'.[424] This latter statement seems to indicate that the market conduct of undertakings would be an additional element in determining the existence of a concerted practice.[425]

While the CJ failed to provide any further guidance on this – the two earlier leading cases on the concept of a concerted practice (*Dyestuffs* and *Suiker Unie*) focused on the element of concertation[426] – the statement did already hint that the threshold for the second element is low and that the concept is not necessarily linked to its effects on the market, as suggested by AG Mayras. In his opinion, a concerted practice could not be dissociated from the effects it has on the market. Conversely, an agreement can be condemned without considering its effects on the market.[427] His interpretation already respected the literal meaning of the notion ('concerted *practice*'), i.e., a concertation that is borne out by the conduct with effects on the market.[428]

---

418. *Ibid.*, para. 45.
419. *Ibid.*, para. 39.
420. *Ibid.*, para. 40.
421. *See* section 4.2.3.
422. *See* Havu and Zupančič (2016), p. 260.
423. *See* section 5.1.
424. Case C-48/69, *Dyestuffs*, para. 65 (emphasis added).
425. *See* Albors-Llorens (2006), pp. 844-845.
426. *See* Ghezzi and Maggioline (2014), p. 654.
427. *See* opinion of AG Mayras in Case C-48/69, *Dyestuffs*, p. 671.
428. *See* Albors-Llorens (2006), p. 844. Cusu (2013, p. 222) notes that 'strictly etymologically, the concerted practice suggests a conscious and deliberate alignment of undertakings to a certain market behaviour'.

4.2.1.c.2 *Anic and Hüls (Requirement of Subsequent and Casual Conduct on the Market)*

Anic and *Hüls*, both appeals of the *Polypropylene* decision,[429] clarified conceptual issues regarding the second element of a concerted practice. It nuanced the previous case law that merely focused on the element of concertation.[430] The CJ clarified that the concept of a concerted practice entails – besides the element of concertation – that there must be: (i) a market conduct following the concertation, and (ii) a causal relationship between that market conduct and the concertation.[431] In other words, the concertation must be implemented on the market.[432] This conduct element makes the concept of a concerted practice different from an agreement which only entails a mental element.[433]

However, the CJ established a rebuttable *presumption* that when an undertaking remains active on the market, it does take account of the information received from the concertation (the so-called Anic-presumption).[434,435] The presumption can be justified on the basis that there is little doubt why competing undertakings would not use such information for their future decision-making.[436] The decision-making of any rational market player will be necessarily influenced by the receipt of such information.[437]

The element of 'practice' conceptually overlaps with the independence doctrine. If the essence of a concertation is the removal of uncertainty regarding the future conduct of competitors, subsequent market conduct is necessarily influenced by information received from concertation. Put differently, the removal of uncertainty regarding the future conduct of competitors that comes with the receipt of such information is irremovable.[438]

There are two ways out of that presumption. The *first* way out is in case the Commission fails to show that the undertaking does not remain active on the market subsequent to the concertation. The *second* way out is when the undertaking shows that it has not taken into account the information received. However, it is hard to envisage circumstances in which the undertaking is able to demonstrate that it was not influenced by information received since it is a proof of negative facts.[439] In *Cimenteries*, for instance, the GC rejected the argument that the party involved in the concertation had escaped the presumption, even though the actual prices charged after

429. Commission decision, *Polypropylene*.
430. *See* Baño Fos (2015), p. 151.
431. *See* Case C-199/92 P, *Hüls*, para. 161; Case C-49/92 P, *Anic*, para. 118.
432. *See* Jones and Sufrin (2016), p. 154.
433. *See* Ghezzi and Maggioline (2014), p. 654. The meeting of minds has been described in section 4.2.1.a.1.
434. *See* Baño Fos (2015), p. 151.
435. *See* Case C-199/92 P, *Hüls*, paras 162 and 167; Case C-49/92 P, *Anic*, para. 121.
436. *See* Bellamy & Child (2018), para. 2.073.
437. *See* Ghezzi and Maggioline (2014), p. 669.
438. *See* Frazer (2013), p. 3.
439. *See* Stroux (2004), pp. 84 and 158; Jones and Sufrin (2016), p. 155; Zampa and Carli (2015), pp. 77-78 note that they have not found any instance where the presumption has been successfully rebutted.

the concertation had been lower than the ones communicated to its competitors.[440] Similarly, in *Bavaria*, the GC rejected the argument that the fact that prices were not increased in accordance with the information exchanged was not able to demonstrate that the information received did not influence the decision-making.[441]

Thus, although the presumption is rebuttable,[442] there is little scope of rebutting it in practice.[443] The rebuttal seems to be more a theoretical construct with little practical relevance. The evidentiary burden is simply too high.[444] However, the case law essentially requires negative proof of facts (i.e., that the undertaking did not take into account the information in its decision-making). Any negative proof is very difficult. This is why some argue that the presumption creates friction with the requirement of Art. 6 ECHR (presumption of innocence).[445] However, such concern is mitigated when one considers that the presumption does not relate to the subject element of the concept of concerted practice (the concertation part). On the contrary, the presumption merely strengthens the conclusion of illegality of subsequent market conduct that was taken after a concertation has been already established.

From the perspective of enforcers, the Anic-presumption has significantly lowered the burden of proof for establishing a concerted practice.[446] Although the CJ has nuanced the case law, which until these two judgments only focused on the concertation part, in a way that the concept of concerted practice also requires the proof of subsequent market conduct (the practice part), it deprived the practice part of the concept of any meaningful practical relevance. It is practically impossible to rebut the Anic-presumption. This shifts the emphasis of proofing a concerted practice to the concertation part.[447]

Furthermore, the CJ also stated that the practice part of a concerted practice does not require to show that the conduct had produced concrete effects of restricting, preventing or distorting competition.[448] The question whether and to what extent a concerted practice has restricted competition is different from the question whether undertakings have engaged in a concerted practice.[449]

While it might be technically true that these issues relate to two separate conditions of Art. 101 TFEU, the fact that the CJ feels the need to comment on it shows the necessary intertwinedness of both concepts. As pointed out by Albors-Llorens this

440. *See* Cases T-25/95, etc., *Cimenteries*, para. 1912.
441. *See* Case T-235/07, *Bavaria*, paras 179-180.
442. In *Eturas* (*see* section 4.2.1.b.4) the CJ clarified that it may be sufficient in an online environment when the 'public distancing' is merely expressed to the online system administrator (*see* Case C-74/14, *Eturas*, paras 47-48). *Eturas* seems to indicate a stronger willingness of the CJ to rebut the Anic-presumption in the online environment (*see* Havu and Zupančič (2016), p. 265). However, it should be kept in mind that the CJ did not have to decide on the substantive outcome of the case since it was a preliminary reference.
443. *See* Baño Fos (2015), p. 151; Zampa and Carli (2015), p. 78.
444. *See* Bellamy & Child (2018), para. 2.075.
445. *See* Rivas and Van De Walle De Ghelcke (2012).
446. *See* Ghezzi and Maggioline (2014), pp. 655-656.
447. *See* Albors-Llorens (2006), pp. 847-847; Jones and Sufrin (2016), p. 156. *See* section 4.2.2.a.1.
448. *See* Case C-49/92 P, *Anic*, paras 119, 122-124; Case C-199/92 P, *Hüls*, paras 163-165.
449. *See* Jones and Sufrin (2016), p. 155.

statement seems to discount the fact that collusion may be deducted from circumstances that are more ambiguous than express manifestations of concertation.[450] Statements like these suggest a mechanical application of Art. 101 TFEU that tries to artificially separate the condition of 'concerted practice' from the conditions of a 'restriction by object/effect', while at closer scrutiny of the case law a more holistic assessment seems to be applied without being explicit about it.[451]

4.2.1.c.3 T-Mobile (Single Meeting Is Sufficient for Presumption)

In *T-Mobile*, the CJ clarified that the Anic-presumption does not only apply when the concertation takes place regularly and lasts over a longer period of time[452] but also when undertakings concert on only one single occasion.[453] Thus, the number, frequency and form of meetings may matter on an evidentiary level (i.e., whether the CJ is convinced that concertation has taken place), but not for the application of the Anic-presumption.[454]

4.2.2 Guidance by the Literature

This section discusses two strands of literature that analyse conceptual issues of a concerted practice. While the jurisprudential literature focuses more on descriptive issues (*see* section 4.2.2.a), the analytical philosophical literature aims to offer a more normative perspective on the concept (*see* section 4.2.2.b).

4.2.2.a The Jurisprudential Literature

4.2.2.a.1 The Importance of the Element of 'Concertation'

The element of 'practice' is *conceptually* important because it distinguishes a concerted practice from an agreement.[455] Only an agreement is prohibited as a mere consensual act. There would be no concerted practice if the parties only plotted to coordinate but did not actually carry out the plot.[456]

---

450. *See* Albors-Llorens (2006), p. 848.
451. This argument is further developed in section 6.5.1.d.3.
452. The statement in Case C-49/92 P, *Anic*, para. 121 and Case C-199/92 P, *Hüls*, para. 162 suggested a narrower application of the presumption that depended on the duration and frequency of the concertation (*see* Bellamy & Child (2018), para. 2.074): 'That is all the more true where the undertakings concert together on a regular basis over a long period, as was the case here.'
453. *See* C-8/08, *T-Mobile*, paras 60-61. On this issue, *see also* Camesasca, Schmidt and Clancy (2010), p. 408.
454. *See* C-8/08, *T-Mobile*, para. 60. The CJ also clarified in this judgment that the presumption forms an integral part of EU law (*ibid.*, para. 52) and thus national courts are not permitted to apply stricter national rules of evidence (*see* Whish and Bailey (2018), p. 117).
455. *See*, e.g., Monti (2007), p. 326.
456. *See* Jones and Sufrin (2016), p. 154.

However, in light of the case law it becomes obvious that the *practical* focus is on the element of 'concertation'. The element of 'practice' is merely a theoretical construction with little practical weight. Not only is there a presumption that subsequent market conduct will follow after a concertation but also the threshold for the rebuttal is extremely high.[457] It seems that the only way to rebut the Anic-presumption is essentially to cease to trade altogether.[458] As demonstrated below,[459] most of the evidentiary difficulties of proving a concerted practice without hard documentary evidence relates to the concertation element.

However, one should not overlook the conceptual linkage between both elements. The Anic-presumption (the practice-element) aligns well with the independence doctrine (the concertation-element). The receipt of strategic information about future conduct will necessarily be taken into account in the decision-making and thus effectively undermine the independence of decision-making that characterises the competitive process. As put by Ghezzi and Maggioline, any card game is hopelessly compromised if a player shows one of his cards to his adversaries.[460] Thus, although both elements are conceptually different, they are also closely linked with each other at the same time.

4.2.2.a.2 The Sources of Concertation

Jones and Sufrin distinguish three sources from which a concertation can be derived:[461]

(1) *Direct contacts*: occurs when commercially sensitive information is passed directly to competitors.[462]
(2) *Indirect contacts*: occurs when commercially sensitive information is not directly passed to competitors but is ultimately received by them. Examples are advance unilateral public announcements[463] or hub-and-spoke arrangements where information is exchanged via a common third party.
(3) *Parallel conduct*: occurs when market data indicates that competitors act in parallel particularly regarding prices.

In the first two situations some kind of information is exchanged, either directly or indirectly. However, the latter situation does not entail any exchange of information.

457. *Ibid.*, pp. 155-156.
458. *See* Monti (2007), p. 328.
459. *See* section 4.2.3.
460. *See* Ghezzi and Maggioline (2014), p. 661.
461. *See* Jones and Sufrin (2016), pp. 156-162. *See also* Ghezzi and Maggioline (2014), pp. 653-654 and 656-659.
462. In *Cimenteries*, the GC clarified that even the mere disclosure of future *intentions* is sufficient to be considered as practical cooperation (*see* Case T-25/95, etc., *Cimenteries*, para. 1852). In *Tate & Lyle*, the GC clarified that it is also sufficient to be regarded as practical cooperation if such future intentions are only revealed by *one* participant at a meeting (*see* Cases T-202/98, etc., *Tate & Lyle*, para. 54). *See* Albors-Llorens (2006, pp. 858 et seq.) for a more in-depth discussion on unlawful contacts between undertakings.
463. *See* section 6.4.

One has to rely solely on circumstantial evidence. The reluctant stance of the EU Courts in deriving concertation from mere parallel conduct explains the current importance of information exchange under Art. 101 TFEU prohibition.[464]

4.2.2.a.3 The Lack of Consensus on the Conceptual Meaning

While the definition given in *Dyestuffs* is somehow intuitive (concerted practice is not an agreement), it is not self-explanatory.[465] In particular, it is not entirely clear what is meant by a 'practical cooperation'.[466] More importantly, this definition may not help to identify the essence of a concerted practice.

This can be seen by the different opinions among legal scholars of what is actually the essence of a concerted practice.[467] Whish and Bailey for instance describe the essence of a concerted practice as a 'mental consensus' whereby practical cooperation is knowingly substituted for competition. He stresses out that this mental consensus does not have to be established verbally, but can be also established through direct or indirect contacts between undertakings.[468] Castillo de la Torre and Gippini Fournier argue that the essence of a concentration is the notion of 'reciprocal contacts' between competitors.[469] Similarly, Jones and Sufrin argue that the concept of concerted practice seems 'to require reciprocal cooperation or a joint intention to conduct themselves in a specific way, disclosed through direct or indirect contact, designed to influence the conduct of an actual or potential competitor or to reveal to them the course of conduct that will or may be adopted on the market'.[470] Faull and Nikpay argue that a concertation requires 'some form of contact between undertakings'[471] and

464. *See* section 5.1.
465. Del Mar (2011, p. 112) for instance argues that this definition 'does not yet tell us a great deal, for we need to know what "form of co-ordination" is of the prohibited kind (i.e., we need to know the evidentiary target), and we need to know under what circumstances, by reference to what kinds of behaviour or materials, we can reasonable infer the likely existence of such a prohibited form of co-ordination (i.e., we need to know the evidentiary platform)'. Thus, he stresses out the importance of the evidentiary questions for a concerted practice.
466. This question was raised very early by Ray Pfeiffer (1974, p. 117).
467. These different interpretations among legal scholars are also observed by Del Mar (2011, p. 116). Conversely, Soames (1996, p. 29) thinks that the concept of a concerted practice is 'well defined'. However, I disagree and think that on a deeper conceptual level the concept of a concerted practice is not as well defined as it could be. Otherwise the definitions and interpretations of legal scholars would not differ so significantly.
468. *See* Whish and Bailey (2018), p. 116. The 'mental element' is also highlighted by Alese (1999, p. 380).
469. *See* Castillo de la Torre and Gippini Fournier (2017), para. 2.046. Similarly, also Vaughan et al. (2006), p. 64; opinion of AG Darmon in Cases C-114/85, etc., *Woodpulp II*, para. 174: 'the concept of concerted practices refers to reciprocal communications between competitors with the aim of giving each other assurances as to their conduct on the market'.
470. Jones and Sufrin (2016), p. 153.
471. Faull and Nikpay (2014), para. 3.131 (the first element to prove a concerted practice).

'some meetings of minds or consensus between the parties to cooperate rather than to compete'.[472]

As can be seen, there is no clear consensus on the essence of a concerted practice. While some put more emphasis on the mental element (Whish and Bailey), others stress out the importance of contacts for establishing a concerted practice. However, (anti-competitive) information exchanges seem to be covered by all these definitions simply because they produce hard evidence of some form of contacts.

4.2.2.a.4 The Two Strands of the Conceptual Meaning

Obudu provides a useful discussion about the different strands on the conceptual meaning of a concerted practice.[473] He argues that there are essentially two conceptions of a concerted practice. The first view is that a concerted practice requires the adoption of *common intention*. Accordingly, the notion of an agreement captures binding expressions of common intention, while the notion of concerted practices captures non-binding expressions of common intention. This conception would fit into the view expressed by the CJ in *Anic*, where the CJ stated that an agreement and a concerted practice have 'the same nature and are only distinguishable from each other by their intensity and the forms in which they manifest themselves'.[474]

However, there are many problems with this conception. First, there is the problem that the CJ has clearly stated in *Suiker Unie* that a concerted practice requires in no way the working out of an actual plan.[475] The Court seems to reject the views of those demanding some kind of mental consensus or common intention. Also, the first conception contradicts with the definition given in *Bayer*, where the GC stated that the concept of an agreement 'centres around the existence of a concurrence of wills between at least two parties, the form in which it is manifested being unimportant so long as it constitutes the faithful expression of the parties' intention'.[476] Thus, the first conception does not add any difference that is not already caught by the (wide) notion of an agreement.

The second conception of a concerted practice is more convincing. It argues that an agreement and a concerted practice have in common that both focus on the potential of various strategies to *reduce uncertainty about the future conduct of competitors*.[477] This view would sit well with the existing case law. In *Dyestuffs*, the CJ concluded that a concerted practice existed once 'undertakings eliminated all uncertainty between them as to their future conduct and, in doing so, also eliminated a large part of risk

472. *Ibid.*, para. 3.131 (the second element to prove a concerted practice). Interestingly, the third element combines what Bellamy & Child (2018, para. 2.069) describe as the second and third elements: the subsequent conduct on the market and the causality between the concertation and market conduct.
473. *See* Obudu (2012), pp. 70-91.
474. Case C-49/92 P, *Anic*, para. 131. *See* already section 4.2.1.a.
475. *See* Cases C-40/73, etc., *Suiker Unie*, para. 173.
476. Case T-41/96, *Bayer*, para. 69.
477. *See* Obudu (2012), p. 82. Supporter of this view is e.g., Albors-Llorens (2006), p. 846; Jones and Sufrin (2016), p. 153.

usually inherent in any independent change of conduct on one or several market'.[478] In *Suiker Unie*, when the CJ established the independence doctrine, it stated that Art. 101 TFEU prohibits 'any direct or indirect contact between such operators, the object or effect whereof is either to influence the conduct on the market of an actual or potential competitor or to disclose to such a competitor the course of conduct which they themselves have decided to adopt or contemplate adopting on the market'.[479] In *Tate & Lyle*, the GC stated that 'uncertainty as to the pricing policies which the other operators intend to practise in the future constitutes the main stimulus to competition'.[480] In other words, risk and uncertainty are an essential part of the competitive process and any practice that aims to reduce it would be regarded as a concerted practice.[481]

However, from the second conception it is neither clear to what types of uncertainties the CJ refers to nor what amount of decrease in uncertainties the CJ had in mind. Although it is commonly understood that it is not required to completely remove all uncertainty as stated by the CJ in *Dyestuffs*,[482] the Court has failed to offer a clear threshold.[483]

Still, the second conception of a concertation provides a useful analytical framework for assessing conduct that is covered by the concept of a concerted practice. The emphasis should be on conduct that aims to reduce the uncertainty of competitors' market conduct. What the CJ seems to protect is the inherent nature of competition, i.e., the uncertainty of the *future* market conduct. The importance of the temporal perspective is not just reflected in the classification of pure information exchanges as either restrictive by object or effect[484] but is yet another example for the close intertwinedness between the concept of concerted practice and the by object/effect classification.[485]

4.2.2.b The Analytical Philosophical Literature

Some argue that the jurisprudential literature sheds little light on the deeper conceptual meaning of a concerted practice.[486] It is therefore also worth to explore the analytical philosophical perspective.[487] Two authors stand out from this literature: Black who argues that the focus should be on communication[488] and Del Mar who argues that the analytical focus should be on evidentiary issues.[489]

478. Case C-48/69, *Dyestuffs*, para. 101.
479. Cases C-40/73, etc., *Suiker Unie*, para. 174.
480. Cases T-202/98, etc., *Tate & Lyle*, para. 46.
481. *See* Obudu (2012), p. 82.
482. *See* Osti (1994), pp. 177-180.
483. *See* already section 4.2.1.b.2 for this critique.
484. *See* section 6.5.1.
485. *See* section 6.5.1.d.3.
486. *See* Black (2005a), p. 142.
487. *See* Page (2007), p. 426 for this categorisation.
488. *See* section 4.2.2.b.1.
489. *See* section 4.2.2.b.2.

4.2.2.b.1 Black: Communication Should Matter

Black rightly criticises that there is cluster of such words – 'concert' (wording of Art. 101(1) TFEU), 'coordinate' (sometimes used by the EU Courts),[490] 'collude' (used by the economic literature)[491] or 'cooperate' (used by game theory)[492] – that are often used without explaining their meaning and relation to each other.[493] Instead, he proposes to use the term 'correlate', which has been not used so far, to offer a fresh new start.

His analysis refers to six 'grades of correlation' that describe the spectrum from independent action all the way to collusion:[494]

(1) *independent action*: each firm does an act entirely independently of the other;
(2) *mutual belief*: firms act, each believing the other is acting in a particular way;
(3) *mutual reliance*: firms act not only believing the others will act in a certain way, but they also rely on them to do so;
(4) *mutual reliance with a common goal*: firms act in reliance on their belief that others will act in a certain way, and in doing so firms have the same goal;
(5) *mutual reliance with a common goal and with knowledge*: firms act knowing that all of the foregoing conditions have been satisfied;
(6) *mutual reliance with a common goal and with knowledge gained, in part, by communication ('joint action')*: firms act knowing that all conditions have been satisfied in part because they have communicated their reliance and their goals to each other.

He argues that only the latter grade (joint action) should be regarded as concertation.[495] Concerted practice does not only involve communication but it is also followed by parallel action to complete the infringement.[496] Thus, the notion of 'communication' should be the decisive element of a concerted practice that distinguishes it from other (lawful) conduct.[497] Communication itself comes in various forms and degrees, ranging from full-blown linguistic communication all the way to a situation 'where one person simply causes another to believe something'.[498] The latter situation (the lowest degree of communication) sets the threshold for condemning a certain conduct as an unlawful concerted practice.

490. *See*, e.g., Case C-48/69, *Dyestuffs*, para. 64; Cases C-40/73, etc., *Suiker Unie*, para. 173.
491. *See*, e.g., Grillo (2002); Fonseca and Normann (2012).
492. *See*, e.g., Paha (2013), p. 198.
493. *See* Black (2005a), pp. 141-142 and 185; Black (2005b), p. 341.
494. *See* Black (2005a), pp. 185-187. This book follows the description given by Page (2007, pp. 426-427) because he describes these grades in a less technical manner than Black (*see also* Del Mar (2011), p. 117 who also follows Page's description).
495. *See* Black (2005b), p. 187.
496. *See* Black (2005a), pp. 159-160 as thoroughly observed by Page (2007), p. 428.
497. Obudu also emphasises the importance of communication to prove a concerted practice: 'If reduction of uncertainty as to the future conduct of others s, or is to become, an accepted and acceptable conception of concerted practice, it must be possible to prove that a reduction of uncertainty has occurred. Communication reduces uncertainty and evidence of communication seems sufficient to establish a concerted practice.' (Obudu (2012), p. 84)
498. Black (2005a), p. 154; Black (2005b), p. 341.

There may be broader support for his conceptual focus on the notion of communication. On the one hand, there is support from the *jurisprudential* literature. Page, for instance, building on the model of Black,[499] points out that there is some, although inconclusive,[500] experimental support for Black's argument that communication should be the decisive element of a concerted practice.[501] On the other hand, there is also support from the *economic* literature. As explained, communication can facilitate collusion by overcoming the equilibrium selection problem.[502] Communication may help to tailor possible retaliation measures.[503] There is consensus among economists that effective and stable price collusion requires both mutual recognition of self-interest and direct communication.[504]

However, Black's test can be criticised because it fails to take into account evidentiary issues.[505] If communication is the essential threshold for condemning conduct, *evidence* of specific communication is necessarily required to prove a concerted practice.[506] His concept also fails to explain if and how the establishment of a concerted practice can be also proven by circumstantial evidence alone. Still, his theory implicitly emphasises the importance of information exchange for the concept of concerted practice because information exchange per definition contains some form of communication.

4.2.2.b.2 Del Mar: Conduct Analysis vs Economic Analysis

Del Mar's analytical philosophical analysis may be useful to explain the current state of law on concerted practices.[507] He identifies two types of analyses currently employed. First, the *conduct* analysis focuses on the conduct of firms and its proof. It can be broken down into 'evidentiary target' and 'evidentiary platform'. The former describes what kind of conduct is prohibited (namely any direct or indirect contact that reduces the uncertainty of the conduct of other undertakings in the market). The latter describes what kind of evidence is needed on which it can be interfered that the

499. *See* Page (2007), p. 406 adopting it for the US: 'I propose building on the recent work of Oliver Black, that the distinguishing characteristic of concerted action is communication among rivals, not only of intentions, but also of firms' reliance on their rivals' actions in choosing a common course of action.'
500. *See*, e.g., Vives (1999), p. 321: 'The research on the effect of communication is not yet conclusive. In repeated games, for instance, in the presence of imperfect monitoring and privately observed signals, it is not known whether full collusion is possible without communication or whether communication is even needed for collusion. However, in general, the presumption is that communication abets collusion.'
501. *See* Page (2007), pp. 433-435.
502. *See* section 3.3.5.b.
503. *See* Grillo (2002), p. 158.
504. *See* Werden (2004), p. 763: game theoretic models 'show that pricing coordination is possible under certain circumstances, but very few economists take the models so literally that they believe coordinated pricing occurs without communication of any form'.
505. *See* Del Mar (2011), pp. 117-118.
506. *See* Page (2007), p. 428.
507. *See* Del Mar (2001), pp. 119-120.

evidentiary target has been met (e.g., participation of meetings). The conduct is only prohibited if there is a link between the evidentiary target and evidentiary platform.

Second, the *economic* analysis applies only when there is no kind of evidence as described in the first type of analysis. Its task is then to consider whether there are any alternative plausible explanations of the parallelism in question. This means he implicitly admits that the economic literature, which tries to derive concertation from market conduct by using econometrical models, has not just a subsidiary role to play when proofing a concerted practice but also a limited role.

His analysis overcomes the limitations of Black's concept by putting more emphasis on the evidentiary challenges of proofing concerted practices. However, one may wonder what new perspective he has to offer compared to the analysis of legal scholars. His notion of 'evidentiary target' can be substituted by the literature on the element of 'concertation',[508] his notion of 'evidentiary platform' with the literature on documentary evidence and his notion of 'economic analysis' with the literature on circumstantial evidence.[509] Thus, at worst he merely gives the various (legal) categories new (philosophical) labels. At best though, he offers a holistic approach that brings together the various issues dispersed in the jurisprudential literature into a coherent and clear-cut analytical framework.

4.2.3 Evidentiary Issues

In contrast to the literature on the substantive meaning of a concerted practice, the literature on evidentiary issues is quite underdeveloped. This is surprising considering the importance of documentary evidence for the long-lasting struggle to tackle mere parallel conduct. This is why this section explores the different evidentiary issues of how to prove a concerted practice.

4.2.3.a Burden of Proof

The burden of proof can be described as the 'burden of persuasion'[510] as it describes *who* has to prove its case and persuade a judge.[511]

There are two types of burden of proof. The evidential burden of proof (also known as subjective burden of proof[512] or *formelle Beweislast*)[513] and the legal burden of proof (also known as objective burden of proof[514] or *materielle Beweislast*).[515,516] The former requires the proponent of a fact to adduce sufficient evidence to raise an

508. *See* particularly section 4.2.2.a.1.
509. *See* section 4.2.3.c for the latter two.
510. *See* Castillo de la Torre and Gippini Fournier (2017), para. 2.009.
511. *See* Bailey (2003), p. 849.
512. *See* Castillo de la Torre and Gippini Fournier (2017), para. 2.008.
513. *See* opinion of AG Kokott in Case C-8/08, *T-Mobile*, fn 60.
514. *See* Castillo de la Torre and Gippini Fournier (2017), para. 2.009.
515. *See* opinion AG Kokott in Case C-8/08, *T-Mobile*, fn 60.
516. An example where the CJ itself differentiates between these two types can be found in Cases C-204/00, etc., *Aalborg*, para. 79.

issue as to the existence of a fact, absent which the factual claim can be dismissed.[517] The latter allocates the negative effects of the ultimate lack of material facts (the *non-liquet* situation).[518] It determines which party ultimately bears the risk of material facts remaining unproven.[519]

Both concepts play together in competition law proceedings. Art. 2 of Regulation 1/2003 states that the burden of proof is on the party alleging the infringement of Art. 101 TFEU (i.e., the Commission in public enforcement cases). Thus, the Commission has 'to adduce evidence capable of demonstrating to the requisite legal standard the existence of circumstances constituting an infringement'.[520] Once 'the factual evidence on which [the Commission] relies may be of such kind as to require the other party to provide an explanation or justification, failing which it is permissible to conclude that the burden of proof has been discharged'.[521] However, a substantiated submission by the Commission can be only overturned by an at least equally substantiated submission by the other party.[522] Thus, if the Commission has drawn certain conclusions on the basis of objective and verifiable evidence, the other party cannot refute these findings by simply disputing them in an unsubstantiated manner.[523]

4.2.3.b Standard of Proof

4.2.3.b.1 Meaning

The standard of proof (or 'requisite legal standard'[524] as commonly referred to by the EU Courts) is the threshold that needs to be exceeded in order to establish, as a matter of law, whether an event has happened or not. It gives the evidential burden of proof 'flesh' in that it concretises the quality and quantity of the evidence required to prove a material fact.[525]

The standard of proof is functionally related with the concept of the *burden* of proof. The stricter the standard of proof, the more often the legal burden of proof applies to solve *non-liquet* situations.[526] It is also functionally related to the standard of *review*, which refers to the intensity of review of Commission decision by the EU

517. *See* Castillo de la Torre and Gippini Fournier (2017), fn 14 in para. 2.008.
518. *Ibid.*, para. 2.009.
519. *See* opinion AG Kokott in Case C-8/08, *T-Mobile*, fn 60.
520. Case C-49/92 P, *Anic*, 86; Case T-442/08, *CISAC*, para. 91.
521. Cases C-204/00, etc., *Aalborg*, para. 79.
522. *See* opinion of AG Kokott in Case C-105/04 P, *FEG*, para. 73.
523. *Ibid.*, para. 74.
524. *See*, e.g., Cases T-77/89, etc., *Società Italiana Vetro*, para. 167; Case C-49/92 P, *Anic*, 86; Case T-442/08, *CISAC*, para. 91. This has been noted by Faull and Nikpay (2014, para. 8.469).
525. *See* Bailey (2003), pp. 854-855. This includes an assessment of the amount, type and probative value of the specific evidence (*see* Bailey (2003), p. 847). Faull and Nikpay provide a useful guidance over the assessment of the probative value of evidence (*see* Faull and Nikpay (2014), paras 8.484-8.500).
526. *See* Castillo de la Torre and Gippini Fournier (2017), para. 2.010.

Courts. Stricter judicial scrutiny tends to require stronger and more compelling evidence to justify the conclusions reached in the decision.[527]

4.2.3.b.2 The Ambiguous Case Law on the Exact Test

The case law on the exact test on the standard of proof is ambiguous. First, the case law refrains from providing a clear threshold or a specific formula. Instead, the language that describes the quality requirement for the evidence varies substantially. The quality of the evidence has been described as 'sufficiently precise and coherent',[528] 'precise and consistent',[529] 'firm, precise and consistent',[530] 'solid, specific and corroborative',[531] 'convincing'[532] or 'cogent',[533] while also taking into account the specific features of the markets in question.[534] It is worth noting though that this quality requirement refers to the body of evidence viewed as a whole, not in isolation from each other.[535] Such holistic view means that certain facts can be established by deduction.[536]

Sir Cristopher Bellamy, former President of the GC, argues that the diversity of legal traditions is probably the main reason for this lack of clear guidance by the EU Courts.[537] While this explanation might be true, it does not help to overcome the problems associated with such ambiguous standard of proof. An ambiguous standard of proof undermines not just the confidence in the correctness of the conclusions drawn, but also in the confidence in the principle of legal certainty.[538]

527. *See* Bailey (2003), p. 850.
528. *See* Cases C-29/83, etc., *Compagnie Royale Asturienne des Mines and Rheinzink*, para. 20; Case T-62/98, *Volkswagen*, para. 43.
529. *See* Case T-36/05, *Coats*, para. 71.
530. *See* Cases C-114/85, etc., *Woodpulp II*, para. 127.
531. *See* Case T-145/89, *Baustahlgewerbe*, para. 74.
532. *See* Case C-105/04 P, *FEG*, para. 60.
533. *See* Cases T-305/94, etc., *PVC II*, para. 644.
534. *See* Case C, *ICI*, para. 68.
535. *See* Cases T-305/94, etc., *PVC II*, paras 768-78; Case C-407/08 P, *Knauf Gips*, para. 47. Exceptionally even a single item of documentary evidence may be sufficient (*see* Case T-191/06, *Hydrogen Peroxide*, para. 122).
536. *See* Case C-407/08 P, *Knauf Gips*, para. 49: 'since the prohibition on participating in anti-competitive practices and agreements and the penalties which infringers may incur are well known, it is normal that the activities which those practices and agreements involve take place in a clandestine fashion, for meetings to be held in secret, frequently in a non-member country, and for the associated documentation to be reduced to a minimum. Even if the Commission discovers evidence explicitly showing unlawful contact between traders, such as the minutes of a meeting, it will normally be only fragmentary and sparse, so that it is often necessary to reconstitute certain details by deduction. In most cases, the existence of an anti-competitive practice or agreement must be inferred from a number of coincidences and indicia which, taken together, may, in the absence of another plausible explanation, constitute evidence of an infringement of the competition rules'. Interestingly, Faull and Nikpay only refer to this judgment in the context of hard-core cartel (*see* Faull and Nikpay (2014), para. 8.470). However, there is no doubt to me that this holistic view also applies when collusion is less obvious.
537. *See* OECD (1996), p. 105.
538. *See* Bailey (2003), p. 848.

Second, the standard of proof in antitrust cases is closer to the standard in criminal law cases ('beyond any reasonable doubt') than to the standard in civil law cases ('balance of probabilities'). *Groupe Danone*[539] is one example where the GC even explicitly mentioned the term 'beyond reasonable doubt'. The CJ appears to have never used this term explicitly though.[540] Furthermore, in *Dresdner Bank* the GC has established the 'benefit of any doubt' doctrine for the undertaking alleged of infringing Art. 101 TFEU.[541] This 'benefit of any doubt' was derived from the presumption of innocence pursuant to Art. 6(2) ECHR[542] and Art. 48(1) of the EU Charter and is now regularly used by the CJ.[543]

Castillo de la Torre and Gippini Fournier argue that the case law suggests that there is no meaningful difference between the standard of proof in antitrust law and criminal law.[544] Sir Cristopher Bellamy essentially agrees; the standard is 'probably very close to the criminal standard'.[545] This may explain the practical importance and weight of documentary evidence. Instead of trying to prove concertation from merely parallel conduct, enforcers are well advised to focus their efforts on finding documentary evidence such as information exchanges.

4.2.3.b.3 The Concept of 'Effort Probatoire'

Ultimately, the function of evidence is to convince judges. The standard of proof and the burden of proof are just abstract theoretical concepts that may have only limited practical value in explaining the persuasiveness of evidence needed to convince judges.[546] Therefore, the literature has proposed the idea of *effort probatoire*.[547] These are factors that influence the 'persuasive effect'[548] of evidence:[549]

- *Temporality*: the standard of proof should be higher for past facts than for future facts.[550]

539. Case T-38/02, *Groupe Danone*, para. 227.
540. *See* Faull and Nikpay (2014), fn 1236 in para. 8.469.
541. Cases T-61/02, etc., *Dresdner Bank*, para. 60: 'Any doubt in the mind of the Court must operate to the advantage of the undertaking to which the decision finding an infringement was addressed.'
542. European Convention on Human Rights ('ECHR'), available at: https://www.refworld.org/docid/3ae6b3b04.html.
543. *See* Cases C-403/04, etc., *Sumitomo*, para. 52; Case C-89/11 P, *E.ON*, para. 72.
544. *See* Castillo de la Torre and Gippini Fournier (2017), paras 2.029-2.030. Faull and Nikpay (2014, para. 8.469) agree with this conclusion.
545. OECD (1996), p. 105.
546. *See* Castillo de la Torre and Gippini Fournier (2017), para. 2.038.
547. *See* Sibony and Barbier de la Serre (2007).
548. *See* Castillo de la Torre and Gippini Fournier (2017), ch 2.G.
549. On the first three factors, *see* Sibony and Barbier de la Serre (2007), paras 749-751. On the third, fourth and fifth factors, *see* Castillo de la Torre and Gippini Fournier (2017), paras 2.038-2.064. *See also* Bailey (2003), pp. 873-885.
550. It is precisely because it requires a higher effort to 'prove' future events, a judge will avoid placing impossible high demands on the Commission to prove these future events (*see* Castillo de la Torre and Gippini Fournier (2017), fn 103 in para. 2.039). In other words, it is impossible

- *Complexity*: the standard of proof should be higher for situations with complex chains of causality.
- *Perception of normality*: the standard of proof should be higher for facts that deviate more from the judge's prior views on the normality (e.g., it is easier to make someone believe that the creature seen in the park was a dog than a lion).[551]
- *Evidence of actions vs evidence of their consequences*: the standard of proof should be higher for questions that relate to whether the undertaking has acted in a certain way than for questions that relate to anti-competitive consequences of those actions and their causation. This can be justified on the principle of personal responsibility and presumption of innocence.
- *Error costs*: the standard of proof should be higher when the risk of getting it wrong is higher. This can be justified on that basis that those situations involve a complex trade-off between the different rights and interests at stake, as well the incentives and disincentives by the judgment for the parties and society.

The concept is appealing for the analysis of a concerted practice. First, the standard of proof in *ex post* antitrust proceedings should be higher than in *ex ante* merger proceedings. The substantive assessment of mergers is based on a predictive analysis of future facts,[552] and the error costs for wrongly concluding an infringement may be higher than for wrongly blocking a merger.[553]

Second, in antitrust proceedings the standard of proof for concerted practice should be lower for documentary evidence than for circumstantial evidence. Documentary evidence can be used as direct evidence of concertation. For instance, why would competing undertakings exchange information about their future pricing intentions if not to collude. It deviates less from the perception of economic reality that such exchange has usually an anti-competitive motive than if it would be argued that such exchange has pro-competitive motives. Conversely, circumstantial evidence can be only used for indirect evidence of collusion. For instance, deriving concertation from parallel conduct entails the risk that competition authorities wrongly assume that firms have concerted, while in fact they have adopted themselves independently on the market (higher error costs).[554] Also, the perception of normality for parallel conduct is not necessarily collusion as there are many alternative plausible explanations for such conduct.[555]

to speak of certainties when making prognoses. Instead, the likelihood of future events must be based on the plausible scenario that can be drawn from an existing situation (Bailey (2003), pp. 874-875).

551. The example was given by Lord Hoffmann and is cited in Castillo de la Torre and Gippini Fournier (2017), para. 2.043.
552. *See* Bailey (2003), pp. 874-875.
553. *See* Castillo de la Torre and Gippini Fournier (2017), para. 2.058.
554. *See* Rivas and Van De Walle De Ghelcke (2012).
555. Such as the transparency or concentrated nature of the market as mentioned in section 3.3.2.c.

4.2.3.c *Types of Evidence*

There are two ways a concerted practice can be proven: by documentary or circumstantial evidence. In general, the less formalised the form of collusion, the more difficult to prove it.[556]

Documentary evidence can be any direct or indirect contact between undertakings[557] (such as the exchange of confidential information,[558] attendance at meetings[559] or discussion via telephone calls).[560] Importantly, when the Commission relies on documentary evidence to prove the concertation, the case law provides that other plausible explanations of parallel conduct on the market are irrelevant.[561] This is because the documentary evidence may be used as direct proof of the actual concertation. The party of the alleged infringement can still show that the evidence the Commission relied on is insufficient, incomplete or inconsistent.[562]

However, undertakings are well aware of the illegality of concertation and will try not to leave behind any trails of incriminating evidence.[563] In that case, if the Commission is not able to provide documentary evidence to prove an infringement, it can also rely on *circumstantial* evidence.[564] It could use for instance econometrical models to show that parallel conduct on the market has to be the result of concertation between the market players. However, such antitrust cases are very difficult to win for the Commission. The recent defeat of the Commission before the GC in *CISAC*[565] is a good example. The case law sets the threshold for circumstantial evidence quite high: it requires that parallel conduct of undertakings must be the only plausible explanation for such conduct (the so-called plausible alternative narrative).[566,567] However, it will be often very easy to find an alternative plausible explanation for the parallel conduct *inter alia* by using a different economic model with different assumptions.[568]

556. *See* Del Mar (2011), p. 112. As Joshua and Jordan has put it: 'At one extreme is proof of direct exchange of assurances between rivals, the classic form of evidence which shows the existence of an agreement. At the other end of the continuum lies economic proof of patterns of behavior, that the participants have followed similar business practices over a period of time.' (Joshua and Jordan (2004), p. 663)
557. *See* Bellamy & Child (2018), para. 2.078. *See also* the guidance by the Commission given in the Horizontal Cooperation Guidelines (paras 60-63).
558. *See* Case C-172/80, *Züchner*, para. 21.
559. *See* Case C-8/08, *T-Mobile*, para. 60. The fact that there were no minutes of the meeting may be a strong indication that the participants had to hide something (*see* Case T-334/94, *Sarrió*, para. 277 which was upheld on appeal: Case C-291/98 P, *Sarrió*).
560. *See* Cases C-40/73, etc., *Suiker Unie*, paras 328 and 393.
561. *See* Cases T-67/00, *JFE*, para. 186 (upheld on appeal: Cases C-403/04, etc., *Sumitomo*).
562. *See* Bellamy & Child (2018), para. 5.028.
563. *See* Albors-Llorens (2006), pp. 850-851.
564. *See* Bellamy & Child (2018), para. 2.081; Castillo de la Torre and Gippini Fournier (2017), para. 2.032.
565. *See* Case T-442/08, *CISAC*.
566. The notion is used by Castillo de la Torre and Gippini Fournier (2017), ch 2.F.3.
567. *See* Cases C-114/85, etc., *Woodpulp II*, para. 71; Case T-442/08, *CISAC*, paras 133 et seq. As Sir Christopher Bellamy puts it, the Court tries in such situations to balance 'the liberty of the subject and the need to ensure economic laws are properly enforced' (*see* OECD (1996), p. 106).
568. *See* Del Mar (2011), p. 120. *See* section 5.1.2 for a further discussion on this.

4.3 THE CLASSIFICATION AS A RESTRICTION OF COMPETITION BY OBJECT OR EFFECT

4.3.1 The Object/Effect Dichotomy

The object/effect dichotomy has been an area of immense discussion and uncertainty in recent years which is surprising given the concept is a fundamental part of the analysis in Art. 101 TFEU for over 50 years.[569] However, the two recent judgments in *Generics*[570] and *Budapest Bank*[571] have clarified some of the fundamental conceptual issues underlying the object/effect dichotomy. The former case concerned a preliminary reference from the United Kingdom (UK) relating to pay-to-delay agreements, where the CJ indicated that the agreement in question may be considered as a restriction by object. The latter case concerned a preliminary reference from Hungary relating to a multilateral interchange fee (MIF) in a credit card payment system, where the CJ raised doubts as to whether the agreement in question could be considered as a restriction by object (as done by the Hungarian competition authority).[572] Both cases seem to have made explicit some of the fundamental elements of the object/effect dichotomy that have merely been indicated by the previous case law.

It should be also mentioned that Ibáñez Colomo's contributions on the interpretation of these two cases and its implications for conceptual issues is significant.[573] Even his contributions before the two recent judgments in *Generics* and *Budapest Bank* seemed to 'predict' some of the solutions to the issues that have now been clarified.[574] What is particularly striking about his contributions is that he tries to emphasise the commonalities between both concepts by exploring the boundaries of the concept of a 'restriction of competition', instead of only the boundaries of the concept of a

569. *See* Whish and Bailey (2018), p. 122; Bruzzone and Capozzi (2016), p. 4.
570. Case C-307/18, *Generics*. For case comments, *see* Ibáñez Colomo (2020a); Henry and van Weert (2020) (more critical of the actual guidance given by the judgment); Rizzuto and Lynch (2020) (who also give a good overview over the pay-for-delay cases pursued by the Commission and pending before the EU Courts); Lahtinen (2020). For an economic perspective on this case, *see* Neven and Siotis (2020). On the pay-for-delay cases pursued by the Commission, *see*, e.g., Killick (2015) and Ska, Werner and Paul (2017), both are critical of the by object classification of the Commission. On the pay-for-delay cases pursued by the Commission, *see also* Ibáñez Colomo (2019b) who focuses on the more dogmatic issues raised by these cases.
571. Case C-228/18, *Budapest Bank*. The opinion of AG Bobek provides further clarity on the object/effect dichotomy (*see* opinion of AG Bobek in Case C-228/18, *Budapest Bank*). For case comments, *see* Bardusco and Juvigny (2020); Pazzi (2020); Nagy (2020); Baldwin (2020); Mandrescu (2020).
572. The Commission has classified MIF agreements in its proceedings as a restriction by effect, not as a restriction by object (*see* Commission decision, *MasterCard*). This view was confirmed by the GC (Case T-111/08, *MasterCard*) and CJ (Case C-382/12 P, *MasterCard*). For comments on these cases, *see* Gee (2012) and De Mattheis and Giordano (2015).
573. *See* particularly Ibáñez Colomo (2020b) and also Ibáñez Colomo (2020c) with regard to the implications for vertical restraints.
574. *See* Ibáñez Colomo (2020d), section 3 on the notion of restriction of competition in Art. 101(1) TFEU; and his joint article with Lamadrid de Pablo (*see* Ibáñez Colomo and Lamadrid de Pablo (2016)).

'restriction by object'.[575] In that sense he gives a holistic perspective on an important element in the Art. 101(1) TFEU analysis, despite criticism by some that argue that even these more recent cases added.[576]

The aim of this section is to lay down the foundation for understanding the commonalities (*see* section 4.3.1.b) and differences (*see* section 4.3.1.c) between both concepts in order to develop a coherent analytical framework for identifying restrictions by object (*see* next section 4.3.2) that is used for the coherent framework for assessing information exchanges (*see* Chapter 6).

4.3.1.a Preliminary Observations

4.3.1.a.1 Distinct Concepts

The EU Courts have derived from the literal interpretation of Art. 101 TFEU ('or') that both concepts are distinct and to be understood alternatively, not cumulatively.[577] A specific conduct infringes Art. 101 TFEU either on the basis that it has a restrictive objective *or* a restrictive effect. In *Budapest Bank*, the CJ merely clarified that a competition authority is not prevented from classifying a conduct as a restriction by object and effect.[578] Although it is thus possible for a competition authority to build a decision on two alternative pillars as precautionary measure, it cannot mix up both concepts and their respective analysis.[579]

The wording of Art. 101 TFEU does not suggest any hierarchical order between both concepts.[580] The CJ has clarified that the classification entails a two-stage process.[581] The first step is whether the conduct has to be classified as a restriction by object (also as referred to as 'prima facie unlawful' conduct);[582] if it does not, whether the conduct has restrictive effect on competition. Thus, the latter is merely a catch-all concept for conducts whose anti-competitive effects are less obvious and thus require a more in-depth effects analysis.

---

575. *See* particularly Ibáñez Colomo (2020d), section 3, which was published before *Generics* and *Budapest Bank*; Ibáñez Colomo (2020b), which takes into account and builds upon *Generics* and *Budapest Bank*. Although it should be mentioned that others have also emphasised the similarities between both concepts (*see*, e.g., Andreangeli (2011) who argued that the CJ used a 'similar pattern' (p. 216) when analysing object and effect cases and moved away from 'dichotomy' towards 'continuum' (p. 238)).
576. *See*, e.g., Baldwin (2020) who argues that *Budapest Bank* provided little practical and operational clarity and argues that one can be cynical in the sense that the CJ has simply packed existing vague language describing the notion of a restriction by object and repacked it in a language that is different but still equally vague.
577. *See* Case C-56/65, *Société Technique Minière*, para. 249.
578. *See* Case C-228/18, *Budapest Bank*, para. 44.
579. *See* Bardusco and Juvigny (2020), p. 164.
580. *See* Zelger (2017), p. 359. *See also* González (2012), p. 9 on the two-step approach.
581. *See* Case C-56/65, *Société Technique Minière*, para. 249. Similarly, in Case C-228/18, *Budapest Bank*, para. 40.
582. *See* Ibáñez Colomo (2019a), pp. 426 and 429-432.

4.3.1.a.2 Linguistic Considerations

Whish and Bailey famously distinguish between the 'object box' and 'effect box' when distinguishing between by object and by effect restrictions.[583] Ibáñez Colomo is sceptical whether these terms are still a good reflection of the case law after *Generics* and *Budapest Bank*. This is because the 'object box' seems to suggest a methodology to identify restrictions by object that appears to be rather abstract and disregards the crucial aspect in the case law that the identification of by object restrictions is a case-specific enquiry.[584]

In *Budapest Bank*, for instance, an abstract analysis could have led to the conclusion that the agreement in question constitutes a restriction by object since, from the outset, a group of competitors coordinated their conduct in relation to prices.[585] However, the CJ carefully considered the specific context of the agreement and raised doubts as to whether the agreement in question could be considered as a restriction by object in this specific context.

In the author's view the terms 'object box' and 'effect box' are still a useful linguistic simplification to the otherwise more complex language of 'restriction by object' or 'by object restrictions'. However, it is only that linguistic simplification that makes them useful. The terms should not carry any methodological meaning as they would, as rightly observed by Ibáñez Colomo, imply a rather mechanical identification of by object restrictions that do indeed not reflect the case law, which was apparent even before *Generics* and *Budapest Bank* (*see* section 4.3.2.b.1 below).

4.3.1.a.3 Normative Justifications for the Dichotomy

The object/effect distinction has also wider policy implications for undertakings, society and enforcers. In *Groupement des cartes bancaires*, AG Wahl has highlighted three normative justifications for the concept of a restriction by object.[586] In other words, these are policy justifications for why the object/effect dichotomy is necessary and why a uniform 'restriction of competition' concept may not be appropriate.

First, for undertakings restrictions by object provide (in theory) legal certainty and predictability of legal consequences.[587] This is because once undertakings engage in a conduct that is regarded as a restriction by object, anti-competitive effects are presumed, and the burden is then on the undertaking to prove the contrary. However, this argument assumes that the legal formula for identifying new restrictions by object is clear and unambiguous,[588] which is not a fully accurate description of the case law and its understanding, even after *Generics* and *Budapest Bank* (in section 4.3.2.b).

583. For this name, *see* Whish and Bailey (2018), p. 122.
584. *See* Ibáñez Colomo (2019c).
585. For that observation, *see* Ibáñez Colomo (2020c), p. 4.
586. *See* opinion of AG Wahl in Case C-67/13 P, *Groupement des cartes bancaires*, para. 35.
587. *See* opinion of AG Wahl in Case C-67/13 P, *Groupement des cartes bancaires*, para. 35. *See also* Italianer (2014), p. 6; Peeperkorn (2015), paras 15-16; Brankin (2016), p. 377; Zegler (2017), p. 363.
588. *See* opinion of AG Wahl in Case C-67/13 P, *Groupement des cartes bancaires*, para. 36.

Furthermore, one should consider that an effects analysis places a high burden on undertakings. Some undertakings may not be in a position to carry out expensive competition law assessments in every situation. This can mean that some undertakings will simply not engage in certain types of conducts that can be beneficial, simply because they are cautious not to be caught by Art. 101 TFEU prohibition (type I errors). In other words, the risk is that an *expansive* use of an effect-based analysis would chill efficiencies enhancing conduct.[589]

Second, the classification of certain conduct as a by object restriction entails a deterrence effect for undertakings. It helps to prevent the occurrence of anti-competitive conduct in the first place.[590] The presumption of restrictive effects should incentivise undertakings to enter into such conduct in the first place.[591] The idea is that undertakings only engage in conducts that are regarded as restrictions by object, if they can justify it based on efficiency considerations. Thus, the by object classification ultimately improves overall welfare and makes societies better off.

However, this argument may overstate the role of the concept of by object restrictions in preventing anti-competitive conduct. Cartels are formed because they are profitable. Other means may be more effective in deterring anti-competitive conduct (such as high fines, whistle-blower programmes, leniency programmes, criminal prosecution of individuals and so on). Still, even if the deterrence contribution of the by object concept may be small, one might argue that a small contribution is still better than no contribution at all.

Third, for competition authorities the concept of restrictions by object is a tool for achieving procedural efficiencies.[592] An effects analysis is often complex, time-consuming and may require substantial resources. If competition authorities have to spend more resources on fewer cases, this could result in general under-enforcement and insufficient deterrence of anti-competitive conduct (type II errors or false negatives).[593,594] Under the object analysis competition authorities do not have to spend their resources on cases which are rarely beneficial in most situations.[595] Furthermore, the fact that undertakings are able to demonstrate that a conduct that does not plausibly restrict competition that would have existed without the agreement, helps to prevent that they do not engage in beneficial conduct simply because this kind of conduct may fall within the object box (type I errors or false negatives).[596,597]

589. *See* Bennet and Collins (2010), p. 313; González (2012), p. 17.
590. *See* opinion AG Wahl in Case C-67/13 P, *Groupement des cartes bancaires*, para. 35. *See also* Bailey (2012), pp. 565-566; Peeperkorn (2015), paras 15-16; Brankin (2016), p. 377; Zegler (2017), p. 363.
591. *See* Wijckmans and Tuytschaever (2015), para. 11.25.
592. *See* opinion of AG Wahl in Case C-67/13 P, *Groupement des cartes bancaires*, para. 35. *See also* González (2012), p. 9; Peeperkorn (2015), paras 15-16; Brankin (2016), p. 377; Zegler (2017), p. 363.
593. False positives occur when an authority wrongly concludes that a pro-competitive conduct constitutes an infringement of competition law (*see* Whish and Bailey (2018), pp. 198-199).
594. *See* Bennet and Collins (2010), p. 313; Smith, Ridyard and Petrescu (2015), p. 36.
595. *See* Bailey (2012), p. 567.
596. False negatives occur when an authority wrongly concludes that an anti-competitive conduct does not constitute an infringement of competition law (*see* Whish and Bailey (2018), pp. 198-199).

On the negative side though, the procedural efficiencies consideration may incentivise competition authorities to disproportionally pursue by object cases.[598] This is encouraged even further because by object cases are normally more robust from a legal standpoint.[599] However, an under-enforcement of by effect cases may be detrimental for the development of the law in new, more complex or more controversial areas where an effects analysis should be employed to further clarify the application of the law in this area.

4.3.1.b Analytical Similarities

4.3.1.b.1 Restriction of Competition vs Restriction in the Freedom of Action

Both concepts aim to protect the 'restriction of competition' and thus to prevent allocative inefficiency.[600] A restriction of competition does not coincide with restriction in the *freedom of action* of undertakings.[601] What matters for the assessment of the restrictive nature under Art. 101(1) TFEU is the impact of a specific conduct on competition, not on the freedom of action of undertakings. The analysis under Art. 101(1) TFEU focuses on the impact of the conduct on firms' incentive to compete.[602]

It may well be that the freedom of action is restricted, while competition is not. This difference becomes important when assessing *inter alia* non-compete obligations or non-challenge clauses in licensing agreements.[603] For instance, while an exclusive dealing agreement restricts the freedom of distributors to sell products of other competing suppliers (i.e., restriction of freedom of action), it may increase inter-brand competitors *inter alia* because the exclusive supplier is able to build up a brand image that exercises more competitive pressure to existing strong brands.[604]

4.3.1.b.2 Relevance of the Counterfactual

Since both concepts protect the restriction of competition, it would seem only logical that both concepts do so by using the same benchmark for assessing the impact of an agreement on competition: that is to assess the scenario that would have existed without the agreement in question (the so-called counterfactual). The relevance of the

597. *See* Bennet and Collins (2010), p. 313; Smith, Ridyard and Petrescu (2015), p. 36.
598. *See* Killick and Jourdan (2014), p. 9. *See also* Dnes (2016), p. 249: 'The point is of particular salience, because of the tendency of some enforcers to favour the object category in order to truncate evidence gathering possibly out of administrative convenience, rather than out of a principled stand on the likely risk posed by the activity in question.'
599. *See* Ibáñez Colomo and Lamadrid de Pablo (2016), p. 18.
600. *See* Obudu (2006), p. 113.
601. *See* Ibáñez Colomo and Lamadrid de Pablo (2016), p. 12; Ibáñez Colomo (2020b), p. 34.
602. *See* Ibáñez Colomo and Lamadrid de Pablo (2016), p. 41. According to Ibáñez Colomo such coordinated loss or reduction of competitive pressure is one of the mechanisms through which anti-competitive effects are manifested (*see* Ibáñez Colomo (2020b), p. 14).
603. For these examples, *see* Ibáñez Colomo (2020b), p. 34.
604. *See* Vertical Guidelines, para. 164 for the efficiency and Ibáñez Colomo and Lamadrid de Pablo (2016), p. 12 for the example of the exclusive dealing agreement.

counterfactual is well established in the case law concerning restrictions by effects.[605] The CJ has now made clear in *Generics* and *Budapest Bank* that the counterfactual is also relevant for assessing restrictions by object.[606]

The counterfactual analysis is an integral part to assess whether there is a restriction of competition at all. The CJ has emphasised the importance of the counterfactual as early as in *Société Technique Minière*.[607] The counterfactual was an important part of CJ's analysis of (early) landmark cases that concerned the necessity of contractual restrictions for the achievement of a legitimate business purpose: *Remia*[608] (non-compete clauses in the context of the sale of a business), *Pronuptia*[609] (restrictions aimed to protect know-how in a franchise agreement), *Nungesser*[610] (territorial protection needed for the necessary investment to penetrate new markets in the context of an exclusive licence) and *Gøttrup-Klim*[611] (restriction of members of a cooperative purchasing association to participate in other purchasing cooperations in direct competition).[612]

Ibáñez Colomo derives from the case law that the counterfactual has an *ex ante* and an *ex post* perspective. When considering the conditions of competition that would have existed without the agreement, one should also consider the incentives of undertakings to invest and innovate (*ex ante* perspective) which may justify certain *ex post* restraints that would have been seen problematic if viewed on their own (*ex post* perspective). In other words (more easily observable) *ex post* restrictions cannot be examined in isolation.[613]

He further derives from the case law that the counterfactual has two main implications. First, the counterfactual requires a causal link between the agreement and the effects on competition. Such causal link does not exist where the absence of

605. *See* Case T-328/03, *O2 Germany*; Case C-382/12, *MasterCard*.
606. *See* Case C-307/18, *Generics*, paras 102-111 (pro-competitive effects would not have materialised absent the agreement) and Case C-228/18, *Budapest Bank*, paras 82-83 (price would have been higher absent the agreement). *See also* Ibáñez Colomo (2020c), para. 8 and Pazzi (2020), p. 235.
607. *See* Case C-56/65, *Société Technique Minière*, p. 250 (emphasised, e.g., by Bruzzone and Capozzi (2016), p. 4).
608. Case C-42/84, *Remia*.
609. Case C-161/84, *Pronuptia*.
610. Case C-268/78, *Nungesser*.
611. Case C-250/92, *Gøttrup-Klim*.
612. For a discussion of these cases *see* Nazzini (2006), pp. 511-513; Jones (2006), pp. 772-778 and 780 (who categorises *Nungesser* as an example for restraints on inter-brand competition, while categorising the other cases as ancillary restraints).
613. *See* Ibáñez Colomo (2020b), pp. 8-9, 29-31 and 63-64. The examples he gives to illustrate his argument are *Nungesser* (Case C-268/78) and *Pronuptia* (Case C-161/84). In *Nungesser*, the CJ took the view that certain *ex post* restraints (territorial protection to the licensee) were justified on the basis of the nature of the product (technology that required years of research) (*see* Case C-268/78, *Nungesser*, paras 56 and 58; this case and its broader context is also more extensively discussed in Ibáñez Colomo (2020d), pp. 124-127). Similarly, in *Pronuptia*, the CJ accepted certain *ex post* restraints resulting from a franchise agreement (such as a non-compete clause) that were linked to the pro-competitive gains of a franchise agreement (allowing the franchisor to benefit from the formula without investing its own capital) (*see* Case C-161/84, *Pronuptia*, para. 15; this case and its broader context is also more extensively discussed in Ibáñez Colomo (2020d), p. 120).

competition is attributable to, for instance, the regulatory context or an intellectual property (IP) rights but not to the agreement.[614] Second, the counterfactual aims to identify those scenarios where a thorough evaluation reveals that the agreement does actually improve the conditions of competition. For instance, when an agreement enables undertakings to engage in a project that they would have not been able to pursue individually (market creation) or where a restrictive clause is objectively necessary for the conclusion of an agreement (ancillary restraint doctrine).[615]

4.3.1.b.3 Relevance of Pro-competitive Effects

Generics and *Budapest Bank* have now clarified (although there were already indications in the case law before the two judgments)[616] that pro-competitive effects resulting from the agreement are also relevant under the restriction by object analysis under Art. 101(1) TFEU, not just for the analysis under Art. 101(3) TFEU.[617] The relevance of pro-competitive effects closely flows from and is closely related to the counterfactual.

In *Budapest Bank*, when the CJ tried to assess how interchange fees would have been developed without the MIF in place (the counterfactual), it ruled that 'contradictory or ambivalent evidence' on the claimed impact on competition cannot be ignored under the by object analysis.[618] AG Bobek emphasised more explicitly that possible pro-competitive effects of the MIF agreement in question cannot be ignored under the restriction by object analysis.[619]

Similarly in *Generics*, the CJ stated that only 'in the absence of any other plausible explanation' can the pay-for-delay agreement in question be classified as a restriction by object.[620] The CJ emphasised that *taking into account* pro-competitive effects under Art. 101(1) TFEU is not a United States (US)-style 'rule of reason' assessment where the anti-competitive harm is *balanced* against the pro-competitive benefits.[621] Instead, the role of 'sufficiently significant' pro-competitive effects under the object analysis of Art. 101(1) TFEU is to cast doubt as to whether an agreement caused harm to competition in the first place.[622]

In other words, the counterfactual analysis cannot just consider the anti-competitive effects of an agreement and completely ignore pro-competitive effects. Since the purpose of the object analysis is to identify the 'precise purpose' of an

---

614. *See* Ibáñez Colomo (2020b), pp. 25-27. Similar dogmatic considerations can be found already in Ibáñez Colomo (2019a), p. 430. In other words, the scope of the intellectual property rights (a legal barrier) determines the scope of application of Art. 101(1) TFEU (*see* Ibáñez Colomo (2019b), p. 592).
615. *See* Ibáñez Colomo (2020b), pp. 27-29.
616. *See* the cases cited in Ibáñez Colomo (2020c), fn 13.
617. *See* Case C-307/18, *Generics*, para. 104 and Case C-228/18, *Budapest Bank*, paras 81-83. *See* on this issue also e.g., Ibáñez Colomo (2020c), para. 7; Bardusco and Juvigny (2020), p. 165; Henry and van Weert (2020), p. 362; Dunne and Maher (2020), p. 337.
618. *See* Case C-228/18, *Budapest Bank*, para. 82.
619. *See* opinion of AG Bobek, Case C-228/18, *Budapest Bank*, para. 78.
620. *See* Case C-307/18, *Generics*, para. 89.
621. *Ibid.*, para. 104.
622. *Ibid.*, para. 107.

agreement,[623] it is only logical that both possible directions on the impact on competition are relevant for both concepts, whether they are negative or positive. However, both concepts differ in the *probability* threshold of these effects on competition (*see* section 4.3.1.c.1 below).

4.3.1.b.4 Context-Specific Assessment

When establishing that a conduct is restrictive on competition by effect, it is clear that it is necessary to appraise the conduct in light of its legal, factual and economic context.[624] *Generics* and *Budapest Bank* have also clarified (again) that the specific context of a conduct is also relevant for the object analysis.[625] As mentioned, in *Budapest Bank*, from the outset it seemed that a group of competitors coordinated their conduct in relation to prices, which would have resulted in the conclusion that the agreement constituted a restriction by object under an abstract/formalistic assessment.[626] However, the CJ did not follow such abstract/formalistic assessment. Instead, it carefully analysed the specific conduct of the agreement and had doubt as to whether the agreement in question could be classified as restriction by object.[627]

The context assessment essentially aims to identify those instances of horizontal cooperation that appear on their face to be plain vanilla cartels, but where the specific context provides a degree of legitimation.[628] It seems now clear that both types of restriction of competition analyses, whether an object or effects analysis, are context-specific and have to be assessed on a case-by-case basis.[629] The necessity to consider the specific legal and economic context of the agreement under the object analysis is further discussed below (*see* section 4.3.2.b.1 below).

4.3.1.c Analytical Differences

4.3.1.c.1 Nature of the Analysis: Plausibility vs Likelihood of Anti-competitive Effects

As mentioned, the concepts of a restriction by object and effect both aim to protect the same thing: the restriction of competition. However, they do so with different means regarding the nature of the analysis.[630]

623. This is emphasised by Ibáñez Colomo (2020a), p. 18.
624. *See* Case C-56/65, *Société Technique Minière*; Case C-23/67, *Brasserie de Haecht*; Case T-35/92, *John Deere*. For instance, in cases where the main concern is foreclosure, what matters is the agreements' contribution to the restrictive effects on competition (*see* Case C-234/89, *Delimitis*; Case C-214/99, *Neste Markkinointi Oy*).
625. *See* Case C-307/18, *Generics*, para. 67; Case C-228/18, *Budapest Bank*, para. 55. Conversely, an abstract and analysis focusing on the formal feature of an agreement is not sufficient (*see* Ibáñez Colomo (2020a), p. 17).
626. For that observation, *see* Ibáñez Colomo (2020c), p. 4.
627. *See* Case C-228/18, *Budapest Bank*, paras 80 et seq.
628. For this description, *see* Dunne and Maher (2020), p. 335.
629. *See* Pazzi (2020), p. 235.
630. *See* González (2012), p. 10; Bailey (2012), p. 583.

Various attempts have been made by the literature on how to distinguish the different nature of the analysis for restrictions by object on the one hand and restrictions by effect on the other hand. Generally, the economic analysis for restrictions by effect has been described as more intensive.[631] Conversely, the economic analysis for restrictions by object is less intense not just because such restrictions usually entail anti-competitive effects[632] but also because they usually lack any sort of plausible efficiency.[633] In other words, the presumption of the existence of anti-competitive effects is so 'self-evident' in case of restrictions by object that it does not need to be established.[634] Some have emphasised that while (potential or actual) anti-competitive effects are presumed in the case of restrictions by object, these effects have to be 'proven' in case of restrictions by effects.[635] Restrictions by object have been also described as 'conduct-oriented' whereas restrictions by effects as 'effect-oriented'.[636] Others have emphasised that the one-sided reliance on evidence of subjective intent only works for by object restrictions. Subject intents of parties are used by the Commission to condemn parties, rather than show that undertakings did not have the object of restricting competition.[637]

One very promising difference between the nature of the analysis is carved out by Ibáñez Colomo (and Lamadrid de Pablo) and relates to the *probability* threshold for anti-competitive effects. While restrictions by object have to be merely 'capable' of restricting competition, restrictions by effects have to 'likely' restrict competition.[638] For the assessment of restrictions by object this difference with regard to the probability threshold for effects has two dimensions. On the one hand, this means for competition authorities that it is sufficient that harm to competition is a plausible outcome.[639] On the other hand, this also means for parties that it is sufficient to show that their agreement is a plausible source of pro-competitive effects on competition or

631. *See* King (2011), p. 273.
632. *See* Case C-67/13 P, *Groupement des cartes bancaires*, para. 51: 'Experience shows that such behaviour leads to falls in production and price increases, resulting in poor allocation of resources to the detriment, in particular, of consumers.' *See also* Art. 101(3) Guidelines, para. 21: 'These are restrictions which in light of the objectives pursued by the Community competition rules have such a high potential of negative effects on competition that it is unnecessary for the purpose of apply Article [101](3) to demonstrate any actual effects on the market.'
633. *See* Peeperkorn (2015), para. 8. *See also* Jones who argues that by object restrictions are at the extreme end of conduct regarding the likely anti-competitive effects (*see* Jones (2010), p. 655). *See* section 4.3.2.c.1 below for the plausible efficiency theory.
634. *See* OECD (2011), para. 72.
635. *See* González (2012), p. 12; Peeperkorn (2015), para. 12. Put differently, an agreement that restricts competition by object is prohibited even if it is not yet implemented (*see* Ibáñez Colomo and Lamadrid de Pablo (2016), p. 17). The presumption of anti-competitive effects does not preclude any sort of competitive analysis. *Some* effects analysis might still be necessary for the assessment within Art. 101(3) TFEU and the determination of the level of fine (*see* Bailey (2012), p. 588).
636. *See* Zelger (2017), pp. 359-360.
637. *See* Bailey (2012), pp. 578-579.
638. *See* Ibáñez Colomo (2020b), pp. 12-13 and 45-52. *See also* Ibáñez Colomo (2019b), pp. 595-596 and his joint paper with Lamadrid de Pablo in 2016 (*see* Ibáñez Colomo and Lamadrid de Pablo (2016), pp. 34-35).
639. *See* Ibáñez Colomo (2020b), p. 47.

that the agreement is incapable of having an impact on competition.[640] Although this conceptual difference is theoretically convincing, the problem is (as Ibáñez Colomo admits himself) that the words 'capable' and 'likely' are sometimes used indistinctly by the CJ. This creates friction between how the two probability thresholds are actually applied in practice (i.e., capability threshold for restrictions by object and likelihood threshold for restrictions by effect) and in the language used by the CJ. This is a potential source of legal uncertainty, and future cases will show whether the language will get more consistent.[641]

4.3.1.c.2 Burden of Proof

The less in-depth analysis in case of restrictions by object means that the burden of proof shifts more easily.[642] Once the competition authority has demonstrated that the conduct in question constitutes a restriction by object (and thus did not need to demonstrate potential or actual anti-competitive effects), it is for undertakings to show that pro-competitive efficiencies outweigh anti-competitive effects (individual exemption) or that the restriction is objectively necessary for the existence of the agreement (object necessity).[643] In both latter cases the burden of proof is on the undertaking claiming it. Particularly in the former case the result is that the effort of gathering factual evidence on the effects on competition lies with the parties engaging in a conduct that has restrictive objective.[644]

*4.3.1.c.3 Appreciability on Competition (*De Minimis *Doctrine)*

For a conduct to infringe Art. 101(1) TFEU it is necessary that it has an appreciable effect on competition. The De Minimis Notice has set out a positive presumption that a conduct does have an appreciable effect on competition, if certain market share thresholds are not exceeded (5% in case of cumulative foreclosure of parallel networks of agreements having similar effects on the market;[645] 10% in case of agreements between competitors;[646] 15% in case of agreements between non-competitors).[647] However, the De Minimis Notice does not apply to restrictions by object.[648]

For restrictions by object, the CJ has very early established in *Völk*[649] that even restrictions by object (in this case an exclusive dealing agreement with absolute territorial protection) may not have an appreciable effect on competition in light of the

640. *Ibid.*, p. 49.
641. *Ibid.*, p. 60.
642. *See* Zelger (2017), p. 361.
643. *See* the various guidance by the Commission on the issue of objective necessity: Art. 101(3) Guidelines, para. 18; Vertical Guidelines, paras 60 and 62; By Object Guidance, pp. 4-5. *See also* Peeperkorn (2015), paras 42-51.
644. *See* Peeperkorn (2015), para. 12.
645. *See* De Minimis Notice, para. 9.
646. *Ibid.*, para. 8 lit a.
647. *Ibid.*, para. 8 lit b.
648. *Ibid.*, para. 13.
649. Case C-5/69, *Völk*.

weak position of the undertakings in question.[650] The case suggests that EU competition law is not intended to deal with only insignificant restrictions of competition, even if it concerns agreements that are designed to restrict competition.[651]

However, the more recent judgment in *Expedia,*[652] which triggered a torrent of literature,[653] has raised doubts as to whether the statement in *Völk* still holds true. Interestingly, the case mainly concerned the role of the De Minimis Notice for national competition authorities. Only one paragraph concerned the issue of appreciability of restrictions by object. This statement was not even necessary in light of the question asked by the French court and was thus merely obiter dictum.[654] In this paragraph the CJ stated that 'an agreement that may affect trade between Member States and that has an anti-competitive object constitutes, by its nature and independently of any concrete effect that it may have, an appreciable restriction on competition'.[655] The CJ failed to provide any further guidance on how this statement interacts with existing case law.[656]

Most scholars argue that both judgments should be read and interpreted complementarily, not contradictorily.[657] They argue that the CJ in *Expedia* has merely clarified that the beneficial presumption of non-appreciability set out by the old De Minimis Notice does not apply in case of restrictions by object.[658] However, in line with *Völk*, an agreement that restricts competition by object can still fall outside the scope of Art. 101(1) TFEU if it fails to produce appreciable effects on competition. However, this is for the parties to demonstrate (i.e., there is no presumption of non-appreciability within safe harbours). In other words, *Expedia* has merely shifted the burden of proof

650. *See* Case C-5/69, *Völk*, para. 5/7.
651. *See* González (2013), p. 461.
652. Case C-226/11, *Expedia*.
653. *See*, e.g., Akman (2013); Bushell and Healy (2013); González (2013); Graham (2013); van der Vijer and Vollering (2013); Zegler (2017).
654. *See* Akman (2013); van der Vijver and Vollering (2013), pp. 1136 and 1139 et seq.
655. Case C-226/11, *Expedia*, para. 37.
656. *See* Bushell and Healy (2013), p. 225.
657. *See*, e.g., Bushell and Healy (2013), p. 225; González (2013), p. 465 who even goes so far as to argue that it is 'more appropriate to consider the judgement as a desirable clarification and even as a simplification of former jurisprudence: object agreements are *presumed* to affect competition appreciably' (emphasis added); van der Vijver and Vollering (2013), pp. 1140-1142; Zegler (2017), pp. 384-388. Akman (2013) and Graham (2013), both are early commentators on the *Expedia* judgment, read the judgment that a by object restriction *always* has an appreciable effect on competition. However, Graham fails to provide any reasoning in support for his interpretation. Akman admits that she is not entirely sure whether the presumption of appreciability is irrebuttable. She is concerned that the judgment is not in line with the modern economic approach. However, such contradiction would only hold true if one takes the view (as she does) that the presumption of appreciability is irrebuttable. Conversely, if one takes the view (like Zegler or Bushell and Healy) that there is merely a *rebuttable* presumption of appreciability, even within the safe harbours, then parties could still demonstrate the non-appreciability of the agreement and thus there would be no contradiction with economics.
658. Zegler's reasoning for this interpretation is quite convincing: 'Due to the fact that, as a matter of principle, no analysis of actual effects is required but rather presumed as soon as an object restriction is established, it would be inconsistent to then let the identified practice benefit from the presumption that such (presumed) effect is however presumed not being appreciable. In other words, to presume that a practice presumably having an anticompetitive effect is in the next step not appreciable, that is, does not have an appreciable effect on competition, seems to bear a contradiction in itself.' (Zegler (2017), p. 387)

regarding the demonstration of appreciability. While for restrictions by effect it is for the competition authority to show that within the safe harbours set out in the De Minimis Notice the agreement does nevertheless appreciably affect competition, undertakings always have to demonstrate the non-appreciability effect on competition in case of restrictions by object.

Nevertheless, for undertakings to show that a by object restriction does affect competition only insignificantly may be as difficult as to demonstrate that the agreement satisfies the conditions for an individual exemption (*see* below). However, as *Völk* has shown, it is not impossible, just very unlikely.[659]

4.3.1.c.4 Likelihood of Exemption

Even a by object restriction can be exempted.[660] From a *theoretical* perspective, this recognises that a by object classification is not intended to be a perfect rule designed to be 100% accurate in predicting the net negative effects.[661] Even an agreement that is generally presumed to produce net anti-competitive effects (object box) may produce efficiencies in exceptional circumstances. The decisional practice of the Commission provides some examples of restrictions by object that were individually exempted.[662]

However, in *practice* an exemption of a restriction by object is generally unlikely for two reasons. First, it is unlikely that a restriction by object can benefit from the safe harbours in one of the BERs. This is because the list of hard-core restrictions[663] in the various BERs reflects what types of conduct in the context of the specific BER were regarded, at the time of the adoption of the BER, as restrictions by object.[664] Still, hard-core restrictions only exemplify rather than limit or define restrictions by object.[665]

Second, although no type of agreement is excluded from the scope of Art. 101(3) TFEU, a restriction by object is unlikely to be individually exempted. This is because one of the main characteristics of restrictions by object is that it usually lacks any sort

659. *See* Zegler (2017), p. 388.
660. *See,* e.g., Case T-17/93, *Matra Hachette,* para. 85; Case C-209/07, *Beef Industry Development Society,* para. 21; Case C-439/09, *Pierre Fabre,* paras 48-59. In other words, by object restrictions are not per se infringements as this would be inconsistent with the structure of Art. 101 TFEU (*see* van der Vijver and Vollering (2013), pp. 1142-1143). This is one of the main differences to US law under the rule of per se infringements (*see* Italianer (2014), p. 4).
661. *See* González (2012), pp. 18-19.
662. *See* Commission decision, *REIMS II* (price-fixing agreement between most of the public postal operators); Commission decision, *CECED* (agreement between suppliers of washing machines to promote the production of energy-efficient washing machines by ceasing the production of inefficient ones); Commission decision, *Visa International – Multilateral Interchange Fee* (multilateral agreement between banks within the Visa card system to fix interchange fees).
663. It should be noted that the Court explicitly pointed out that Art. 101 TFEU does not use the notion of 'hard-core restriction' (*see* Case C-439/09, *Pierre Fabre,* para. 32). Still, in practice they are used synonymously (*see* Bailey (2012), p. 573).
664. *See* Peeperkorn (2015), paras 15 and 43.
665. *See* Bailey (2012), p. 573.

of plausible efficiency which justifies the classification in the first place.[666] Although theoretically there is scope for possible efficiency claims under Art. 101(3) TFEU, the practical relevance of such claims is rather limited.[667]

4.3.2 Identifying Restrictions by Object

This section explores the identification of restrictions by object. While this was a relatively straightforward task in the early days of EU competition law, it has become quite a minefield for competition lawyers in recent years due to mainly two relatively recent cases (*T-Mobile* and *Allianz Hungária*). However, *Groupement des cartes bancaires, Generics* and *Budapest Bank* have significantly contributed to clarify how to identify restrictions by object. This section discusses how the case law on the restriction by object was perceived in the past (*see* section 4.3.2.a) and how it can be described now after *Groupement des cartes bancaires, Generics* and *Budapest Bank* (*see* section 4.3.2.b). Interestingly, recent cases triggered an interesting academic discussion that has resulted in essentially three theories exploring the very foundation of the concept of a restriction by object (*see* section 4.3.2.c).

4.3.2.a The Case Law in the Past: Emphasis on 'Category-Building' and Abstract Legal Formulas

4.3.2.a.1 Category-Building and the Steady Shift Away from It

One of the features of the traditional doctrine of by object restrictions was what Nagy describes as 'category-building'.[668] There was a relatively exhaustive list of hard-core restrictions that was cautiously developed by the Commission (particularly through the hard-core restrictions in the various BERs) together with the EU Courts. Whish therefore proposed the concept of an 'object box' which contains these categories of harmful conduct.[669] A classification within the object box was established by reference to precedences.[670] The anti-competitive harm of these types of conduct was so obvious

666. *See* Art. 101(3) Guidelines, para. 46; Vertical Guidelines, para. 47; By Object Guidance, p. 4. As put by Bailey (2012), p. 593: 'Finding examples of such agreements is a difficult as it is easy to state the principle.' He also discussed those cases that were classified as restrictions by object but individually exempted (*see* Bailey (2012), pp. 595-597).
667. *See* Jones (2010), p. 663. The presumption created by the classification as a by object restriction is simply too strong to be rebutted in practice and sufficiently substantiate claimed efficiencies (*see* Jones (2010), pp. 669-670).
668. *See* Nagy (2013); Nagy (2015).
669. *See* Whish and Bailey (2018), p. 122.
670. *See* Mahtani (2012), p. 28. While this provided legal certainty, it also lacked flexibility and was rather formalistic (*see* King (2011), p. 274).

that EU Courts did not feel the need to require a detailed analysis of the context.[671] The scope of the object box thus developed was relatively reliable and predictable.[672]

However, *T-Mobile* and *Allianz Hungária*, both were preliminary references given to national courts that struggled to apply the classification, indicated a shift in that approach.[673] Instead of cautiously expanding the object box to new categories of restrictions, the CJ seemed to encourage a case-by-case analysis that some feared comes close to an effects analysis. While the old case law seemed to be relatively clear, these cases caused considerable confusion.[674] Scholars have raised concerns that these cases undermined the very nature of the conceptual difference and that the concept of by object restrictions therefore became a 'loose cannon'.[675] Particularly *Allianz Hungária* felt short of being a 'model of clarity'.[676] These cases have exposed the lack of robust conceptual foundation on how to identify restrictions by object in light of the rather formalistic classification through category-building.

In *Groupement des cartes bancaires* the CJ offered more clarity. It indicates a clearer demarcation between restrictions by object and effect.[677] Some consider the judgment even as an important turning point for the object analysis.[678] The judgment marks an important brake to the expansive interpretation of restrictions by object,[679] something the CJ emphasised again in *Budapest Bank*.[680] It was the first time the CJ has set aside a Commission decision on the basis of a false classification as a restriction by object.[681] As put by Italianer, former Director-General for Competition at the Commission, the judgment 'warns against an overenthusiastic finding of "by object" infringements'.[682] Although the CJ did not completely eliminate previous rulings (*Allianz Hungária* was still cited six times in the judgment), it has changed its tone towards a more cautious contextual approach.[683] Thus, the recent development in the case law can be described as two steps towards blurring the conceptual distinction (*T-Mobile* and *Allianz Hungária*) and one step back towards clarifying it (*Groupement des cartes bancaires*).

---

671. *See* Nazzini and Nikpay (2014), p. 159. Jones even argues that the assessment of by object restrictions was left behind by the modernisation and continued to be applied rather formalistic (*see* Jones (2010)).
672. *See* Nagy (2015), pp. 154-155; Alvin Sng (2016), pp. 180-183.
673. *See*, e.g., Nazzini and Nikpay (2014), pp. 159-162; Fattori (2015), pp. 23-24.
674. *See* Killick and Jourdan (2014), p. 4. *See also* Nagy (2013), pp. 561-563 with regard to *Allianz Hungária*.
675. *See* Nagy (2015) for this expression.
676. *See* Collin (2017), p. 49 for this expression.
677. *See* Dnes (2016), pp. 246 and 248.
678. *See* Bruzzone and Copozzi (2016), p. 2.
679. *See* Murray (2015), p. 47. For a more moderate interpretation of the judgment, *see* Nazzini and Nikpay (2014), p. 157: 'the judgement does not fundamentally alter the law for the object cases. Rather the judgement attempts to clarify apparent ambiguities and discrepancies in the case law and provides a more structured framework than previously existed for determining whether an agreement is restrictive by object'.
680. *See* Case C-228/18, *Budapest Bank*, para. 54.
681. *See* Killick and Jourdan (2014), p. 6.
682. Italianer (2014), p. 3.
683. *See* Nagy (2015), pp. 155-157.

The Commission has accelerated the shift away from category-building. On the one hand, the decisional practice suggests that the Commission has extensively used the concept of by object restrictions probably prompted by the desire to achieve procedural economy.[684] On the other hand, the legal nature of the By Object Guidance sends a clear signal to those hoping that the Commission returns to the cautious approach of category-building. Although the By Object Guidance provides a useful illustrative list of by object restrictions, it 'is without prejudice to any developments in the case law and in the Commission's decisional practice'.[685] Thus, the By Object Guidance is not the typical soft law instrument that binds the Commission. Instead, the Commission abstains from promising an 'investigative abstinence' as to novel restrictions.[686] As a result, the By Object Guidance may be understood as a move away from the slow and cautious category-building towards case-by-case analysis for by object restrictions.

The Commission seems to be willing to apply the concept of a restriction by object even in 'untested territories' which some argue creates friction with the general aim of applying a more economic approach.[687] However, viewed more positively, this can give the CJ more opportunities to clarify some of conceptual issues of a restriction by object. The area of pay-for-delay agreements, which are settlement agreements between pharmaceutical companies and producers of generic medicines, is a good example for such 'untested territory'. In its decisions in *Lundbeck*[688] and *Servier*,[689] the Commission has classified certain pay-for-delay agreements as restrictions by object. The GC confirmed the Commission's view with regard to the classification as a restriction by object; appeals before the CJ are still pending.[690] It is however noted that the CJ has already dealt with pay-for-delay agreements for the first time in *Generics*, a preliminary reference ruling given to the UK, where it indicated that it considered the specific pay-for-delay agreement in question as a restriction by object.[691]

684. *See* Pradelles et al. (2014), p. 3.
685. By Object Guidance, p. 5.
686. *See* Nagy (2015), p. 158.
687. *See* Alvin Sng (2016), p. 181.
688. Commission decision, *Lundbeck*.
689. Commission decision, *Servier*. While the *Lundbeck* decision only concerned the application of Art. 101 TFEU, the *Servier* decision also concerned the application of Art. 102 TFEU.
690. Case T-472/13, *Lundbeck* (appeal pending in Case C-591/16 P, *Lundbeck*); Case T-691/14, *Servier* (appeal pending in Cases C-176/19 P and C-201/19 P, *Servier*). The opinion of AG Kokott has been already published in *Lundbeck*, where AG Kokott agrees with the Commission's and GC's view that the pay-for-delay agreements were restrictions by object (*see* opinion of AG Kokott, Case C-591/16 P, *Lundbeck*, paras 114-172). For a discussion of these two decisions and the respective rulings of the GC, *see*, e.g., Rizzuto and Lynch (2020), pp. 151-153. For a case comment of the *Servier* ruling of the GC, *see* Killick, Jourdan and Pêcheux (2019).
691. Case C-307/18, *Generics*, paras 59-111.

4.3.2.a.2 *The Long-Lasting Struggle to Settle on an Abstract Legal Formula*

The case law before *Groupement des cartes bancaires* is ambiguous, confusing and fails to provide a clear legal test to identify by object restrictions.[692] Instead, the case law provided a wide range of different tests. There are at least five legal formulas that can be found in the case law before *Groupement des cartes bancaires* for identifying restrictions by object:[693]

(1) restrictions that are by their 'very nature' injurious to the proper functioning of competition[694] (most often cited);
(2) restrictions that reveal a 'sufficient degree of harm' to competition[695] (also adopted by the Commission in its Guidelines);[696]
(3) restrictions that have a 'sufficiently deleterious effect' on competition[697] (substantively identical to the second test);[698]
(4) restrictions that constitute 'obvious' restrictions of competition[699] (only cited once by the GC); and
(5) restrictions that have the 'potential' to have negative impact on competition[700] (this test is considered an outliner).[701]

Most people read the judgment in *Groupement des cartes bancaires*, in which the CJ disagreed with the by object classification of the GC, in a way that it at least 'clarified' the previous case law in which some cases have blurred the line between both concepts (particularly *T-Mobile* and *Allianz Hungária*).[702] Thus, the CJ has not

692. *See* Murray (2015), p. 48. *See also* Baño Fos (2015), p. 28 who asks the (conceptually) more fundamental question why the GC got something as fundamental to the application of Art. 101 TFEU as the distinction between by object and effect restriction wrong after 50 years of case law.
693. *See* Brankin (2016), pp. 378-380 who identifies the first four tests. He essentially criticised that these tests are substantively 'empty' and thus fail to provide a robust legal test. *See also* the discussion by Murray (2015), p. 48.
694. *See* Case C-19/77, *Miller International Schallplatten*, para. 7; Case C-209/07, *Beef Industry Development Society*, para. 17; Case C-8/08, *T-Mobile*, para. 29; Case C-226/11, *Expedia*, para. 36; Case C-32/11, *Allianz Hungária*, para. 36.
695. *See* Cases C-501/06 P, etc., *GlaxoSmithKline*, para. 55; Cases C-403/08, etc., *Premier League*, para. 135; Case C-32/11, *Allianz Hungária*, para. 34.
696. *See* Art. 101(3) Guidelines, para. 21; Horizontal Cooperation Guidelines, para. 24.
697. *See* Case C-56/65, *Société Technique Minière*, para. 235; Case C-8/08, *T-Mobile*, para. 28.
698. This is because the CJ cites in *GlaxoSmithGline* (para. 55), which refers to the second test, the paragraph in *T-Mobile* (para. 28), which lays down the third test. Thus, the Court considers these two tests as identical.
699. *See* Cases T-374/94, etc., *European Night Services*, para. 126.
700. *See* Case C-8/08, *T-Mobile*, para. 31; Case C-32/11, *Allianz Hungária*, para. 38. A discussion of this test and the relevance for information exchanges can be found in González (2012), pp. 41-44.
701. *See*, e.g., Jones and Sufrin (2016), p. 683.
702. *See*, e.g., Fattori (2015); Murray (2015); Peeperkorn (2015) who also mentions these two judgments in para. 27 (*Allianz Hungária*) and fn 16 (*T-Mobile*); Brankin (2016). Nagy emphasises though that the Court has not overruled *Allianz Hungária*, but simply applied it more cautiously. The difference comes down to a different tone, while the language remains the same (*see* Nagy (2015), pp. 155 and 159).

revolutionised the classification with *Groupement des cartes bancaires* but merely readjusted it. The following two formulas set out in that judgment reflect that clarification. They cannot be found in this form in previous case law[703] and have been repeated in *SIA Maxima Latvija,*[704] in *Budapest Bank*[705] and (mostly) in *Generics:*[706]

- Restrictions that 'reveal a sufficient degree of harm to competition that it may be found that there is no need to examine their effects'.[707] While the former part of the statement already existed in the case law (sufficient degree of harm),[708] the combination with the latter part is novel.[709]
- Restrictions that are 'so likely to have negative effects, in particular on the price, quality of the goods and services, that it may be considered redundant, for the purpose of applying Art. [101(1) TFEU], to prove that they have actual effects on the market [...]. Experience shows that such behaviour leads to falls in production and prices increases, resulting in poor allocation of resources to the detriment, in particular, of consumers'.[710] In *Generics*, the CJ has repeated the second part (the importance of experience), but not the first part.[711]

4.3.2.a.3 The Challenges of Employing an Abstract Legal Formula

The discussion in the literature about the various legal formulas used by the EU Courts to identify a restriction by object is certainly interesting, but also frustrating.[712] The long-lasting struggle may have at best carved out the challenges of using an abstract legal formula. At worst it has exposed the fundamental flaw of an analytical approach that merely focuses on an abstract legal formula. Whatever view one takes, the strong emphasis on abstract legal formulas is probably not (anymore) the best description of the current state of the case law on restrictions by object. Instead, the contextual and cautious approach better reflects the current state of the case law (*see* section 4.3.2.b below).

There are several challenges in employing an abstract legal formula to identify restrictions by object. These theoretical considerations may offer one explanation for the ambiguous case law and the struggle to get the legal test 'right'. First, it has been

703. *See* Brankin (2016), p. 380.
704. *See* Case C-345/14, *SIA Maxima Latvija*, paras 18-19. In this case, the CJ did not qualify the relevant clauses of lease agreements as a restriction by object because the restrictive clauses were necessary to invest in the first place and thus they were at least potential positive net effects (*see* Brankin (2016), pp. 382-383).
705. *See* Case C-228/18, *Budapest Bank*, paras 35-36 and 54.
706. *See* Case C-307/18, *Generics*, paras 64 and 67.
707. Case C-67/13 P, *Groupement des cartes bancaires*, para. 50.
708. Which has not even been the most relevant test (*see* Murray (2015), p. 48).
709. *See* Brankin (2016), p. 380.
710. Case C-67/13 P, *Groupement des cartes bancaires*, para. 51.
711. *See* Case C-307/18, *Generics*, para. 64.
712. *See*, e.g., MacCulloch (2020), p. 363 who argues that such abstract formula leaves as many questions as answers and gives little guidance and that an approach based on taxonomy is not well aligned with the approach away from legal formalism.

pointed out by the economic and jurisprudential literature[713] that the *context* of the conduct should be decisive for the classification. For instance, while the exchange of price-related information may be necessary and thus justified in a joint commercialisation agreement,[714] the same exchange could be also used as an effective means to facilitate a cartel. In other words, whether EU Courts have put forward an abstract formula in the context of a cartel investigation or in other contexts makes a huge (in some cases even decisive) difference. Thus, an abstract legal formula necessarily falls short of taking into account the specific context of the case. General statements that are uncoupled from its context in which they were given are doomed to be misunderstood.[715]

Second, abstract legal formulas given by the CJ may also entail the risk of a too loose application by the various actors that apply EU competition law in the decentralised enforcement system (national courts, national authorities, arbitrators, etc.).[716] It is interesting to note that the 'outliners' are cases given in form of a preliminary reference judgment (*T-Mobile* and *Allianz Hungária*), while the 'constrainer' was given on appeal of GC's judgment (*Groupement des cartes bancaires*).[717] In the former cases the language was broad and expansive,[718] while in the latter narrower and more precise. Guidance that is given in a preliminary reference necessarily amplifies the abstract nature and thus deemphasises the specific context for the classification. This raises the question whether an abstract legal formula is (still) suitable in a decentralised enforcement system. The recent landmark rulings in *Generics* and *Budapest Bank*, both preliminary reference rulings, show that such fear is unfounded as they clarified many of the doctrinal controversies about the notion of a restriction by object.[719] Particularly *Budapest Bank* may be a good example after *Groupement des cartes bancaires* of how the CJ tried to put the genie invoked by *Allianz Hungária* back into the bottle.[720]

4.3.2.b The Current Case Law: The Importance of Context and Experience

4.3.2.b.1 Contextual Approach: The Context Is Everything[721]

Particularly after *Generics* and *Budapest Bank*, there is now no doubt that even a restriction by object analysis requires a context-specific enquiry into the legal and economic context of a conduct (*see* already in section 4.3.1.b.4 above).[722] The objective

713. *See*, e.g., Peeperkorn (2015), para. 9; Brankin (2016), pp. 378-379.
714. *See* Horizontal Cooperation Guidelines, para. 244.
715. Similarly Dunne (2020), p. 377.
716. *See* Alvin Sng (2016), p. 184.
717. *See* Nagy (2015), pp. 157-158.
718. *See* Dnes (2016), p. 245 who also points out that *Allianz Hungária* invites authorities to even place vertical agreement into the object box. Similar criticism is raised by Nagy (2013), p. 561.
719. *See* Ibáñez Colomo (2020c), para. 5.
720. *See* Nagy (2020).
721. For this expression, *see* Murray (2015), p. 48.
722. *See* Case C-307/18, *Generics*, paras 67-68; Case C-228/18, *Budapest Bank*, paras 51-52, 55 and 59. *See also* Ibáñez Colomo (2020c), para. 6, in the context of these two cases.

of a conduct cannot be ascertained in vacuum by merely using an abstract formula.[723] Instead, the objective must be put and understood in its legal and economic context, which the CJ has emphasised as early as in *Société Technique Minière*.[724] The context of the conduct has significant weight in the case law.[725] It could be the reason why the EU Courts do not feel the need to settle on a specific abstract formula, even though more recent cases seem to repeat (more or less) the formulas set out in *Groupement des cartes bancaires*. While the discussion about an abstract formula is academically interesting it does not seem to be decisive; the specific legal and economic context seems to be though.

In *Groupement des cartes bancaires* the CJ laid down a list of factors that need to be considered for the classification as a restriction by object: (i) the content and objectives of the agreement, (ii) the economic and legal context of which it forms a part, (iii) the nature of the goods or service affected and (iv) the 'real conditions' of the functioning and structure of the market or markets in question.[726] These factors have been repeated in *Generics*[727] and *Budapest Bank*.[728] Although intentions of the parties do not have to be considered necessarily, they still can be considered.[729] The intentions may be useful for instance when enforcers try to figure out whether a conduct aims to achieve efficiencies or not.[730] The CJ has also emphasised that the context analysis is not the same as the analysis of the relevant market.[731] The assessment of the economic and legal context is wider and includes factors that do not play a role when defining the relevant market.[732]

It is not so much the specific list as such that is important. The individual factors may well be interpreted formalistically in a way that would require a full effects analysis for the classification as a restriction by object.[733] Instead, *Groupement des cartes bancaires* provides a useful example for the limits of the context analysis. In *Allianz Hungária*, the Court went too far in requiring a de facto effects analysis for the classification as a by object restriction.[734] This is why the Court in *Groupement des*

---

723. *See* Bailey (2012), p. 582.
724. *See* Case C-56/65, *Société Technique Minière*. This has been also noted by the literature (*see*, e.g., King (2011), pp. 277-284 who identifies a 'more analytical approach' in the case law with a strong focus on the legal and economic context).
725. Andreangeli (2011), p. 242 saw that trend in the case law even before *Groupement des cartes bancaires, Generics* and *Budapest Bank*. He argued the CJ has moved away from the stark distinction between object and effects analysis and embraced a concept of restriction by object as a spectrum ranging from more to less serious competition infringements (*ibid.*, pp. 242-243).
726. *See* Case C-67/13 P, *Groupement des cartes bancaires*, para. 53.
727. *See* Case C-307/18, *Generics*, paras 67-68.
728. *See* Case C-228/18, *Budapest Bank*, para. 51.
729. *See* Case C-67/13 P, *Groupement des cartes bancaires*, para. 54; Case C-228/18, *Budapest Bank*, para. 53.
730. *See* Peeperkorn (2015), para. 35. *See* section 4.3.2.c.1 for the plausible efficiency theory.
731. *See* Case C-67/13 P, *Groupement des cartes bancaires*, paras 76-79.
732. *See also* Nazzini and Nikpay (2014), p. 165 on this point.
733. *See* Peeperkorn (2015), para. 31.
734. *See* Case C-32/11, *Allianz Hungária*, para. 48: 'In order to determine the likelihood of such a result, that court should in particular take into consideration the structure of that market, the existence of alternative distribution channels and their respective importance and the market power of the companies concerned.' For the conclusion of a de facto effects analysis, *see* the opinion of the AG Wahl in Case C-67/13 P, *Groupement des cartes bancaires*, para. 51; Killick

cartes bancaires cited *Allianz Hungária* only selectively.[735] The selective recalling demonstrates that the CJ is well aware of the conceptual blurring and offers exactly what was needed to stop further dilution: a concrete example when a context analysis blends over into an effects analysis.[736]

CJ's review of GC's substantive assessment in *Groupement des cartes bancaires*[737] demonstrates that the CJ was *inter alia* dissatisfied with the direction of the analysis (assessment of effects instead of the context)[738] and the limited breadth of the analysis (focused only on one side of the two-sided market).[739] The judgment suggests that the CJ is not concerned with the depth of the analysis required to identify the specific context and purpose of the conduct. The 'saving' of the analysis merely relates to the effects analysis, not to the context analysis.[740] In other words, the by object analysis does not necessarily put constraints on finding out the precise scope and purpose of the conduct.[741]

In line with the cautious approach (discussed in the next section 4.3.2.b.2), one could argue that an extensive context analysis may be already an indication that the restriction in question should be classified as a restriction by effect.[742] A restrictive interpretation of the scope of the object box aims to prevent false positives.[743] *Groupement des cartes bancaires* and *Budapest Bank* both concerned a rather complex assessment of a two-sided market. If an extensive context analysis comes close to a light effects analysis, then it is only logical to argue that the former is already an indication that a classification as restriction by object is not appropriate. This is what

---

and Jourdan (2014), p. 3; Fattori (2015), p. 24. Nagy has described para. 48 of the judgment as 'disastrous' (*see* Nagy (2013), p. 561). For Nazzini and Nikpay it seems that the Court looked for causality between the agreement and the likely negative effects on competition, rather than merely assessing the economic context (*see* Nazzini and Nikpay (2014), p. 161). However, a more favourable interpretation for the Court and the case law is that para. 48 is merely a poorly drafted attempt by the Court to enunciate the test for less obvious restrictions (*see* Nazzini and Nikpay (2014), p. 162). This case is one of those cases where the practice seems to be unproblematic from a formal standpoint, but upon closer scrutiny may conceal significant anti-competitive potential (*see* Ibáñez Colomo and Lamadrid de Pablo (2016), p. 7).

735. Noted by Murray (2015), p. 49: For instance, the CJ in *Groupement des cartes bancaires* did not cite the last part of para. 48 of the *Allianz Hungária* judgment which suggests that market power of the parties should not be part of the context analysis.
736. *See* Murray (2015), p. 49.
737. *See* particularly Case C-67/13 P, *Groupement des cartes bancaires*, paras 59-94.
738. Noted by Italianer (2014), p. 14. *See*, e.g., Case C-67/13 P, *Groupement des cartes bancaires*, para. 65: 'Although it is apparent from the judgment under appeal that the General Court took the view that the restrictive object of the measures at issue could be inferred from their wording alone, the fact remains that it did not at any point explain, in the context of its review of the lawfulness of the decision at issue, in what respect that wording could be considered to reveal the existence of a restriction of competition "by object" within the meaning of Article [101(1) TFEU].'
739. Noted by Killick and Jourdan (2014); Nazzini and Nikpay (2014); Collin (2017), p. 53.
740. This is also the understanding of Peeperkorn (2015), para. 29.
741. *See* Loozen (2010), p. 148. Camesasca, Schmidt and Clancy also read *T-Mobile* in a way that makes those parts of the judgment softer that suggest a more formalistic language (*see* Camesasca, Schmidt and Clancy (2010), p. 414).
742. *See* similarly Pradelles et al. (2014), p. 4.
743. *See* Nazzini and Nikpay (2014), p. 166.

AG Bobek meant when he argued in his opinion in *Budapest Bank* that the difference between the object and effects analysis is more of degree than of kind.[744]

A good understanding of the specific context is closely linked to the counterfactual analysis that is required even under the object analysis[745] (on the counterfactual *see* already section 4.3.1.b.2 above). In *Budapest Bank*, the CJ explained to the referring national court that the scenario without the MIF agreement in place needs to be explored in order to understand whether the level of interchange fees resulting from competition would have been lower or higher.[746] In other words, had the MIF agreement not been concluded, how would the actual competitive context look like particularly with regard to prices.[747] Following a formal and abstract assessment, the agreement in *Budapest Bank* looked like a cartel (undertakings coordinated their prices). However, the CJ carefully analysed the specific context and raised doubts as to whether the agreement in question constituted a restriction by object.[748]

One interesting view on the notion of 'obviousness' of anti-competitive restrictions is also explored by Killick and Jourdan. They argue that obviousness entails two perspectives. The anti-competitive restriction can be obvious for the enforcer as well as for the parties of an arrangement. While the parties should be able to assess *ex ante* whether their conduct constitutes a restriction by object, enforcers need the in-depth scrutiny of the context analysis in order to identify the anti-competitive nature of the conduct *ex post*. In short, they argue that if the classification as a restriction by object is not obvious for the parties, it should not be classified as a restriction by object.[749] Their argument emphasises that the context analysis merely helps enforcer to identify the obviousness of anti-competitive conduct more easily and reliable when it is not so obvious at first sight. Consequently, the context analysis has little to offer for the parties as they already know the economic and legal context in which they operate.

On a theoretical level, the contextual approach is able to justify the consequences of by object restrictions as discussed above (plausibility threshold for effects, de facto shift of burden of proof, presumption of appreciable effects, etc.). One of the main characteristics of by object restrictions is the lack of obvious and plausible efficiencies.[750] While a cartel lacks any sort of efficiencies, a horizontal cooperation agreement is concluded to materialise significant efficiencies. This consideration helps to explain

744. *See* opinion of AG Bobek in Case C-228/18, *Budapest Bank*, para. 50.
745. Baldwin (2020) also argues that the counterfactual analysis is closely linked to the purpose and context of an agreement and makes an interesting comparison to negotiation theory. The counterfactual is similar to the Best Alternative To a Negotiated Agreement (also known as BATNA).
746. *See* Case C-228/18, *Budapest Bank*, paras 81-83.
747. *See* Pazzi (2020), p. 233.
748. *See* Case C-228/18, *Budapest Bank*, particularly paras 80-85.
749. *See* Killick and Jourdan (2014), pp. 8-9.
750. *See* Peeperkorn (2015), para. 8. Loozen argues that this entails two categories of evidence: (1) evidence where the practice 'clearly' reveals that the effect on competition will be deleterious since it is the 'typical' cartel; and (2) evidence that requires a more in-depth examination to find out whether the practice reveals a deadweight loss (*see* Loozen (2010), p. 149). However, this classification essentially refers to the issue of whether a classification of a similar practice has been done before or not. In other words, whether the conduct is not listed in the non-exhausted list of by object restrictions listed by the Commission in its By Object Guidance.

why some restrictions are instinctively[751] ('you know when you see them')[752] considered as by object restrictions: not so much because of some abstract legal formula, but because (after the appraisal of the specific circumstances of the case) the conduct lacks any meaningful efficiency.[753]

4.3.2.b.2 Cautious Approach: The Importance of Sufficient Experience (or in Dubio Pro Effectu*)*

The language of the CJ in *Groupement des cartes bancaires* is probabilistic. Only those restrictions are regarded as restrictions by object that have 'generally' net negative effects.[754] There is no 'reasonable expectation' that the conduct in question has net positive effects.[755] In the words of AG Wahl and AG Bobek, only those restrictions fall within the object box that are 'easily identifiable'[756] (*Groupement des cartes bancaires*) or 'clearly defined'[757] (*Budapest Bank*). In *Budapest Bank*, AG Bobek was struck by the fact that the parties themselves could not explain without ambiguity the type of competitive harm that will result from the MIF agreement in question, as the parties' arguments jumped 'from one market to another and from one type of harm to another, without the necessary clarity and precision'.[758]

The probabilistic language can be justified by the policy rationales of by object restrictions. This suggests that the CJ endorses a *teleological* interpretation to distinguish both concepts. What matters for the classification of by object restrictions is whether the avoidance of a full-blown effects analysis is justified.[759] If the quality of the competitive predication, i.e., net negative effects on competition (or in more economic terms, the impact on allocative efficiency),[760] is already sufficiently good, then the costs of further investigation of the specific effects can be saved. Conversely, where the further gathering of evidence on the possible effects of a conduct would lead to a better overall decision-making an effects analysis is more appropriate.[761] This is also what Ibáñez Colomo refers to as the main difference between a restriction by object and a restriction by effect: the probability of anti-competitive effects. While the case law seems to follow a (lower) plausibility threshold for restrictions by object, the case law seems to require a (higher) likelihood threshold for restrictions by effect.[762]

751. For that expression, *see* Brankin (2016), p. 379.
752. *See* Murray (2015), p. 50.
753. On the problem of applying an abstract test to determine the anti-competitive objective, *see also* González (2012), p. 13.
754. *See* Peeperkorn (2015), paras 8, 17 and 22.
755. *See* Brankin (2016), pp. 380-381. *See also* Niels, Jenkins and Kavanagh (2016), para. 5.06 who argue that cartels usually produce no or very limited efficiencies.
756. *See* opinion of AG Wahl in Case C-67/13 P, *Groupement des cartes bancaires*, para. 56.
757. *See* opinion of AG Bobek in Case C-228/18, *Budapest Bank*, para. 56.
758. *Ibid.*
759. *See* Brankin (2016), pp. 380 and 383.
760. *See* Obudu (2006), p. 114.
761. *See* Dnes (2016), p. 251.
762. *See* Ibáñez Colomo (2020b), pp. 12-13, 45-51 and 54-55. Although he admits that the words 'capable' and 'likely' are sometimes used indistinctly in the case law which is a source of potential legal uncertainty (*ibid.*, p. 60).

Classifications as restrictions by object should also not come out of the blue. This would undermine legal certainty and predictability of the concept.[763] In *Budapest Bank*, the CJ makes clear that the classification as a restriction by object must rely on 'sufficiently reliable and robust experience'[764] or 'sufficiently general and consistent experience'[765] of the harmfulness of the conduct. The notion of 'experience' is mainly understood with reference to economics. As put by AG Bobek, 'sufficient consensus among economists' would seem of utmost importance to the classification as restriction by object.[766] Similarly, Ibáñez Colomo points out that mainstream economics can provide valuable insights.[767] Even before *Budapest Bank*, the literature has emphasised the importance of experience and economics. Peeperkorn argues that it is prudent to base the classification on sufficient experience or other empirical evidence.[768] Similarly, Alvin Sng points out that such experience normally correlates with the conclusion drawn by economic theory.[769] Obudu also emphasises the importance of sufficient experience for presuming allocative inefficiency.[770] It is only then that measurement and prediction can be avoided because 'such an analysis would only confirm what logic and experience tell us is virtually certain outcome'.[771]

Crucially, this teleological interpretation suggests a cautious approach for new types of restriction. When authorities have yet to gather experience on how to deal with such new types of restriction,[772] when it involves complex restrictions where the truncated by object analysis is not appropriate[773] (such as the one in *Groupement des cartes bancaires* or in *Budapest Bank*), where an abridged competitive analysis is felt necessary to consider whether there is a credible theory of harm,[774] or when it concerns

763. *See* Killick and Jourdan (2014), p. 8.
764. Case C-228/18, *Budapest Bank*, para. 76. Baldwin (2020) and Mandrescu (2020) are both sceptical though what this term actually means. Baldwin argues that if one takes the cynical view the CJ simply unpacks existing vague language and repacks it in a different although similarly vague language.
765. Case C-228/18, *Budapest Bank*, para. 79.
766. *See* opinion of AG Bobek in Case C-228/18, *Budapest Bank*, para. 72.
767. *See* Ibáñez Colomo (2020c), para. 9. *See also* Bardusco and Juvigny (2020, p. 165) who argue that the notion of restriction by object is 'the daughter of experience' and requires 'sufficiently common, constant, robust and reliable' experience.
768. *See* Peeperkorn (2015), paras 22-25. Not just the Court explicitly refers to the word 'experience' (*see* above) but also AG Wahl in his opinion (Case C-67/13 P, *Groupement des cartes bancaires*, para. 55). The word 'experience' has been also noted by others (*see*, e.g., Fattori (2015), p. 24 who concludes at p. 26: 'the judgement could have important implications for all conducts for which – given the novelty or the complexity of the case, and the consequently lack of "experience" by the Courts – the legal characterization results difficult').
769. *See* Alvin Sng (2016), p. 183. On the importance of experience of the classification as a restriction by object, *see also* Bailey (2012), p. 565, who refers to para. 21 of Art. 101(3) Guidelines for this idea.
770. Obudu (2006), p. 114, who describes such approach as 'induction based presumptions'.
771. *Ibid.*, p. 115.
772. *See* Peeperkorn (2015), para. 24 using the example of retail most favoured customer clauses. Bailey refers to this as the 'analogy method' where restrictions by object are established by reference to decided cases. However, he points out that this approach may be misused to refrain from classifying new conduct as a restriction by object that has never been classified as a restriction by object before (*see* Bailey (2012), pp. 574-575).
773. *See* Pradelles et al. (2014), p. 3. In the context of *Budapest Bank*, *see* Pazzi (2020), p. 235.
774. *See* Bailey (2012), p. 586.

a 'borderline' case where a more nuanced economic appraisal of facts is necessary,[775] a classification as a restriction by object is not appropriate. Dnes for instance argues that as a rule of thumb the more information gathering on the effects of the conduct is felt necessary, the less appropriate a classification as a restriction by object.[776] AG Bobek noted in his opinion in *Budapest Bank* that the more variables that are included in the equation in terms of structural complexity in terms of number of actors active in several markets over a long time, the less likely it is generally to classify the conduct in question as a restriction by object.[777] Thus, the depth of the context analysis and its complexity suggested that a restriction by object is simply not appropriate.

Murray argues that the tone of the judgment in *Groupement des cartes bancaires* can be understood as indicating a 'visceral test'. If the restriction in question does not obviously restrict competition, one should apply the benefit of the doubt and conduct an effects analysis.[778] This consideration would align well with the explicit statement of the CJ that the concept of by object restrictions should be understood restrictively (and thus explicitly rejecting the view of the GC that it should be understood not strictly).[779] This statement of the restrictive interpretation was repeated by the CJ in *Budapest Bank*.[780]

The cautious approach does not mean though that new types of restrictions can never be classified as a restriction by object. Even novel types of restriction can be classified restrictions by object if the specific context has been carefully considered and leads to the conclusion that the anti-competitive harm is obvious. Thus, the cautious approach does not mutually exclude the contextual approach, but rather complements it. This is the lesson learned from *Generics* involving pay-for-delay agreements. On the one hand, pay-for-delay agreements are settlement agreements which are an effective means to put an end to IP disputes and are thus a potential source of efficiency.[781] On the other hand, pay-for-delay agreements bear also similarities with cartel-like conduct.[782] The CJ carefully considered the specific context of this case and indicated that the specific pay-for-delay agreement can be classified as restriction by object. It observed *inter alia* the 'very appreciable' decline of prices once the IP right has expired[783] and that the original manufacturer and the generic producers cannot be

775. *See* Murray (2015), p. 47; Dnes (2016), p. 247.
776. *See* Dnes (2016), p. 249.
777. *See* opinion of AG Bobek in Case C-228/18, *Budapest Bank*, para. 62.
778. *See* Murray (2015), p. 50. Alvin Sng concludes that such test would offer 'sufficient flexibility without being too limiting in practice' (Alvin Sng (2016), p. 184). This is also the understanding of the Commission: 'Cartes Bancaires says "only use by object if you are pretty sure that it's there." [...] We also need to think twice before finding that agreements that may have a legitimate aim, such as preventing free riding, are a restriction by object. [...] This will be more demanding for new, unfamiliar types of agreement or conduct, but will be normally rather straightforward for established types of restrictions by object such as cartels.' (Italianer (2014), pp. 13-14)
779. *See* Case C-67/13 P, *Groupement des cartes bancaires*, para. 58.
780. *See* Case C-228/18, *Budapest Bank*, para. 54.
781. *See* Ibáñez Colomo (2020a), p. 2.
782. *Ibid.*, p. 13.
783. *See* Case C-307/18, *Generics*, para. 69.

unaware that the medicine sector is particularly sensitive to market entry delays.[784] In other words, the specific context of the pay-for-delay agreement was the extension of the period of monopoly prices caused by the pay-for-delay agreement. As pointed out by Ibáñez Colomo, this aspect was central to make sense of the purpose behind the pay-for-delay agreement.[785]

The interplay between the cautious and contextual approach in the case law has been wonderfully described by AG Bobek in *Budapest Bank* with his fish metaphor: 'Simplified to a metaphorical extreme, if it looks like a fish and it smells like a fish, one can assume that it is fish. Unless, at the first sight, there is something rather odd about this particular fish, such as that it has no fins, it floats in the air, or it smells like a lily, no detailed dissection of that fish is necessary in order to qualify it as such. If, however, there is something out of the ordinary about the fish in question, it may still be classified as a fish, but only after a detailed examination of the creature in question.'[786]

4.3.2.c *The Theoretical Perspective*

4.3.2.c.1 The Plausible Efficiency Theory (Positive Theory)

Ibáñez Colomo and Lamadrid de Pablo[787] argue that an abstract definition of a restriction by object achieves little in practice (top-down approach). Instead, one should take the opposite perspective and derive from the case law building blocks that, once they are put together, produce a clearer picture of the common theme among those conducts that have been classified as restrictions by object (bottom-up approach). One should read between the lines of these judgments because EU Courts are not always explicit on what they actually do. Abstract definitions and formulas fail to capture the principles EU Courts follow upon closer scrutiny.[788]

They propose to classify those practices as restrictions by object which do not entail 'plausible' pro-competitive effects in their economic and legal context.[789] This

784. *Ibid.*, para. 70.
785. *See* Ibáñez Colomo (2020a), p. 8.
786. Opinion of AG Bobek in Case C-228/18, *Budapest Bank*, para. 51.
787. *See* Ibáñez Colomo and Lamadrid de Pablo (2016), particularly section 3.
788. *Ibid.*, p. 28. *See* their conclusion on p. 43: 'Discussions about the notion of restriction of competition have often been dominated by a sense of frustration. This piece shows that this widespread view may not be justified. A bottom-up analysis of the case law suggests that authorities, courts and practitioners are equipped with sufficient elements to assess the restrictive object and/or effects of a practice. Confusion about the notion is not, it would seem, so much the consequence of the lack of guidance from the EU courts, but of the fact that the principles have not always been presented systematically in the case law.'
789. *Ibid.*, p. 21. This concept is emphasised in more recent papers of Ibáñez Colomo (*see*, e.g., Ibáñez Colomo (2019a), p. 429). A similar idea has been described by Mahtani (2012), pp. 32-35 and Dnes (2016), pp. 248-249. Bailey already indicated a similar idea by referring to the notion of 'plausible' on this context several times. But he failed to further develop this (*see* Bailey (2012), pp. 563 and 565). Similarly, Jones already mentioned the idea of plausible efficiencies when comparing EU's approach with US's approach, but also failed to further develop the theory (*see* Jones (2010), p. 663). Fai Kwok clarifies that a claimed efficiency is 'plausible' if there is sufficient evidence to suggest that it is 'pretextual' and follows a legitimate purpose related to consumer welfare (*see* Fai Kwok (2018), p. 484). However, the notion of

test does not ask whether the practice entails 'likely' or even 'certain' pro-competitive effects.[790] Any practice that fails to be a 'credible' source of efficiency gain is unlikely to have net positive effect on competition.[791] Thus, it is then safe to presume that the practice serves an anti-competitive purpose.[792] In other words, if a rational and profit-maximising firm engages in a practice that lacks any credible pro-competitive benefits, then the prospect of restricting competition is at least a plausible one.[793] This presumption shifts the evidentiary[794] burden of proof to the firms which then have to show that the practice has net pro-competitive effects.[795]

In a more recent paper, which also takes into account *Generics* and *Budapest Bank*, Ibáñez Colomo still interprets the case law in a way that restrictions by object follow a (lower) plausibility threshold, while restrictions by effect require a (higher) likelihood threshold (*see* already section 4.3.1.c.1).[796] For the classification as a restriction by object, it is sufficient that anti-competitive harm is a 'plausible' outcome.[797] However, he admits that the words 'capable' and 'likely' are sometimes used by the CJ indistinctly which is a source of potential legal uncertainty that can be exploited by parties.[798]

Their theory may suggest that the classification as a restriction by object takes place somewhere in the middle of the abstractness scale. Neither should the classification merely deduct the conduct from an abstract formula (i.e., be highly abstract) nor should the classification consider all the situation-specific circumstances and their likely impact on competition (i.e., be highly concrete). Instead, the classification should apply what one could refer to as an 'objectified context standard'. What matters for the classification is the *objectified* benchmark, i.e., what can be usually expected from a similar arrangement in the same context according to mainly economic theory and experience.[799] The context analysis aims to identify this objectified standard. If there are exceptional pro-competitive circumstances that can be only identified if one goes beyond the context analysis, this should not exclude the possibility of the classification as a restriction by object since these special circumstances can be assessed under Art. 101(3) TFEU.

However, one crucial issue Ibáñez Colomo and Lamadrid de Pablo fail to explore is what types of *sources* parties can use to support their claims of pro-competitive

'legitimate purpose' may be misleading because it usually refers to non-competition law related aims (*see*, e.g., Case C-309/99, *Wouters*).

790. *See* Ibáñez Colomo and Lamadrid de Pablo (2016), p. 24.
791. *Ibid.*, p. 21.
792. *Ibid.*, p. 24.
793. *See* Ibáñez Colomo (2019a), p. 430. Obudu argues that Art. 101(1) TFEU is concerned with the allocative inefficiency and therefore obligates companies not to engage in economic activity that causes allocative inefficiency (*see* Obudu (2006), p. 102).
794. *See* Fai Kwok (2018), p. 482 for this clarification.
795. *See* Ibáñez Colomo and Lamadrid de Pablo (2016), p. 24.
796. *See* Ibáñez Colomo (2020b), pp. 12-13, 45-51 and 54-55.
797. *Ibid.*, p. 47.
798. *Ibid.*, p. 60.
799. *See* similarly Bailey (2012), p. 560 who concludes: 'The case law reveals a process of classification in which the EU courts engage in a judgement as to how much the conduct deviates from the competitive norm.'

plausible justifications. After all, parties and enforcers may have different conceptions about the type of efficiencies that are suitable to escape the by object classification. Bailey for instance identifies three broad categories of sources: (1) economic research, (2) enforcement experience and (3) policy judgments. The first source refers to all theoretical and empirical economic researches that show that this type of conduct is likely to distort competition.[800] The second source refers to all practical experiences gained from enforcement activities.[801] The third category refers to policy considerations that go beyond economic consideration (such as the market integration objective in the EU).[802]

Two comments should be made on these three sources. First, they clearly suggest that the objectified standard is multifaceted. In some situations, only one source may be relevant for the classification as a restriction by object, in other situations more than that. Although economic theory is very influential, competition law is like a sponge open to influences beyond economic theory.[803] Second, these sources suggest some flexibility and dynamic adaptability. If economic theory on a specific issue changes over time, competition law should not be afraid to adopt accordingly and expand or narrow the scope of by object restrictions.[804] For instance, this might be the case with the exchange of future intentions. While such type of exchange was initially systematically underestimated by game theoretical models and dismissed as merely cheap talk, economic theory and empirical research have now recognised the harmfulness for the competitive process.[805]

Critics of the plausible efficiency theory point out that as a positive theory it does not provide an explanation for all those situations where even a pro-competitive justification does not save the arrangement from by object condemnation.[806] However, such criticism that essentially demands to perfectly explain all by object cases seems to be asking too much from a bottom-up theory. After all, a robust positive theory that helps to explain most, even if not all, cases is still a valuable contribution to the ambiguous case law on by object restrictions.

800. This source has also been mentioned by Jones who refers to 'accepted economic principles' (*see* Jones (2010), p. 655). On this source, *see also* Ibáñez Colomo (2020c), para. 9; Alvin Sng (2016), p. 183.
801. Nagy points out that judicial experience was one of the characteristics of the traditional category-building which cautiously expanded the scope of the object box (*see* Nagy (2013), p. 563).
802. *See* Bailey (2012), pp. 564-565. Killick and Jourdan also note that the Court for the first time explicitly referred to the notion of 'experience' in *Groupement des cartes bancaires* (in para. 51). While this notion has appeared before in opinions of AGs and in the Commission's Guidelines, the recognition by the Court gives it more weight (*see* Killick and Jourdan (2014), p. 6). The importance of experience has been repeated by the CJ in *Budapest Bank* (*see* Case C-228/18, *Budapest Bank*, paras 76 and 79).
803. *See* Ezrachi's thought-provoking articles about his 'sponge theory' (*see* Ezrachi (2015)). He argues that competition law is like other legal disciplines a social construct that has the ability to stretch and narrow its application in order to protect a wide range of social goals (sponge property). At the same time, the sponge-like property of competition law uses economic theory as a constant benchmark (economic membrane).
804. *See* similarly Jones (2010), p. 661.
805. *See* already section 3.3.5.
806. *See* Fai Kwok (2018), p. 469.

4.3.2.c.2 The Intended Ends Theory (Normative Theory)

Another interesting theory has been recently proposed by Fai Kwok.[807] It is a normative theory (as opposed to the positive theory discussed in section 4.3.2.c.1) because it aims to explain *why* certain arrangements are regarded as restrictions by object.

Essential for his theory is the distinction between intended *means* (the proximate purpose) and intended *ends* (the ultimate purpose). He takes such means-end distinction from the English common law. He argues that only those arrangements should fall within the object box that lack a pro-competitive *ultimate* purpose. Conversely, those arrangements that entail anti-competitive proximate purposes but pursue pro-competitive ultimate purposes (what he describes as arrangements with conflicting purposes) should be assessed under the effects analysis. For instance, although the fee arrangement in *Groupement des cartes bancaires* had the anti-competitive purpose of limiting output, such purpose was only proximate not ultimate. The ultimate purpose was to discourage freeriding and thus pro-competitive.[808] Similarly, one could argue that the ultimate purpose of the MIF agreement in *Budapest Bank* ensured the proper and smooth functioning of the system.[809]

His theory is valuable but not revolutionary. The idea of arrangements with conflicting purposes has strong resemblances with the concept of ancillary restraints where essentially anti-competitive 'side-effects' are inevitable to achieve the greater pro-competitive rationale.[810] In this sense, he uses something that already exists in a different context and re-conceptualises it for the by object classification.

His theory also complements the plausible efficiency theory. It clarifies that the plausibility of the efficiencies should refer to the *ultimate* purpose of the arrangement, not the proximate purpose. This may also help to explain why the EU Courts seem to be unwilling to constrain the context analysis. In order to find out the ultimate purpose of the arrangement in situations where it is not obvious, an extensive context analysis is needed for its revelation. The context analysis is then a necessary but merely preliminary step for the classification exercise.[811] It only helps to figure out if the specific purpose of a conduct is proximate or ultimate, but not whether the goal as such is anti-competitive.

807. *Ibid.* In a similar vein goes the theory proposed by Mahtani that one way to establish the classification as a restriction by object is the reference to its 'objective' (*see* Mahtani (2012), pp. 29-32).
808. *See* Fai Kwok (2018), pp. 472-474.
809. *See* opinion of AG Bobek, Case C-228/18, *Budapest Bank*, para. 76. *Budapest Bank* was not taken into account by Fai Kwok, as the judgment was published later. Nagy (2020) argues similarly that the MIF agreement could be considered as ancillary to the effective operation of the payment card system and as serving the purpose of creating balance in the system. Mandrescu (2020) also argues that the economic rationale of the MIF agreement was to maintain an optimal ratio between platform participants. Similarly, Colangelo and Maggiolino argue that the MIF is a form of autoregulation to maintain an equilibrium in a system that is threatened by conflicts of interests between issuers and acquirers (*see* Colangelo and Maggiolino (2018), p. 122).
810. *See* the Ancillary Notice by the Commission on this issue.
811. For this though, *see also* Fai Kwok (2018), p. 478.

4.3.2.c.3 The Risk Offence Theory (Normative Theory)

Another normative theory has been explored by AG Trstenjak in *Beef Industry Development Society*[812] and AG Kokott in *T-Mobile.*[813] They argue that restrictions by object are similar to risk offences (*Gefährdungsdelikt*) that exist in most national criminal or administrative laws. AG Kokott provides the example of a driver who is under the influence of alcohol or drugs. Such driver is liable to penalty *irrespectively* of whether he has endangered another road user *in concreto* or whether he has caused an accident *in concreto*. It is the engagement in the conduct that is under punishment, not the actual harm caused by the conduct. It is general experience with similar incidents that justifies the prohibition based on precautionary considerations.[814]

Baño Fos further develops this theory for competition law purposes by distinguishing three types of risk offences: (1) *abstract* risk offences, (2) *concrete* risk offences and (3) *abstract-concrete* risk offences. The example of drunk driving given by the AG Kokott falls within the first category. The prosecutor only has to show that the driver was drunk, but not that he has actually harmed someone. An example for the second category is reckless driving. The prosecutor has to show that the driver has posed a concrete danger to the values protected by the legal prohibition. It is not sufficient to merely demonstrate the engagement in that practice. He also has to show that the conduct is likely to result in concrete danger to other drivers. An example for the third category is hazardous material spill. This type of risk offence includes abstract elements (the spilling of a person) and concrete element (the spilling of a substance that is dangerous to the environment).[815]

He argues that these concepts developed in continental criminal law should be used for competition law. Restrictions by object align well with abstract risk offences because it is established case law that there is no need to demonstrate any effects (they are presumed); much like there is no need to demonstrate actual harm under abstract risk offences. Restrictions by effect where the enforcer is able to demonstrate potential effects align well with concrete-abstract risk offences. Although there is no need to show actual effects (abstract element), by taking into account the particular circumstances of the case, there must be a real concrete danger that harm will occur (concrete element). Restrictions by effect where the enforcer is able to demonstrate actual effects lie somewhere between harm offences (if actual harm has already occurred to consumers) and concrete risk offences (due to the uncertainties of predicting a hypothetical future under the counterfactual analysis). Thus, he argues that competition law prohibits a continuum of conduct that endangers the competitive process where the exact boundaries are necessarily blurred.[816]

The risk offence theory is a valuable contribution in order to justify the conceptual distinction between restrictions by object and effect. It offers an interesting

812. *See* opinion of AG Trstenjak in Case C-209/07, *Beef Industry Development Society*, para. 46.
813. *See* opinion of AG Kokott in Case C-8/08, *T-Mobile*, para. 47.
814. *See* Bailey (2012), pp. 563-564. This theory has also been noted by practitioners (*see*, e.g., Killick and Jourdan (2014), pp. 2 and 10).
815. *See* Baño Fos (2015), pp. 183-186.
816. *Ibid.*, pp. 188-190.

comparative analysis with criminal law. However, the classification of conducts in competition law is less prescribed by detailed legal rules than in criminal law. This gives competition law more flexibility to adapt to different factual situations. One explanation for this more 'open-textured' nature of competition law rules is the influence of economic theory on competition law. While criminal law is mostly shaped by the protection of values that are not necessarily linked to economic values (such as the protection of physical integrity or personal freedom), competition law is mainly driven by economic values (such as consumer welfare). This also becomes clear in light of the emphasis of sufficient 'experience' in recent cases[817] for the classification as a restriction by object, which is mainly understood as reference to mainstream economics.[818] Furthermore, it is not surprising that due to the vast amount of risk offences in criminal law its literature is more advanced than in competition law. Thus, one should be careful to not overenthusiastically implement concepts that have been developed in a specific legal context (criminal law) into another context (competition law).

817. *See* particularly Case C-228/18, *Budapest Bank*, paras 76 and 79. But *see also* Case C-67/13 P, *Groupement des cartes bancaires*, para. 51 and Case C-307/18, *Generics*, para. 64.
818. *See* Ibáñez Colomo (2020c), para. 9; Alvin Sng (2016), p. 183.

CHAPTER 5

The Importance of Information Exchanges for the Implementation of Economic Collusion Theories in Art. 101 TFEU

5.1 PARALLEL CONDUCT AND CIRCUMSTANTIAL EVIDENCE

This section discusses how the EU Courts have dealt with issue of parallel conduct. It aims to lay the foundation for understanding the importance of information exchange for collusion theories in Art. 101 TFEU. Parallel conduct is perceived particularly in concentrated market as a major competition policy problem (the 'oligopoly problem'). The desire to tackle mere parallel conduct, without any further documentary evidence of concertation, has mainly emerged from the rich economic literature on collusion. However, there are fundamental differences between the economic and legal approach on how to deal with parallel conduct (*see* section 5.1.1). The case law shows that EU Courts were and still are extremely reluctant to condemn parallel conduct based on economic collusion theories under Art. 101 TFEU (*see* section 5.1.2). This leaves information exchange as the most important and most relevant manifestation of collusion theories in Art. 101 TFEU (*see* section 5.1.3). This section offers a broader explanation for how and why information exchange has become so important for Art. 101 TFEU.

5.1.1 The Legal Challenges of Tackling Mere Parallel Conduct

5.1.1.a The Legal Challenge of Solely Relying on Circumstantial Evidence

The concept of a concerted practice gives the Commission more evidentiary leeway to establish an infringement than the concept of an agreement does because the former also covers less formalised types of collusion. It is not necessary for the establishment of a concerted practice to show that the anti-competitive intention of one party has been *formally* expressed, like the case law requires for the establishment of an agreement.[819] Instead, the practical focus is also on the proof of the subjective element of 'concertation'.[820]

A concertation can be derived either from direct or indirect contacts between undertakings (documentary evidence) or from mere parallel conduct on the market (circumstantial evidence). However, in the latter scenario the challenge from a legal perspective is to correctly distinguish between unlawful collusion ('practical cooperation') and lawful market adoption ('intelligent adoption on the market' or conscious parallelism).[821] The crucial issue is not how to determine the specific form of collusion but *how to prove* the existence of collusion.[822] As the CJ has put it in *Anic*: 'The only essential thing is the distinction between independent conduct, which is allowed, and collusion, which is not, regardless of any distinction between types of collusion.'[823]

There are two types of risks that can arise when competition authorities solely rely on circumstantial evidence: The risk of 'false positives' and 'false negatives'.[824] On the one hand, if a concerted practice is only derived from parallel conduct, the risk is that undertakings may get fined simply because they operate in an oligopolistic market without concerting (false positive).[825] Art. 101 TFEU condemns concertation, not rational adoption that is caused by the structure of the market (i.e., parallel conduct in

819. *See* section 4.2.1.a.1.
820. *See* section 4.2.2.a.1.
821. As Joshua and Jordan put it: 'the same parallel pricing pattern could be invoked with apparent conviction as proof of either cut-throat competition or of the darkest conspiracy. Viewed from the outside, the absence of competition could be the manifestation of anything from a common sense recognition by the individual operators that there is no point in competing vigorously, to a full-blown price fixing cartel meeting in the traditional smoke-filled room'. (Joshua and Jordan (2004), p. 661)
822. *See* Albors-Llorens (2006), p. 850.
823. Case C-49/92 P, *Anic*, para. 108.
824. *See* Whish and Bailey (2018), p. 199 in the context of Art. 102 TFEU: 'A false positive occurs where a competition authority incorrectly concludes that pro-competitive behaviour is abusive. [...] A false negative occurs where a competition authority incorrectly concludes that the anti-competitive behaviour is not illegal and therefore permits it.'
825. *See also* Cucu (2013), p. 224: 'If the price uniformity represents the result of the logical action within an oligopoly and there is no secret agreement, then sanctioning the undertakings is neither rational nor fair. The issue is no longer *behavioural* in the sense that the parties engage in a behaviour different from that which would exist under normal conditions within the same type of market, but the issue is *structural*, meaning that this type of market normally generates this type of response' (emphasis added). He also argues that the problem of parallel behaviour may not just happen in oligopolistic markets but also in cases of price leadership of a powerful firm and on transparent markets; on the oligopoly: 'An oligopolistic competition market is characterized by the existence of a small number of competitors that hold close market shares, without being able to speak about a considerable force of one of them in relation to the others. In such market conditions (for example, the mobile operating market) there is a close link between the competitors' behaviour, the action of one of them is followed by a corresponding response from the others and each change of strategy is achieved by taking into account the probable response of the competitors. Consequently, the specific features of the oligopolistic market can determine the price alignment (therefore without a concerted practice between competitors).' (*ibid.*, p. 225)

concentrated markets).[826] On the other hand, when the standard of proof for circumstantial evidence is set too high, undertakings that concert, which is so sophisticated that no documentary evidence of concertation can be found, may never get fined (false positive). This would result in under-enforcement of cartel activities. Thus, there is an inherent tension between both types of risks for optimal competition policy. As shown below, the EU Courts have preferred to take the latter risk and essentially require documentary evidence to prove concertation.[827]

5.1.1.b The Differences Between the Legal and Economic Analysis

There are two major differences between the economic and legal perspective on parallel conduct under Art. 101 TFEU. First, the terminology is different. The economic literature distinguishes tacit and explicit collusion. For Posner, the main difference between both forms is the type of evidence used.[828] While explicit collusion can be proven with documentary evidence, tacit collusion is proven with economic circumstantial evidence.[829] Conversely, a concerted practice can be also proven by circumstantial evidence.[830] This means that the (economic) concept of tacit collusion is narrower than the (legal) concept of a concerted practice. This difference is rather formalistic as it comes down to a difference of terminology (tacit collusion vs concertation) as both the economic and the legal literatures refer to the same type of evidence used to prove the collusion (circumstantial evidence).

Second, the main concern of economic theory is different. In economics, collusion refers to a situation where the prices are higher than some competitive benchmark.[831] Economics is concerned with the *outcome* (higher prices than some competitive benchmark)[832] and not with the form or means through which that outcome has

826. *See* OECD (2007a), p. 9. Since the problem then is structural, this paper indicated that market investigations like in the UK might be the solution: 'In industries in which supracompetitive outcomes can be observed but where it is difficult to establish that oligopolists engaged in culpable conduct, alternative approaches which do not require the establishment of unlawful agreement or culpability may be more appropriate. One example is the instrument of market investigations under the UK Enterprise Act, which allows the Competition Commission to examine the structure of the market and conduct of the players within the market, and to impose solutions *without the need to identify culpable conduct* or the possible imposition of sanctions.' (OECD (2007a), p. 10, emphasis added)
827. *See* section 5.1.2.
828. *See* Posner (1969), p. 1578. The OECD defines explicit collusion as any form of direct contact between firms (*see* OECD (2012a), para. 21).
829. *See* Petit (2013), p. 27. *See also* Alese (1999), p. 382: 'once a competitor(s) in non-collusive oligopoly decides to seek another in order to influence decisions on price and output, the method used in acting on the message is almost irrelevant, as the rules of non-collusive oligopoly would have been broken. In fact it is almost sufficient to rely on economic theory in stating that apart from "contact" between competitors, there is no other requirement needed to convert a non-collusive parallel conduct into concerted practice'.
830. *See* already section 4.2.3.c.
831. *See* Motta (2004), p. 138.
832. It is not even clear which benchmark should be used, in particular, whether marginal costs or a competitive Nash equilibrium should be used as a benchmark. Even if one agrees on one type of benchmark, it may be questioned whether courts or competition authorities are able to

been attained.[833] Thus, economic literature does also not distinguish between parallel conduct that is the result of an unlawful concertation or the result of a lawful conscious parallelism based on 'intelligent adoption' on the market.[834] From an economic perspective, in both scenarios the welfare loss is the same and thus there is no need to distinguish.[835] Instead, economics merges the two conditions of Art. 101 TFEU (concerted practice and by object/effect restriction on competition) and merely assesses whether the conduct is economically efficient or not, that is whether prices are higher than some competitive benchmark suggests.[836]

While the means through which supra-competitive outcomes have been achieved does not matter from an economic perspective, it does from a legal perspective. An infringement of Art. 101 TFEU comes with several consequences such as significant fines and (more recently also) damages claims. Thus, from a legal perspective it is crucial to assess whether the parallel conduct is a manifestation of an underlying concertation between undertakings. Competition law cannot force rivals to compete.[837] It is the competitive process that incentivises them to do so. If one is merely concerned about the anti-competitive effects of parallel conduct on the market (economic perspective), Art. 101 TFEU may not be the right tool to tackle the problems arising from parallel conduct. This is because the source of the tacit collusion problem is primarily a structural one (particularly concentrated markets).[838]

5.1.2 The Leading Cases: A Lost Fight to Tackle Parallel Conduct under Art. 101 TFEU?

5.1.2.a The Early Days: 1950s and 1960s

In the US, the issue of tacit collusion and the possible interference with section 1 of the Sherman Act (the US equivalent to Art. 101 TFEU) has started much earlier than in the EU. Parallelism was perceived as an important problem for the US industry. Particularly in the 1960s, there was a lively doctrinal debate between the Harvard school (Turner), which focused on the market structure, and the Chicago school (Posner), which focused on the firms' behaviour.[839]

In the EU, the inclusion of the notion of 'concerted practice' in the Treaties was the result of the influence of US antitrust law.[840] The meaning of that term was unclear at that time and interpretations varied substantially among scholars.[841] Interestingly though, while the debate in the US on tacit collusion in the 1960s already focused on

identify the 'correct' benchmark since reality is much more complex than a simple economic model (*see* Wagner-von Papp (2012), p. 25).

833. *See* Grillo (2002), p. 153; OECD (2012a), para. 10.
834. *See*, e.g., Heimler (2010), p. 402.
835. *See* Petit (2013), p. 13. *See* already section 3.3.1.b.
836. *See* Page (2007), p. 429 who uses the economic reasoning of Carlton et al. (1997) as an example.
837. *See* Heimler (2010), p. 402.
838. *See* already section 3.3.2.c.
839. *See*, e.g., Stroux (2004), pp. 38-42; Filippelli (2013), pp. 10-16.
840. *See* Albors-Llorens (2006), p. 843.
841. *See* Filippelli (2013), p. 78 that mentions some of the scholar's opinions.

competition policy for oligopolistic markets, the debate in Europe was still merely academic.[842] It took until the 1970s until the notion of a concerted practice and the issue of tacit collusion were examined by the CJ: the *Dyestuffs* judgment in 1972 and the *Suiker Unie* judgment in 1975.

5.1.2.b The Dyestuffs *Case*

In *Dyestuffs*,[843] several producers of dyestuffs increased their prices in different members simultaneously and by identical proportions on three separate occasions (1964, 1965 and 1967). The Commission concluded in its decision that these price increases were the result of a concerted practice.[844] The parties challenged the decision and invoked the so-called oligopoly defence.[845] They argued that the price increases were merely the result of an oligopolistic market structure, not the result of collusion.[846] In other words, they argued that they should not be condemned for what constitutes a natural market phenomenon (price leadership by one undertaking).[847]

The CJ dismissed the appeal. In doing so the CJ addressed the issue whether parallel conduct may be used as evidence to prove a concerted practice. It gave an important statement of principle: 'Although parallel behaviour may not by itself be identified with a concerted practice, it may however amount to strong evidence of such a practice if it leads to conditions of competition which do not correspond to the normal conditions of the market, having regard to the nature of the products, the size and number of the undertakings, and the volume of the said market.'[848] The Court further stated that the conclusion that parallel conduct is proof of a concerted practice is particularly true 'if the parallel conduct is such as to enable those concerned to attempt to stabilize prices at a level different from that to which competition would have led, and to consolidate established positions to the detriment of effective freedom of movement of the products in the [Internal] Market and of the freedom of consumers to choose their suppliers'.[849] In other words, parallel conduct may be indeed used as

842. *See* Filippelli (2013), p. 80. Joshua and Jordan (2004, p. 657) also note that European attitudes towards cartel activity generally focused on the outcome of the cartel conduct rather than its characteristic. Regulatory efforts were directed towards compliance based on recommendations and persuasion rather than public enforcement. The control of cartel activity was a matter of soft law back then.
843. Case C-48/69, *Dyestuffs*.
844. Commission decision, *Dyestuffs* (not available in English).
845. *See* Petit (2013), p. 27.
846. *See* Case C-48/69, *Dyestuffs*, pp. 638-639: 'It observes that in order for a concerted practice to exist it is not enough that undertakings operating on an oligopolistic market consciously adopt a parallel attitude. [...] The Commission's reasoning to the effect that every case of similar conduct on an oligopolistic market entails a strong presumption that there is a concerted practice represents a misunderstanding of how an oligopolistic market really works.' (p. 638)
847. *See* Petit (2013), p. 27.
848. Case C-48/69, *Dyestuffs*, para. 66. The CJ has referred to the statement in *Tournier* (Case C-395/87, *Tournier*, para. 24) and *Lucazeau* (Cases C-110/88, etc., *Lucazeau*, para. 18), both judgments are preliminary reference rulings requested from French courts.
849. Case C-48/69, *Dyestuffs*, para. 67 (emphasis added). Alese notes though that in most non-collusive oligopolies price stability can co-exist with active competition (*see* Alese (1999), pp. 380-381). Thus, the stability of the prices should not be an *indicium* for collusion.

evidence of a concerted practice,[850] but it would be only one evidentiary aspect.[851] However, the language used by the CJ is quite vague and one may wonder what is exactly meant by 'strong evidence' or 'normal' market conditions.[852]

On the substantive appraisal of the facts, the CJ found that the price increases could not be explained by independent competitive behaviour.[853] It concluded so after analysing the market conditions of the dyestuffs market. It found that the market for dyestuffs consisted of different national markets, each of them with different price levels and an oligopolistic market structure.[854] The Court's argument was that despite the national scope of dyestuffs markets, price announcements and their implementations were not just done on very similar dates but also to very similar extents.[855]

Both the CJ and the Commission relied on three important indicia: the fact that the price increases were identical for all Member States,[856] that they concerned the same dyestuffs[857] and that they were executed at the same or almost the same time.[858]

However, what is striking is the fact that the Commission relied on *more* indicia for establishing a concerted practice than the Court did.[859] The Court did not mention two other indicia on which the Commission relied on; namely the fact that certain letters, which were sent by the suppliers to their respective subsidiaries, were almost identical[860] and the fact that the producers met several times, particularly in London and Basel.[861] This is surprising because the Court itself stated that 'the question whether there was a concerted action in this case can only be correctly determined if the evidence upon which the contested decision is based is considered, not in isolation, but as a whole, account being taken of the specific features of the market in the products in question'.[862] Why would the Court state that all the evidence available has to be considered, but then simply ignore strong indicia of a concertation?[863]

850. *See* Stroux (2004), p. 72.
851. *See* Albors-Llorens (2006), p. 853.
852. Jones mentions the concern raised by some scholars after the judgment that also purely rational parallel conduct may be caught. However, she emphasises that the Commission provided significant evidence of direct and indirect contacts between the parties. Thus, this was a 'hybrid case' in which the Commission relied both on documentary evidence and circumstantial evidence (*see* Jones and Sufrin (2016), pp. 694-695). Van Gerven and Varona therefore argues that 'the judgement was not so much worrying because of its definition of a concerted practice but more because it so easily assumed, without a detailed study of the market characteristics and without evidence of concertation, that parties had cooperated'. (Van Gerven and Varona (1994), p. 590).
853. Case C-48/69, *Dyestuffs*, paras 69-124.
854. *Ibid.*, paras 76-81.
855. *Ibid.*, para. 109.
856. Commission decision, *Dyestuffs*, p. 12; Case C-48/69, *Dyestuffs*, paras 83 et seq.
857. Commission decision, *Dyestuffs*, p. 12; Case C-48/69, *Dyestuffs*, para. 90.
858. Commission decision, *Dyestuffs*, p. 12; Case C-48/69, *Dyestuffs*, para. 88.
859. Noted by Korah (1973), pp. 221 and 225. She argues therefore that 'there is some concern that the notion of a "concerted practice" may not require any element of collusion and that any method of raising prices when there are only a few suppliers in the market is risky'. (*ibid.*, p. 221)
860. Commission decision, *Dyestuffs*, p. 13.
861. *Ibid.*, p. 13.
862. Case C-48/69, *Dyestuffs*, para. 68.
863. Joshua, part of the Commission back then, and Jordan further highlight that it is 'significant in historical terms that the *Dyestuffs* cartel had been one of the most notorious organized

In general, the judgment was not well received by the literature and criticised for being rather formalistic. Korah for instance argued that it is not clear whether collusion can be interfered from these indicia. For instance, once a market with few producers has been broken up geographically, it may remain fragmented for decades without any collusion needed.[864] Joliet, who was Judge-Rapporteur in *Woodpulp II* (discussed below), argues that the overall economic analysis of the Court was weak.[865] Albors-Llorens adds that the Court merely looked 'superficially' at the characteristics of the dyestuffs market to conclude a concerted practice.[866] Petit emphasises that the Court failed to consider the situation that would have prevailed under 'normal' market conditions (the counterfactual).[867] Concerns were raised that the judgment may be understood too broadly and render mere parallel conduct illegal without a robust economic analysis.[868]

In light of the criticism and subsequent case law, the judgment is only an unreliable precedent.[869] Surely, one can argue that the fact that the Court has to give one single judgment for a complex multifaceted cartel may have prevented the Court from producing a better reasoning.[870] However, the judgment does certainly not live up to the depth of the economic reasoning and the level of judicial scrutiny of subsequent case law.[871]

5.1.2.c The **Suiker Unie** *Case*

In *Suiker Unie,*[872] the Commission found that the main producers of sugar in Germany, Belgium and the Netherlands had engaged in concerted practice that was aimed to control the supply of sugar into the Netherlands. On the facts of the case, the CJ reached the conclusion that the conducts of the undertakings in question were not the

international cartels dating from the late 1920s. Its durability was underlined by the fact that the main players had all been members of the original pre-war arrangements. The record of both the Commission and European Court is strangely silent as to the sinister historical antecedents of the cartel. A reading of the decision and judgments almost leaves the impression that although orchestrated, the price-fixing that occurred between 1964 and 1967 was a spontaneous and "one-off" event. The Commission had been alerted of the cartel by complaints from customer trade bodies. Although it had conducted some inspections, and there was some evidence of meetings being held in Basel and elsewhere, the Commission had obviously not managed to obtain any damning documentary evidence. Its decision to prosecute ultimately relied on the similarities of timing and amount in the announced price increases as well as an "expert's report" concluding that the only explanation was prior concertation'. (Joshua and Jordan (2004), pp. 658-659)

864. *See* Korah (1973), p. 224.
865. *See* Joliet (1974), p. 285.
866. *See* Albors-Llorens (2006), p. 854.
867. *See* Petit (2013), p. 28.
868. *See* Stroux (2004), pp. 74-75.
869. *See* Monti (2007), p. 332.
870. *See* Korah (1973), p. 225 who suggests this theory as one explanation.
871. *See* Soames (1996), p. 25.
872. Cases C-40/73, etc., *Suiker Unie.*

result of independent decision-making, but that of a concerted practice whereby they knowingly substituted practical cooperation for the risk of competition.[873]

On a more conceptual level, the judgment is important because the Court has established the independence doctrine where undertakings which 'adopt themselves intelligently to the existing and anticipated conduct of their competitor'[874] do not fall within the scope of Art. 101 TFEU.[875] The independence doctrine marks a decisive choice of how to treat parallel conduct under Art. 101 TFEU. The Court used the doctrine to significantly narrow the scope for parallel conduct to be used as evidence for a concerted practice.[876] It stated *inter alia* that '[t]he fact that a vendor aligns his price on the highest price charged by a competitor is not necessarily evidence of a concerted practice but may be explained by an attempt to obtain the maximum profit'.[877] This statement makes clear that parallel conduct itself is not sufficient to prove a concerted practice.[878]

At the time of the judgment, concerns have been raised that the judgment in *Dyestuffs* may be an indication that the Court's understanding of a concerted practice focuses on consequences rather than culpability of the conduct.[879] Even back then, scholars have already argued that an infringement of Art. 101 TFEU should be based on *culpable* anti-competitive conduct (rule-oriented approach), and not on a strict liability for ostensibly non-competitive markets (result-oriented approach).[880] Although there are some indications in *Dyestuffs* that suggest that the Court favoured a rule-oriented approach (namely the insertion of the word 'knowingly'),[881] other statements suggest the opposite (namely the statement that parallel conduct may amount to 'strong evidence' of a concerted practice).[882] In any way, it has become clear in the subsequent case law that Art. 101 TFEU only condemns culpable anti-competitive conduct and thus follows a rule-oriented approach.

5.1.2.d The **Zinc Producer Group** *Decision vs the* **Cartonboard** *Decision*

It is also interesting to compare the *Zinc Producer Group* decision[883] with the *Cartonboard* decision[884] because it shows the importance of documentary evidence for

873. *Ibid.*, para. 191.
874. *Ibid.*, para. 174. This formula has been repeated in Case C-172/80, *Züchner*, para. 14.
875. *See* already section 4.2.1.b.2.
876. This is the interpretation of Petit (2013), p. 28.
877. Cases C-40/73, etc., *Suiker Unie*, para. 285.
878. *See* Albors-Llorens (2006), pp. 854-855.
879. *See* Ray Pfeiffer (1974), p. 117.
880. *Ibid.*, pp. 115-116 and 118-120: 'On a practical level, the difference between concerted practice and conscious parallelism can be recognized only by the application of workable standards of proof which differentiate honest, sustained efforts by competing enterprises to abide by the rules of the economic system, on the one hand, from the planned coordination of cooperating enterprises to override it on the other. Such standards have yet to be articulated.' (*ibid.*, para. 115)
881. *See* Case C-48/69, *Dyestuffs*, para. 64; noted by Soames (1996), p. 26.
882. *See* Case C-48/69, *Dyestuffs*, para. 66; noted by Albors-Llorens (2006), p. 853.
883. Commission decision, *Zinc Producer Group*.
884. Commission decision, *Cartonboard*.

condemning parallel conduct. In the former case, parallel conduct on prices was regarded as lawful; in the latter it was seen as part of a wider cartel. The difference of substantive outcomes comes down to the lack of documentary evidence in the former case.

In the *Zinc Producer Group* decision, the Commission found insufficient evidence to qualify the parallel conduct in question as a concerted practice.[885] It accepted the argument that parallel conduct could be explained by 'barometric price leadership':[886] 'This does not remove from undertakings the ability to "determine independently the policy which (they intend) to adopt on the common market". Under such circumstances, parallel pricing behaviour in an oligopoly producing homogeneous goods will not be in itself sufficient evidence of a concerted practice.'[887]

Conversely, in the *Cartonboard* decision, the Commission found documentary evidence that the major producers formed a cartel and agreed in advance that one of them would lead the increase and then the others would follow (collusive price leadership). The reason was simple. Price leadership makes collusion less obvious and without hard evidence almost difficult to prove.[888] The Commission explained that had 'they been challenged, the producers could as a result of this elaborate scheme of deception have attributed the series of uniform, regular and industry-wide price increases in the cartonboard sector to the phenomenon of "oligopoly behaviour". They could argue that it made sense for all the producers to decide of their own volition to copy an increase initiated by one or other of the market leaders as soon as it became publicly known; unlawful collusion as such would not necessarily be indicated. Customers might well suspect and even accuse them of operating a cartel; and given the relatively large number of producers, economic theory would be stretched to its limits and beyond, but unless direct proof of collusion were forthcoming – and they went to some lengths to ensure it was not – the producers must have had hopes of defeating any investigation into their pricing conduct by the competition authorities by invoking the defence of oligopolistic interdependence'.[889]

The conclusion that one has to derive from both decisions is that without documentary evidence, parallel pricing can be easily explained with barometric price leadership (*Zinc Producer Group* decision). Conversely, if the Commission finds hard evidence of a wider cartel scheme, parallel conduct is simple proof of its execution. The fact that cartel members try to cover up the cartel by using a system of barometric price leadership merely demonstrates the sophistication of the cartel (*Cartonboard* decision).[890]

885. *See* Commission decision, *Zinc Producer Group*, para. 76.
886. *See* section 3.3.2.c for that notion.
887. *Ibid.*, para. 75.
888. *See* Stroux (2004), p. 81.
889. Commission decision, *Cartonboard*, para. 73.
890. *See also* Stroux (2004), pp. 81-82 on contrasting these two decisions.

5.1.2.e The Compagnie Royale Asturienne Des Mines *Case*

In *Compagnie Royale Asturienne des mines,*[891] two producers of rolled zinc products delivered large quantities of these products to a Belgian undertaking. These large quantities were meant for the sale in Egypt at prices close to those for the Belgian market. However, the Belgian undertaking relabelled the products and sold them in Germany for prices lower than normally charged in Germany. When two employees of one of the producers found out that its products were relabelled and sold in Germany, both producers ceased to deliver to the Belgian undertaking. The Commission concluded that both producers engaged in a concerted practice aimed at protecting the higher price level in the German market.

However, the CJ disagreed and stated that 'it is sufficient for the applicants to prove circumstances which cast the facts established by the Commission in a different light and which thus allow another explanation of the facts to be substituted for the one adopted by the contested decision'.[892] In this case, the termination of deliveries could be also explained by the non-payment of invoices by the Belgian undertakings.[893]

The case shows that the Commission cannot rely on insufficient evidence to prove a concerted practice and ignore alternative commercial explanations.[894] The Commission has to provide a coherent set of facts in order to demonstrate that parallel conduct is the result of a concerted practice.[895]

5.1.2.f The Woodpulp II *Case*

In *Woodpulp II,*[896] the CJ extensively examined many of the issues that remained unclear after *Dyestuffs.*[897] It is one of the clearest judgments on the relationship between concerted practice and parallel conduct.[898] It is considered as the end of a controversial debate that lasted over 15 years on whether mere parallel conduct falls within the scope of Art. 101 TFEU.[899]

One of the issues of this case was the issue of whether parallel conduct could be used to prove the existence of a concerted practice.[900] Several producers of woodpulp

891. Cases C-29/83, etc., *Compagnie Royale Asturienne des mine.*
892. *Ibid.*, para. 16.
893. *Ibid.*, paras 18-21.
894. *See* Jones (1993), p. 275.
895. *See* Albors-Llorens (2006), p. 855. Faull and Nikpay (2014, para. 3.142) also mention that case but merely conclude that the Commission has to consider other plausible explanations for the facts on which it establishes parallel conduct.
896. Cases C-114/85, etc., *Woodpulp II.* In the earlier preliminary judgment in 1988 the CJ upheld the extraterritorial application of EU competition law to undertakings outside the EU because the conduct has been implemented in the EU (Cases C-89/85, etc., *Woodpulp I*).
897. *See* Albors-Llorens (2006), p. 856.
898. *See* Joshua and Jordan (2004), p. 666; Jones and Sufrin (2016), p. 695.
899. *See* Stroux (2004), p. 77.
900. There were two other issues: (1) the concertation within the Pulp, Paper and Paperboard Export Association of the United States, which was essentially an export cartel; and (2) the concertation within Fides, a research and information centre of the European pulp and paper industry. These two accusations by the Commission were based on documentary evidence.

followed a system of quarterly price announcements in which prices were announced simultaneously or almost simultaneously (announced prices). As a result, prices of woodpulp in the internal market developed in parallel and thus were almost the same with only minor deviations (transaction price).[901]

The Commission concluded that a concerted practice between the woodpulp producers had taken place. However, the Commission provided no documentary evidence of contacts or information exchanges between the producers.[902] Instead, it derived its conclusion solely from circumstantial evidence: (i) the system of quarterly price announcements, (ii) the simultaneity or near-simultaneity of the price announcements and (iii) the price parallelism of announced prices.[903]

The Commission had two hypotheses. The first was that the system of quarterly price announcements *in itself* constitutes an infringement of Art. 101 TFEU.[904] The second was that the system of quarterly price announcements constitutes *evidence* of a

Since they are not relevant for the matter of parallel conduct, this book will not discuss them further (they are discussed, e.g., by Kühn and Vives (1995), pp. 88-91; Motta (2004), pp. 213-214; Møllgaard and Overgaard (2006), p. 120).

901. *See* Petiti (2013, p. 29) for the difference between transaction and announced prices.

902. The Commission decision relied also on documentary evidence (telefaxes). However, the Court excluded these documents from its consideration because the Commission was unable to specify its relevance (*see* Cases C-114/85, etc., *Woodpulp II*, paras 68-69). Joshua and Jordan, the former was part of the Commission at that time of the decision, paint a different picture. They criticise that the Court too easily rejected hard evidence and then concluded rather mechanically that the little circumstantial evidence that was left was not sufficient: 'Besides some fairly unambiguous evidence of face to face meetings implicating, in particular, many of the Scandinavian producers, it was clear that the whole industry shared an awareness of the need for one region to support another's prices so as to achieve stability and a uniform price level for pulp. Even if there were some shadowy areas in the evidence on price fixing, one might have been forgiven for thinking, based on the *Dyestuffs* case, that this was a clear case of price signaling. Advance price announcements and the universal adoption of a basing point system must have facilitated the achievement of the remarkable pattern of uniform price increases. In its judgment, however, the Court annulled virtually all of the Commission's findings. The tone of the Court's judgment was intensely hostile to the Commission, and the Commission was not helped by the ambiguity of its decision as to whether the nub of its case was a classic cartel or simply price signaling, even if the low fines imposed were indicative of the latter. [...] The Court then dismissed the separate "collusion" hypothesis out of hand by rejecting all the hard evidence of meetings and contacts. The court said that for each and every document relied upon, the Commission had to specify between which producers and for what period the collusion established by that document had occurred. The implication is that collusion evidence has no relevance outside its own intrinsic facts. Because the Commission had insisted that circumstantial evidence was not susceptible to such mechanical analysis, the Court held that this collusion evidence was completely inadmissible, stating tersely and in a baffling nonsequitur that "in the light of that reply those documents must be excluded from consideration."' (Joshua and Jordan (2004), pp. 667-668)

903. *See* Cases C-114/85, etc., *Woodpulp II*, para. 70.

904. *Ibid.*, paras 59 et seq. The Commission has brought forward two arguments for its first hypothesis. First, the system gave other producers the opportunity to adopt their prices before actually applying them to their customers at the beginning of each quarter, and second, it created an artificial price transparency in the woodpulp market (*ibid.*, paras 60-61). This case is also discussed in section 6.4 from the perspective of signalling via public announcements.

concertation at an earlier stage. The former hypothesis considered price announcements as an element of a concentration, while the latter considered them as circumstantial evidence.[905]

The CJ disagreed with the Commission's substantive appraisal of facts and concluded that producers had determined their market conduct independently. In addressing the first hypothesis the Court referred to the independence doctrine.[906] It concluded that communication from public price announcements did not in itself constitute market behaviour that lessened uncertainty as to the future attitude of other competitors.[907] The Court indirectly criticised the Commission's non-robust theory of harm on price announcements that failed to take into account that public announcements to *customers* are generally vital for market economies.[908]

The Court also dismissed the second hypothesis of the Commission. It stated as a matter of principle that 'parallel conduct cannot be regarded as furnishing proof of concertation unless concertation constitutes the only plausible explanation for such conduct'.[909] This is a new formula that cannot be found before in the case law. It can be analysed from three different perspectives. On an *evidentiary* level, this formula sets a high standard of proof for the use of circumstantial evidence.[910] However, the judgment does not state how compelling the evidence put forward must be to rule out any plausible explanation.[911] On an *argumentative* level, the formula is somehow circular in its logic. In order to prove a concerted practice from parallel conduct, one has to show that parallel conduct can be the only logical result of collusion.[912] On a more *jurisprudential* level, this formula carefully balances the need for some control over parallel conduct in oligopolistic markets, which entails detrimental effect on overall welfare, with the freedom of enterprise to act commercially rational.[913]

The Court ensured that its judgment was based on sound economic reasoning following the conclusions drawn by a panel of economists, who had examined the parallelism of prices (first report)[914] and the characteristics of the woodpulp market (second report).[915] The depth of the economic analysis compared to *Dyestuffs* is

905. *See* Osti (1994), p. 179.
906. *See* Cases C-114/85, etc., *Woodpulp II*, para. 63.
907. *Ibid.*, para. 64. Jones (1993, p. 275) argues therefore that price signalling should not be considered per se an infringement of Art. 101 TFEU, unless the public exchange of information establishes reciprocal communication between the undertakings.
908. *See* opinion of AG Darmon in Cases C-114/85, etc., *Woodpulp II*, paras 180-181. *See also* Osti (1994), p. 179 on this issue. *See* already section 3.1.1 on benefits of vertical market transparency.
909. Cases C-114/85, etc., *Woodpulp II*, para. 71.
910. *See* Albors-Llorens (2006), p. 857.
911. *See* Stroux (2004), p. 78.
912. *See* OECD (2012a), para. 49.
913. *See* Ray Pfeiffer (1974, p. 121) who mentions this balance in a slightly different context, namely what is the protective function of Art. 101 TFEU.
914. *See* Cases C-114/85, etc., *Woodpulp II*, para. 31 (first report). This has been noted by e.g., Albors-Llorens (2006, p. 857); Petit (2013, p. 29). *See* paras 73-127 of the judgment for the extensive analysis of the Court regarding parallel pricing. Alese argues that it is doubtful whether the Court would have gone to such lengths in the economic analysis if the Commission would have been able to provide documentary evidence (*see* Alese, pp. 382-383).
915. *See* Cases C-114/85, etc., *Woodpulp II*, para. 32 (second report).

astonishing.[916] It reflects the increasing tendency to include in-depth economic analyses.[917] It thoroughly analysed the market for woodpulp and concluded that concertation was not the only plausible explanation for the parallel conduct: 'the *system of price announcements* may be regarded as constituting a rational response to the fact that the pulp market constituted a long-term market and to the need felt by both buyers and sellers to limit commercial risks [...] the *similarity in the dates of price announcements* may be regarded as a direct result of the high degree of market transparency, which does not have to be described as artificial [...] the *parallelism of prices* and the price trends may be satisfactorily explained by the oligopolistic tendencies of the market and by the specific circumstances prevailing in certain periods'.[918]

Both economic reports were extremely damaging to the case of the Commission and much of the Court's conclusions were based on them.[919] The economic analysis of the two reports and economic reasoning of the Court are not free of criticism though. For instance, the Court speaks of oligopolies without properly defining the relevant market.[920] Also, it is questionable why large concentrated buyers would want to share their prices with competitors if, in doing so, they would deprive themselves of their competitive disadvantage (i.e., the secret price cuts they were granted).[921] Furthermore, the patterns of price levels (high levels in 1976, 1977 and 1981, and abrupt falls in 1977 and 1982) might also suggest collusive outcomes with subsequent punishment phases.[922] Also, the lockstep price increases were viewed by the experts as natural in light of the market transparency. However, one could have argued that the

916. Soames (1996, p. 29) and Petit (2013, p. 29) both note that the fact that Professor Joliet, who heavily criticised the Court's economic analysis in *Dyestuffs*, was now Judge-Rapporteur in *Woodpulp II* played an important part in the outcome of the case.
917. *See* Jones (1993), p. 277.
918. Cases C-114/85, etc., *Woodpulp II*, para. 126 (emphasis added).
919. *See* Stroux (2004), p. 78; Jones and Sufrin (2016), p. 696.
920. *See* Petit (2013), p. 30.
921. *See* Kaplow (2011), p. 775. Thus, one may question the explanation of the economic report regarding large buyers and why they were not able to get better prices: 'the experts explain why, in their view, very large orders for pulp did not lead to sharp price cuts. Such orders do not enable significant cost savings to be made for various reasons: first, wood pulp is normally a standard product delivered from anonymous stock; secondly, producers are in the habit of installing storage capacity at the great receiving ports; finally, because they use a wide range of pulps, the paper manufacturers prefer, when placing orders for large quantities, to have the pulp delivered in several consignments. Ultimately, the economies of scale associated with very large orders are confined to overheads and administrative costs.' (Cases C-114/85, etc., *Woodpulp II*, para. 123)

    On the other hand, one can question whether prices that were *actually* charged were the same as the announced ones. As Motta (2004, p. 219) points out: 'it is far from clear that in this industry the collusive outcome can be easily reached. Firms can coordinate on list prices, but the effective transaction prices are determined by the bargaining between a buyer (some of them were buying large quantities, although the published documents do not offer precise information) and a seller. Apparently, secret price cuts were widespread in the industry, and announced and effective prices did not generally coincide (although the actual divergence is somehow disputed in the proceedings), which results in the market shares of producers varying during the period at issue'.
922. *See* Motta (2004), p. 217.

system was artificial and a deliberate and avoidable action on part of all undertakings.[923] Finally, the report also failed to distinguish between private and public market transparency. While the scope for collusion may be the same in both scenarios, only in the latter scenario a more lenient treatment is justified because it materialised significant efficiencies for customers.[924]

This landmark case now set the standard for assessing parallel conduct. Two main conclusions can be drawn from it. First, the *evidentiary* conclusion relates to the standard of proof that the Court demands when the Commission solely relies on circumstantial evidence.[925] The Court went far beyond merely requiring an overall robust and sound economic analysis. The Court required that concertation is the 'only plausible explanation' for the parallel conduct. As mentioned, this is quite a high standard of proof. It will be often very easy in practice to find an alternative plausible explanation for parallel conduct.[926] One may even wonder whether one can practically ever find an infringement solely based on parallel conduct.[927]

The judgment provides guidance for oligopolists on how to escape Art. 101 TFEU. Essentially, do not produce any hard evidence of collusion. This is because if the Commission is left with merely parallel conduct, oligopolists can simply invoke the oligopoly defence. The interdependence of undertakings in oligopolistic markets is then regarded as a plausible explanation for parallel conduct.[928]

Second, the *policy* conclusion that can be drawn from the judgment is that it indirectly suggests that Art. 101 TFEU should not be used to tackle the problems caused by parallel conduct in oligopolistic markets.[929] If the Commission has only gathered

923. *See* Joshua and Jordan (2004), p. 669.
924. *See* Kühn and Vives (1995), pp. 92-93; Wijckmans and Tuytschaever (2015), para. 11.58. *See* already section 3.1.4 on the weight of vertical market transparency for competition policy.
925. The Commission interpreted the outcome of the case in one of its later published Guidelines as following: 'in the wood pulp market, the Court has found that unilateral quarterly price announcements made independently by producers to users constitute in themselves market behaviour which does not lessen each undertaking's uncertainty as to the future attitude of its competitors and hence, in the absence of any preliminary concerted practice between producers, do not constitute in themselves an infringement of Article [101](1) of the Treaty' (*see* 2008 Maritime Guidelines, para. 43; discussed in section 6.1.1.d).
926. *See* Del Mar (2011), p. 120. Jones (1993, p. 277) seems to equate 'plausible' with 'convincing' explanation. The author of this book would not go so far. For him, a convincing explanation would set a higher threshold than mere plausible explanations.
927. *See* Motta (2004), pp. 218-219: 'At this point, one can ask the broader question of whether one can ever find an infringement of anti-trust laws by simply looking at parallel conduct. The answer is that this is possible, but the standard of proof is (rightly) high, as one should prove that communication and/or coordination of some kind among the firms must be the only plausible explanation for parallelism. In *Dyestuffs* [...], firms were found sending similar price instructions to their agents and subsidiaries basically at the same hour and day. The probability that this could happen without firms having previously talked to each other was nil: concertation was in that case the only plausible explanation for parallel conduct.' *See also* Alese (1999), p. 383: 'in reality it now seems that it is almost impossible for concerted practice to be deduced from evidence focusing solely on parallel conduct. Unless there is documented evidence of collusion between identifiable parties, it now seems that the Commission would be reluctant to bring parties to book for concerted practice'.
928. *See* Stroux (2004), p. 80.
929. *See* Kühn and Vives (1995), pp. 89-90 and Jones (1993), p. 278: 'The Treaty of Rome provides no obvious solution for the control of oligopolies. Since Article [101] is aimed at collusive

circumstantial evidence of parallel conduct, it should try to also gather documentary evidence, or otherwise not pursue the case at all under Art. 101 TFEU.[930] Art. 101 TFEU is not the right tool to tackle the structural problem of oligopolistic markets. This is certainly a gentle but powerful policy message to the Commission.[931]

5.1.2.g The BPB *Case*

In *BPB,*[932] four producers of plasterboards operated a complex cartel that started with a meeting in London when they decided to end the fierce competition that existed up to this point. Following this meeting, an information exchange system was set up where the undertakings repeatedly exchanged information. One of the arguments of the undertakings on appeal of the Commission decision was that the Commission had not shown that the (parallel) prices after the meeting in London were not taken independently.

The GC dismissed the argument. It stated that 'even if the intervals between the various price rise announcements may have enabled the undertakings to ascertain those price rises by information from the market and even if those rises were not always exactly of the same level, the near-simultaneity of the price rise announcements and the parallelism of the prices announced amount to strong evidence of concerted action prior to those announcements, since those rises were made in a context characterised by the fact that, as the Commission found in the contested decision, the [undertakings] agreed at the London meeting at the beginning of 1992 to put an end to the price war on the four European markets'.[933] The latter part of the statement is the decisive difference to *Woodpulp II.* While the Commission was not able to provide any documentary evidence of collusion in *Woodpulp II,* the Commission was able to show in *BPB* that the undertakings have participated in a meeting with anti-competitive objective.

---

behaviour it would seem a peculiar means of trying to regulate rational market behaviour. The CJ decision in *Woodpulp [II]* has now ruled this Article out as such a tool of control. Since the problem is essentially a structural one then, of the two Articles, Article [102] might at first sight appear to be a more appropriate tool. [...] Sanctions and prohibitions are inappropriate means of controlling malfunctioning markets. Better, would be an investigative system which does not condemn, but which provides a means of correcting such malfunctionings.' Also, Soames (1996, p. 25) argues similarly: 'because of the limitations placed on the application of the principle of concerted practice under Article [101] to oligopolistic parallel behaviour, the Commission is left with little opportunity to control such behaviour except in circumstances in which it can prove that it was a result of collusion, or in extreme cases that the existence of collusive behaviour (that is, concertation) was the only plausible explanation for the parallel conduct in question'.

930. Stroux (2004, pp. 80 and 85) seems to come to the same conclusion. She concludes that 'the possibility of controlling oligopolistic behaviour with an anti-competitive outcome, with specific evidence of collusion, under Article [101] seems to be limited. [...] This means that under European Law, as it stands today, tacit collusion cannot be effectively controlled by means of Article [101 TFEU]'. (*ibid.*, p. 85)

931. *See* Albors-Llorens (2006), p. 856.

932. Case T-53/03, *BPB.*

933. *Ibid.*, para. 144.

The case is a good example for the argument that once the Commission is able to provide documentary evidence of concertation (such as the attendance of meetings between competitors with anti-competitive objectives), subsequent parallel conduct is merely a conformation of the substantive conclusion that concertation has already taken place.[934]

5.1.2.h The CISAC *Case*

The *CISAC*[935] case concerned the Commission decision[936] that found that 24 EEA-based collecting societies have engaged in a concerted practice. Collecting societies manage copyrights on behalf of authors. The case concerned only the management and licensing of authors' public performance rights of musical works. The 24 collecting societies were all members of the International Confederation of Societies of Authors and Composers (CISAC). CISAC provided a model contract which served as a template for the reciprocal representation agreements between the CISAC members for the licensing of public performance rights of musical works. The decision did not challenge the existence of the reciprocal representation agreements as such, but two of their clauses: (i) a clause that prevented authors from changing their collective society (the membership clause) and (ii) a clause that granted each collecting society an absolute territorial protection (the exclusivity clause). Furthermore, the Commission also argued that there was a concerted practice among the collecting societies because there is no other explanation for the strict and systematic domestic territorial delineation.

On appeal, the GC disagreed with the Commission. First, the GC clarified the different evidential burden of proof required for documentary evidence as well as for circumstantial evidence. When the Commission relied its case merely on *circumstantial* evidence 'it is sufficient for the applicants to prove circumstances which cast the facts established by the Commission in a different light and thus allow another explanation of the facts to be substituted for the one adopted by the Commission'[937] (lower effort for parties). However, when the Commission provides *documentary* evidence 'the burden is on the applicants not merely to submit another explanation for the facts found by the Commission but to challenge the existence of those facts established on the basis of the documents produced by the Commission'[938] (higher effort for parties). Essentially, the GC is saying that the evidential burden of proof for

934. Bellamy & Child (2018, para. 2.082) is one of the few scholars mentioning this case at all. The importance of this case for the issue of parallel conduct is rather limited as *Woodpulp II* concerns the more extreme case (i.e., solely circumstantial evidence).
935. Case T-442/08, *CISAC*. *See also* the case comments by Whelan (2013), the perspective of a competition lawyer, and Quintais (2013), the perspective of an IP lawyer.
936. Commission decision, *CISAC*. A good comment on the decision can be found in Andries and Julien-Malvy (2008).
937. Case T-442/08, *CISAC*, para. 99.
938. *Ibid.*, para. 99.

the Commission is higher when the case relies on circumstantial evidence. In other words, it is much easier for the applicants to refute evidentiary claims of the Commission in case of circumstantial evidence. Although this is rather intuitive, the clarification is welcomed.

The GC then held that the Commission had not provided documentary evidence.[939] It continued to assess whether the explanations put forward by the applicant for the parallel conduct provided a plausible alternative to a concerted practice.[940] The GC concluded that there was indeed a plausible alternative explanation, namely 'the need to ensure the effectiveness of the fight against the unauthorised use of musical works'.[941] Competition between two collecting societies in one country may undermine the incentives to ensure monitoring and enforcing the rights to exploit musical works.[942] In other words, the monopolisation of the national markets (the one-territory/one-society model)[943] was a commercially plausible scenario and offered an alternative explanation to concertation.[944]

The judgment not only sets a very high *standard* of proof, but it also sets a high threshold for the evidential *burden* of proof for the Commission. The GC stated that 'the Commission cannot criticise the applicant for failing to provide further specifics regarding its other explanation, inasmuch as it is the Commission which must prove an

939. *Ibid.*, paras 102-131.
940. *Ibid.*, paras 132 et seq.
941. *Ibid.*, para. 181.
942. *See* the thorough analysis of the Court: 'Furthermore, it must be pointed out that the Commission did not answer the question of who would manage the general monitoring of the market in order to require users to request licences – not merely the monitoring of licences which have already been granted – if the collecting societies were not involved in the execution of that task. Without being contradicted by the Commission, the applicant claims that one of the tasks of collecting societies is to require unauthorised users of musical works to request the necessary licence. According to the applicant, the collecting society best able to carry out that task is, for each territory, the local collecting society, which has the most thorough knowledge of the market of the country in which it is established. Yet if that collecting society had no guarantee of recovering – by the revenue it receives from granting licences – the expenses related to the monitoring which it carries out, that activity would simply not be viable. That guarantee would be threatened if several collecting societies could grant, for the same territory, licences covering the same repertoires. It must be stated that the Commission has not provided any information capable of undermining the credibility of the applicant's argument in that respect. [...] In addition, the Commission has not been able to explain how there could be cooperation between collecting societies which would be competing to grant licences in respect of repertoires which overlap and cover the same territories. [...]. In particular, in order to be able to grant a licence covering the worldwide repertoire, a collecting society must cooperate with all the other collecting societies. Yet the contested decision fails to provide any element to explain how – between collecting societies which have become competitors, as called for by the Commission – the cooperation which the Commission considers to be necessary, inter alia, for certain monitoring activities and for the prosecution of infringements, would take place.' (Case T-442/08, *CISAC*, paras 150-151)
943. For this term, *see* Quintais (2013), p. 682.
944. The decision would have improved the chances of commercial user to obtain a licence that would have covered more than one country. Thus, it would have increased competition by incentive collecting societies to improve their efficiency and quality of service (*see* Andries and Julien-Malvy (2008), p. 55). However, the Court was not convinced that Art. 101 TFEU is the right means to execute such 'structural' solution.

infringement. Therefore, if the Commission, at the administrative stage, considers that the applicant had not sufficiently substantiated its explanation, it must continue the examination of the case or find that the concerned parties have not been capable of providing the necessary information'.[945] Castillo de la Torre and Gippini Fournier argue that this paragraph suggests that it is sufficient for the parties to be 'fairly passive' when coming up with alternative explanations.[946] In this case, the parties have not provided any specific documents that substantiated their alternative explanations. The GC was fine with that despite the fact the production of such documents would have been easier for the parties. Thus, the GC makes clear that it is the task of the Commission to search for, substantiate and scrutinise all kinds of possible alternative explanations. Alternative explanations from parties should only be seen as 'inspirations' for the Commission. But they do not shift the evidential burden of proof.[947]

The depth of judicial scrutiny by the GC is considerable. It sets an extremely high standard of proof for circumstantial evidence. One may wonder whether the 'plausible alternative narrative' merely offers a theoretical possibility of proving a concerted practice by solely relying on circumstantial evidence. It seems that the threshold for circumstantial evidence is simply impossible to exceed in practice.[948]

What was already indicated in *Woodpulp II* is now confirmed in *CISAC*. The resources of the Commission are likely to be wasted on cases that solely rely on circumstantial evidence. If the Commission is not able to produce sufficient documentary evidence, it is not worth to pursue such cases. Thus, one should not be surprised if *CISAC* may be the last example of a 'dying species', i.e., a case in which the Commission was brave enough to try to prove a concerted practice by solely relying on circumstantial evidence.

945. Case T-442/08, *CISAC*, para. 161.
946. *See* Castillo de la Torre and Gippini Fournier (2017), para. 2.085.
947. *Ibid.*, para. 2.086: 'In a nutshell, even if the judgement appears to be based on the premise that the undertaking has a certain burden to provide *prima facie* alternative explanations, in reality the General Court did not require the party to provide specific evidence to substantiate the alternative explanation. That evidence must be gathered by the Commission. This appears strange in a context where the information about plausible explanations is likely to be in the hands of the parties themselves which is precisely the reason why typically there has been a shift in the evidential burden of proof in such cases.'
948. Whelan (2013, p. 488) comes to the same conclusion: 'This fact underlines the significant difficulties facing the Commission when it attempts to establish the existence of a concerted practice without adequate "documentary evidence" [...]. In such circumstances, a concerted practice will only be deemed to exist if the Commission establishes the implausibility of parallelism being contributable to anything other than collusion. In future, this may prove to be a hurdle which is too high for the Commission (and indeed other EU competition law enforcers) to overcome.'

5.1.3 Concluding Remarks

5.1.3.a The Descriptive Perspective: Parallel Conduct Is Merely Weak Circumstantial Evidence

It is clear from the case law that parallel conduct as such is not prohibited by Art. 101 TFEU. The EU Courts are very cautious to derive a concerted practice from circumstantial evidence.[949] Although it is in theory possible to prove a concerted practice solely by circumstantial evidence, it has little practical application as shown by the strict case law.[950] The standard of proof is simply too high to be exceeded in practice. Particularly in concentrated markets, where parallel conduct caused by a high degree of interdependency is to be expected, the 'oligopoly defence' can be successfully invoked by firms.[951] Thus, Art. 101 TFEU has no teeth in controlling mere parallel conduct.

On the positive side though, the strict stance by the EU Courts prevents false positive errors (i.e., condemning parallel conduct that is not attributable to concertation between firms).[952] This strict stance provides legal certainty for undertakings. Even oligopolists do not have to fear that their pricing policies infringe Art. 101 TFEU simply because the market structure enables parallel conduct by the easier anticipation of competitors' strategies. What matters is whether they produce hard evidence of concertation (such as the exchange of information). Parallel conduct is then merely the manifestation of such concertation that further strengthens the conclusion of the existence of concertation.

5.1.3.b The Normative Perspective: Is the Strict Stance When Solely Relying on Circumstantial Evidence Justified?

Although the strict stance of the EU Courts on circumstantial evidence means that the risk of false negatives errors (i.e., the risk that undertakings get away with concertation) is higher than the risk of false positives errors (i.e., the risk that undertakings get fined for merely adopting intelligently on the market), it can be justified from a legal perspective with the idea of *effort probatoire*.[953] Compared to the *ex ante* merger control regime, the *ex post* infringement regime of Art. 101 TFEU relates to: (i) evidence of actions and (ii) past facts. The former difference means that the error costs for wrongly concluding an infringement may be higher than for wrongly blocking a merger. An infringement of the cartel prohibition comes with severe consequences for undertakings (fines, damages claims, etc.) that outweigh possible consequences for blocking a merger. This justifies a higher standard of proof for infringements under Art. 101 TFEU.

949. Ghezzi and Maggioline (2014, p. 652) argue that one of the central issues of the concept of concerted practice has always been the difficult relationship between concertation and parallel conduct.
950. This is also the conclusion by Stroux (2004), pp. 84-85.
951. *See* Monti (2007), p. 334; Petit (2013), pp. 27-30.
952. *See* Stroux (2004), p. 85.
953. *See* already section 4.2.3.b.3.

Put differently, the presumption of innocence 'trumps' the (non-existing) right to merge. The standard of proof should be higher for past facts since they can be theoretical proven with a higher level of certainty. It is easier to reconstruct the past than to predict the future. Consequently, a higher standard of proof for Art. 101 TFEU is justified.

The idea of *effort probatoire* suggests though that economic theory on the collusion has little to offer for *enforcers* when relying on circumstantial evidence under Art. 101 TFEU. The liability that comes with an infringement under Art. 101 TFEU might be a valid reason not to condemn undertakings because economic models suggest it. Economic models are just theoretical models whose outcome heavily relies on assumptions and the design of the model.[954] Instead, economic models are a powerful way that can be used by *parties* to weaken possible theories of harm put forward by the enforcer. The beauty of modelling is that one can always construct a model that provides a plausible alternative explanation for parallel conduct.[955] The clear lesson from the case law on parallel conduct is that economic factors are no substitute for hard evidence of concertation.[956] Even Motta, an economist himself, argues that neither parallel conduct, nor parallelism plus (i.e., parallel conduct coupled with some facilitative practice), nor the presence of periods of price wars should be used as an evidence of concertation. Econometric techniques, as sophisticated as they might be, should not be the decisive factor for condemning conduct without any hard evidence of concertation. Only such a strict approach on circumstantial evidence offers the legal certainty necessary for Art. 101 TFEU.[957]

5.1.3.c The Prescriptive Perspective: The Implications for Competition Policy

There are three implications for competition policy that can be derived from the strict stance of the EU Courts on circumstantial evidence. First, the Commission should shift its focus towards acquiring the right enforcement tools to be able to actually *discover* cartel activities (dawn raids, whistle-blowers, leniency programme, etc.).[958] Leniency programmes for instance are (according to game theory) very effective means to make collusion less stable because of the incentives to confess.[959] Of course, this is an arm's race. As enforcers are equipped with better tools to discover concertation, firms get more and more sophisticated in their efforts to conceal concertation. As Joshua and Jordan conclude, the debate on tacit collusion has shifted 'from a purely "economic" approach – as manifested in the academic and scholastic debates surrounding the *Dyestuffs* saga – to one based on condemning bad behavior and bad attitude'.[960]

954. *See also* Kühn (2001), pp. 172-180.
955. *See* Motta (2004), p. 189 who provides the example of the US railroad cartel where one model suggested a collusion, while the other model (under different assumptions) did not.
956. *See* Joshua and Jordan (2004), p. 670.
957. *See* Motta (2004), pp. 185-190.
958. *See also* Motta (2004), pp. 192 et seq. on the issues of dawn raids and leniency programmes.
959. *See* for this analysis Monti (2007), pp. 332-334.
960. Joshua and Jordan (2004), p. 679.

Without any hard evidence of actual concertation, the Commission will likely waste its limited resources on cases that are almost impossible to win before the EU Courts.

Second, the Commission should employ more *ex ante* competition policy and try to prevent the occurrence of 'tacit collusion' in the first place. Obviously, one immediately thinks about merger control as an effective tool to prevent collusion.[961] Merger control routinely assesses potential coordinated effects.[962] Since economic theory provides that the creation of certain structural market characteristics makes collusion easier and more likely, it is only logical to tackle the problem structurally (European Merger Regulation (EUMR)) and not conduct-based (Art. 101 TFEU).[963] However, a sole focus on merger control oversees the preventive analytical approach that underlies many pure information exchange cases that were considered as a restriction by effect.[964] A thorough analysis of these cases suggests that Art. 101 TFEU has been indeed used as a tool for *ex ante* competition policy. What is required is a simple analytical framework to make this more obvious. This is why this book further develops the concept of a facilitative practice to prohibit certain types of pure information exchanges that causally make tacit collusion easier.[965]

Third, the Commission should focus its attention on conduct that produces *hard* evidence (such as information exchange). This also helps to explain the recent shift of academic attention away from parallel conduct towards information exchange.[966] Economic theories on tacit collusion have found its way into the assessment of information exchanges, at least regarding those information exchanges that have been regarded as restrictive by their effect.[967]

5.2 FACILITATIVE PRACTICES IN THE COMMISSION GUIDELINES

This section discussed the various facilitative practices discussed in the Guidelines, namely the Horizontal Cooperation Guidelines (*see* section 5.2.1), the Vertical Guidelines (*see* section 5.2.2) and the TT-Guidelines (*see* section 5.2.3). The purpose of this section is to argue that the exchange of information is the most relevant manifestation of the concept of facilitative practice (*see* section 5.2.4).

961. *See* the conclusion by Monti (2007), pp. 344-345 in this regard: 'The most significant is that even if economics teaches us to predict harm (tacit collusion) there may be no remedy available, because we cannot design a remedy where the authority can be confident that the gain (eliminating tacit collusion) is greater than the loss (harm to allocative, productive and dynamic efficiency as a result of the market's structure and the firm's actions). This explains why ex ante we can design merger law to prevent the creation of market structures prone to tacit collusion, but ex post competition authorities are more sceptical about the benefits of law enforcement: any rule to block efforts at tacit collusion seems likely to yield significant Type 1 errors and to be expensive to enforce.'
962. *See* Horizontal Merger Guidelines, paras 39-57.
963. *See* Stroux (2004), p. 85.
964. *See* section 6.3 for these cases.
965. *See* section 6.5.2.
966. *See* Capobianco (2004), p. 1258.
967. *See* section 6.3.

5.2.1 Horizontal Cooperation Guidelines

The Horizontal Cooperation Guidelines lay down an analytical framework for the six most common[968] forms of horizontal cooperation between competitors. Facilitative practices that result in 'collusive outcome' may be caught in the context of R&D agreements (*see* section 5.2.1.a), production agreements (*see* section 5.2.1.b), joint purchasing agreements (*see* section 5.2.1.c), joint commercialisation agreements (*see* section 5.2.1.d) and standardisation agreements (*see* section 5.2.1.e). Pure information exchanges are discussed in Chapter 6. It is noted that the notion of 'agreements' used in the Horizontal Cooperation Guidelines also covers the notion of a concerted practice.[969]

5.2.1.a R&D Agreements

R&D agreements cover a wide range of different cooperations on R&D.[970] The Horizontal Cooperation Guidelines distinguish three types of R&D cooperations when discussing the definition of the relevant market: (1) R&D cooperations that may result in products or technologies that directly compete with existing products without necessarily replacing them;[971] (2) R&D cooperations that may result in products or technologies that initially keep competing with existing products but will replace them over time;[972] (3) R&D cooperations that may aim to invent something completely new which is in no competitive relationship with existing products or technologies.[973]

The collusion concern raised by the Horizontal Cooperation Guidelines relates to the first two types of R&D cooperations and is directed towards existing product or technology markets. R&D cooperations may make collusion on those markets easier that relate to the R&D activities.[974] However, the risk of collusion may also arise outside the scope of those markets to which the R&D activities relate. This is why the R&D-BER for instance set out a positive condition that aims to prevent extensive production and distribution agreements beyond the scope of the jointly developed products (Art. 3(3) R&D-BER) or provides that any imposed restriction of the freedom to carry out R&D outside the scope of the cooperation would be considered a hard-core restriction (Art. 5(a) R&D-BER).

968. *See* Horizontal Cooperation Guidelines, para. 5.
969. *Ibid.*, para. 1.
970. *Ibid.*, para. 111. *See also* the broad definitions given in the R&D-BER of a 'R&D agreement' (Art. 1(1)(a) which covers jointly R&D agreements as well as paid-for R&D agreements) and 'R&D' (Art. 1(1)(c): 'means the acquisition of know how relating to products, technologies or processes and the carrying out of theoretical analysis, systematic study or experimentation, including experimental production, technical testing of products or processes, the establishment of the necessary facilities and the obtaining of intellectual property rights for the results').
971. *See* Horizontal Cooperation Guidelines, para. 113. *See also* Faull and Nikpay (2014), para. 7.146.
972. *See* Horizontal Cooperation Guidelines, para. 114. *See also* Faull and Nikpay (2014), para. 7.147.
973. *See* Horizontal Cooperation Guidelines, para. 119. *See also* Faull and Nikpay (2014), para. 7.148.
974. *See* Horizontal Cooperation Guidelines, para. 127.

5.2.1.b Production Agreements

Production agreements can provide that the production of a certain good is carried out by only one party (horizontal subcontracting agreement) or by two or more parties (joint production agreement usually by way of a joint venture).[975] The Horizontal Cooperation Guidelines set out a safe harbour for those agreements where the parties have a combined market share of not more than 20%.[976]

The Horizontal Cooperation Guidelines provide two collusion concerns regarding production agreements.[977] First, production agreements may increase the commonality of costs (i.e., the proportion of variable costs that undertakings have in common) to a level that enables the parties to collude. The production agreement may then tip the balance towards collusion, but only when production costs constitute a large proportion of their variable costs.[978] The parties have little incentive to compete on price, if their costs are the same to a large extent. However, the likelihood of a collusive outcome depends on the parties' market power and the characteristics of the relevant market.[979] Second, the production agreement may also involve the exchange of commercially sensitive information.[980]

5.2.1.c Joint Purchasing Agreements

Joint purchasing agreements involve several undertakings jointly purchasing products, normally with the aim of creating buying power against their suppliers.[981] Such agreements have possible effects on two different markets: the upstream market, where they buy the input, and the downstream market, where they sell their products.[982] The Horizontal Cooperation Guidelines set out a lower threshold for the safe harbour of joint purchasing agreement (15%) than for production agreements (20%).

The collusion concerns relate to the selling market where parties are direct competitors. The concerns are very similar to the concerns raised with regard to production agreements: The joint purchasing may increase the commonality of variable costs to a level that is high enough to enable collusion and may also entail the exchange of commercially sensitive information beyond what is necessary for the joint

975. *See* Horizontal Cooperation Guidelines, para. 150. The Guidelines only provide guidance for horizontal subcontracting agreements (*ibid.*, para. 154).
976. *Ibid.*, para. 169.
977. *Ibid.*, paras 175-182.
978. *Ibid.*, paras 176-180 and 187 (example 1).
979. *Ibid.*, paras 158 and 175. The wording of Guidelines suggests that the two economic conditions for the concern to materialise (market power and certain structural market features) relate to both the collusion concerns (commonality of costs *and* information exchange). However, the guidance given for the assessment of joint purchasing and joint commercialisation agreements suggests that these two conditions only relate to the first collusion concern (commonality of costs) but not to the second one (information exchange); *see* for that para. 213 for joint purchasing agreements, para. 243 for joint commercialisation agreements and para. 36 in more general. *See* already section 3.3.1.d for these structural market characteristics.
980. *Ibid.*, paras 181-182.
981. *Ibid.*, para. 194.
982. *See* Faull and Nikpay (2014), para. 7.364.

purchasing agreement (such as sales prices).[983] This similarity is not surprising since the 'economic effect' of both the production agreement and the joint purchasing agreement is the same. In both cases, the firms use the same input. Thus, the source of the input cannot be used as a differentiating factor in downstream market on which they sell their products.

The Horizontal Cooperation Guidelines provide two examples on the issue of commonality of costs and the importance of market power for the assessment of collusion.[984] In the first example, parties lack market power:[985] 150 small retailers conclude a joint purchasing agreement that obligates them to purchase a minimum volume through a joint venture which accounts for roughly 50 % of each retailer's total costs. Together, the retailers have a combined market share of 23 % on both the purchasing and selling markets. They have two main competitors, one with a market share of 25 % and the other with a market share of 35 %. The Horizontal Cooperation Guidelines conclude that in this example, even though the retailers achieve a high degree of commonality of costs, collusion is unlikely. This is because retailers lack market power due to the market presence of the other two main competitors.

Conversely, in the second example the parties enjoy market power:[986] Two supermarket chains conclude a joint purchasing agreement for products which accounts for roughly 80 % of their variable costs. On the purchasing market they have a market share between 25 % and 40 %. On the selling market their market share is 60 %. There are four other significant retailers, each of them with a market share of 10 %. The Horizontal Cooperation Guidelines conclude that in such case a collusive outcome is likely because of: (i) their market power on both the selling and purchasing market and (ii) their high degree of commonality of costs. Collusion is particularly likely if the cost structure was already similar before the joint purchasing agreement. However, the example assumes that market entry is unlikely which reinforces the incentives to collude.

On the issue of the exchange of commercially sensitive information, the Horizontal Cooperation Guidelines also provide an example:[987] Three competing manufacturers set up an independent joint purchasing venture that is responsible for the purchasing of a product which is an intermediate product used by all three parties. The joint venture does not compete with the parties on the selling market of the final product. The parties are obligated to disclose all information necessary for the purchase (such as quality specifications, quantities, delivery dates, maximum purchase prices and so on). The joint venture negotiates prices with suppliers. The Horizontal Cooperation Guidelines conclude that in this example the joint venture does not facilitate collusion between the parties. The conclusion suggests that the specific design of the cooperation matters. In this example, the parties disclose information

983. *See* Horizontal Cooperation Guidelines, paras 213-216.
984. *See also* Faull and Nikpay (2014), paras 7.385-7.388 who stress that the difference between these two examples is downstream market power.
985. *See* Horizontal Cooperation Guidelines, para. 221.
986. *Ibid.*, para. 222.
987. *Ibid.*, para. 224.

only to the joint venture, but not directly to the parties. The parties also have only limited access to the information disclosed to the joint venture.

5.2.1.d Joint Commercialisation Agreements

Joint commercialisation agreements involve cooperation between competitors in the selling, distribution or promoting of their products. The scope of the cooperation ranges from the determination of all commercial aspects necessary for the sale of products (including prices) to more limited form of cooperations that merely cover certain sales aspects (such as after-sales services or advertising).[988]

The two collusion concerns raised by the Horizontal Cooperation Guidelines are the same as with production and joint purchasing agreements: commonality of variable costs and exchange of commercially sensitive information.[989] On the former concern, the Horizontal Cooperation Guidelines (again) stress out that the risk of collusion only increases if the parties have market power and if the commercialisation constitutes a large proportion of the variable costs of the product.[990] On the latter concern, the Horizontal Cooperation Guidelines admit that 'some degree' of information exchange of commercially sensitive information (such as prices and marketing strategy) may be necessary in order to implement the agreement.[991] However, it cannot go beyond what is necessary for the implementation.[992]

5.2.1.e Standardisation Agreements

Standardisation agreements have as their primary objective the definition of technical or quality requirements in relation to products, production processes, services or methods.[993] Many standardisation agreements are adopted by recognised standard-setting organisations at EU or national level and thus involve a large number of market players.[994]

The collusion concern raised by the Horizontal Cooperation Guidelines is that the discussions that are required to make the conclusion of a standardisation agreement possible may entail spill-over effects that could result in a collusive outcome.[995] The participants of the discussion may (mis)use the occasion to exchange commercially sensitive information on issues not directly related to the standardisation.[996] However, in that regard the theory of harm is not specific to standardisation agreements. Any occasion where competitors come together (such as meetings of trade associations, industry fairs and so on) can be used by competitors to collude with each other.

988. *Ibid.*, para. 225.
989. *Ibid.*, paras 242-245.
990. *Ibid.*, para. 243.
991. *Ibid.*, para. 244.
992. *Ibid.*, para. 245.
993. *Ibid.*, para. 257.
994. *See* Faull and Nikpay (2014), para. 7.510.
995. *See* Horizontal Cooperation Guidelines, para. 265.
996. *See* Faull and Nikpay (2014), para. 7.513.

5.2.1.f Other Types of Horizontal Cooperation Agreements

The Horizontal Cooperation Guidelines provide another theory of harm that is not discussed in the respective sections of the specific types of horizontal cooperation agreements. The horizontal cooperation agreement may require parties to contribute certain assets which might undermine or reduce their decision-making independence.[997] This could increase the likelihood of collusion and make coordination more stable.[998]

There are two interpretations why this theory of harm is not concretised in the other sections and only discussed in the introduction. On the one hand, one could argue it is quite vague and abstract. It might be quite difficult to concretise the theory of harm for a specific type of efficiency-generating horizontal agreement. On the other hand, one could also argue that this theory of harm is a general warning with regard to the scope of the cooperation. At worst, it may call into question more closer forms of cooperation (such as closer joint venture). At best though, it may simply require a more in-depth assessment of possible efficiencies for closer forms of cooperation.

5.2.1.g Conclusion

There are essentially only two theories of harm on how horizontal cooperation agreements may facilitate collusion between competing undertakings:

(1) *Commonality of costs*: it is problematic if variable costs are increased by an agreement to such a level that enables the parties to collude on the condition: (i) that the parties have market power and (ii) that the market is characterised by certain structural feature that makes collusion likely.
(2) *Information exchange*: it is also problematic if the exchange of commercially sensitive information goes beyond what is necessary for the implementation of the specific efficiency-aiming agreement (negative spill-over effects).[999]

5.2.2 Vertical Guidelines

This section discusses collusion concerns raised by the Vertical Guidelines in a vertical context. The Vertical Guidelines discuss the most common forms of 'vertical restraints' (*see* section 5.2.2.a for the definition). Facilitative practices are discussed by the Vertical Guidelines with most but not all forms of vertical restraints (*see* sections 5.2.2.b-5.2.2.i).

997. *See* Horizontal Cooperation Guidelines, para. 33.
998. *Ibid.*, para. 37.
999. For the notion of 'spill-over effects' in this context, *see*, e.g., Faull and Nikpay (2014), para. 7.513.

5.2.2.a *Definition and Scope*

The exact definition of the notion of 'vertical restraints' is necessary because it sets the scope of application of the Vertical Guidelines. This rather technical approach is necessary because of the BER in the vertical context, the Vertical BER. The horizontal context lacks a general BER. Instead, there are two context-specific BERs in the horizontal context, the R&D-BER and Specialisation BER. However, even if a horizontal cooperation agreement falls outside the scope of one of the horizontal BERs, it is still able to fall within the scope of the Horizontal Cooperation Guidelines. Thus, while the scope of the Guidelines and the block exemption is aligned in the vertical context, it is not in the horizontal context.[1000] This is why this section briefly discussed the scope of the Vertical BER.

The scope of the Vertical BER and thus also the scope of the Vertical Guidelines are defined rather technically in Art. 1 of the Vertical BER. A vertical restraint is a restriction of competition in a 'vertical agreement' (Art. 1(b) Vertical BER). A vertical agreement is defined as 'an agreement or concerted practice entered into between two or more undertakings each of which operates, for the purposes of the agreement or the concerted practice, at a different level of the production or distribution chain, and relating to the conditions under which the parties may purchase, sell or resell certain goods or services' (Art. 1(a) Vertical BER).

This definition entails four elements.[1001] While the first two conditions concern the general application of Art. 101 TFEU, the latter two are more specific to the vertical context. First, the definition not just covers agreements but also concerted practices. However, it should be noted that most cases that concerned the exact delimitation between conduct that is covered by Art. 101 TFEU and unilateral conduct, which falls outside the scope of Art. 101 TFEU, centred around the concept of an agreement and not around the concept of a concerted practice.[1002]

Second, the vertical agreement must be between two 'undertakings' which exclude *inter alia* agreements with consumers.

Third, the vertical agreement must be between two undertakings which 'operate at different levels of the supply chain'. It is sufficient though that these undertakings only operate at different supply levels 'for the purpose of the agreement'. One of the consequences of this element is that firms that operate a dual distribution network are not excluded from the scope. For instance, a manufacturer may sell its goods not just through independent retailers (vertical relation with retailers) but also through its own shops (horizontal relation with retailers).[1003] In this case, only the former relation is dealt under the Vertical BER and Vertical Guidelines.

Fourth, the vertical agreement must relate to the conditions under which the supplier and buyer may purchase, sell or resell certain goods. This element entails that

1000. *See* Horizontal Cooperation Guidelines, para. 8.
1001. *See* Vertical Guidelines, para. 25.
1002. *See*, e.g., Whish and Bailey (2018), pp. 109-115.
1003. *See also* the two exemptions of Art. 2(4) of the Vertical BER and para. 28 of the Vertical Guidelines.

only purchase and distribution agreements are covered. Thus, the main purpose of the agreement is 'down' and not 'up'. This is why for instance subcontracting agreements, which concern the production of certain goods by an upstream subcontractor for the downstream contractor, are not covered by the definition.[1004]

5.2.2.b Agency Agreements

An agent is a person vested with the power to negotiate and/or conclude contracts on behalf of another person (the principal) either in the name of the agent or the principal.[1005] Only if the agent does not bear any or only insignificant financial or commercial risks relating to the selling and purchasing of goods,[1006] the agreement is considered as an 'agency agreement' that falls outside the scope of Art. 101 TFEU.[1007]

However, even if the agent does not bear any or only insignificant risk (and thus would fall within the definition of an 'agency agreement'), the agency agreement still falls within the scope of Art. 101 TFEU if it facilitates collusion. The concern is that the commonality of an agent is used as a means to enable collusion between principals (hub-and-spoke collusion). The Vertical Guidelines provide the following examples: when several principals use the same agents while collectively excluding others from using these agents; or when they use the same agents to collude on marketing strategy or to exchange commercially sensitive information.[1008]

5.2.2.c Single Branding Agreements

Single branding agreements have as their main characteristic the obligation of the buyer to concentrate its orders for a particular type of product with one supplier. This includes *inter alia*: (i) non-compete clauses, where the buyer is obligated to purchase more than 80% of its supplies of a specific product from one supplier, (ii) quantity-forcing clauses, where the incentives of the agreements make the buyer purchase to a large extent from one supplier, and (iii) so-called English clauses, where the buyers are

1004. *See* Vertical Guidelines, para. 22.
1005. *Ibid.*, para. 12.
1006. *Ibid.*, paras 13 et seq. The Guidelines provide a non-exhaustive black list of risks which, if incurred by the agent, would disqualify the agreement as an agency agreement (*ibid.*, para. 16 for the list and para. 17 for the methodology of assessment). Importantly, there are three types of risks (*ibid.*, para. 14): contract risks (risks that are directly related to the contracts concluded, such as the financing of stocks), market risks (risks that are related to market-specific investments, which are usually sunk costs) and other risks that relate to activities undertaken on the same product market. The example of a petrol station given by Faull and Nikpay (2014, fn 50 in para. 9.47) illustrates the different nature of these risks quite well: contract risks are, e.g., the costs of financing the purchase of petrol or the non-payment of customers; market risks are, e.g., the costs relating to the installation and maintenance of the tanks and pumps; the risks for other activities on the same product market are relevant if the 'agent' is required to sell the petrol at its own risk.
1007. *See* Vertical Guidelines, para. 18.
1008. *Ibid.*, para. 20.

obligated to report any better offer and allow the buyer to accept such offer only when the supplier does not match it.[1009]

The Vertical Guidelines raise the concern that such agreements may facilitate collusion between suppliers when they are used cumulatively.[1010] This is when several major suppliers enter into single branding agreements with a significant number of buyers.[1011] The collusion concern comes hand in hand with the concern of foreclosure. The more foreclosed the relevant product market, the more stable a possible collusion.

5.2.2.d Exclusive (Territorial) Distribution Agreements

Exclusive distribution agreements usually contain restrictions for both the supplier and distributor. On the one hand, the supplier is obligated to sell its products to only one distributor for resale in a particular territory. On the other hand, the distributor is usually limited in its active selling into other (exclusively allocated) territories.[1012]

The concern raised by the Vertical Guidelines is that in a market where most or all suppliers employ exclusive distribution systems, it may facilitate collusion on the suppliers' and distributors' level,[1013] particularly when the undertakings are similar in terms of market share, capacity and distribution network.[1014] Similar to single branding agreements, the collusion concern only materialises when exclusive distribution systems are used cumulatively. The likelihood then depends on the structure of the market.[1015]

Concerns are also raised by the Vertical Guidelines when several suppliers use the same exclusive distributor in a given territory.[1016] Similar to agency agreements, the commonality of a third party may facilitate indirect collusion (hub-and-spoke collusion). However, the Vertical Guidelines fail to explain why the exclusive distribution situation is different from any other distribution arrangement in which suppliers regularly use the same retailer to sell their goods. The risk of hub-and-spoke collusion is not specific to exclusive distribution, but more generally a risk in the vertical context.

5.2.2.e Exclusive Customer Allocation Agreements

The term 'exclusive distribution agreement' normally refers to the territorial exclusivity of a distributor. However, the exclusivity of a distributor cannot just relate to a specific territory but also to a specific group of customers (exclusive customer allocation

1009. *Ibid.*, para. 129.
1010. *Ibid.*, para. 130.
1011. *Ibid.*, para. 134.
1012. *Ibid.*, para. 151.
1013. *Ibid.*, para. 151.
1014. *Ibid.*, para. 154.
1015. *See* already section 3.3.1.d.
1016. *Ibid.*, para. 154.

agreements).[1017] Under such agreements, the supplier agrees to sell its products to only one distributor for the resale to a specific group of customers, while the distributor is usually limited in its active selling to other (exclusively allocated) groups of customers.[1018]

Since the economic logic of exclusive customer allocation agreements is similar to exclusive (territorial) distribution agreements, the collusion concern is the same. Only when exclusive customer allocations are used cumulatively, they may facilitate collusion at the suppliers' or customers' level.[1019]

5.2.2.f Selective Distribution Agreements

On an abstract level, selective distribution agreements have in common with exclusive distribution agreements that they restrict the number of distributors that can resell their products on the one hand and the possibilities of resale on the other hand.[1020] However, these two means of distribution differ in terms of their scope and nature. First, the restriction of the number of distributors does not depend on the number of exclusively allocated territories or customer groups, but on the criteria for the selection normally linked to the nature of the product. Second, the restriction on resale does not relate to the restriction of active sales but to the restriction of all sales (active and passive)[1021] to unauthorised distributors, leaving only other authorised distributors or final customers as possible buyers.[1022]

Collusion concerns only materialise when selective distributions are used by the majority of main suppliers.[1023] Due to the closed nature of the selective distribution network, it is particularly well suited to avoid pressure by price discounters on the margins of suppliers and other distributors. The Vertical Guidelines fail to provide further guidance on this theory of harm. But one could think about a market where selective distribution networks are used by most suppliers in order to systematically exclude price discounters and thus raise prices. The cumulative use of selective distribution agreements is then just a means to collude on prices.

Furthermore, Art. 5(1)(c) of the Vertical BER sets out that 'any direct or indirect obligation causing the members of a selective distribution system not to sell the brands of particular competing suppliers' is excluded from the benefit of the Vertical BER

1017. Customers are usually identified on the basis of objective criteria such as turnover, quantities ordered or nature of the activity (e.g., *final user vs reseller*) (*see* Faull and Nikpay (2014), para. 9.245).
1018. *See* Vertical Guidelines, para. 168.
1019. *Ibid.*, para. 168.
1020. *See* the definition of a selective distribution system in Art. 1(e) of the Vertical BER: 'a distribution system where the supplier undertakes to sell the contract goods or services, either directly or indirectly, only to distributors selected on the basis of specified criteria and where these distributors undertake not to sell such goods or services to unauthorised distributors within the territory reserved by the supplier to operate that system'.
1021. For the difference between these two types of sales, *see* Vertical Guidelines, para. 51 (general) and paras 52-54 (specifically for internet sales).
1022. *See* Vertical Guidelines, para. 174.
1023. *Ibid.*, paras 175 and 178.

(excluded restriction).[1024] While, the Vertical BER does cover the combination of selective distribution agreements with non-compete clauses, which obligate authorised distributors not to sell competing brands *in general*, it does not cover the 'targeted exclusion' of *specific* competing brands.[1025] The Vertical Guidelines explain that the rationale for this provision is driven by collusion concerns. On the one hand, leading suppliers may decide to systematically exclude certain brands that are not part of the collusion.[1026] The targeted exclusion then relates to the external stability of the collusion. On the other hand, targeted exclusion may be also used as an effective means of retaliation for colluding undertakings. The exclusion then relates to the internal stability of the collusion.

5.2.2.g Upfront Access Payments

Upfront access payments are fixed fees paid by a supplier to a distributor in advance in order to get access to the distribution network. This includes phenomena such as slotting allowances, which are fixed fees charged in order to get access to the distributor's shelf space, or pay-to-stay fees, which are lump sum payments made to ensure the continued presence of an existing product on the shelf for some further time.[1027] Upfront access payment is mainly the result of increasing buyer power on the distributors' side.[1028]

The collusion concern materialises on the downstream level of distributors. The Vertical Guidelines provide that because upfront access payments increase (upstream) costs of the product for the supplier, it might lead to higher (downstream) prices. This will ultimately reduce incentives for distributors to compete on prices on the downstream market.[1029]

However, this theory of harm is economically not entirely convincing. It fails to consider the horizontal competitive pressure among distributors. Even if distributors are able to extract more profits from suppliers due to their buyer power, this does not mean that distributors are also able to charge higher prices from their customers. The

1024. This is one of the three so-called excluded restrictions (grey list). Excluded restrictions in Art. 5 of the Vertical BER are different from the hard-core restriction in Art. 4 of the Vertical BER (black list) in two ways: First, the inclusion of excluded restrictions in the vertical agreement does not prevent the application of the Vertical BER to the rest of the agreement, while the inclusion of hard-core restrictions also deprives the rest of the agreement from the benefit of the Vertical BER (*see* Vertical Guidelines, para. 65). Second, the inclusion of excluded restrictions does not result in a presumption of illegality of such excluded restrictions under the individual assessment of Art. 101(3) TFEU (*see* Faull and Nikpay (2014), para. 9.153). In other words, there is no double negative presumption like for hard-core restrictions which are presumed to fall within Art. 101(1) TFEU and are presumed to also not benefit from Art. 101(3) TFEU (*see* Vertical Guidelines, para. 47).

1025. *See* Vertical Guidelines, para. 69.

1026. *Ibid.*, para. 182.

1027. *Ibid.*, para. 203.

1028. *See* Faull and Nikpay (2014), para. 9.275 who also point out that the lack of attention to increasing buyer power was one of the main criticisms of the old regime on vertical agreements before 2000.

1029. *See* Vertical Guidelines, para. 206.

price levels on the downstream market depend on the competitive pressure from other distributors. If the competitive downstream pressure is high enough, extracted profits may actually reduce downstream prices (it has to be passed on in order to remain competitive). All this theory of harm can provide then is that upfront access payment may be merely a sign of concentrated downstream market (buyer power) which is a structural factor that makes collusion easier.[1030]

5.2.2.h Category Management Agreements

Category management agreements provide that a distributor entrusts a supplier (the category captain) with the marketing of a category of products that also includes products that compete with the category captain's products. The supplier's ability as a category captain may include *inter alia* product placement, product promotion and product selection.[1031]

The collusion concerns raised by the Vertical Guidelines relate to both the distributors' and suppliers' level. On the one hand, if a supplier serves as the category captain for most or all distributors, category management agreements may facilitate collusion among distributors.[1032] This theory of harm seems to have elements of a hub-and-spoke collusion via a common third party and elements of a collusion theory that only materialises when the practice is used cumulatively. This makes it an interesting hybrid theory of harm. It is not just the cumulative use of category management agreements as a specific type of vertical agreement that triggers the collusion concern (like single branding, selective distribution, exclusive territorial distribution or exclusive customer allocation), but it is the combination with the hub-and-spoke collusion theory (i.e., it must be a *common* category captain among distributors).

On the other hand, category management agreements may also facilitate collusion among suppliers through the increased opportunity to exchange commercially sensitive information via those distributors that are under the influence of a category captain (hub-and-spoke collusion).[1033] In other words, category captains may be more tempted to exchange commercially sensitive information with other suppliers because it can be done less obvious than without a category management agreement.

5.2.2.i Resale Price Restrictions

The Vertical Guidelines discuss collusion concerns in the context of resale price maintenance and recommended prices. Only resale price maintenance includes practices that use direct or indirect means to 'enforce' the objective of the supplier to establish fixed or minimum prices (such as making the grant of rebates conditional on

1030. *See* already section 3.3.1.d.2.
1031. *See* Vertical Guidelines, para. 209.
1032. *Ibid.*, para. 211.
1033. *Ibid.*, para. 212.

the observance of a given price level; or using threats, intimidations, warnings, penalties, delays or even suspensions of deliveries).[1034]

Resale price maintenance may facilitate collusion among distributors because it eliminates intra-brand price competition (i.e., distributors cannot differentiate themselves from other distributors by offering a lower price for products of a certain supplier).[1035] However, in this situation one has to distinguish between the effect and culpability. While economists are concerned with the former, the latter matters for the application of Art. 101 TFEU.[1036] Even if the effect of resale price maintenance is the same as if collusion among distributors would have taken place (higher downstream prices), resale price maintenance does not equal collusion among distributors. The infringement of resale price maintenance lies in the vertical relationship between the supplier and its distributors but not in the horizontal relationship between distributors. Thus, a theory of harm based on collusion *between distributors* is not convincing on the basis of resale price maintenance.

Recommended prices may facilitate collusion among distributors because recommended prices may be used as a focal point to collude. Such focal point could be followed by distributors and thus lead to aligned prices.[1037] However, recommended prices are then, if at all, only a small puzzle in facilitating collusion. They merely relate to the first economic condition necessary for collusion, namely the condition to reach a common understanding on the terms of the coordination.[1038]

5.2.2.j Conclusion

The Vertical Guidelines essentially provide four theories of harm on how vertical agreements might facilitate collusion either on the upstream supplier level or on the downstream distributor level. While the first two concerns are not specific to one type of vertical agreement, the latter two concerns are specific:

(1) *Hub-and-spoke collusion*: the commonality of a third party among competitors (common agent, common exclusive distributor, common category captain) may facilitate collusion because it offers an increased opportunity to indirectly exchange commercially sensitive information.
(2) *Cumulative use*: certain types of distribution may facilitate collusion either on the supplier level (single branding and selective distribution), the distributor level (category management) or on both the supplier and distributor level (exclusive territorial distribution and exclusive customer allocation) when they are used widely in the market.
(3) *Targeted exclusion of certain competitors*: this concern was only raised in the context of selective distribution networks. The concern is that colluding

1034. *Ibid.*, paras 48 and 223.
1035. *Ibid.*, para. 224.
1036. *See* already section 3.3.1.b.
1037. *See* Vertical Guidelines, para. 227.
1038. *See* already section 3.3.1.c.

suppliers use the targeted exclusion of certain competitors in vertical agreement to either decide to systematically exclude non-members of the collusion (external stability) or retaliate cheating members (internal stability).

(4) *Focal point*: this concern was only raised in the context of recommended prices. The concern is that recommended prices may be used as a focal point to enable collusion among distributors.

5.2.3 Technology Transfer Guidelines

The TT-Guidelines set out the analytical framework for assessing 'technology transfer agreements' (*see* section 5.2.3.a). Collusion concerns are raised by the TT-Guidelines in the context of licensing agreements (*see* section 5.2.3.b) and technology pools (*see* section 5.2.3.c).

5.2.3.a Definition and Scope

In general, technology transfer agreements concern the licensing of technology rights where the licensor permits the licensee to exploit the licensed technology rights for the production of goods or services.[1039] However, the definition and scope of application of the TT-Guidelines is not aligned with the TT-BER. The TT-Guidelines also provide guidance for agreements that are not covered by the (narrower) definition of technology transfer agreement under the TT-BER (Art. 1(1)(c) of the TT-BER).

First, the TT-BER only covers technology transfer agreements between *two* parties.[1040] This limitation comes from Regulation 19/65 in which the Commission is only empowered to block exempt technology transfer agreements between two parties. However, the TT-Guidelines also provide guidance for licensing agreement between more parties. The most prominent example is a 'technology pool' which falls outside the scope of the TT-BER but is extensively discussed in the TT-Guidelines (*see* section 5.2.3.c).

Second, the TT-BER only covers technology transfer agreements for the *production* of contract products.[1041] Contract products are goods or services produced on the basis of the licensed technology rights.[1042] This condition is satisfied when the technology is used in the production process or when the technology is incorporated into the product itself.[1043] When the purpose of the agreement is not the production of the contract good (the TT-Guidelines provide the example where the purpose is to merely block the development of a competing technology),[1044] not even the TT-Guidelines apply.

1039. *See* TT-Guidelines, para. 1.
1040. *Ibid.*, paras 54-57.
1041. *Ibid.*, paras 58-66.
1042. *See* Art. 1(1)(g) in connection with Art. 1(1)(f) of the TT-BER.
1043. *See* Faull and Nikpay (2014), para. 10.69.
1044. *See* TT-Guidelines, para. 59.

Third, the TT-BER only covers those agreements that involve the *transfer* of technology.[1045] However, this does not require an 'active' flow of technology rights. Normally, such transfer takes the form of licensing where the licensor grants the licensee the right to use its technology rights against paying royalties.[1046] The TT-BER also covers assignments where part of the risk associated with the exploitation of the technology rights remains with the assignor,[1047] and even non-assertion agreement where the licensor commits not to exercise its technology rights against the licensee.[1048]

Fourth, the TT-BER does not cover all IP rights.[1049] Again, the limitation flows from Regulation 19/65 which only empowers the Commission to block exempt 'industrial property rights'. Therefore, the TT-BER does only cover *'technology rights'* that are exhaustively listed in Art. 1(1)(b) of the TT-BER: know-how,[1050] patents, utility rights, topographies of semiconductor products, supplementary protection certificates for medicinal products or other products for which such supplementary protection certificates may be obtained, plant breeder's certificates and software copyrights. Other types of IP rights (such as trademarks or copyrights other than software copyrights) are not covered by the TT-BER. While the Commission will apply similar principles for the copyrights other than software copyrights as set out for those types of IP rights that are covered by the TT-Guidelines,[1051] it will not do so for trademark licensing.[1052]

5.2.3.b Licensing Agreements

Licensing agreements are one of the most important examples of technology transfer agreements. This is why most of the analysis in the section that provides guidance on technology transfer agreements outside the scope of the TT-BER (section 4 of the TT-Guidelines) relates to licensing agreements.

The TT-Guidelines identify two levels at which collusion may take place in case of licensing agreements. First, collusion can occur at the upstream level of *licensers*.[1053] This level is about inter-technology competition (i.e., competition between suppliers of substitutable technologies). Licensing agreements between suppliers of substitutable technologies may facilitate collusion, particularly in highly concentrated markets. The TT-Guidelines first set out the four conditions necessary for collusion.[1054] They then mention four ways in which collusion can be achieved in this context: increasing market transparency, controlling certain behaviour, raising barrier to enter the market and achieving a high degree of commonality of costs. None of these theories is specific

1045. *Ibid.*, paras 51-53.
1046. *See* Art. 1(1)(c)(i) of the TT-BER and TT-Guidelines, para. 51.
1047. *Ibid.*, para. 52.
1048. *See* TT-Guidelines, para. 53.
1049. *See*, e.g., Faull and Nikpay (2014), para. 10.73.
1050. As defined in Art. 1(1)(i) of the TT-BER.
1051. *See* TT-Guidelines, para. 48.
1052. *Ibid.*, para. 50.
1053. *Ibid.*, para. 171.
1054. *See* already section 3.3.1.c.

to the licensing setting. For the latter theory of harm, the TT-Guidelines even refer to the Horizontal Cooperation Guidelines.

Second, collusion can also take place at the downstream level of the *licensees*.[1055] This level is about intra-technology competition (i.e., competition between undertakings that produce on the basis of the same technology). However, the TT-Guidelines fail to flesh out in which ways collusion may occur.

The TT-Guidelines also raise collusion concerns regarding two specific types of licensing restraints, namely exclusive licensing and non-compete obligations. First, exclusive licensing agreements are agreements where the licensor is not permitted to either produce himself on the basis of the licensed technology rights or to license the licensed technology rights to third parties. This means that only the licensee is allowed to produce on the basis of the licensed technology.[1056] The TT-Guidelines raise the concern that reciprocal exclusive licensing agreements between competitors may facilitate collusion if the parties have significant market power. Under such agreements the parties would mutually commit not to license their competing technology rights to third parties. The concern of collusion only materialises when the parties have significant market power. This is because only when they engage in these types of agreements would the parties be essentially the only source of output based on these competing licensed technologies. This would enable the parties to collude *inter alia* on prices or output.[1057]

Second, non-compete obligations in licensing agreements result in a situation where the licensee commits not to use third-party technologies that compete with the licensed technology. Thus, such clauses constrain the licensee in what alternative technologies can be used to produce a product.[1058] The concern is that non-compete obligations may facilitate collusion between licensors when they are used cumulatively. The collusion concern comes hand in hand with the foreclosure concern. The more foreclosed the market to third-party technologies is, the more stable a possible collusion is. This economic logic is very similar to single branding agreements in the vertical context.

5.2.3.c Technology Pools

Technology pools are arrangements whereby two or more parties agree to pool their respective technologies and license them as a package. This package of technology rights is not just licensed to the contributors of the pool but also to third parties. The structure of the technology pools covers a wide range of different forms, from simple arrangements between a few players to complex organisational arrangements with separate entities responsible for solely organising the process.[1059]

1055. *Ibid.*, para. 173.
1056. *Ibid.*, para. 190.
1057. *Ibid.*, para. 192.
1058. *Ibid.*, para. 226.
1059. *Ibid.*, para. 244.

The TT-Guidelines stress out that the way technology pools are formed, organised and operated can significantly reduce competition law concerns.[1060] The TT-Guidelines set out four factors for the assessment of anti-competitive risks. One of the factors is whether there are sufficient safeguards against the exchange of sensitive information.[1061] On the one hand, the TT-Guidelines recognise that output and sales data may need to be disclosed to independent experts or to licensing bodies in order to calculate and verify royalties. This is why independent experts or licensing bodies play a crucial part in not disclosing the information they receive to undertakings competing on affected markets.[1062] Put differently, these actors should not facilitate hub-and-spoke collusion. On the other hand, the TT-Guidelines also emphasise that 'special care' should be put into creating safeguards when interested parties participate simultaneously in an effort to form pools of competing standards. Interested undertakings may use the discussions as an opportunity to disclose information to undertakings with competing technologies that are either not relevant or not necessary for the creation of the technology pool (spill-over effects).[1063]

The guidance by the TT-Guidelines on the institutional design may have even wider application than just technology pools. In particular, the guidance may be highly relevant for trade associations whose institutional task is similar.[1064] When trade associations collect information for statistical purposes, they should ensure that they have safeguards against anti-competitive spill-over effects. These safeguards should include (in light of the guidance on technology pools) *inter alia* openness of participation to all non-members, voluntariness of participation for members and an independent management body responsible for the collection and aggregation of the data.[1065]

5.2.3.d Conclusion

If one compares the analytical framework of the TT-Guidelines with those of the Vertical Guidelines and Horizontal Cooperation Guidelines, it becomes obvious that the collusion concerns regarding licensing agreements are similar to vertical agreements, while the collusion concerns regarding technology pools are similar to horizontal cooperation agreements.

Collusion concerns regarding *licensing agreements* only materialise when either the parties have market power (exclusive licensing agreements) or the licensing restraint is used cumulatively (non-compete obligations). This aligns well with the

1060. *Ibid.*, para. 248.
1061. The other three factors are: open participation (*ibid.*, para. 249), selection and nature of the pooled technology (*ibid.*, paras 250-255) and selection and function of independent experts (*ibid.*, paras 256-258).
1062. *Ibid.*, para. 259.
1063. *Ibid.*, para. 260.
1064. *See* on the issue of trade associations and information exchange Bissocoli (2000). His argument is that trade association should follow similar suggestions: exchange is open to non-members, voluntary nature of exchange, aggregation of data, etc. (*see* Bissocoli (2000), p. 102).
1065. *See* Capobianco (2004), p. 1261.

collusion concerns raised by the Vertical Guidelines for exclusive distribution agreements and single branding agreements. This would also mean that many of the more sophisticated and more elaborated theories of harm under the Vertical Guidelines may also apply to licensing agreements.

Collusion concerns regarding *technology pools* focus on the risk of exchanging confidential information between competitors. Information exchange is one of the main collusion concerns of the Horizontal Cooperation Guidelines raised under almost all types of horizontal cooperation. In that sense technology pools merely offer competitors another opportunity to exchange commercially sensitive information in a less obvious way. The crucial question for technology pools is the same as for most types of horizontal cooperation: Does the information that has been exchanged go beyond what is relevant and necessary for the purpose of the efficiency-enhancing cooperation?

5.2.4 Concluding Remarks Regarding Information Exchanges

5.2.4.a Information Exchange Is the Most Relevant and Universal Manifestation of a Facilitative Practice

It becomes obvious from the discussion of the relevant Guidelines (Horizontal Cooperation Guidelines, Vertical Guidelines and TT-Guidelines) on the possible application of Art. 101 TFEU to facilitative practices that information exchange is the common theme among all of them. This suggests that information exchange is not just the most relevant legal manifestation of the concept of a facilitative practice (it is used most often in the Guidelines), but also the most universal facilitative practice (it is used in different context in all three relevant Guidelines).

The Horizontal Cooperation Guidelines essentially mention two theories of harm in regard to facilitating collusion: information exchange and commonality of costs. While the issue of commonality of costs is only mentioned on three occasions (production, purchasing and commercialisation agreement), the exchange of commercially sensitive information is mentioned in *every* type of horizontal cooperation that is discussed in the Guidelines (R&D, production, purchasing, commercialisation and standardisation agreement).

Even in the Vertical Guidelines the *horizontal* exchange of information is used as one of the most prominent manifestations of facilitative practices. Although the most mentioned facilitative practice is the cumulative use of certain types of distribution (single branding distribution, exclusive territorial distribution, exclusive customer distribution, selective distribution and category management agreements), the concern of hub-and-spoke collusion does not fall far behind (agency agreement, exclusive territorial distribution and category management agreements). Thus, even if the context is a vertical one (i.e., between suppliers and distributors), the exchange of information does ultimately take place at a horizontal level (either between suppliers or between distributors). This suggests that vertical agreements merely offer another temptation to misuse the commonality of a third party to exchange commercially sensitive information between competitors. In this regard vertical agreements are not different from other occasions where competitors come together (such as meetings within the institutional structure of trade associations). It is just a way to make the collusion less obvious and thus hide it more easily from enforcers.

The TT-Guidelines represented an interesting hybrid in regard to collusion theories. While the economic setting of licensing agreements is similar to vertical agreements, the economic setting of technology pools is similar to horizontal cooperation agreements.

This is why information exchange plays a more prominent role in case of technology pools (much like in horizontal cooperation agreements). In essence, the TT-Guidelines require sufficient safeguards against the exchange of commercially sensitive information between competitors beyond what is relevant and necessary for the creation of the specific technology pool.

With regard to licensing agreements, it is interesting to note that the exchange of information as a possible theory of collusive harm is not mentioned at all. On the one hand, one could argue that the concern of anti-competitive spill-over effects raised in the context of vertical agreements can also be applied to licensing agreements. The information shared on the basis of a licensing agreement may also go beyond what is necessary to produce the product in question. On the other hand, one could object the application of that concept on the basis that the scope of the information exchange covered by the licensing agreement is so wide (*see* the definition of know-how in Art. 1(1)(i) TT-BER) that it necessarily has to cover information about sales and prices of that product to calculate the licensee fees. Thus, there would be little practical scope of the concept of spill-over effects. However, this still leaves room to apply Art. 101 TFEU in those situations where the licensing agreement is merely used as 'cover' to exchange commercially sensitive information that does not at all relate to the product to which the licensing agreement relates.

5.2.4.b The Scope and Nature of Ancillary Information Exchange

It is also worth discussing two conceptual issues that relate to ancillary information exchanges[1066] raised by the Horizontal Cooperation Guidelines and the TT-Guidelines. The first issue relates to the *scope* of the concept (i.e., when an information exchange is regarded as ancillary) and the second to its *nature* (i.e., the issue of proportionality and institutional design).

On the first issue, the types of horizontal cooperation agreements in Horizontal Cooperation Guidelines as discussed above[1067] clearly relate to ancillary information exchanges, not to pure information exchanges. This is because the exchange is part of

1066. *See* already section 2.1.1 for that concept.
1067. Not section 2 of the Horizontal Cooperation Guidelines which relate to pure information exchanges (*see* section 6.1.3).

the broader cooperation that does not solely aim to exchange information. Instead, the primary aim is *inter alia* to produce, purchase or commercialise something more efficiently. The information exchange is merely ancillary to facilitate the efficiency-enhancing rationale of the cooperation.

With regard to technology pools, it is less obvious that the TT-Guidelines only deal with ancillary information exchanges. One could argue that the information exchange is ancillary to the broader objective of pooling technologies and selling them as package. Similar to the efficiency-enhancing objectives of horizontal cooperation agreements, the efficiency-enhancing objective of technology pools is to pool technologies and sell them as packages. This makes it different *inter alia* from the collection of firms' performance data in order to provide aggregated industry data, which is considered as a pure information exchange.[1068] This is because it requires more intellectual effort to pool technologies than merely collecting and aggregating data. However, when the technology pool becomes less institutionalised and efforts to achieve the pooling are not particularly high, one may even categorise technology pools as pure information exchanges (or at least as weak types of ancillary information exchanges).

On the second issue, the Horizontal Cooperation Guidelines implicitly recognise that some degree of information exchange is necessary to achieve the efficiencies aimed by the cooperation. However, the extent of the exchange cannot go beyond what is necessary for the materialisation of the efficiencies (spill-over effects). This is an expression of the broader principle of proportionality. The extent of information exchange obviously depends on the specific type of horizontal cooperation. While the Horizontal Cooperation Guidelines are sceptical that the exchange of sales prices is necessary for joint purchasing agreements,[1069] they are more reluctant to permit such exchange for joint commercialisation agreements.[1070] One could also argue that the substantive assessment of ancillary information exchange depends on the context of the broader *arrangement* of which they are part of, while the substantive assessment of pure information exchanges depends on the market context.[1071] This also means that any abstract conceptual statement about ancillary information exchanges is doomed to fail because one always has to analyse the broader efficiency-enhancing arrangement.

A further observation on the second issue is that when the cooperation that aims to materialise efficiencies becomes *more institutionalised*, the rules and design of the institutional system gain more weight in the overall assessment. This becomes obvious from the TT-Guidelines and their guidance on technology pools. The TT-Guidelines provide that the institutional design should offer safeguards to reduce the temptation of participating undertakings to engage in exchanging commercially sensitive information

1068. *See* already section 3.1.1 for that type of efficiency.
1069. *Ibid.*, para. 215.
1070. *Ibid.*, para. 244.
1071. *See* section 6.2.2.b for the latter argument.

that is not necessary. On a more abstract level, such guidance can be applied in analogy to other forms of more institutionalised cooperation between competitors (such as trade associations).[1072]

1072. *See* the policy debate at the OECD level on trade associations: 'Participation in trade and professional associations' activities provide ample opportunities for companies in the same line of business to meet regularly and to discuss business matters of common interest. Such meetings and discussions, even if meant to pursue legitimate association objectives, bring together direct competitors and provide them with regular opportunities for exchanges of views on the market, which could easily *spill over* into illegal coordination. Casual discussions of prices, quantities and future business strategies can lead to agreements or informal understandings in clear violation of antitrust rules. It is for this reason that trade associations and their activities are subject to close scrutiny by competition authorities around the world. [...] Competition enforcement is increasingly focussed on trade associations' practices that facilitate collusion among the members. Unduly restrictive membership rules, *exchange of detailed and sensitive commercial information*, exclusive or closed industry standards, marketing restrictions, and 'ethical' codes regulating pricing or other trading practices that limit the members' ability to compete freely are among the antitrust-sensitive issues which most affect the activities of trade associations today.' (OECD (2007b), pp. 8-9, emphasis added)

CHAPTER 6
Pure Information Exchange

6.1 THE COMMISSION'S VIEW

This section explores the view of the Commission on the assessment of pure information exchanges. Early policy statements by the Commission can be traced back until as early as 1968 (*see* section 6.1.1). The early decisional practice on information exchanges focused on ancillary information exchanges that were part of a broader anti-competitive scheme. It failed to develop pure information exchanges as a distinct analytical category (*see* section 6.1.2). It is only recently that Commission provides extensive guidance on assessing pure information exchanges in the current 2011 Horizontal Cooperation Guidelines (*see* section 6.1.3).

6.1.1 Early Policy Statements

6.1.1.a 1968 Notice

The first policy statement of the Commission on information exchanges between competitors can be traced back to the 1968 Notice concerning Agreements, Decisions and Concerted Practices in the field of Co-operation Between Enterprises (the '1968 Notice'). Already in this Notice the Commission tried to distinguish between pro-competitive and anti-competitive information exchanges. For instance, the Commission raised the concern that the exchange of individualised data is more problematic due to the higher risk of collusive outcomes.[1073] It also identified that an exchange of

1073. *See* 1968 Notice, p. 4: 'Wenn aber die Handlungsfreiheit der Unternehmen eingeschränkt oder das Marktverhalten ausdrücklich oder im Wege aufeinander abgestimmter Verhaltensweisen koordiniert wird, kann eine Wettbewerbseinschränkung vorliegen. Das ist insbesondere der Fall, wenn Empfehlungen *konkreter* Art ausgesprochen oder Schlußfolgerungen so *präzisiert* werden, daß dadurch ein gleichförmiges Verhalten im Markt zumindest eines Teils der beteiligten Unternehmen herbeigeführt wird. [...] Gemeinsame Marktforschung sowie

information is more problematic in oligopolistic market involving homogeneous products.[1074]

Although the 1968 Notice was quite short (only four pages) and lacked any sophisticated analytical framework,[1075] the policy statements are still seen as economically sound.[1076] It already emphasised that even information exchanges between competitors are able to produce pro-competitive effects and are thus not necessarily unlawful. It also vaguely indicated that much of the competitive assessment of information exchange depends on the nature of the information exchange (level of aggregation of the information), the structure of the market (market concentration of the market) and nature of the products concerned (homogeneity of products), although economic theory is not as clear on the issue of the homogeneity of products as suggested by the 1968 Notice.[1077]

6.1.1.b 1977 Report

The 7th Report on Competition Policy (the '1977 Report') had a dedicated section on 'information agreements'.[1078] Compared to the 1968 Notice the analytical framework became more sophisticated and the level of guidance increased. For instance, while in the 1968 Notice the issue of aggregation of data was merely indirectly indicated, the 1977 Report elaborated in more detail on where to draw the line between pro-competitive and anti-competitive exchanges.[1079] It explicitly recognised the pro-competitive potential that could come with increased market transparency by information sharing.[1080] Thus, it endorsed a case-by-case analysis to assess possible anti-competitive effects.[1081]

Betriebs- und Branchenvergleiche dienen der Sammlung von Material sowie der Feststellung von Fakten und Marktverhältnissen und berühren für sich allein, ohne eine darüber hinausgehende Zusammenarbeit der beteiligten Unternehmen, den Wettbewerb nicht.' (emphasis added)

1074. *See* 1968 Notice, p. 4.
1075. *See* Peeperkorn (1996), p. 11.
1076. *See* Capobianco (2004), pp. 1249-1250; OECD (2011), fn 64.
1077. As mentioned in section 3.3.1.d, while the Commission still points out in its current Guidelines that it is easier to reach a collusive outcome if products are homogeneous (*see* Horizontal Merger Guidelines, para. 45; Horizontal Cooperation Guidelines, para. 82), the economic literature on product homogeneous is less clear. For instance, although it is harder to punish firms for deviations if products are heterogeneous (cheating firm would still be left with some demand even after a significant price war) it is for the same reason that deviating is also costlier (since the deviating firm has to offer a significant price cut to gain market shares) (*see* Motta (2004), p. 146).
1078. *See* 1977 Report, paras 5-8. *See also* the comment by Niemeyer (1993), p. 152.
1079. *See* 1977 Report, paras 5 and 7: 'A distinction can be drawn between agreements which are for purely statistical purposes and those which identify individual firms – depending on how the central reporting agency collates and passes on the information. [...] The provision of collated statistical material is not in itself objectionable from the point of view of competition policy. The Commission has no fundamental objection where national trade associations representing the same economic interests in different countries exchange statistics, either direct or through a reporting agency, which set out production and sales figures for the industry in question without identifying individual businesses, as is the practice in official statistics. [...] On the other hand, the organized exchange of individual data from individual firms, such as

However, the 1977 Report failed to provide guidance on the importance of the structure of the market that goes beyond the 1968 Notice.[1082] The 1977 Report also failed to distinguish between pure and ancillary information exchanges, even though this distinction already appeared in the decisional practice of the Commission.[1083] The Commission was also willing to deviate from economic theory regarding the concern that even aggregated information may be sufficient in certain markets to enable monitoring of collusive outcomes.[1084]

The 1977 Report has to be seen in light of *Suiker Unie*, which established the independence doctrine for the first time.[1085] Information exchanges are able to undermine the independence of decision-making of undertakings. The 1977 Report can be appraised for further recognising the importance of the specific circumstances in order to assess information exchanges.[1086] This is the key lesson from the economic literature on information exchange (*see* already 3.3.1.d.4).

6.1.1.c 2001 Horizontal Cooperation Guidelines

The 2001 Horizontal Cooperation Guidelines explicitly excluded pure information sharing agreements between competitors from their scope.[1087] However, they still provided guidance on ancillary information exchanges that were part of the wider horizontal cooperation.[1088]

6.1.1.d 2008 Maritime Guidelines

The 2008 Maritime Guidelines were the first more elaborate[1089] guidance by the Commission on *pure* information exchanges.[1090] However, the guidance was limited to a very specific context: the maritime transport sector. It was questionable to what extent the sector-specific guidance had more general applicability beyond the area of maritime transport services. Although general consensus was that the guidance was not just context-specific, the exact degree of transferability remained unknown. This created legal certainties for undertakings.[1091]

figures on quantities produced and sold, prices and terms for discounts, higher and lower rates, credit notes and general terms of sale, delivery and payment, will generally be regarded by the Commission as practices which have as their object or effect the restriction or distortion of competition within the common market, and which are therefore prohibited.'
1080. *See* 1977 Report, para. 7 (point 3).
1081. *See* Stroux (2004), p. 147.
1082. *See* 1977 Report, para. 7 (point 2).
1083. *See* Capobianco (2004), pp. 1250-1251.
1084. *See* Peeperkorn (1996), p. 12.
1085. This is emphasised by OECD (2011), para. 33. *See* already section 4.2.1.b.2.
1086. *See* Capobianco (2004), p. 1250.
1087. *See* 2001 Horizontal Cooperation Guidelines, para. 10.
1088. *Ibid.*, para. 146 regarding commercialisation agreements.
1089. *See* for this Wagner-von Papp (2012), fn 19.
1090. *See* 2008 Maritime Guidelines, paras 38-59.
1091. *See* Seitz (2011), p. 456 on the issue of transferability.

Still, the 2008 Maritime Guidelines laid down an analytical framework that is in many regards similar to the current framework laid down by the Commission in its current 2011 Horizontal Cooperation Guidelines. For instance, the 2008 Maritime Guidelines already distinguished between ancillary and pure information exchanges and only provided guidance for the latter.[1092] In line with economic theory, they also recognised that information sharing can create significant efficiencies (such as better planning and more efficient use of capacity).[1093] They also emphasised the ambiguous nature of market transparency (i.e., increased transparency may be more problematic in concentrated market)[1094] and discussed the role of the market structure[1095] as well as the characteristics of the information exchange.[1096]

However, it became obvious that the Commission had a very specific type of pure information exchange in mind: market information systems that principally aim to generate efficiencies but where their specific design may entail anti-competitive effects. This is why the 2008 Maritime Guidelines defined information exchange systems as 'arrangements' and thus excluded any looser forms of concertation.[1097] In other words, the 2008 Maritime Guidance did not provide any guidance on information sharing that went beyond efficiency-aiming market information systems, but did also fall short of full-blown cartels. The 2008 Maritime Guidelines did not anticipate that there is room for information exchanges as self-standing by object infringements outside broader cartel arrangements.[1098] This perception has shifted with the current 2011 Horizontal Cooperation Guidelines which also elaborate on the danger of 'collusive outcomes' that fall within the object box.

6.1.2 Early Decisional Practice

In the early decisional practice of the Commission in the 1970s and 1980s one can find several decisions where the exchange of information in question was scrutinised.[1099] These decisions condemned information exchanges together with other anti-competitive conduct that was considered as a restriction by object (such as price-fixing or market-sharing).

However, even though information exchanges were not 'pure', they were also not always 'ancillary' to other anti-competitive conduct. The information exchange was instead one element in the overall anti-competitive conduct.[1100] This ambiguous classification reflects the early underdeveloped analytical framework for assessing information exchanges at the time.

1092. *See* 2008 Maritime Guidelines, para. 42.
1093. *Ibid.*, paras 39 and 58.
1094. *Ibid.*, paras 39 and 48.
1095. *Ibid.*, paras 47-49.
1096. *Ibid.*, paras 50-57.
1097. *Ibid.*, para. 38.
1098. *See* Baño Fos (2015), pp. 122-123.
1099. These early cases are also briefly discussed in Niemeyer (1993), pp. 152-154; Capobianco (2004), pp. 1263-1264; Stroux (2004), pp. 143-149; Whish (2006), pp. 31-33).
1100. Also noted by Niemeyer (1993), p. 152; Peeperkorn (1996), p. 10; Bissocoli (2000), p. 84.

Although these decisions do technically not concern pure information exchanges, they have certainly influenced the policy statements of the Commission on information exchanges, particularly the focus on disaggregated information and information exchange in oligopolistic markets.[1101] This is why it is still worth briefly discussing these decisions.

The *Cimbel* decision[1102] concerned *inter alia* the exchange of information on projected capacity expansion. The exchange was clearly ancillary to the overall market-sharing and quota-fixing agreement and aimed at preventing one firm to gain an advantage over competitors by investing in newer production facilities with more capacities.[1103]

The *Cobelpa* decision[1104] concerned a notification by the Belgian and Dutch paper industry federations (Cobelpa and VNP) of a practice between the Belgian and Dutch manufacturers of printing paper and stationery[1105] that involved the exchange of statistical data,[1106] as well as the exchange of prices and general terms of sale, supply and payments (including discounts, price increases and reductions and rebates).[1107] The Commission classified all of these exchanges as a concerted practice that had the object of restricting competition.[1108] On the issue of the exchange of statistical data the Commission stated that the exchange in question was too disaggregated and 'crossed the threshold which separates a lawful information agreement from a practice intended to restrict and distort competition'.[1109] However, it also recognised, in line with the 1977 Report, that the exchange of statistical data does not raise concerns as long as the conduct of individual undertakings could not be identified.

The *Vegetable Parchment* decision[1110] concerned, besides market-sharing[1111] and price-fixing,[1112] the exchange of statistical data that was complemented by individualised data.[1113] The Commission concluded that the practices constituted restrictions by object.[1114] It is questionable though whether the information exchange as such would have been considered a restriction by object. However, it can be assumed that the information exchange was ancillary to the other hard-core restrictions due to their temporal alignment.

The *White Lead* decision[1115] concerned various practices aimed at protecting home markets and allocating quotas to export markets.[1116] The monthly exchange of

1101. These two elements are also emphasised by Stroux (2004), pp. 144-145.
1102. Commission decision, *Cimbel*.
1103. *Ibid.*, pp. 33-34.
1104. Commission decision, *Cobelpa*.
1105. *Ibid.*, para. 1.
1106. *Ibid.*, paras 25-28.
1107. *Ibid.*, paras 29-30.
1108. *Ibid.*, para. 24.
1109. *Ibid.*, para. 27.
1110. Commission decision, *Vegetable Parchment*.
1111. *Ibid.*, paras 55-62.
1112. *Ibid.*, paras 71-73.
1113. *Ibid.*, para. 64.
1114. *Ibid.*, para. 69.
1115. Commission decision, *White Lead*.
1116. *Ibid.*, para. 11.

disaggregated quantities delivered was merely a means to monitor the collusive outcome and detect deviating firms.[1117] Thus, the exchange in question can be classified as ancillary to the overall market-sharing agreement.

The *Atka* decision[1118] concerned an agreement which stipulated the disaggregated exchange of quantities sold to individual customers.[1119] The Commission concluded that the exchange created a 'system of solidarity and reciprocal influence'.[1120] The information exchange agreement was supplemented by other hard-core restrictions (such as customer allocation, market-sharing and price-fixing).[1121] Thus, the exchange was merely ancillary to the overall practice that had the object of restricting competition.

The *Benelux Flat Glas* decision[1122] concerned the exchange of sales figures. The Commission concluded that the aim of the exchange was not just to be better informed about the general state of the market, but also to monitor each other and react if necessary.[1123] Again, the information exchange was one facet in a wider system of hard-core infringements.

In conclusion, these decisions offer only very limited guidance on how to assess pure information exchanges. They were quite formalistic and did often not go beyond the mere accumulation of general statements. In particular, the line between restrictions by object/effect as well as the line between pure and ancillary information exchanges are often ambiguously drawn. Furthermore, none of these decisions faced judicial scrutiny. They are mostly cited in literature that predated the 2011 Horizontal Cooperation Guidelines.[1124] For these reasons, the early decisional practice of the Commission has only a limited weight in light of the subsequent case law[1125] that offers a more sophisticated analytical framework for pure information exchanges.

6.1.3 2011 Horizontal Cooperation Guidelines

6.1.3.a Introduction

The current 2011 Horizontal Cooperation Guidelines – in contrast to the 2001 Horizontal Cooperation Guidelines[1126] – contain a dedicated section for the assessment of (pure) information exchanges.[1127] This section has been added not just because of the strong demand from stakeholders but also because of the institutional change that has

1117. *Ibid.*, para. 25.
1118. Commission decision, *Atka.*
1119. *Ibid.*, paras 38 and 78-78.
1120. *Ibid.*, para. 78.
1121. *Ibid.*, paras 80-82.
1122. Commission decision, *Benelux Flat Glas.*
1123. *Ibid.*, para. 45.
1124. *See*, e.g., Whish (2006) and Capobianco (2004).
1125. *See* sections 6.2 and 6.3.
1126. *See* already section 6.1.1.c.
1127. *See* Horizontal Cooperation Guidelines, section 2, paras 55-110.

occurred since the last revision of the Guidelines (i.e., the decentralised application of EU competition law).[1128]

The 'highly diverse and complex field'[1129] of information exchange has been an 'area of legal uncertainty'[1130] for most lawyers. The Horizontal Cooperation Guidelines are an attempt to codify and clarify the case law and decisional practice on information exchange.[1131] Overall, the systematic set of rules has been welcomed by the literature.[1132]

The Horizontal Cooperation Guidelines are heavily influenced by the economic literature on information exchange.[1133] The analytical framework is also in line with the Commission's more economic approach. The Horizontal Cooperation Guidelines follow an economically sound competition policy approach.[1134] The aim is to try to strike a balance between encouraging those information exchanges that are efficiency enhancing, while at the same time deterring undertakings from engaging in anti-competitive information exchanges.[1135]

One disputed area after the publication of the first draft Guidelines was the by object/effect classification. The final version of the Guidelines expresses a more cautious approach on the scope of the object box.[1136] In the earlier draft of the Guidelines, the Commission has taken an extensive view on the scope of the object box to also capture exchanges about current conduct that reveals intentions on future behaviour. This broader view was criticised by the literature,[1137] but ultimately did not made it into the final version. Thus, the final version of the Guidelines restricts the scope of the object box and thus indirectly endorses a more effect-based economic approach as the common theme. Robertson for instance notes that the Guidelines limit the finding of a restriction of competition by object to very specific cases, while the majority of information exchanges should be analysed based on their effects on the market.[1138]

It should be emphasised that the Horizontal Cooperation Guidelines only apply to *pure* information exchanges.[1139] They do not apply to ancillary information exchanges

1128. *See* Wijckmans and Tuytschaever (2015), para. 11.03.
1129. *See* Camesasca, Schmidt and Clancy (2010), p. 417.
1130. *See* Seitz (2011), p. 455.
1131. *See* González (2012), p. 50.
1132. *See* Camesasca and Schmidt (2011); Wagner-von Papp (2012).
1133. *See* Kühn (2010).
1134. *See* Wagner-von Papp (2012), p. 5.
1135. *See* Robertson (2013), p. 460.
1136. One of the articles that heavily criticised the scope of the object box in the draft Guidelines was Camesasca, Schmidt and Clancy (2010). *See also* the subsequent article by Camesasca and Schmidt (2011) that praises the change in the final version.
1137. *See* Camesasca, Schmidt and Clancy (2010), p. 406; Camesasca and Schmidt (2011), p. 228.
1138. *See* Robertson (2013), p. 461. Robertson also notes that the scope of the 'by object box' is even narrower in the final Guidelines than in the initial draft (*ibid.*, p. 462).
1139. *See*, e.g., Robertson (2013).

that are either part of horizontal cooperation agreement or a wider cartel arrangement.[1140] However, the exact boundaries are fluent in those situations where the information exchange is considered as a restriction by object.[1141]

6.1.3.b Analytical Framework

The Horizontal Cooperation Guidelines provide an analytical framework to assess the restrictive effects of pure information exchanges. The framework should be viewed as a dynamic and moveable system[1142] that is flexible enough to consider the individual circumstances of a case. There are essentially two perspectives that have to be considered when assessing the anti-competitive effects: the characteristics of the market and the characteristics of the information exchange itself.

In the first step, the Commission assesses the characteristics of the market. According to the Horizontal Cooperation Guidelines collusion is easier to achieve and maintain when the market is characterised by the following structural features:

- *Market transparency*: the more transparent the market, the more likely collusive outcomes.[1143]
- *Market concentration*: the more concentrated the market, the more likely collusive outcomes.[1144]
- *Complexity (in terms of number of products, extent of product differentiation, etc.)*: the more complex the market environment, the more likely collusive outcomes.[1145]
- *Demand and supply conditions*: the more stable demand and supply conditions, the more likely collusive outcomes.[1146]
- *Firms' symmetry (in terms of costs, demand, market shares, product ranges, capacities, etc.)*: the more symmetric firms on the market, the more likely collusive outcomes.[1147]

1140. *See* Horizontal Cooperation Guidelines, paras 56 and 59: 'information exchange can be part of another type of horizontal co-operation agreement (for example, the parties to a production agreement share certain information on costs). The assessment of the latter type of information exchanges should be carried out in the context of the assessment of the *horizontal co-operation* agreement itself. [...] communication of information among competitors may constitute an agreement, a concerted practice, or a decision by an association of undertakings with the object of fixing, in particular, prices or quantities. Those types of information exchanges will normally be considered and fined as *cartels*. Information exchange may also facilitate the implementation of a cartel by enabling companies to monitor whether the participants comply with the agreed terms. Those types of exchanges of information will be assessed as part of the cartel'. (emphasis added)
1141. *See* section 6.3.
1142. *See* Robertson (2013), p. 463.
1143. *See* Horizontal Cooperation Guidelines, para. 78.
1144. *Ibid.*, para. 79.
1145. *Ibid.*, para. 80.
1146. *Ibid.*, para. 81
1147. *Ibid.*, para. 82.

- *Firms' extent of discounting their future profits*: the lower firms discount their future profits, the lower the value of short-term profits from deviating and thus the more likely collusive outcomes.[1148]
- *Firms' duration on the market*: the longer the firms operate or tend to operate in the same market, the more likely collusive outcomes.[1149]

However, this list of market factors is neither complete nor fully supported by economic theory.[1150] On the one hand, the Horizontal Cooperation Guidelines fail to mention other structural factors that do facilitate collusion, such as buyer power or market barriers (i.e., the weaker buyers' power and the higher market barrier, the more likely collusion).[1151] On the other hand, not all of the factors mentioned by the Guidelines are unambiguously supported by economic theory. For instance, although it is harder to punish firms for deviations if products are heterogeneous (the cheater would still be left with some demand even after a significant price war), it is for the same reason that deviating is also costlier (since the cheater has to offer a significant price cut to gain market shares).[1152]

In the second step, the Commission assesses the characteristic of the information exchange itself. In accordance with the conceptual framework laid down in Chapter 2, two levels can be distinguished:

(1) *Inner lawyer*: the more strategic (i.e., data that reduces strategic uncertainty in the market),[1153] individualised (as opposed to more aggregated data),[1154] recent (as opposed to historic data)[1155] and private (as opposed to data that is available publicly),[1156] the more likely are collusive outcomes.
(2) *Outer layer*: the more frequent[1157] and the less public[1158] the exchange takes place, the more likely collusive outcomes. Also, the larger the extent of the firms' market coverage, the more likely the information exchange will result in collusive outcomes.[1159]

Although the Horizontal Cooperation Guidelines provide a sound analytical framework, the order of steps must be questioned. The starting point should be the

1148. *Ibid.*, para. 83
1149. *Ibid.*, para. 84.
1150. *See* already section 3.3.1.d for factors that facilitate collusion.
1151. Interestingly the Guidelines mention them in example 2 as a structural factor (*ibid.*, para. 107).
1152. *See* Motta (2004), p. 146.
1153. *See* Horizontal Cooperation Guidelines, para. 86.
1154. *Ibid.*, para. 89. Kühn argues that any exchange that involves individualised data should raise serious suspicion because 'it is very difficult to justify information exchange of individualized data in theory and in individual cases. It is very hard to construct hypothetical situations in which very disaggregated data on past actions is really necessary to achieve substantial efficiency gains' (Kühn (2001), p. 196).
1155. *See* Horizontal Cooperation Guidelines, para. 90.
1156. *Ibid.*, paras 92-93.
1157. *Ibid.*, para. 91.
1158. *Ibid.*, para. 94.
1159. *Ibid.*, paras 87-88.

characteristics of the exchanged information. As explained below, the analytical framework should start with whether the information exchange in question should be classified as a restriction by object or effect.[1160] For such assessment the characteristics of the information exchange are more relevant than the structural features of the market. Although the analysis of the context is also required for the classification, such assessment does not entail a full effects analysis considering all relevant structural factors of the market.

Only if it does not become obvious from the assessment of the characteristics of the information exchanged, in light of the legal and economic context, that the exchange has an anti-competitive objective, one should engage in a more in-depth economic analysis.[1161] This reversed analytical approach would give the Horizontal Cooperation Guidelines greater clarity. They already indicate such approach, although not clearly enough, under the section that explains the Commission's approach on the scope of the object box.[1162]

6.1.3.c Collusion Concerns

Information exchanges can increase market transparency. This is a double-edged sword. On the one hand, increased market transparency brings significant efficiencies and can make markets more competitive.[1163] On the other hand, market transparency is also one of the factors that facilitate collusion.[1164]

The Horizontal Cooperation Guidelines provide three possible narratives on *how* information exchange can facilitate collusion. First, information exchange can help to reach a common understanding about the terms of the coordination. Agreeing on prices that are mutually beneficial and sustainable between firms with different cost structures and different products may be difficult.[1165] Information exchanges can help to overcome those difficulties by creating 'mutually consistent expectations regarding the uncertainties present in the market'.[1166]

The most useful information for collusion is that about firms' *future* intentions because it allows competitors to communicate where they would like a coordinated outcome to be, without actually having to commit to the coordinated equilibrium.[1167]

1160. *See* section 6.5.1 for the proposed analytical framework for identifying restrictions by object.
1161. *See* section 6.5.2 for the proposed analytical framework to assess pure information exchanges that are restrictive to competition by effect.
1162. *See* Horizontal Cooperation Guidelines, paras 73-74 (emphasis added): 'Exchanging information on companies' *individualised* intentions concerning future conduct regarding prices or quantities is particularly likely to lead to a collusive outcome. [...] Information exchanges between competitors of *individualised* data regarding intended future prices or quantities should therefore be considered a restriction of competition by object. In addition, *private exchanges* between competitors of their individualised intentions regarding future prices or quantities would normally be considered and fined as cartels because they generally have the object of fixing prices or quantities.'
1163. *See* already section 3.1.
1164. *See* already section 3.3.
1165. *See* Faull and Nikpay (2014), para. 7.414.
1166. Horizontal Cooperation Guidelines, para. 66.
1167. *See* Kühn (2001), p. 196; Faull and Nikpay (2014), para. 7.415.

This explains why the Horizontal Cooperation Guidelines provide that any exchange of information about individualised intentions concerning future conduct is most problematic and has to be assessed under the object box.[1168]

Conversely, if the exchange does not concern future intentions, the anti-competitive effects of the exchange have to be assessed (effect box). This is illustrated by the second example given in the Guidelines.[1169] Even though the exchange concerns recent data about output and prices and even though the structural market conditions tend to facilitate collusion (concentrated and non-complex market with homogeneous products), the exchange does not constitute a restriction by object. Instead, the anti-competitive effects have to be considered (which exist in this example).

Second, information exchange can also increase the internal stability of collusion. This is because increased transparency enables members of the collusion to monitor and thus punish those firms that deviate from the collusive outcome.[1170] If firms are not able to detect cheating, collusion is not sustainable and will break down.[1171]

Third, information exchanges can also increase the external stability of collusion. This is because increased transparency enables members of the collusion to observe when and how new firms enter the market.[1172] In other words, market transparency can enable colluding firms to target new players and thus prevent them from undercutting the collusive outcome in the first place.[1173] This collusion narrative is connected with the foreclosure concern.[1174]

Although the theories of harm on collusion are economically sound,[1175] the analytical framework lacks a holistic approach that would have been desirable. One the one hand, the Horizontal Cooperation Guidelines fail to offer any guidance on how to *balance* the anti-competitive concerns with the efficiency-enhancing potential,[1176] despite the fact that this is one of the common themes in the case law.[1177] On the other hand, the Guidelines also fail to emphasise the importance of the indispensable test when choosing between different means to achieve efficiencies.[1178] Economic literature considers that the exchange of *aggregated* data achieves similar efficiencies as the exchange of individualised data but entails significantly less collusion concern. Similarly, the *public* exchange of future conduct on important competitive parameters (particularly price and quantity) may have the same collusion potential but materialises significant efficiencies through vertical market transparency. It is astonishing that the Horizontal Cooperation Guidelines completely fail to emphasise this.

1168. *See* Horizontal Cooperation Guidelines, para. 73.
1169. *Ibid.*, para. 107.
1170. *Ibid.*, para. 67.
1171. *See* Faull and Nikpay (2014), paras 7.417.
1172. *See* Horizontal Cooperation Guidelines, para. 68.
1173. *See* Faull and Nikpay (2014), paras 7.420.
1174. *See* Horizontal Cooperation Guidelines, para. 68.
1175. *See* already section 3.3.4 for a more extensive review of the economic literature on market transparency.
1176. *See* Wagner-von Papp (2012), pp. 5-6 and 31.
1177. *See* section 6.2.2.c.
1178. *Ibid.*, p. 31.

6.1.3.d Conclusion

The Horizontal Cooperation Guidelines represent the first policy statement by the Commission that offers more than just context-specific guidance on the assessment of information exchanges. The Guidelines are cautious though in their guidance. For the most parts, it merely codifies the decisional practice and case law. In that sense it is a first step in the right direction. However, the Horizontal Cooperation Guidelines lack a more comprehensive and sophisticated analytical framework for making the assessment of pure information exchanges even more straightforward. This is why this book, after the discussion of the relevant case law and decisional practice (*see* sections 6.2-6.4), proposes a refined analytical framework for pure information exchanges (*see* section 6.5).

6.2 RESTRICTIONS BY EFFECT CASES

This section discusses the case law and decisional practice on pure information exchanges that were considered as restrictions by effect (*see* section 6.2.1). Two perspectives are subsequently offered. The *descriptive* perspective identifies common themes in the case law (*see* section 6.2.2). The *normative* perspective explores the issue of safe harbours and their suitability for pure information exchanges (*see* section 6.2.3).

6.2.1 Case Law and Decisional Practice

6.2.1.a The John Deere *Case*

John Deere[1179] is the first case where the Commission carried out a comprehensive assessment of potential anti-competitive effects of a pure information exchange system.[1180] It is one of the cases around the UK Agricultural Tractor Registration Exchange in the late 1980s and 1990s.[1181] The case concerned two information exchange systems that were administrated by the Agricultural Engineers Association (AEA), a trade association open to all manufacturers and importers of agricultural tractors operating in the UK and with approximately 200 members at the time. The first information exchange system was notified to the Commission in 1988. It replaced an information exchange system from 1975 that has not been notified. The application for negative clearance was rejected by the Commission. This led to the notification of a second (alternative) information exchange system in 1990. Out of the approximately 200 members of the AEA, eight traders (which held a market share of 87%-88% on the

1179. Case T-35/92, *John Deere*; Case C-7/95 P, *John Deere* (appeal dismissed).
1180. *See* Niemeyer (1993), p. 152; Stroux (2004), p. 153; Møllgaard and Overgaard (2006), p. 121; Lévêque (2007), p. 233; OECD (2011), para. 34.
1181. There is another case that concerns the same information exchange: Case T-34/92, *Fiatagri*; Case C-8-95 P, *New Holland Ford* (appeal dismissed).

UK tractor market) participated in the first information exchange and five traders in the second one.[1182]

A dedicated data-processing company was responsible for collecting the data that has been given to the British Ministry of Transport to obtain a licence plate for a new tractor (*inter alia* manufacturer, model, selling dealer and postcode of keeper of the vehicle). The data was prepared and provided to the members of the information exchange system. It contained information about aggregate industry sales (including a breakdown by horsepower or driveline), sales of each member (number of units and market shares in various geographical areas) and sales made by dealers in the distribution network of each member (which enabled to identify imports and exports between different dealers' territories).[1183] The data exchange related to past conduct of the members and did not involve future intentions.[1184]

The system was not regarded as having an anti-competitive object,[1185] which is why the GC considered possible anti-competitive effects on the agricultural tractor market. First, the GC analysed the characteristics of the *market*. On the supply side, the market was characterised as concentrated[1186] (four main suppliers with market shares between 75% and 80% that have been relatively stable over time) with high barriers to enter (also because of customers' brand loyalty)[1187] and products that were regarded as sufficiently homogeneous.[1188] On the demand side, buyers were dispersed with little buyer power.[1189]

Second, the GC also analysed the characteristics of the *information exchange*. The information exchange concerned fairly recent sales[1190] made by each dealer in their respective territory (private data).[1191] The data could only be accessed by members of the information exchange (private exchange).[1192] The data enabled the identification of individual sales of individual competitors and dealers.[1193] The exchange also took place frequently and regularly.[1194]

1182. *See* Case T-35/92, *John Deere*, paras 1-5.
1183. *Ibid.*, paras 13-16.
1184. *See* Stroux (2004), p. 151.
1185. *See* Case T-35/92, *John Deere*, paras 47 and 93. As noted by Robertson, this would be consistent with the approach of the Horizontal Cooperation Guidelines since the exchange concerned past sales data and not future intentions (*see* Robertson (2013), p. 469).
1186. In *Thyssen Stahl* the CJ emphasises that concentration is not the only factor that should be considered in analysing information exchanges and any argument that merely looks at the level of concentration is flawed (*see* Case C-194/99 P, *Thyssen Stahl*, para. 86).
1187. *See* Case T-35/92, *John Deere*, para. 74.
1188. *Ibid.*, paras 51 and 78-80. Scholars have pointed out that the products may have not been as homogeneous as assumed by the Court and the Commission (*see* Robertson (2013), p. 470).
1189. *See* Case T-35/92, *John Deere*, paras 74 and 80.
1190. The exchange did not involve future intentions (*see* Kühn (2001), p. 194).
1191. *See* Case T-35/92, *John Deere*, para. 81.
1192. *Ibid.*, para. 84. This was the crucial difference to *Woodpulp II* which involved a system of quarterly price announcement that was accessible to all market players (*see* Case T-35/92, *John Deere*, para. 91). As noted by Albors-Llorens, this fact was highly significant to determine the boundaries between unlawful coordination and legitimate business practices (*see* Albors-Llorens (2006), pp. 862-863).
1193. *See* Case T-35/92, *John Deere*, para. 92.
1194. *Ibid.*, para. 81.

The GC concluded that the information exchange system was restricting competition (i) by raising barriers to enter the market and (ii) by increasing market transparency.[1195] On the first issue, even though the information exchange system was open to all members, the system constitutes a significant barrier for non-members of the exchange system (such as new traders from other EU countries). Whenever a new trader decided not to join, he did not gain access to important market knowledge. This gave participating firms a competitive advantage. Conversely, when he decided to join, he immediately revealed his business strategy to his biggest competitors. This made it easier for bigger competitors to attack him more targeted.[1196] Thus, the information exchange reduced the competitive pressure mainly coming from new traders from other EU countries.[1197]

On the second issue, the GC concluded that the increased transparency about the market positions and strategies of their competitors reduced 'the degree of uncertainty regarding the operation of the market, which would have existed in the absence of such an exchange of information'.[1198] This statement has to be seen in light of the concentrated market structure. An increased market transparency in an already highly concentrated market would likely prevent any residual competition between participants of the exchange and thus restricted internal competition.[1199]

The GC also identified a vertical issue with indirect horizontal effects. The increased transparency enabled manufacturers to monitor their distribution system and thus to confer absolute territorial protection on their dealers.[1200] The indirect horizontal effect was that this made sustaining collusion at the suppliers' level easier because any deviation from the territorial market-sharing was more likely to be detected.[1201]

John Deere is the first case where a pure information exchange system was condemned to infringe Art. 101 TFEU because of the specific design of the information sharing system in a structurally problematic market context.[1202] As noted by Lévêque, the information exchange is no longer viewed as a way to move from a non-collusive equilibrium to a collusive equilibrium (concertation), but instead from one non-collusive equilibrium to another non-collusive equilibrium that is less beneficial for customers. The system in place reduced the incentive to attack other competitors.[1203]

1195. *Ibid.*, para. 98.
1196. *Ibid.*, para. 84.
1197. *See* OECD (2011), p. 19.
1198. Case T-35/92, *John Deere*, para. 81.
1199. *See* OECD (2011), p. 19.
1200. *See* Case T-35/92, *John Deere*, paras 49 and 96.
1201. *See* Bissocoli (2000), p. 96.
1202. *See* Kühn (2001), p. 194.
1203. This becomes clear from the Commission decision, *UK Agricultural Tractor Registration Exchange*, para. 43: 'In the absence of the Exchange, firms would have to compete in a market with some measure of uncertainty as to the exact place, degree and means of attack by rivals. This uncertainty is a normal competitive risk bringing about stronger competition because reaction and reduction of prices cannot be limited to the absolute minimum degree necessary to defend an established position. Uncertainty would lead the firms to compete more strongly than if they knew exactly how much of a response was necessary to meet competition. They

It effectively prevented residual competition ('surprise effect') between the participants of the system.[1204] In this sense, the competition analysis can also be understood in light of military strategies making combats less daring.[1205]

From an economic perspective, the reasoning of the GC is for the most parts robust and sound.[1206] The GC's conclusion would be not just consistent with earlier Commission policy statements[1207] but also with the approach of the current 2011 Horizontal Cooperation Guidelines.[1208] Economic theory clearly suggests that even the exchange of data on past conduct can facilitate collusion if it enables the detection of deviations from the collusive outcome.[1209] There was no justification that the degree of disaggregation (across the regional submarkets as well as products) was necessary to achieve the efficiency gains.[1210] The argument that the exchange in question was indispensable for the warranty or bonus claims is flawed since one could have designed the exchange differently so that the origin of the sales could not have been identified.[1211]

However, there are also substantive conclusions made by the GC whose economic robustness can be questioned. Kühn and Vives for instance criticise the conclusion that the information exchange in question created a barrier to enter the UK market. Instead, economic theory provides that information exchanges only impact market entrance if it facilitates coordinated *predatory* conduct, which is conduct that aims at making entrance more difficult.[1212] Furthermore, one could criticise the judgment because it upheld the Commission's decision on the basis of assumed or potential effects and thus merely applied a simplistic checklist approach.[1213] The

---

would have to exceed a minimum response, for instance by offering more favourable discounts to move their stock or by offering discounts for more products and in more territories.'

1204. *See* Capobianco (2004), p. 1252.
1205. *See* Lévêque (2007), pp. 233-234.
1206. *See* Jones and Sufrin (2016), pp. 685-686. *See also* Peeperkorn (1996), pp. 16-17 who notes that it fits well with game theory.
1207. For this observation, *see* Capobianco (2004), p. 1251.
1208. *See* Robertson (2013), p. 470. However, she notes that although the final conclusion under the Guidelines would be the same, the legal appraisal would be different: 'the analysis under the Guidelines diverges from the Court's appraisal in so far as the Court primarily viewed the *reduction of uncertainty* regarding the operation of the market as a competition concern that was strong enough to warrant the conclusion that there were (potential) effects of restricting competition. The concern that less secrecy and uncertainty in the market will automatically lead to an anti-competitive outcome is not founded in economics, and is not present as such in the Guidelines. Instead, the Guidelines clearly regard *transparency* as problematic where it is combined with a tight oligopoly, and where other competitive harms would be adduced' (emphasis added).
1209. *See* Kühn and Vives (1995), p. 99. *See* already section 3.3.4 about the collusion concerns caused by increased market transparency.
1210. *See* Kühn (2001), p. 195.
1211. *See* Kühn and Vives (1995), p. 100; Møllgaard and Overgaard (2006), p. 121.
1212. *See* Kühn and Vives (1995), pp. 101-102. For a less critical, although legal perspective, on this issue, *see* Capobianco (2004), p. 1252 who identifies the creation of market barriers caused by the information exchange as one of the main anti-competitive effects. For such strategy, *see* *Fatty Acids* decision in section 6.3.1.a.
1213. *See* Robertson (2013), p. 471.

Commission had not shown that actual anti-competitive effects took place.[1214] Niemeyer criticises the judgment because it suggests the establishment of per se violation for information exchanges in highly concentrated markets.[1215] While this conclusion may be overexaggerated, the fact remains that any exchange of information in concentrated market is more problematic. However, the case still leaves room for lawful information exchanges in concentrated markets if they do not enable the identification of individual market conduct of competitors.

6.2.1.b The Eudim *Decision*

The *Eudim* decision[1216] provides a useful example for an information exchange system in a non-oligopolistic market. Eudim Group was an association of wholesalers for installation materials – which consists of plumbing, heating and sanitary products (PHS)[1217] – with the aim of promoting European wholesaling through the exchange of information.[1218] The association consisted of only 12 European wholesalers out of over 3,000.[1219]

From the perspective of wholesalers two markets were relevant: the sales market and the purchase market for installation materials. The *sales* market tended to be mostly national and highly fragmented. Even though members of Eudim were among the biggest wholesalers (ranging from being number one to number four), they only had a market share between 1.3% and 12%. Furthermore, the market for installation materials covered a product range of over 1 million products in Europe with variations by country between 30,000 and 300,000. The *purchase* market on the other hand tended to be EU-wide and quite concentrated. Suppliers were generally specialised in certain segments and had EU-wide market shares of up to 80%.[1220] Thus, from the perspective of wholesalers, the structural conditions of the market did not facilitate collusion.

Members of Eudim exchanged information that related to both the sales and purchase market. Most of the information related to the *purchase* market where members of Eudim exchanged information about purchase prices and conditions (such as terms of delivery, terms of payment, discounts, costs and stocks and quantities). In relation to the *sales* market, members of Eudim exchanged know-how and other commercially sensitive information about sales markets (such as ratios about costs, profitability, stock, turnover, sales, sales trends and market penetration).[1221]

1214. Case T-35/92, *John Deere*, para. 92: 'the fact that the Commission is not able to demonstrate that the information exchange system at issue produces an *actual* anti-competitive effect on the United Kingdom agricultural tractor market does not affect the outcome of the case since Article [101](1) of the Treaty prohibits both actual anti-competitive effects and purely potential effects, provided that they are sufficiently appreciable' (emphasis added).
1215. *See* Niemeyer (1993), p. 155.
1216. Commission decision, *Eudim*.
1217. *Ibid.*, para. 5.
1218. *Ibid.*, para. 3.
1219. *Ibid.*, para. 6.
1220. *Ibid.*, paras 6-7.
1221. *Ibid.*, paras 9-10.

The role of Eudim ranged from setting-up a central database containing all the information that was exchanged, to providing the venue that facilitated the meetings between the members. Since the information exchange also took place directly between members of Eudim, this case can be described as a hybrid between direct and indirect information exchange.

The Commission concluded that the information exchange on neither of these two markets restricted competition to an appreciable extent, even though the information was highly individualised.[1222] With regard to the exchange on the *purchase* market, the Commission followed the argument made by Eudim that the exchange was necessary to strengthen the position of its members vis-à-vis their suppliers in order to obtain the best purchase prices.[1223] With regard to the exchange on the *sales* market the decisive factor for the substantive conclusion was the non-oligopolistic market structure at the level of wholesalers. The Commission noted that the 'exchange of confidential and individual information such as sales volumes and market shares, which is normally not divulged to competitors may restrict competition, in particular on an oligopolistic market. However, although all Eudim members take prominent positions on their national markets, the wholesale PHS market is too fragmented (there are more than 3 000 European wholesalers) to be considered oligopolistic.'[1224]

The decision demonstrates the importance of the market structure for assessing pure information exchanges. Even highly individualised data may not restrict competition to an appreciable extent if the exchange took place among players in a fragmented market.[1225] The substantive conclusion is economically sound. There was a lack of concentration at the wholersalers' level, and wholesalers faced significant market power from supplier. Both elements are factors that make collusion less likely.[1226]

Capobianco even goes so far as to argue that the decision seems to suggest a presumption of legality for information exchanges in competitive environments.[1227] However, it is not wise to merely focus on one factor that facilitates collusion. The analytical framework for assessing information exchanges is too multifactored. Still, the decision can be used as an example that it is more difficult in fragmented markets to demonstrate anti-competitive effects.

An interesting issue is also the relationship between the disaggregation of information and the fragmented nature of the market (the market covered a product range of over 1 million products). As explained,[1228] economic theory provides that product heterogeneity on its own has an ambiguous effect on the likelihood of collusion. However, when individualised information is exchanged in markets with product heterogeneity, collusion concerns are less pronounced than in market with

1222. *Ibid.*, paras 11-13.
1223. *Ibid.*, paras 9 and 12. *See also*, on this issue, Capobianco (2004), p. 1255 who identifies this as crucial for the outcome of the case.
1224. Commission decision, *Eudim*, para. 13.
1225. Noted also by Carle and Johnsson (1998), p. 76; Bissocoli (2000), pp. 98-99.
1226. *See* already section 3.3.1.d.
1227. *See* Capobianco (2004), p. 1267.
1228. Section 3.3.1.d.

product homogeneity. This is because commercially sensitive information is more difficult to interpret and utilise for collusion purposes if products are differentiated.[1229]

6.2.1.c The **CEPI-Cartonboard** *Decision*

The *CEPI-Cartonboard* decision[1230] concerned a modified information exchange system where CEPI-Cartonboard, the trade association of European board producers with members representing roughly 90% of the total European Cartonboard market,[1231] collected statistical data for its members. The system was modified after the Commission found in its *Cartonboard* decision that the old information exchange system facilitated a price and market-sharing cartel arrangement that existed among Cartonboard producers for five years.[1232] The aim of the new notified system was to continue to collect, collate and disseminate useful statistical information for its members.[1233] Only after some changes to the original notified system, the Commission gave negative clearance.[1234]

The original notified system provided a number of safeguards to address collusion concerns. Only historic data on consumption, production, capacity, order-inflows and order-backlog was collected. It did no longer cover prices and forecast regarding production and capacity utilisation. The individualised data received from its members were also no longer distributed to them in an individualised form. Also, the data was no longer discussed at meetings.[1235]

Still, the Commission raised concerns that some reports (namely on consumption and order-inflows) would have enabled the identification of individual producers. The concern was addressed by further aggregating some of the data.[1236] In this case the aggregation of at least three producers was seen as sufficient to prevent identification of firms' conduct.[1237] While this may be a useful rule of thumb for most situations, it does not protect undertakings from scrutiny (i.e., there is no safe harbour) since the individual circumstances may justify an even stricter approach.[1238] However, the decision emphasises the importance of disaggregation for Commission's enforcement priorities.[1239]

More generally, the decision is a good example for the importance of data aggregation when collecting statistical data.[1240] Even though commercially sensitive data was exchanged, it was sufficiently aggregated to prevent the identification of individual producers. In other words, the sufficient aggregation of the data was crucial

1229. *See* Carle and Johnsson (1998), p. 77; Capobianco (2004), p. 1268; OECD (2011), para. 62.
1230. Commission decision, *Cartonboard.*
1231. *Ibid.*, para. 3.
1232. *See* Commission decision, *Cartonboard*; Commission decision, *CEPI-Cartonboard*, paras 1-2.
1233. *See* Commission decision, *CEPI-Cartonboard*, para. 10.
1234. *Ibid.*, para. 19.
1235. *Ibid.*, paras 10-15.
1236. *Ibid.*, paras 16-18.
1237. *See* Carle and Johnsson (1998), p. 76; Bissocoli (2000), p. 99.
1238. On this *see also* Capobianco (2004), p. 1254.
1239. *See* Stroux (2004), pp. 154-155.
1240. *See* OECD (2011), para. 36.

for the substantive assessment that anti-competitive collusion concerns only played a minor role when weighted against the pro-competitive efficiencies (such as market knowledge and benchmarking).

6.2.1.d The **Wirtschaftsvereinigung Stahl** *Decision*

In the *Wirtschaftsvereinigung Stahl* decision,[1241] an information exchange system was notified to the Commission by the Wirtschaftsvereinigung Stahl, the German steel industry trade association, and 16 of its members.[1242] The role of the trade association was to collect data. Although at the time of the notification only 16 of its members participated (out of 74), the plan was that all members should join in the near future.[1243]

Analysing the characteristics of the information exchange, several elements of the exchange were seen as problematic. With regard to the *inner* layer of the information exchange, the exchange entailed individualised and commercially sensitive information (data about market shares and data on deliveries broken down by quality and consumer industries).[1244] The participating firms received data not only for the sector in which they produced, but also for sectors in which they did not produce anything.[1245] The data was also fairly recent (one month old).[1246] With regard to the *outer* layer of the information exchange, only those firms that participated in the exchange received the data. It was subsequently not made available to other players.[1247] The exchange took place quite frequently (every month).[1248]

The structure of the steel market was problematic and structurally prone to collusion. The steel market was concentrated[1249] with high barriers to enter due to significant investments required at the initial phase.[1250] Several structural links existed among steel producers.[1251] The products made by producers were homogeneous and the different competitive parameters (delivery time, transport costs, etc.) were relatively easy to compare.[1252]

The Commission concluded that the information exchange in question restricted competition. It concluded that the system enables competitors to identify those undertakings that tried to increase their market share and take retaliatory measures against them.[1253] Therefore, it ordered to refrain from implementing the notified exchange.

1241. Commission decision, *Wirtschaftsvereinigung Stahl.*
1242. *Ibid.*, para. 1.
1243. *Ibid.*, para. 19.
1244. *Ibid.*, para. 13.
1245. *Ibid.*, para. 14.
1246. *Ibid.*, para. 17.
1247. *Ibid.*, paras 14 and 18.
1248. *Ibid.*, para. 17.
1249. *Ibid.*, para. 45.
1250. *Ibid.*, para. 22.
1251. *Ibid.*, para. 45.
1252. *Ibid.*, para. 24.
1253. *Ibid.*, paras 45 and 60.

On the issue of market transparency, it should be noted that the exchange did not aim to increase market transparency for *prices*, whose benefits normally also materialise at the customers' level (such as lower search costs and more choice). Steel producers were already required to publish their price lists by EU law.[1254] Instead, the information exchange increased market transparency for *other factors* (namely market shares and deliveries) for which there was no obvious benefit for customers. Thus, the lack of efficiencies for customers is also an important element in this case.

Although the exchange of delivery data is generally not as useful for collusion,[1255] it was crucial for monitoring collusive outcomes in this specific market.[1256] The theory of harm developed by the Commission deviated from what economic theory generally suggests. However, the risk categories proposed by the economic literature are only intended to provide a rough guidance. Deviations are possible but should be justified in the effects analysis. The deviation from general economic theory may have been justified in this case due to the specific features of the steel market (competition for quantities and importance of delivery data for monitoring quantities).

On appeal though, the GC annulled the decision in its entirety because of two factual inaccuracies. The first related to the fact that the Commission stated in its decision that the notified system involved the exchange of market shares, while in reality the system involved the exchange of sales data for certain (not all) steel producers and thus only *indirectly* enable the calculation of approximate market shares.[1257]

The first factual inaccuracy would have not resulted in the annulment.[1258] However, the second did. The Commission based its assessment on questionnaires which did not form part of the notified information exchange.[1259] The Commission also failed to provide any proof that the exchange in these questionnaires had actually taken place.[1260] Since these questionnaires (which wrongly were considered as part of the notified agreement) provided the most detailed and accurate data,[1261] and thus were an important part of the conclusion that the notified system was anti-competitive, the GC had to annul the decision.[1262]

In conclusion, the Commission created a hypothetical scenario that did not align with the actual notified agreement. Based on the facts of that hypothetical scenario though, the Commission would have had good reasons to consider the agreement as anti-competitive. The decision would have complied well with economic theory.[1263] However, since the Commission's conclusion rested upon significant factual errors, the case can now mostly be used as an example for the effective judicial scrutiny of the GC.

1254. *Ibid.*, para. 25.
1255. *See* already section 3.3.6.b.
1256. *See* Capobianco (2004), p. 1254.
1257. *See* Case T-16/98, *Wirtschaftsvereinigung Stahl*, paras 27-29.
1258. *Ibid.*, para. 30.
1259. *Ibid.*, para. 31.
1260. *Ibid.*, para. 31.
1261. *Ibid.*, para. 37.
1262. *Ibid.*, para. 45.
1263. *See*, e.g., OECD (2011), para. 37 only discussing the economic analysis of the decision.

6.2.1.e *The* Thyssen Stahl *Case*

In the *Steel Beams* decision[1264] (also referred to as the *Thyssen Stahl* case), the Commission fined several undertakings on the market for steel beams for a series of agreements, decisions and concerted practices which had as their object *inter alia* the fixing of prices and allocation of quotas. One separate issue from these cartel activities was an information exchange system about current data of orders and deliveries where the level of aggregation was regarded as insufficient.[1265] The figures showing deliveries and orders received by each individual undertaking were updated every week and circulated rapidly among them.[1266] The Commission concluded that the exchange in question established a 'system of solidarity and cooperation designed to coordinate business activities'[1267] in light of the oligopolistic market structure.

While one could argue that the information exchange could have been dealt as part of the overall cartel, the Commission treated the information exchange system as a *separate* infringement. This separate treatment was confirmed by the GC[1268] and the CJ.[1269] The case is used by the literature ever since as an authority to argue that an information exchange in itself can constitute an infringement of Art. 101 TFEU.[1270]

On the substantive appraisal of facts, the GC confirmed the Commission's view that the level of disaggregation enabled the identification of the conduct of each undertaking,[1271] particularly since the information was very recent and the exchange took place frequently.[1272] The exchange was also limited to the participating undertakings (private market transparency).[1273] The information exchange was also regularly discussed on several occasions.[1274] Thus, the information exchange system in place was an effective means to monitor each other's conduct.[1275] The regime ultimately undermined the independence of decision-making of each of the participating undertaking because it facilitated the establishment and maintenance of collusion outcomes.[1276]

6.2.1.f *The* EATA Decision *(Borderline Case)*

In the *EATA* decision,[1277] the parties have notified to the Commission the establishment of the Europe Asia Traders Agreement (EATA) which concerned the scheduled

1264. *See* Commission decision, *Steel Beams*.
1265. *Ibid.*, paras 263-271.
1266. *Ibid.*, para. 267.
1267. *Ibid.*, para. 269.
1268. *See* Case T-141/94, *Thyssen Stahl*, paras 385-412.
1269. *Ibid.*, paras 58-90.
1270. *See*, e.g., Faull and Nikpay (2014), para. 8.43. *See* already section 2.1.1 on the conceptual difference between pure and ancillary information exchanges.
1271. *See* Case T-141/94, *Thyssen Stahl*, para. 394.
1272. *Ibid.*, para. 395.
1273. *Ibid.*, para. 398.
1274. *Ibid.*, para. 402.
1275. *Ibid.*, para. 402.
1276. *Ibid.*, para. 406.
1277. Commission decision, *EATA*.

maritime transport services for the carriage of containerised cargo from North Europe to Far East.[1278] The aim was to establish a 'capacity management programme' under which parties agreed not to use a proportion of the space on their vessels for the carriage of goods on a particular route.[1279] One of the recitals in the agreement provided that the objective was an 'improvement of revenue' and to remedy the 'consistently depressed freight rates'.[1280] The Commission hesitated though to classify the agreement as a restriction of object. Instead, it left the question open and concluded that the EATA had the 'object or effect' of restriction competition.[1281]

One aspect of the decision was the information exchange of disaggregated data.[1282] The Commission concluded that the exchange enabled the parties to learn about competitors' actual liftings of cargo, their capacity, their level of capacity utilisation as well their forecasts on non-scope cargo and capacity.[1283] One could argue that the information exchange as such should have been classified as a restriction by effect. However, one could also argue that the information exchange was part of the overall EATA and therefore ancillary. If the exchange was ancillary, it did not shift the market equilibrium towards a non-collusive equilibrium that made collusion more likely. Instead, collusion in the form of EATA (capacity allocation) did already take place.

The decision is rarely cited[1284] even though it is much more recent than the *UK Agricultural Tractor Registration Exchange* decision (*1999 vs 1993*). This has good reasons. The decision is not just conceptually underdeveloped but also substantially ambiguous. Neither the classification as a pure and ancillary information exchange (should have been probably ancillary) nor the classification as a restriction by object or effect (should have been probably a restriction by object) is clear. If the decision demonstrates one thing, it is that without a proper analytical framework the assessment of information exchanges is made unnecessarily complex.

6.2.1.g The **Asnef-Equifax** *Case*

In *Asnef-Equifax,*[1285] the CJ was asked by a Spanish court to provide a preliminary reference on the legality of the information exchange system on debtor information for which Asnef-Equifax submitted a request to grant an exemption under Spanish competition law.

1278. *Ibid.*, para. 2. *See* section 6.4.2.b for a subsequent commitment decision in this sector regarding the issue of signalling via public announcements.
1279. *Ibid.*, para. 29 for this definition.
1280. *Ibid.*, para. 9.
1281. *Ibid.*, para. 151.
1282. *Ibid.*, paras 154-155. This aspect was also mentioned by Whish (2006), p. 33.
1283. *See* Commission decision, *EATA*, para. 155.
1284. One of those few citations of these decisions can be found in Capobianco (2004), fn 50; Whish (2006), p. 33.
1285. Case C-238/05, *Asnef-Equifax*.

The purpose of the system was to provide solvency and credit information relating to the risks in lending and credit activities.[1286] The proposed credit information exchange system would have provided lenders with negative information (e.g., non-payment) as well as positive information (e.g., outstanding credit balances, collaterals, guarantees and securities, leasing transactions or temporary disposal of assets) about borrowers.[1287] The Spanish Tribunal de Defensa de la Competencia (contrary to the administrative body responsible for the protection of competition) granted such exemption on two conditions: The register (1) must be accessible to all financial institutions on a non-discriminatory basis against payment of a fee and (2) must not disclose the information to lenders.[1288]

The CJ concluded that the proposed register did not have as its object the restriction of competition.[1289] Therefore it was necessary to assess its anti-competitive effects. Before assessing the structure of the market and the nature of the information exchange, the CJ emphasised three important principles. First, the national court had to consider the actual context in which the proposed register occurs; particularly the legal and economic context, the structure of the market and the nature of the goods.[1290] This required a holistic assessment of the facts in light of the actual economic reality. The proposed system could not simply be assessed in the abstract. Second, the national court could not confine itself to only consider its actual effects, but it also had to consider its potential effects.[1291] This is in line with *John Deere* and the criticised simplistic checklist approach. Third, the CJ also emphasised that the benchmark for an information exchange system to be anti-competitive is the reduction of 'the degree of uncertainty as to the operation of the market in question'.[1292] This is in line with the independence doctrine as established in *Suiker Unie* outside the context of information exchanges.[1293]

Although it was for the national court to assess whether the proposed register had the effect of restricting competition (the nature of a preliminary reference), the CJ nevertheless proceeded with its own analysis and left little margin for the national court to decide differently.[1294] The market was fragmented (as opposed to concentrated), the identity of lenders was not revealed and the access was non-discriminatory.[1295] Although the proposed register was liable to reduce the uncertainty of the credit risk (an efficiency),[1296] it was not liable to reduce the uncertainty as to the

1286. *Ibid.*, para. 7.
1287. *Ibid.*, para. 46.
1288. *Ibid.*, para. 8.
1289. *Ibid.*, paras 48, 54 and 57. This would be consistent with the approach of the Guidelines because the system did not concern the exchange of future intentions (*see* Robertson (2013), p. 475).
1290. *See* Case C-238/05, *Asnef-Equifax*, paras 49 and 54.
1291. *Ibid.*, para. 50.
1292. *Ibid.*, para. 51.
1293. *See* already section 4.2.1.b.2.
1294. This was also noted by Robertson (2013), p. 473.
1295. *See* Case C-238/05, *Asnef-Equifax*, paras 58-60.
1296. *Ibid.*, paras 55-56.

future market conduct of competitors.[1297] Therefore, the CJ concluded that the proposed register was not liable to have the effect of restricting competition.[1298]

The overall appraisal of the register can be summarised as follows: the overall design of the information exchange (the two conditions required by the Spanish Tribunal de Defensa de la Competencia) and the market context (fragmented market) enabled the materialisation of significant efficiencies on the Spanish lending market (overcoming the problem of information asymmetry) without having any significant anti-competitive effects.[1299] The CJ identified a market failure (information asymmetry) that was addressed via a sound system of information exchange.[1300] The judgment must be appraised on its sound economic analysis on carefully analysing the anti-competitive effects of the information exchange in question. The guidance in the Horizontal Cooperation Guidelines would have resulted in the same substantive conclusion.[1301]

6.2.2 Descriptive Perspective: Identifying Some Common Themes

6.2.2.a The Issue of Disaggregation

The Commission identified very early that one of the main problematic features of any information exchange is the level of disaggregation of the data exchanged. The issue was already raised by the first policy statement of the Commission in 1968.[1302] It was also the common theme of the early decisional practice of the Commission.[1303]

Thus, it is not surprising that the level of disaggregation of the information exchange is also the common theme in the more recent case law and decisional practice. For instance, in *John Deere* the high degree of disaggregation was regarded as one reason why residual competition between participants of the information exchange system had been eliminated. One of the main modifications of the information exchange system in the *CEPI-Cartonboard* decision was the higher level of aggregation required by the Commission in order to give negative clearance. In *Thyssen Stahl*, the exchanged data about orders and deliveries was viewed as insufficiently aggregated because it enabled the identification of the conduct of each individual undertaking on a market where prices had to published.

While the level of disaggregation was already identified by the early literature as one of the main obstacles for the legality of pure information exchanges (mainly in reference to the early decisional practice),[1304] more recent literature points out to the

1297. *Ibid.*, para. 62.
1298. *Ibid.*, para. 61.
1299. *See also* OECD (2011), para. 39; Smith, Ridyard and Petrescu (2015), p. 37; Jones and Sufrin (2016), p. 689.
1300. *See* Ibáñez Colomo (2019b), p. 595.
1301. *See* Robertson (2013), pp. 476-477.
1302. *See* already section 6.1.1.
1303. *See* already section 6.1.2.
1304. *See*, e.g., Niemeyer (1993), p. 153 who notes that 'the Commission does not object to trade associations exchanging statistics which give an aggregate picture of the production and sales

economic robustness of such view.[1305] According to economic theory detailed and disaggregated information about each other's conduct increases the internal stability of collusion. This is because deviations can be attributed to specific firms and be punished more targeted. This makes punishment not just more likely but also cheaper.[1306]

It should be noted that the approach taken by the Commission and the EU Courts is rather conservative. Economic theory also provides that in certain circumstances (particularly when markets are highly concentrated) even the exchange of *aggregated* data may be sufficient to increase the internal stability of collusion.[1307] The idea is that the fact that colluding firms are able to observe that a cheat has occurred, irrespective of the attribution of the deviation to a specific firm, may be sufficient to facilitate collusion. This would then trigger punishment mechanisms and deter cheating to occur in the first place.

However, the conservative approach taken by the Commission and the EU Courts can be justified from a legal perspective. It provides clear guidance for undertakings on how to design information exchanges that aim to materialise the benefits derived from the exchange of statistical data. The legal certainty of such clear rule provides the right incentive effects for undertakings in an *ex post* assessment system of Art. 101 TFEU.[1308]

In this sense the stricter position taken by the Horizontal Cooperation Guidelines that even the exchange of disaggregated information may be problematic in certain situations[1309] can be criticised on the basis that it overlooks this consideration. The formulation in the Horizontal Cooperation Guidelines 'was more geared towards catching every possible anticompetitive effect ex-post rather than looking at what is relevant: the ex-ante incentive effect'.[1310] It has to been seen whether the stricter position taken by the Horizontal Cooperation Guidelines will find its way into the decisional practice and case law. It would certainly not be desirable from the perspective of legal certainty.

of the relevant industry. These data can be broken down by product, country and period of time. It is, however, necessary to avoid that the information, although aggregate data, allows indirectly the identification of the output or sales of individual undertakings. Thus, trade associations should not reveal data in their statistics or reports if less than three companies sold the product in question during that specific period of time.' Similarly, Bissocoli (2000, p. 81) argues that '[o]bviously, the dissemination of detailed non historical price information is most likely to have anti-competitive effects'.

1305. *See*, e.g., González (2012), pp. 36-38; Smith, Ridyard and Petrescu (2015), p. 38.

1306. *See* already section 3.3.4.b.

1307. *See*, e.g., Wagner-von Papp (2012), pp. 268-269.

1308. *See* Kühn (2010), p. 420.

1309. *See* Horizontal Cooperation Guidelines, para. 89: 'Nevertheless, the possibility cannot be excluded that even the exchange of aggregated data may facilitate a collusive outcome in markets with specific characteristics. Namely, members of a very tight and stable oligopoly exchanging aggregated data who detect a market price below a certain level could automatically assume that someone has deviated from the collusive outcome and take market-wide retaliatory steps. In other words, in order to keep collusion stable, companies may not always need to know who deviated, it may be enough to learn that "someone" deviated.'

1310. Kühn (2010), p. 420.

6.2.2.b *The Importance of the Market Structure Analysis*

The market structure plays an important part in the substantive appraisal on whether an information exchange is considered as anti-competitive or not. In particular the level of concentration and market barriers play a crucial role in the assessment (*see* for instance *John Deere* or *Wirtschaftsvereinigung Stahl*).[1311] While other factors sometimes further support a substantive conclusion (such as brand loyalty in *John Deere*), they are not as important in practice.

Conversely, if the market is fragmented there seems to be more willingness to recognise significant efficiencies. The best example for this is the *Eudim* decision, where the Commission concluded that the information exchange did not entail any anti-competitive effects because the downstream sales market was highly fragmented, and the firms' collective market power was significantly constrained by the upstream market which tended to be concentrated. The Commission recognised the efficiency of leveraging the bargaining position to achieve better purchase prices, despite the fact that the exchange involved highly disaggregated data. In *Asnef-Equifax*, the fragmented market structure was also one crucial element in the overall substantive appraisal that the information exchange brings significant efficiencies to the Spanish lending market (by overcoming the market failure of information asymmetry).

The importance of the market structure puts a relatively high burden on undertakings operating in an oligopolistic market on how to design the information exchange in a way that it falls outside the scope of Art. 101 TFEU. Particularly since it is sufficient for enforcers to demonstrate that the information exchange results in merely potential effects on competition.[1312] However, the case law does not seem to indicate that *any* information exchange in concentrated market will be scrutinised. Instead, the focus is on the level of disaggregation of the data. Both *John Deere* and *Wirtschaftsvereinigung Stahl* concerned information exchanges with disaggregated data that enables the identification of individual market conduct of competitors.

The emphasis on the market structure is also perfectly consistent with economic theory. Market concentration and market entry are two of the main factors that facilitate collusion.[1313] Market concentration increases the internal stability of collusion because if there are few players in the market cheating can be detected more easily. Even small changes may be attributed to certain players. Market entry on the other hand increases the external stability of collusion. The higher the barriers to enter, the lower the threat of potential competitors threatening the collusive outcome.

If the rationale of prohibiting such types of information exchanges in markets that are structurally prone to collusion is to prevent the emergence of conditions that make collusion easier to achieve, the approach has a *preventive* character. It resembles similarities with the assessment of coordinated effects in merger control. What is prohibited is not actual collusion, but the likely prospective of collusion caused by

1311. *See* Lenares (1997), p. 67; Capobianco (2004), p. 1266; Whish (2006), pp. 29-31; Vives (2006a), p. 92; Kyprianides (2012), p. 409; Jones and Sufrin (2016), p. 687.
1312. *See* Stroux (2004), p. 156.
1313. *See* already section 3.3.1.d.

certain market conditions. While in merger control the change of the market condition is caused by the merger, under Art. 101 TFEU the change is caused by the information exchange. Such preventive approach seems to be pragmatic from a legal point of view because it aims to pre-empt the legal challenges faced by enforcers when trying to condemn mere parallel conduct.

6.2.2.c The Lack of Using of Art. 101(3) TFEU

Another interesting observation from the case law is the lack of use of Art. 101(3) TFEU. Instead, the focus has been on Art. 101(1) TFEU.[1314] Those information exchange systems that generated significant efficiencies (*Eudim* and *Asnef-Equifax*) were viewed as not to entail any anti-competitive effects at all. Consequently, there was no need to consider Art. 101(3) TFEU. In other cases, the claim by parties that restrictive effects of the information exchange were outbalanced by efficiencies was dismissed. In *John Deere*, for instance, the GC rejected the argument that the information exchange was indispensable for warranty or bonus claims since the exchange could have been designed differently so that the origin of the sales could not have been identified.

One could argue that the analysis in Art. 101(1) TFEU already entails the assessment of the indispensability of the information exchange. If there are other less restrictive means available in order to achieve similar efficiencies, then *not* using those less restrictive means makes the information exchange anti-competitive. The importance of the principle of indispensability has been already emphasised by the economic literature. For instance, if firms want to achieve efficiencies that come with exchanging past data on prices or quantities (such as benchmarking), the exchange of aggregated data is normally sufficient to achieve these efficiencies.[1315]

While the GC has explicitly rejected that EU competition law employs a 'rule of reason' under Art. 101(1) TFEU,[1316] where pro- and anti-competitive effects are weighed with each other, the inclusion of the principle of indispensability in the analysis of Art. 101(1) TFEU seems to question that. If the analysis under Art. 101(1) TFEU not just limits itself to assess the anti-competitive nature of the information exchange, but also assesses which other means are available to achieve similar efficiencies, this indirectly resembles elements of a rule of reason approach.

6.2.3 Normative Perspective: Are Safe Harbours Desirable?

6.2.3.a Safe Harbours Based on Market Shares

The Commission has currently not established safe harbours based on market shares for pure information exchanges. The idea would be that those information exchanges

1314. *See* Whish (2006), pp. 40-41.
1315. *See* already section 3.3.6.c.
1316. *See* Case T-328/03, *O2 Germany*, para. 69.

that do not exceed a certain market share threshold would fail to appreciably affect competition.

The Commission has already established market share thresholds in various Guidelines and BERs with the aim to provide legal certainty for undertakings. If those market share thresholds are not exceeded, the conduct either falls outside the scope of Art. 101(1) TFEU (in case of a BER such the Specialisation BER or R&D-BER) or it is very unlikely to be pursued by the Commission (in case of safe harbours set out by Guidelines).

The idea of appreciability that is associated with safe harbours can be found in the *Eudim* decision. The Commission concluded that the information exchange in question did not restrict competition to an appreciable extent, even though the exchanged information was highly disaggregated. For the upstream purchase market, the information exchange enabled wholesalers to gain a better bargaining position and thus negotiate better prices. For the downstream sales market, the Commission concluded that the exchange did not appreciably restrict competition because the downstream market was too fragmented (more than 3,000 European wholesalers). The underlying idea in both markets was that the increased market power by wholesalers did not produce appreciable effects on competition, either because the market power was offset by more powerful players (concentrated upstream market) or insufficient to be employed effectively (fragmented downstream market). Thus, the decision raises the question whether market share thresholds should not also be used for information exchanges.

Furthermore, the Horizontal Cooperation Guidelines provide that only those information exchanges may entail restrictive effects on competition that 'cover a sufficiently large part of the relevant market'.[1317] Otherwise undertakings that do not participate in the exchange are able to constrain the participating undertakings and thus threaten the external stability of the collusive outcome.[1318]

However, there are several arguments why safe harbours based on market share thresholds are *not* desirable for information exchanges. First, market share thresholds give insufficient weight to the individual circumstances of the case. They may lead to type II errors where an anti-competitive information exchange is not condemned simply because it does not exceed a market share threshold. It is that simplicity and inflexibility of market share thresholds that runs counter to the necessary analytical flexibility.[1319] The *Eudim* decision should be understood as an example for the need of a flexible analytical approach that is able to consider the specific circumstances of the information exchange and the market structure.

Second, another risk with market share thresholds is that they provide wrong incentives for undertakings which result in detrimental outcomes for society overall. This argument refers to type I errors where a pro-competitive information exchange is wrongly condemned. Undertakings may get the wrong impression that information

1317. Horizontal Cooperation Guidelines, para. 87.
1318. *See* Horizontal Cooperation Guidelines, para. 87.
1319. *See* already section 3.3.1.d.4 for that desirable analytical approach.

exchange regimes above a certain market share threshold suddenly become anti-competitive. This might even result in a situation where firms refuse to share information with other firms simply because of the fear of competition law scrutiny that might come with the exceedance of a certain threshold.[1320] Such thresholds would therefore shift the analytical focus away from more important factors for assessing information exchanges (certain problematic characteristics such as the high level of disaggregation) to less important factors (the market coverage). This runs counter to the holistic analytical approach necessary for information exchanges. Such market share thresholds would also distract from the significant potential for efficiencies of information exchanges that have wide market coverage (such as benchmarking). What matters in such situation is not *if* the information exchange takes place but *how* it takes place (e.g., exchange of aggregated information instead of disaggregated information).

Third, any level of market share threshold for information exchanges is arbitrary. The thresholds set out in the Horizontal Cooperation Guidelines and the BERs for cooperation agreements follow the logic that the closer the cooperation is to the final customer, the lower the threshold (25% for R&D agreements, 20% for specialisation agreements, 15% for purchasing and commercialisation agreements). Information exchanges do not fit in this logic because they can occur in all these contexts. However, some authors have suggested that a market share threshold of 20% might be sensible.[1321] It is a sensible starting point because the threshold should in any case be set above the thresholds in the De Minimis Notice (10% in a horizontal setting, 15% in a vertical setting). Still, even the Horizontal Cooperation Guidelines abstain from providing any concrete market share threshold for information exchanges.[1322]

The fundamental problem remains that any market share threshold has the inherent problem of trying to provide a catch-all solution to a problem that deserves a tailor-made assessment. For instance, while economic theory risk classifies exchanges of deliveries generally lower than exchanges of prices, the exact opposite has been concluded in *Eudim* and *Thyssen Stahl*. While the former case concerned the exchange of price but was not considered anti-competitive, the latter case merely concerned the exchange of delivery but was considered anti-competitive.

Thus, the introduction of safe harbours based on market shares is a policy trap. At first sight it seems to offer legal certainty and clarity to an area that is widely considered as highly complex. However, at closer scrutiny such type of safe harbour would make the assessment of information exchange less logical and even more complicated. Less logical because safe harbours based on market shares would contradict the economic framework which requires a holistic analytical approach where the market coverage is only one small puzzle. More complicated because undertakings (and lawyers) do then have to consider the interplay between the rather

1320. *See* Käis (2013), p. 358.
1321. *See*, e.g., Bennet and Collins (2010), p. 332; OECD (2011), para. 77; Käis (2013), p. 357.
1322. *See* Horizontal Cooperation Guidelines, para. 88: 'What constitutes "a sufficiently large part of the market" cannot be defined in the abstract and will depend on the specific facts of each case and the type of information exchange in question.'

formalistic market share based safe harbours and the rather flexible economic framework on assessing pure information exchanges. All these arguments suggest that such type of safe harbour is not desirable for pure information exchanges.

6.2.3.b *Safe Harbours for Certain Types of Information Exchange*

The second type of safe harbours that can be considered for information exchanges are those that only apply to certain types of information exchanges. Kühn argues that optimal competition policy should cover certain types of information exchanges by safe harbours irrespectively of appreciability considerations. Two ideas are central for his argument. First, competition policy on information exchange should consider the '*ex ante* incentive effect' that safe harbours would offer. Instead of catching every possible anti-competitive effect that information exchange may entail, one should focus on what types of conduct competition law should deter. There are strong incentives for firms to stay within the boundaries of safe harbours because any information exchange regime that goes beyond it requires a timely and costly assessment of tangible benefits to prevent competition law scrutiny.[1323]

Second, competition policy on information exchange should also consider the 'costs of avoidance' which Kühn describes as the idea that 'where the avoidance of the type of information exchange scheme has small costs because the alternatives have almost the same value for firms, but where the dangers that the information can facilitate collusive behaviour are particularly large'.[1324] For example, while the removal of disaggregated data about current demand and production from a spreadsheet entails some costs for the collecting firm, it prevents significant social costs that would come with exchanging individualised information. Thus, a safe harbour for the exchange of aggregated information about current demand and production can be justified because the exchange of individualised information would materialise the same efficiencies, it would entail significant anti-competitive effects.[1325]

Kühn identifies *inter alia* the following types of information exchanges on current or past data (not future intentions) suitable for safe harbours:[1326]

- *Exchanges that occur sporadically*: if a firm has received information about the conduct of a competitor sporadically, this does not enable the systematic monitoring required to make collusion likely.
- *Exchanges of delivery data*: even the exchange of highly disaggregated delivery data is not useful to monitor competitors' conduct in contract negotiations because what matters for the competitive process are quantities and prices.

1323. *See* Kühn (2010), pp. 420-422.
1324. Kühn (2010), p. 421. A similar expression of this idea has been also mentioned by das Nair and Mncube (2013): 'If the information exchange is found to be anticompetitive, the appropriate remedy need not necessarily be an outright ban of the information exchanged, but to eliminate "unnecessary" information exchange, or increase aggregation of the shared information.'
1325. *See* Kühn (2010), pp. 421 and 427-430.
1326. *Ibid.*, pp. 425-428.

- *Exchange of cost data*: the exchange of cost data is generally irrelevant for monitoring competitors' conduct because only the knowledge about prices and sales enables firms to identify cheaters (and thus to explain lost sales).
- *Exchange of demand and production data that is sufficiently aggregated*: although the exchange of such data makes the market more transparent (and thus improve the abilities to monitor each other), it enables the materialisation of significant horizontal efficiencies for firms (such as benchmarking).

Käis adds two further types of conduct to the safe harbour list:[1327]

(1) *Exchange of historic information*: historic information has lost its commercial value, and its exchange is irrelevant for collusion.
(2) *Exchange of publicly available data*: the exchange of public information does not have any impact on market transparency and thus is not able to facilitate collusion.

It is hard to dispute that most of these types of information exchange are less problematic according to economic theory. However, the theoretical economic perspective only tells half of the story. The challenges lie on a *practical* level. First, it is very difficult to draw an exact line between exchanges that fall within such safe harbour and those that do not. For instance, it is not always clear-cut when an information exchange is 'sufficiently aggregated'. The level of aggregation heavily depends on the specific industry and other available information. The contradiction is that one tries to establish a safe harbour in abstract, while the assessment of information exchanges should consider the specific context. The establishment of such safe harbours would then not achieve the level of legal certainty they aim to achieve.[1328]

Second, it may be questioned from a competition policy perspective whether competition policy should really exclude all forms of aggregated information exchanges from its scrutiny. It is one thing not to prioritise the pursuing of these cases. However, it is an entirely different issue to exclude all forms of aggregated information exchange from competition law scrutiny. Wagner-von Papp for instance argues that even aggregated information may be sufficient to achieve collusion (through untargeted punishment mechanism) in fairly concentrated markets.[1329] Thus, there are also substantive objections against such a one-size-fits-all approach.

Third, some types of information exchange mentioned above are problematic to exempt. For instance, the 'sporadic category' is not really practical because it entails the risk that the discovered information exchange may *seem* sporadic simply because the full extent of the (problematic) information exchange has not been discovered. At

1327. *See* Käis (2013), pp. 356-357. These two categories have been also classified by Capobianco (2004), pp. 1269-1270 as a 'permitted exchange', although he does not explicitly refer to as safe harbours.
1328. *See also* Wagner-von Papp (2012), pp. 21 and 31. Peeperkorn also emphasises that it may be wise to provide a clear-cut rule on when information is considered 'historic' and thus not relevant for competition law anymore (*see* Peeperkorn (1996), p. 6).
1329. *See* Wagner-von Papp (2007), p. 269.

worst, a sporadic information exchange could be an evidence of a successfully operating cartel. A safe harbour would be used as a defence by undertakings to effectively increase the burden of proof for enforcers. This would lead to under-enforcement. Safe harbours should not produce such negative side effects.

In conclusion, Kühn's ideas of '*ex ante* incentive effects' and 'costs of avoidance' are valuable from a theoretical perspective. Particularly the latter idea may explain why the Commission has not yet taken a case that condemned an information exchange of aggregated data. However, his ideas are not suitable for the catch-all-nature of safe harbours. The economic analysis of information exchanges is simply too multifaceted.[1330]

6.2.3.c 'Safe Zones'

A third way to exclude unproblematic pure information exchanges from competition law scrutiny is by using what Wijckmans and Tuytschaever refer to as 'safe zones'. In these safe zones a given information exchange is unlikely to restrict competition.[1331] Although the likelihood of competition scrutiny is also on the lower end, it is still more likely than in case of safe harbours. Safe zones consider the specific circumstances of a case to a greater extent than safe harbours. This makes them more flexible in their application. Furthermore, safe zones merely provide a 'rough' abstract substantive guidance. This makes them less formalistic in their application.

The Horizontal Cooperation Guidelines provide for instance that the exchange of historic data is unlikely to restrict competition because it has lost its commercial value.[1332] Also, the exchange of genuinely public information is unlikely to have restrictive effect because such information can be collected with ease from the market.[1333] Similarly, the exchange of aggregated data is unlikely to entail anti-competitive effects because it does not enable the identification of competitors' conduct.[1334]

All these types of information exchange mentioned by the Horizontal Cooperation Guidelines are also mentioned by Kühn and Käis in their safe harbour list. However, the scope of the Guidelines is narrower. For instance, the Guidelines do not cover information exchanges of cost and delivery data. This suggests that the Commission is more conservative regarding the scope of generally unproblematic information exchanges, even though it merely refers to safe zones instead of safe harbours. A possible explanation for this cautious approach regarding cost data can be found in economic theory. Cost data might enable the better evaluation of future conduct of firms because costs form the basis for pricing strategies. Furthermore, the *Wirtschaftsvereinigung Stahl* decision offers a precedent for the cautious approach regarding

1330. *See also* Wagner-von Papp (2012), p. 21.
1331. *See* Wijckmans and Tuytschaever (2015), paras 11.46 and 11.61.
1332. *See* Horizontal Cooperation Guidelines, para. 90.
1333. *Ibid.*, para. 92.
1334. *Ibid.*, para. 89.

delivery data. In this decision firms used the exchange of delivery data to identify those firms that tried to increase their market shares.

A conservative list of safe zones is the right policy approach to provide some abstract guidance for identifying unproblematic information exchanges. On the one hand, safe zones do not create the same expectation as safe harbour regarding the unlikeliness of scrutiny. Although scrutiny is generally less likely, it is still more likely than in case of safe harbours. On the other hand, a narrow list of a few safe zones does not give the impression that the (desirable) context-specific analytical approach is completely substituted by safe zones. Although the holistic analytical approach should always play a role in the assessment of information exchanges, the practical weight of such approach is more limited in the scope of application of (more abstract) safe zones.

6.2.3.d Conclusion

Since information exchange can occur in a wide variety of different contexts, the catch-all approach by safe harbour is not suitable. It would undermine the analytical importance of assessing information exchanges holistically and context-related. Although safe zones do not overcome all these problems, they mitigate most of them. On the one hand, safe zones provide for *undertakings* some abstract guidance on identifying unproblematic information exchanges without spending too much resources on the assessment. On the other hand, safe zones also set priorities for *enforcers* because those cases within safe zones require particularly thorough economic analyses that justify any intervention. Consequently, safe zones are a pragmatic approach for generally unproblematic pure information exchanges.

6.3 RESTRICTIONS BY OBJECT CASES

This section discusses those pure information exchanges that were considered as restrictions by object (*see* section 6.3.1). It then tries to identify some common themes in the case law (*see* section 6.3.2). Finally, it discusses two discrepancies on the scope of the object box between the case law on the one hand and the Horizontal Cooperation Guidelines as well as economic theory on the other hand (*see* section 6.3.3).

6.3.1 Case Law and Decisional Practice

6.3.1.a The Fatty Acid *Decision (Borderline Case)*

The *Fatty Acid* decision[1335] is a borderline case between a hard-core cartel agreement and a pure information exchange.[1336] The Commission viewed the case as cartel

1335. Commission decision, *Fatty Acids*.
1336. *See* Carle and Johnsson (1998), fn 12.

agreement relating to quota-fixing.[1337] Still, even though the classification as a pure information exchange is disputed, the case can be used as an example of how fluent the boundaries are between ancillary and pure information exchange agreements.

The case concerned an information sharing agreement between the three largest producers of oleochemicals, oleine and stearine in the EU (Unilever, Henkel and Oleofina).[1338] All three undertakings had together about 60% market share on the European fatty acid market. They were all part of a trade association (l'Association des Producteurs d'Acides Gras (APAG)) which represented about 90% of the production of fatty acids.[1339] The rest of the market was fairly fragmented with smaller and mostly local producers.[1340] The agreement was concluded at a time of an economic recession with overproduction on the market.[1341]

The trigger for the conclusion of the information sharing agreement was that Unilever, the market leader with 30% market share, planned a merger which would have inevitably involved rationalisation and reduction of capacity on the market.[1342] Unilever was concerned that its merger plans would be 'misinterpreted' as a signal of its withdrawal from the market and thus would have intensified competition even more.[1343] It therefore initiated setting-up an information sharing agreement between these three undertakings, which existed in parallel to the already existing information exchange systems in the framework of the APAG.[1344] This latter information exchange agreement between all members of the APAG was not objected by the Commission.[1345]

The agreement between the three undertakings entailed the exchange of past[1346] data about quantities sold on the market; first on an annual basis, later on a quarterly basis.[1347] Unilever itself described the objective of the agreement as a tool to enable the three undertakings to monitor major changes in their relative position as a result of the unilateral reduction of capacity of Unilever.[1348] Attempts by one of the three undertakings to win one of their respective customers by price cuts were considered as 'stolen' sales.[1349] There was a common understanding between the undertakings that the best way of solving the overcapacity problem was the exit of smaller producers.[1350] The Big

1337. *See* Commission decision, *Cartonboard*, para. 134. However, this conclusion does not seem to reflect the conclusion of the Commission in the *Fatty Acids* decision itself: 'agreement bears a strong resemblance to that of an outright quota-fixing agreement' (Commission decision, *Fatty Acids*, para. 39) in contrast to 'this illustrates at best that the parties' commitment to market stabilization did not amount to an outright quota-fixing arrangement' (*ibid.*, para. 45).
1338. A fourth party to the agreement was then integrated into the operations of Unilever (*see* Commission decision, *Fatty Acids*, para. 2).
1339. *Ibid.*, para. 7.
1340. *See* Kühn and Vives (1995), p. 94.
1341. *See* Commission decision, *Fatty Acids*, para. 40.
1342. *Ibid.*, para. 11.
1343. *Ibid.*, paras 11 and 25.
1344. *See* Commission decision, *Fatty Acids*, para. 42. The information exchange operated by the APAG was not objected by the Court.
1345. *See* Kühn and Vives (1995), p. 94.
1346. *See* explicitly in Commission decision, *Fatty Acids*, para. 29.
1347. *See* Commission decision, *Fatty Acids*, para. 12.
1348. *Ibid.*, para. 14.
1349. *Ibid.*, para. 26.
1350. *Ibid.*, para. 27.

Three were indeed able to increase their combined market share by 10% to almost 80%. While Unilever's market share stagnated, the shares of Henkel and Oleofina grew significantly.[1351]

The Commission considered the information sharing agreement as a restriction by object.[1352] The agreement was an effective means to monitor each other.[1353] It enables the undertakings to identify more precisely and more quickly the competitive conduct and thus 'artificially'[1354] increased market transparency.[1355] The agreement was further facilitated by regular contacts.[1356] However, there was no evidence that the parties had actually agreed on fixing quotas.[1357]

The decision is a good example for how an information exchange system can be employed as an effective means to collude. The firms refrained from competing harshly on their established customers, while intensifying competition on the residual market to induce the exit of smaller firms. This 'predatory strategy' seems to be at the heart of the agreement.[1358] The fact that the market share of Unilever remained the same, while the share of the other two undertakings grew is also consistent with economic theory of how to effectively run a cartel.[1359]

The decision is also a good example of efficient competition enforcement. While there may have been evidence for a broader collusive agreement,[1360] the exchange of individualised current data about quantities was the easier way to establish the infringement.[1361] In other words, while the Commission did not find the smoking gun on quota-fixing, it did find one of the most problematic types of information exchange according to economic theory (highly disaggregated information in a concentrated market).[1362]

From an economic perspective, the decision takes into account the game theoretical perspective on the prisoner's dilemma. Unilever was afraid to be misunderstood by its competitors and to provoke a price war.[1363] The information exchange system was an effective means to overcome the prisoner's dilemma.

However, the decision may have less weight than subsequent cases because it did not face judicial scrutiny. It would have been interesting to see whether the EU Courts would have agreed with the Commission on the classification as a restriction by object. As shown below, subsequent case law suggests that only the exchange of *future* intentions (and not the exchange of current data even if highly disaggregated) falls

1351. *Ibid.*, para. 28.
1352. *Ibid.*, paras 33-47.
1353. *Ibid.*, paras 36 and 45.
1354. For this wording, *see* Commission decision, *Fatty Acids*, para. 45.
1355. *Ibid.*, para. 37.
1356. *Ibid.*, para. 38.
1357. *Ibid*, para. 39. In other words, there was no direct evidence of an underlying cartel (*see* Bissocoli (2000), p. 94).
1358. *See* Kühn and Vives (1995), p. 95; Vives (2006a), p. 93.
1359. *See* Kühn (2001), p. 193.
1360. An indication of this can be found in Commission decision, *Fatty Acids*, para. 39.
1361. *See* Kühn (2001), p. 193.
1362. *See* Stroux (2004), pp. 149-150.
1363. *See* Peeperkorn (1996), p. 13.

within the object box. Thus, this case may be an outliner and should therefore be relied only cautiously.

A different reading of the decision is that the case was not just about an information exchange. Instead, the exchange was just one powerful indicia of a concertation. Put differently, the specific context and sequence of the establishment of the information exchange (planned merger) seems to suggest that the information exchange was merely a manifestation of the underlying 'understanding' between the undertakings to avoid price wars. This is not the typical information exchange scenario where an effects analysis seems to be appropriate. The decision did not aim to prevent the likely emerge of collusion. Instead, it prohibited actual collusion where the information exchange system was merely the most powerful indicia of the underlying concertation.

6.3.1.b The **Tate & Lyle** *Case*

Tate & Lyle[1364] (also referred to as *British Sugar)*[1365] was the first case about the unilateral disclosure of future intentions.[1366] It concerned the British sugar market in the 1980s. At the time, there was a Community sugar scheme designed to support and protect the production of sugar with the EU. This involved *inter alia* minimum prices and national production quotas.[1367]

British Sugar was the only British producer of sugar beet and the entire British beet sugar quota was allocated to it. Despite British Sugar being by far the largest market player in the UK on the downstream market, it faced competition from Tate & Lyle which imported sugar mainly from outside the EU. Together both undertakings produced roughly the volume necessary for satisfying the demand for sugar in the UK. Thus, the market was highly concentrated.[1368] British Sugar had an advantage over cane-refiners (such as Tate & Lyle) because it processed the original sugar beet and thus enjoyed higher margins. As a consequence, British Sugar was the price leader and other distributors (such as Tate & Lyle) were merely price followers.[1369]

Between 1984 and 1986 British Sugar was fined by the Commission for abusing its dominant position by engaging in a price war with abnormally low prices.[1370] In June 1986 a meeting took place between British Sugar and Tate & Lyle in which the former announced to end the price war in the UK. Subsequently, several other meetings, which not just Tate & Lyle but also other customers of British Sugar attended,

1364. Cases T-202/98, etc., *Tate & Lyle*. On appeal to the CJ (Case C-359/01 P, *British Sugar*) the parties did not claim that the GC wrongly concluded the existence of a concerted practice. This is why the judgment of CJ is not discussed here.
1365. *See*, e.g., Baño Fos (2015), p. 153.
1366. *See* Baño Fos (2015), p. 153.
1367. *See* Cases T-202/98, etc., *Tate & Lyle*, paras 1-2.
1368. *Ibid.*, paras 3-4.
1369. *See* Camesasca, Schmidt and Clancy (2010), p. 409.
1370. Commission decision, *Napier Brown – British Sugar*.

took place. In those meetings British Sugar unilaterally disclosed its *future* prices for industrial sugar.[1371]

The GC concluded that the purpose of this meeting was the restriction of competition by coordinating pricing policies.[1372] There was no justification for British Sugar to reveal its future pricing intentions with its competitors.[1373] The GC rejected the argument that there was no room for price competition. Despite the existence of the Community sugar scheme there was still room for price competition between the minimum price offered by the scheme and the price set by British Sugar.[1374] Thus, the revelation of future prices in these meetings had an anti-competitive purpose. The GC also rejected the argument that each operator had already acquired all the information necessary to understand the commercial policy of competitors *before* the revelation due to the highly concentrated market environment. Despite the fact that commercial policies of competitors are easier to predict in oligopolistic markets, uncertainty still remains as to exact future pricing policy of competitors.[1375] The revelation of future intentions enables market players to more simply, rapidly and directly get the information compared to the situation where the future conduct has to be interpreted based on past market conduct.[1376]

The GC stated that for the establishment of a concerted practice it is sufficient that only one of the participants at the meetings with anti-competitive purpose reveals its intentions regarding its future conduct.[1377] This is because once such information is revealed, each participant could not fail to take into account the information obtained.[1378] In other words, the mere receipt of information concerning future conduct of a competitor is sufficient.[1379] There is no need to show that the recipients have actually acted upon it.

The case differs from the typical cartel case in that it merely entails unilateral disclosure of price intentions of one market player.[1380] The information exchange acted as focal point to eventually achieve a collusive outcome, but not as a means to execute an already existing common plan to fix prices (like in a typical hard-core cartel). In other words, the exchange of information is aimed at *achieving* collusion, not at maintaining it.

1371. *See* Cases T-202/98, etc., *Tate & Lyle*, paras 9-11.
1372. *Ibid.*, para. 53.
1373. *Ibid.*, para. 49.
1374. *Ibid.*, paras 44-45.
1375. *Ibid.*, para. 46.
1376. *Ibid.*, para. 60.
1377. *Ibid.*, para. 54.
1378. *Ibid.*, para. 67.
1379. *Ibid.*, para. 58.
1380. *See* Baño Fos (2015), pp. 153-154.

6.3.1.c *The* T-Mobile *Case*

T-Mobile was a preliminary reference ruling requested by a Dutch court. The case concerns a meeting where (the only)[1381] five operators on the Dutch mobile telecommunication market exchanged information on one single meeting in June 2001. They discussed to reduce the standard commission paid to dealers for brokering post-paid mobile subscriptions as of 1 September 2001.[1382]

The case is interesting because it neither fits in the typical pure information exchange setting nor in the typical hard-core cartel setting. On the one hand, it has elements of a hard-core cartel because it lacks any sort of efficiency that normally justifies information exchange agreements (*see* particularly *Asnef-Equifax* above).[1383] On the other hand, it differs from the typical hard-core cartel because the exchanged information merely concerned production costs (i.e., commissions paid to dealers) but not actual prices charged to customers.

Although the final assessment whether the information exchange in question constituted a restriction by object lied with the referring national court, the language of the judgment leaves little room to not regard the information exchange in question as a restriction by object.[1384] The main reason for such classification was because it related to future intentions.[1385] It seems that the fact that the content of the information exchange did merely relate to production costs (but not to actual prices) did not matter. The classification was also reached despite the statement of the CJ that restrictions by object are generally only those severe forms of collusion that 'by their very nature, as being injurious to the proper functioning of the normal competition'.[1386] One may wonder whether the harmonisation of production costs is one of the most severe forms of collusion. Maybe the CJ reached that conclusion because of the special market circumstances of the Dutch mobile telecommunication market (oligopolistic, quite homogeneous products and no market entry possible[1387] since the market was essentially closed).[1388]

The wider scope of the 'object box' underlying the judgment creates friction with the narrower approach taken in the Horizontal Cooperation Guidelines. Since the

1381. *See* Case C-8/08, *T-Mobile*, para. 10. The entrance of a sixth operator was unlikely since there were no further licences issued.
1382. *Ibid.*, para. 12.
1383. *See* Robertson (2013), p. 480.
1384. *See* Case C-8/08, *T-Mobile*, paras 41: 'an exchange of information which is capable of removing uncertainties between participants as regards the timing, extent and details of the modifications to be adopted by the undertaking concerned must be regarded as pursuing an anti-competitive object, and that extends to situations, *such as that in the present case*, in which the modification relates to the reduction in the standard commission paid to dealers'. (emphasis added)
1385. *Ibid.*, particularly para. 43: 'An exchange of information between competitors is tainted with an anti-competitive object if the exchange is capable of removing uncertainties concerning the intended conduct of the participating undertakings.' *See* section 6.3.2.d for more on this.
1386. *Ibid.*, para. 29.
1387. It was unlikely that a sixth licence would have been issued (*see* Camesasca, Schmidt and Clancy (2010), p. 407).
1388. *See* Robertson (2013), p. 479.

information exchanged did merely relate to production costs (and not to actual prices) it would *not* be regarded as a restriction by object under the Horizontal Cooperation Guidelines, even though it related to future intentions.[1389]

Scholars have therefore argued that the judgment has significantly widened the scope of the object box and created uncertainties with regards to the conceptual limits of restrictions by object.[1390] Critics of the judgment also view it as a setback for the (generally desirable) more economic approach because it advocates a per se prohibition thinking,[1391] *inter alia* because of its broad statements, lack of economic analysis and very formalistic analytical approach.[1392] Some also criticise that the CJ explained not sufficiently why this specific exchange was regarded as restriction by object.[1393]

However, an alternative reading of the judgment could be that it should be seen more from a cartel perspective and less from a typical information exchange perspective.[1394] The parties competed for the procurement of services of dealers which has been eliminated by the information exchange.[1395] One should read between the lines and understand the language of the judgment in light of the economic circumstances of the case.[1396] Accordingly, the judgment should be given little weight when assessing pure information exchanges that aim to materialise efficiencies. This view would have the advantage of preventing friction with the approach taken by the Commission in the Horizontal Cooperation Guidelines. It would also help to explain why the CJ's language is so different from other cases about pure information exchange agreements.

Furthermore, the substantive appraisal of the facts is economically sound, even though the language might suggest a more formalistic approach.[1397] An *actual* unilateral reduction by any operator would have put its market share at risk since other operators may not follow (first mover disadvantage). Once a competitor has lowered its remuneration fee, other competitors have the incentive not to lower their remuneration in order to attract new dealers. This dilemma was solved by the concertation.[1398] Even a single meeting was sufficient to take away the uncertainty a unilateral remuneration reduction would have entailed.[1399] As pointed out by Wagner-von Papp, a one-time exchange of future intentions was indeed sufficient to transform the market that is not conducive to tacit collusion into one that is, when the main problem for collusion was

1389. *See* Horizontal Cooperation Guidelines, para. 73. Noted by Robertson (2013), pp. 478-479.
1390. *See* Jones (2010), p. 658; Nazzini and Nikpay (2014), p. 159.
1391. *See* Meyring (2010), p. 30. The OECD (2011, para. 40) also notes the 'strict view' on information exchanges taken by the Court.
1392. *See* Meyring (2010), p. 31; Bailey (2012), p. 589; Robertson (2013), p. 481; Ezrachi (2018), p. 145. *See also* Jones and Sufrin (2016), p. 680 who argue that the Court went further than was perhaps required in this case. Dnes argues that the effect of the single information exchange is likely to be relatively modest (*see* Dnes (2016), p. 242).
1393. *See* MacCulloch (2020), p. 369.
1394. *See* Meyring (2010), p. 32.
1395. *See* Mahtani (2012), pp. 23 and 35.
1396. *See* Kyprianides (2012), p. 409.
1397. *See* Camesasca, Schmidt and Clancy (2010), p. 408 who note that the Court did analyse the context of the information exchange.
1398. *See* Loozen (2010), p. 149.
1399. *Ibid.*, p. 150.

the equilibrium selection.[1400] In other words, the single meeting was an effective and sufficient means to tip the market towards a collusive outcome.

It is also worth comparing *T-Mobile* with the *Eudim* decision. The *Eudim* decision has in common with *T-Mobile* that both exchanges had as the objective to reduce production costs. However, there are two crucial differences between both cases: the market concentration and market coverage. While the market was highly fragmented in *Eudim*, the market was highly concentrated in *T-Mobile* with no possible entry in the near future. While the parties and their exchanges merely covered a small percentage of the market in *Eudim*, the information exchange in *T-Mobile* covered the entire market. Thus, both cases are extremes among a spectrum of possible levels of market concentration and market coverage. However, these sharp differences help to explain why the exchange in *T-Mobile* was regarded as a restriction by object, while the exchange in the *Eudim* decision was not even considered as a restriction by effect.

6.3.1.d The **Two Bananas** *Cases*

The *Dole*[1401] and also the *Del Monte*[1402] case (both of which are referred to as the *Banana* cases)[1403] concerned the Commission decision that fined several banana producers and importers for exchanging pre-pricing information relating to bananas marketed in Northern Europe for a period of three years. The decision was upheld by the GC whose judgment was upheld by the CJ. The case provides detailed insights on the operations of the information exchange in question due to the fact that one of the participating undertakings (Chiquita) applied for immunity under the leniency programme.[1404]

There were three tiers of perceived qualities for bananas pursuant to their brand: premium Chiquita bananas, second-tier bananas (Dole and Del Monte) and third-tier banana (from several other brands). The brand division was reflected in the price.[1405]

The banana business in Northern Europe was organised in weekly cycles with banana shipments from Latin America to Northern Europe approximately every week. The main banana importers set their *quotation* prices for their brands each week on Thursday morning. However, the *actual* prices paid by retailers and distributors for bananas were different either because of weekly negotiations or because of supply contracts that provided for pre-established pricing formulas.[1406] Still, the quotation price served as a powerful signal of the intended development of actual prices.[1407]

1400. *See* Wagner-von Papp (2012), p. 22.
1401. Case T-588/08, *Dole*; Case C-286/13 P, *Dole* (appeal dismissed). This is the case more often cited by the literature than *Del Monte*.
1402. Case T-587/08, *Del Monte* and Cases C-293/13 P etc, *Del Monte* (the CJ has merely reduced the fine by 10%).
1403. *See* Frazer (2013). Sometimes *Dole* is referred to as 'the Banana' case (*see* Baño Fos (2015), pp. 171 et seq.; Jones and Sufrin (2016), p. 157). However, it is better to refer to *Dole* as one of the two Banana cases.
1404. *See* Case T-588/08, *Dole*, para.2.
1405. *See* Camesasca, Schmidt and Clancy (2010), p. 410.
1406. *See* Case T-588/08, *Dole*, paras 11-14.
1407. *See* Camesasca, Schmidt and Clancy (2010), p. 411.

The Commission found bilateral exchanges between Chiquita and Dole (two of the largest Banana producers in the world) as well as between Dole and Weichert (a marketing company which was, for parts of the infringement, under the decisive influence of Del Monte).[1408] These bilateral exchanges included 'pre-pricing information' which took place before actual prices were set and related to future quotation prices (*inter alia* price-setting factors, price trends and indications of quotation prices for the forthcoming week). The undertakings also exchanged their quotation prices after they have been set. Certainly, the information exchange went beyond what one would describe as 'industry gossip'.[1409] The communication took place over the phone, normally on Wednesday or Thursday morning. The former communication was ultimately designed and aimed[1410] to reduce uncertainty relating to the setting of their quotation prices. The latter communication enabled them to monitor their individual pricing decisions. The Commission concluded that these bilateral exchanges were restrictions by object.[1411]

The GC upheld the Commission decision in its entirety and provided clarifications on many issues surrounding direct information exchanges. Different from *T-Mobile,* which was a preliminary reference, the GC had to actually decide on the merits of the case. First, the GC rejected arguments by the applicants aimed to narrow the scope of the object box.[1412] It rejected the argument that a restriction by object can only be ascertained if the information exchange forms part of a 'broader cartel arrangement', such as cartels to fix actual prices or share markets. It did so with reference to the independence doctrine established in *Suiker Unie*. What matters for the classification as a restriction by object is the reduction or removal of uncertainty as to the future price-setting of competitors.[1413] It also rejected the argument that a restriction by object can only be ascertained if there is a direct connection between the practice and consumer prices.[1414]

Second, the GC ruled that the Commission was right in ascertaining that the bilateral exchanges in question constituted a restriction by object.[1415] It rejected the argument that the Commission drew an artificial distinction between 'pre-pricing' communication and 'ex post' communication.[1416] What mattered for the classification as a restriction by object was the fact that the communication related to the *future*

1408. *See* for that description Camesasca, Schmidt and Clancy (2010), p. 410.
1409. Zampa and Carli for instance indicate that this might have been merely industry gossip (*see* Zampa and Carli (2015), p. 76).
1410. This has been emphasised by Mahtani (2012), p. 31.
1411. *See* Case T-588/08, *Dole,* paras 15-21 and 54.
1412. *Ibid.*, paras 51-66.
1413. *Ibid.*, paras 59-63.
1414. *Ibid.*, paras 64-65.
1415. *Ibid.*, paras 67-71, 86-118 (rejecting the argument that the Commission could not rely on the evidence provided by the leniency applicant because of its allegedly lack of credibility), 119-248 (upholding the theory of the Commission that the objective of these bilateral exchanges were to ultimately coordinate their quotation prices) and 249-585 (upholding the Commission's factual assessment that the Commission has identified and classified the various information exchanges correctly).
1416. *Ibid.*, paras 72-85.

course of conduct, even though it merely involved pre-pricing information and not actual prices.[1417]

The CJ upheld the judgment of the GC in its entirety. It particularly rejected the claim that the GC distorted the facts relating to the economic context of the infringement[1418] and inadequately assessed the evidence.[1419]

Robertson concludes that the case gives a textbook example of an information exchange that falls within the scope of Guidelines' narrow object category.[1420] While *T-Mobile* is an example for their discrepancy, Dole is a good example for their alignment. The case is generally seen as less controversial because the exchange resembles more the usual price-fixing setting than *T-Mobile* does.[1421]

Frazer on the other hand argues that the case suggests that (what he calls) 'concerted practice by object' applies to much broader categories of situations than just prices. It applies to areas which have been considered relatively safe to talk about (such as the impact of changes in tax or regulation on the market).[1422] More broadly framed, this interpretation would mean that any talk with competitors about future developments that affect the competitive process could fall within the object box. What matters is the temporal orientation of the information exchanged (future conduct) and not the closeness to the actual prices charged (merely pre-pricing information). This interpretation sits well with the independence doctrine which regards the reduction of uncertainty of conduct of market players as the decisive test. Obviously, uncertainty lies in the future not in the past. The exchange of future intentions necessarily reduces the uncertainty in a way that the exchange of past information (even if it is very recent) is not able to achieve.

However, the danger of such test that focuses on the exchange of future intension is that it is loose.[1423] It needs to be complemented by an appreciability threshold. An information exchange only then falls in the object box, if it relates to future conduct that has an appreciable effect on one of the main variables of competition (such as price, output, product quality, product variety or innovation).[1424] Pre-pricing information falls in that category. But so does the exchange about a competitor's interpretation

1417. *Ibid.*, para. 78.
1418. *Ibid.*, paras 62-75.
1419. *Ibid.*, paras 75-135.
1420. *See* Robertson (2013), p. 484.
1421. *See* Jones and Sufrin (2016), p. 683.
1422. *See* Frazer (2013). Concern of the possible wide application is also raised by Smith, Ridyard and Petrescu (2015), p. 42; Zampa and Carli (2015), p. 76.
1423. *See* Case T-587/08, *Del Monte*, para. 346, where the GC has differentiated between talks about the weather and other issues that relate more on the competitive process: 'The individual assessment by a banana importer of a climatic event affecting a region of production, information which is public and available, should not be confused with the joint evaluation by two competitors of that event, in combination, as the case may be, with other information on the state of the market, and of its impact on the development of the sector, very shortly before their quotation prices are set.'
1424. Jones and Sufrin (2016), pp. 683-684 develop that argument in the context of restrictions by effect, i.e., there must be an appreciable adverse impact on at least one of the parameters of competition.

of the impact of certain future developments that appreciably shape the competitive process. There is certainly a scope for clarification in future cases.

Another criticism that has been raised is that the case blurs the line between pure and ancillary information exchanges.[1425] The GC itself described in *Dole* the bilateral information exchanges in one paragraph as a 'cartel arrangement'.[1426] Dunne has also described the conduct to lay on the boundaries of 'cartel behaviour'.[1427] This blurriness makes it difficult to assess under which circumstances a pure information exchange infringes Art. 101 TFEU.[1428]

However, one could argue that not the distinction between pure and ancillary information exchanges is important, but only the distinction between restrictions by object and effect. Only the latter entails legal significance and should be delimited properly. The classification as a restriction by object can be justified in this case because the exchange did not involve any meaningful efficiencies.[1429]

6.3.1.e The E-Book Commitment Decision

The *E-Book* commitment decision[1430] is one of the most high-profile cases in 2012 and was pursued by the Commission in parallel to the investigations pursued by the US Department of Justice.[1431]

A commitment decision is a new enforcement instrument (Art. 9 of Regulation 1/2003)[1432] that is different from an infringement decision (Art. 7 of Regulation 1/2003). It makes commitments offered by the undertakings under investigation as to their future behaviour legally binding without making a finding as to whether there has been an infringement.[1433] It is only appropriate when the Commission does not intend to impose a fine.[1434] It allows the Commission to more efficiently use its limited resources (procedural economy).[1435]

The Commission initially opened proceedings against Apple and five major book publishers (Hachette, Harper Collins, McMillan, Penguin, and Simon & Schuster) in December 2011. These publishers were five of the six largest English-language

1425. *See* Case T-588/08, *Dole*, para. 76.
1426. *Ibid.*, para. 52.
1427. *See* Dunne (2020), p. 398.
1428. *See* Robertson (2013), pp. 484 (specifically mentioned in the discussion of the *Dole* case) and 485-486 (mentioned in a more broadly context).
1429. *See* Barnkin (2016), p. 382; Niels, Jenkins and Kavanagh (2016), para. 5.34.
1430. Commission decision, *E-Books*.
1431. *See* Buettner et al. (2013), p. 283.
1432. Article 9(1) of Regulation 1/2003: 'Where the Commission intends to adopt a decision requiring that an infringement be brought to an end and the undertakings concerned offer commitments to meet the concerns expressed to them by the Commission in its *preliminary* assessment, the Commission may by decision make those commitments binding on the undertakings. Such a decision may be adopted for a specified period and shall conclude that there are *no longer grounds for action* by the Commission.' (emphasis added)
1433. *See* Whish and Bailey (2018), p. 264.
1434. *See* Faull and Nikpay (2014), paras 2.127-2.128.
1435. *See* Whish and Bailey (2018), p. 264.

publishers.[1436] The Commission adopted a commitment decision pursuant to Art. 9 of Regulation 1/2003 in December 2012 (for five of them) and July 2013 (for Penguin).

The background of the case was that at the time, Amazon was the largest online retailer of e-books through its dedicated Kindle reader. It was selling e-books under a 'wholesale model'. Under such model Amazon paid publishers a wholesale price and independently set retail prices. In the US, Amazon was selling some best-sellers under a low-price policy at just USD 9.99.[1437]

Apple was about to launch its iBookstore as it had just released the iPad in 2010. The Commission found in its preliminary assessment that Apple initially contacted these five publishers on an individual basis regarding its intention to start selling e-books via its iBookstore. In parallel to the initial contact by Apple, some of the five publishers contacted each other directly regarding their respective discussions with Apple. Apple at first considered entering the market under a wholesale model. However, some of the five publishers proposed an agency model for the sale of e-books in order to raise retail prices of e-books above Amazon's retail price. Apple subsequently changed its mind and regarded the agency model as the preferred model in order to achieve its goal of eliminating meaningful retail price competition with Amazon. Apple simultaneously informed the five publishers about its decision one month later.[1438]

Shortly afterwards, Apple submitted its proposed draft agency agreement to the publishers. It contained *inter alia* a retail price most favoured clause (MFN clause) and maximum retail price grids for new releases.[1439] Apple also ensured throughout its negotiations that each of the five publishers knew that they were negotiating on the same pricing terms,[1440] that they were informed about the status of the negotiations,[1441] and that they understood that Apple intended to roll out the iBookstore on a global scale (including the EEA) on the basis of the same agency model and with the same key pricing terms.[1442] Through the negotiations the publishers were in direct contact and disclosed information about the course of conduct contemplated or adopted by each other, particularly on pricing.[1443]

In January 2010 each of the five publishers signed agency agreements with Apple in the US, each containing the same key terms.[1444] When publishers entered into negotiations with Apple concerning the agency agreement in the UK, France and Germany, they used the agency agreement in the US as a template for their global strategy.[1445] The agency agreements for these countries were then signed a few months

1436. *See* Buettner et al. (2013), p. 284.
1437. *Ibid.*, p. 284.
1438. *See* Commission decision, *E-Books*, paras 33-34.
1439. *Ibid.*, paras 35-36.
1440. *Ibid.*, para. 37.
1441. *Ibid.*, para. 37.
1442. *Ibid.*, para. 39.
1443. *Ibid.*, para. 38.
1444. *Ibid.*, para. 40.
1445. *Ibid.*, para. 45.

later[1446] containing the same key terms (*inter alia* the same retail MFN clauses, similar maximum retail pricing grids and same commission fee for Apple).[1447]

Apple then launched its iBookstore in the UK, France and Germany. However, the publishers understood that this was only a first step by Apple. Apple had informed them of its intentions to launch the iBookstore in other EEA countries shortly after.[1448]

In its preliminary assessment, the Commission concluded that the publishers and Apple had engaged in a *concerted practice* to either raise retail prices of e-books in the EEA or to prevent the emergence of lower prices for e-books in the EEA by jointly concerting to move from the sale of e-books via a wholesale model to an agency model with the same key pricing terms on a global basis.[1449] This conclusion rested essentially on four arguments. First, the parallel conduct in the US and EEA between Apple and the publishers (*inter alia* on the process of negotiation and the content of the agency agreements).[1450] Second, the direct and indirect contacts between Apple and the publishers that disclosed their future course of conduct (*inter alia* with the aim of raising prices of e-books above Amazon's level and convert the sale of e-books from a wholesale to an agency model).[1451] Third, such conduct did not correspond with the normal conditions of competition whereby each publisher would be unaware of their respective negotiations with Apple and the key terms of their agency agreements.[1452] Fourth, the decision of the publishers to enter into an agency agreement with Apple on the same key pricing terms could have been not explained other than by a concerted action.[1453]

The Commission considered the concerted practice as a *restriction by object* because it related to price-fixing (i.e., to increase the retail prices of e-books in the EEA and prevent the emergence of lower retail prices).[1454]

In order to meet the preliminary concern of the Commission, the parties offered the following main commitments:[1455]

- termination of all agency agreements between the five publishers and Apple for the sale of e-books in the EEA;
- termination of all other agency agreements concluded with retailers other than Apple in the EEA for the sale of e-books that either restrict retailer's ability to set retail prices or that contain price MFN clauses;
- two-year cooling-off period within which the price-setting discretion of retailers to determine prices for e-books is not restricted; and
- five-year ban on retail price MFN clauses for e-books.

1446. *Ibid.*, paras 47-49 (between May and August 2018).
1447. *Ibid.*, para. 51.
1448. *Ibid.*, para. 50.
1449. *Ibid.*, para. 86.
1450. *Ibid.*, para. 75.
1451. *Ibid.*, paras 76-80.
1452. *Ibid.*, paras 81-83.
1453. *Ibid.*, paras 84-85.
1454. *Ibid.*, paras 90-93.
1455. The commitments were made binding first Apple, Hachette, HarperColins, Holtzbrinck/Macmillan and Simon & Schuster and very similar commitments also later for Penguin.

The Commission considered that the mere termination of the agency agreements was not sufficient to re-establish the conditions of competition that existed before the concerted practice. Without the latter two conditions the publisher would simply replicate the pricing terms from their concerted practice or use them as a focal point.[1456] The time period would be sufficiently long enough to enable a 'competitive reset' and create enough uncertainty regarding the future choice of business model by publishers and retailers (*wholesale model vs agency model vs other novel models*).[1457]

The case suggests that the publishers concerted due to mainly two reasons. First, publishers feared that the low retail pricing policy of Amazon would have further strengthened Amazon's position on the retail market and allowed it to eventually enter upstream (and thus become a direct competitor of publishers). Second, publishers also feared that the low retail pricing policy of Amazon would deflate prices generally as consumers become used to pay less for e-books.[1458] Thus, publishers saw the entrance of Apple as a one-off chance to collectively leverage their position against Amazon in order to increase retail prices.[1459] Apple was merely a *coordinating actor* that facilitated the concertation (including the constant flow of information between publishers).[1460] The MFN clause was merely a collective *commitment device* since each publisher was aware that the others were negotiating similar terms.[1461] As Buettner et al. put is 'Apple's facilitating role mitigated the publishers' fears of moving alone in a switch to agency, allowing them instead to move as a block, and significantly strengthening their bargaining position vis-à-vis Amazon. The coordinated move to agency was effective, in the sense that Amazon was forced to adopt the agency model (after an initial showdown with one of the publishers, McMillan), first in the US, and later in the EEA.'[1462]

It is also worth stressing out two points about the categorisation of the case. First, the case was mainly a 'horizontal case'. The vertical setting (the launch of Apple's iBookstore) was merely the trigger for a horizontal concertation among publishers. What was decisive in this case was the objective of the concertation (increase retail prices), not the possible anti-competitive effects arising from agency models or MFN clauses more generally. Second, the case relied upon documentary evidence (not merely on circumstantial evidence) and can thus be different from mere parallel conduct. Although some parts of the Commission decision suggest that the case was one of the typical 'parallel conduct cases',[1463] the Commission found hard evidence of direct contacts and information exchanges (*inter alia* information exchanges between Apple and the publishers and direct contacts between publishers outside the direct negotiation setting with Apple).

1456. *See* Commission decision, *E-Books*, paras 108-109.
1457. *Ibid.*, para. 112.
1458. *See* Buettner et al. (2013), pp. 284-285.
1459. *Ibid.*, p. 288.
1460. *Ibid.*, p. 287.
1461. *Ibid.*, pp. 286-288.
1462. *Ibid.*, p. 287.
1463. *See* Commission decision, *E-Books*, particularly paras 75 and 84-85.

6.3.1.f *Foreign Exchange Spot Trading Cartels (Forex Cartels)*

In two recent cartel settlement decisions five banks (Barclays, RBS, Citigroup, JPMorgan and MUFG Bank) have been fined for engaging in two foreign exchange (Forex or FX) spot trading cartels.[1464] Another bank (UBS) has been granted immunity because it revealed the existence of the two cartels to the Commission. Forex refers to the trading of currencies. Forex trading is for the most part speculative and the largest market in the world with a global daily turnover of around 4.5 billion.[1465]

Although the full decisions have not been published, summaries of the decisions and the press release give some insights into the case. The first decision concerned the exchange of certain commercially sensitive information that took place in three private Bloomberg chatrooms between five banks on a recurrent basis between December 2007 and June 2013[1466] (what the Commission called the 'Forex-Three Way Banana Split' cartel). The second decision concerned the exchange of certain commercially sensitive information that took place in two private Bloomberg chatrooms between five banks on a recurrent basis between December 2009 and July 2012[1467] (what the Commission called the 'Forex-Essex-Express' cartel). Most of the traders participating in the chatrooms also knew each other on a personal basis.

The press release and the two summaries leave no doubt about the seriousness of the infringement. Both conducts were classified as by object restrictions (the press release explicitly speaks of 'cartels').[1468] It seems that the conduct only refers to information exchanges of 'certain current or forward-looking' commercially sensitive information in private and mostly multilateral chatrooms that informed the traders about the positions, intentions and constraints of their competitors.[1469] More specifically, the exchanges revealed: (i) their open risk positions (the currency they needed to sell or buy in order to convert their portfolios into their bank's currency) that could have provided them with insights into each other's hedging conduct, (ii) their existing or intended bid-ask spreads, which ultimately disclosed the price quoted by the traders for specific currency pairs and trade sizes, and (iii) current or planned trading activities and outstanding customers' orders (i.e., the amount that a client wanted to exchange and the specific currencies involved, as well as indications on which client was involved in a transaction).[1470]

1464. *See* initial press release by the Commission on 16 May 2019, IP/19/2568, 'Antitrust: Commission fines Barclays, RBS, Citigroup, JPMorgan and MUFG €1.07 billion for participating in foreign exchange spot trading cartel.' Although the full decision is not yet available, two summaries of the Commission decision have been published (*see* summary of Commission decision, *Forex-Three Way Banana Split*; and summary of Commission decision, *Forex-Essex Express*).
1465. *See* Paukste (2019).
1466. *See* summary of Commission decision, *Forex-Three Way Banana Split*, paras 12-13.
1467. *See* summary of Commission decision, *Forex-Essex Express*, paras 12-13.
1468. *See* summary of Commission decision, *Forex-Three Way Banana Split*, para. 1; *see* summary of Commission decision, *Forex-Essex Express*, para. 1.
1469. *See* summary of Commission decision, *Forex-Three Way Banana Split*, paras 13-14; *see* summary of Commission decision, *Forex-Essex Express*, paras 13-14.
1470. *See* summary of Commission decision, *Forex-Three Way Banana Split*, para. 14; *see* summary of Commission decision, *Forex-Essex Express*, para. 14.

The infringement seems to rely solely on the (written) exchange of sensitive information between traders of competing banks. It does seem from this that these information exchanges were not part of a broader cartel scheme where parties are systematically monitored and where mechanisms have been established to punish those undertakings that deviate from the agreed understanding. Thus, these two cartels seem to be looser forms of concertation. However, according to the two case summaries these information exchanges created a 'tacit underlying understanding'[1471] between the traders that was meant to affect two basic parameters of competition in the Forex spot trading: price and expert risk management.[1472]

Since the exchanged information referred to specific transactions and specific banks, it was highly disaggregated. Not only was the information exchanged in private, the exchange also took place privately. The traders used professional chat rooms on their Bloomberg terminals. Most of the traders also knew each other on a personal basis.

More interestingly, the exchanged information not just related to existing/current trading activities but also to future/intended trading activities. Thus, the Commission seems to have made the conceptual distinction between the exchange of past information (even if current) and future intentions. One could argue that this indicates that the Commission had two theories of harm in mind. First, a relatively simple theory of harm that competitors should not exchange *future* intentions unless their objective is to achieve efficiencies (i.e., efficiency-generating horizontal cooperation). The secret exchange of commercially sensitive information in online chat rooms gave the exchange an 'illegal appearance'. Second, the Commission may have also developed a more complex theory of harm that relates to the exchange of *past* information. Even though these types of information exchange were probably efficiency-enhancing (traders have made more informed market decisions), they also enabled traders to tacitly collude. This theory of harm would conceptually align well with the concept of a facilitative practice.[1473] It remains to be seen in the final decision whether this conclusion was reached only in connection with the exchange of future intentions. In other words, whether the classification as a restriction by object of conduct involving the exchange of past information was only reached *because* it was done so together or even inextricably linked with the exchange of future intentions.

On the one hand, one could argue that this case adds more clarity to the 'labelling' of the information exchange. When the exchange relates to *future* intentions and lacks any justification, it seems that the Commission does not hesitate (anymore) to call such exchange what it is – cartel conduct that lacks any sort of efficiency. While

1471. Such tacit understanding rested upon four elements: '(i) such information could be used to the traders' respective benefit and in order to identify occasions to coordinate their trading; (ii) such information would be shared within the private chatrooms; (iii) the traders would not disclose such shared information received from other chatroom participants to parties outside of the private chatrooms; and (iv) such shared information would not be used against the traders who shared it' (summary of Commission decision, *Forex-Three Way Banana Split*, para. 13; summary of Commission decision, *Forex-Essex Express*, para. 13).

1472. *See* summary of Commission decision, *Forex-Three Way Banana Split*, para. 13; *see* summary of Commission decision, *Forex-Essex Express*, para. 13.

1473. *See* section 3.3.3.

the Commission was more cautious in labelling the exchange in the two *Bananas* cases as a 'cartel', the Commission made this very clear in the *Forex* case. This would suggest that any information exchange that is considered as restriction *by object* can be labelled as a 'cartel'.

On the other hand, the case also adds confusion because it also involved in the exchange of *past* information. This creates to a certain extent friction with the Commission's approach in the Horizontal Cooperation Guidelines where only the exchange of 'individualised intensions concerning future conduct regarding prices or quantities' is considered as a restriction by object.[1474] Surely, one could argue that the exchange of past information was 'consumed' in this case by the exchange of future intentions, i.e., in view of the overall 'tacit underlying understanding' in light of the exchange of future intentions the additional exchange of past information was simply part of that overall understanding. However, the problem remains that this is not clear from the case summaries. Furthermore, some argue that in the Forex market there is generally a very thin line between information necessary for market research or direct trades and information exchange aimed at collusion when using chatrooms, and that the case has not clarified the exact boundaries of illegality in this context.[1475] Thus, these issues have to be re-evaluated once the full decision will be published.

6.3.2 Descriptive Perspective: Identifying Common Themes

6.3.2.a The Market Context Matters

One of the common themes in the case law is that the information exchange concerned the biggest market players in rather concentrated markets. This is rather similar to the effect box cases.[1476] In *Fatty Acid*, *Bananas* and in the *E-Book* commitment decision the exchange involved the largest producers. In *Tate & Lyle*, the unilateral disclosure of future intentions was done by the British incumbent which was the only British producer of sugar beet. In *T-Mobile*, the Dutch telecommunication market was essentially temporarily closed due to legal barriers.

Some commentators have suggested that the market concentration mattered for the substantive appraisal of these cases.[1477] However, while the market context (particularly market concentration and market barriers) should not be the decisive factor for the classification of an information exchange as a restriction by object, there seems to be a preference by the enforcer to choose such cases. One explanation might be that in those situations, economic theory suggests that collusion can be more easily sustained. Another explanation might be that the harm to consumers is normally bigger the larger the market coverage of the information exchange. Since in all those cases the information exchange covered most of the market, it is only sensible as an enforcer to pick those cases where the harm to consumers seems to be most pronounced.

1474. *See* Horizontal Cooperation Guidelines, para. 73.
1475. *See* Paukste (2019); Zampa and Carli (2015), pp. 80-81.
1476. *See* section 6.2.2.b.
1477. *See*, e.g., Camesasca, Schmidt and Clancy (2010), p. 407.

6.3.2.b *The Lack of Plausible Efficiencies*

Another common theme in the case law is the lack of plausible efficiencies. The only plausible rationale in these cases seems to be the restriction of competition.[1478] In the *Fatty Acid* decision, the information exchange was aimed at effectively monitoring each other's conduct in a declining market. In *Tate & Lyle* and *T-Mobile* it is not convincing from an economic perspective why competitors need future prices or production costs to become more efficient or how this would have benefited consumers. In the *Bananas* cases one could argue that the exchange enabled firms to better predict future demand. However, it is not comprehensible why this would also require the exchange of price-related information. In the *E-Book* commitment decision, publishers essentially used the negotiations with Apple to move away from the low-price Amazon model towards a higher-price distribution model.

The lack of plausible efficiencies is conceptually an important element for the classification of an information exchange as a restriction by object.[1479] In *Groupement des cartes bancaires* the CJ emphasised the importance of a thorough context analysis (as opposed to an effects analysis) in order to *inter alia* find out if the conduct in question is at least at first sight capable of producing possible efficiencies.[1480] If it does, the conduct should be assessed within the effects-analysis; if not, enforcers can save time and resources and presume the anti-competitive effect.

In this sense, these cases have a certain cartel-alike character. The parties of these information exchange fell short of convincingly providing efficiency claims to justify the exchange of information. This justifies the strict classification as a restriction by object. Put differently, in order to avoid the classification as a restriction by object, parties of an information exchange should be prepared to plausibly explain why the information exchange is efficiency-enhancing.

6.3.2.c *The Practical Importance of the Concept of a Concerted Practice*

The case law does also seem to suggest a correlation between the concept of a concerted practice and the classification as a restriction by object.[1481] If the information exchange is classified as concerted practice, chances are high that it is classified as restriction by object. The unilateral disclosure of information in *Tate & Lyle*, the exchange of information in one single meeting in *T-Mobile*, the regular bilateral exchange of information in *Bananas* and the negotiations with Apple in the *E-Book* commitment decision were all regarded as concerted practices. The only exception is the *Fatty Acid* decision where the information was exchanged on the basis of an agreement.

1478. *See* Ibáñez Colomo and Lamadrid de Pablo (2016), pp. 26-27 regarding *T-Mobile* and *Bananas*.
1479. *Ibid.*, p. 26; Flores (2017). *See also* Smith, Rodyard and Petrescu (2015), p. 43; Niels, Jenkins and Kavanagh (2016), para. 5.06.
1480. *See* already section 4.2.1.
1481. *See*, e.g., Dunne (2020), p. 384 who argues that the concept of a concerted practice has provided a means to bring the various information exchanges within the 'cartel sphere'.

One explanation might be the increased awareness of competition law due to compliance efforts by undertakings. Undertakings are aware of the unlawfulness of cartel arrangements. If undertakings still decide to concert, they have to do so in a less obvious and less formal way. This is why the concept of a concerted practice has gained more practical weight for cartel-alike conduct. The inherent nature of a concerted practice is that it is a residual clause for more loose forms of collusion.[1482] The fact that most cases that are classified as restrictions by object are also regarded as concerted practices merely reflects the trend towards less formal and more sophisticated cartel-alike arrangements.

Another explanation might be the lack of confidence of the parties to argue that the exchange entails plausible efficiencies. Conversely, if the parties have the confidence to make the exchange formal (i.e., conclude a more formal agreement) because they are confident that the information exchange is efficiency-enhancing, the information exchange is unlikely to be classified as a restriction by object. In that sense, information exchanges that are classified as restrictive by object are more similar to hard-core cartel infringements due to their 'cartel-alike' character (lack of efficiencies, secret nature, etc.).

Also, the theory of harm is different from the effect box cases. The theory of harm is not just about preventing the creation of structural condition that makes collusion more likely. Instead, it is about condemning the engagement in collusive conduct that is detrimental to consumer. Thus, these types of information exchanges are 'more downstream' and 'more immediate' in their actual harm to consumers.

These considerations also seem to be the underlying rationale of the EU Courts for classifying the object box cases as a concerted practice. Even though both elements are analytically distinct, their appraisal by the EU Courts is fluid.[1483] Once EU Courts have decided on the classification of the conduct as restriction by object, the conclusion as a concerted practice follows naturally.[1484] One might even go so far that in assessing information exchanges the distinction between both elements is somehow artificial, if not redundant. It follows from the independence doctrine and the case law on parallel conduct that any exchange of information (as documentary evidence of some form of contact) falls within the scope of Art. 101 TFEU. While the EU Courts are reluctant to derive proof of a concertation from mere circumstantial evidence, the EU Courts are more willing to do so when documentary evidence is presented.

6.3.2.d The Temporal Perspective: Future Intentions Are Problematic

There is also another common theme observable in the case law. Except for the *Fatty Acid* decision (as mentioned above, an outliner regarding many common themes), all cases concerned the exchange of future intentions. *Tate & Lyle* concerned the unilateral disclosure of future price intention by the British incumbent. In *T-Mobile*, the only five Dutch mobile telecommunication providers discussed their future intentions to reduce

1482. *See* already section 4.2.1.a.2.
1483. *See* Wijckmans and Tuytschaever (2015), para. 11.84.
1484. *See* Rivas and Van De Walle De Ghelcke (2012), section 1.2.

the standard commission paid to dealers. In the *Banana* cases, the banana producers exchanged pre-pricing information that related to their future quotation prices. In the *E-Book* commitment decision, the publishers used the negotiations with Apple to exchange information about their future course of conduct with the aim of raising the prices for e-books above Amazon's level.

The importance of the temporal perspective for the classification as a restriction by object has been also emphasised by the literature.[1485] It is also an important factor for cases that were assessed under the effect standard. For instance, the information exchange in the *Eudim* decision and *T-Mobile* case both related to production prices. However, while the former related to past production prices, the latter concerned the intended prices. The comparison suggests that there is something inherently more harmful in exchanging future intentions than (just) exchanging information about past conduct.[1486]

Furthermore, a broad reading of the recent *Banana* cases seems to indicate that the classification as restriction by object is not just limited to exchanges of future intentions relating to prices, quantities or production costs. In fact, any exchange of future intentions that affect the competitive process could fall within the scope of the object box. The conceptual rationale for this strict stance can be found in the independence doctrine. The exchange of future intentions is logically more capable to reduce uncertainty about future conduct than the exchange of past information (even if that information is relatively recent).

Economic theory based on game theory systematically underestimated the importance of communication about future conduct for the success of collusion. Game theory has argued that it is merely cheap talk that is neither binding nor verifiable. However, more recently economics have pointed out that communication about future conduct may be indeed quite harmful because it solves the equilibrium selection problem.[1487] There are only very few instances where the exchange of past information is sufficient to overcome that selection problem.[1488] Thus, the strict stance regarding the exchange of future intentions does find support in the economic literature. In fact, it is quite effective in finding collusive outcomes because such exchange is costless. As pointed out by commentators in the *T-Mobile* case, without the exchange of future intentions undertakings have to unilaterally increase prices in an attempt to signal their willingness to collude and thus fear losing sales to competitors if they do not follow.

It should be noted that the exchange of future intentions must be *individualised* to fall within the object box.[1489] Intentions about sufficiently aggregated data may entail significant efficiencies (such as demand forecasts). This suggests that

1485. *See*, e.g., González (2012), pp. 34-35; Smith, Ridyard and Petrescu (2015), p. 38; Bergman (2006), p. 12; Caffarra and Kühn (2006), p. 140; Whish (2006), pp. 37-38. This has been also noted by economists (*see* Niels, Jenkins and Kavanagh (2016), para. 5.35). For a more critical view, *see* OECD (2011), para. 73.
1486. *See also* Ibáñez Colomo and Lamadrid de Pablo (2016), p. 26.
1487. *See* already section 3.3.5.
1488. *See* Wagner-von Papp (2007), p. 269.
1489. *See* Horizontal Cooperation Guidelines, para. 73; Wijckmans and Tuytschaever (2015), para. 11.17.

it is not the exchange of future intentions as such that results in the classification as a restriction by object, but the combination with the efficiency argument. The decisive test for the classification is not just the temporal perspective but also the absence of plausible efficiencies that these cases have in common.[1490]

6.3.2.e *The Means of Communication: Private Communication Is Problematic*

At the heart of the independence doctrine is the reduction of uncertainty regarding the future conduct of other competitors. However, this aspect may not tell the entire story why these cases were considered as restrictions by object. Bennet and Collins point out that from an economic perspective uncertainty has no role in economic models of perfect competition because they assume that firms and consumers have perfect information. In these economic models, it is the *lack* of information that distorts competition.[1491] Furthermore, the economic literature shows that reductions in uncertainty may even be beneficial depending on the type of uncertainty, the type of competition and the firm's expectation.[1492]

This suggests that one has to look beyond the mere reduction of uncertainty and identify another common theme in the case law: in all of these cases, the exchange was done privately. Thus, the means of communication is another crucial factor for the classification as a restriction by object.[1493] EU Courts seem to be more comfortable to derive concertation from private communication than from public communication.[1494]

The stricter treatment of private communication can be explained with the principle of indispensability. The principle of indispensability, which seems to be one of the underlying rationales of the EU Courts, condemns the selection of the most anti-competitive means to achieve efficiencies.[1495] Although private exchanges do achieve similar efficiencies for undertakings than public exchanges, only the latter enable significant efficiencies for customers and further increase upstream competition.[1496] Thus, it seems only reasonable to incentivise undertakings, with the classification as a restriction by object to exchange future intention only publicly.

1490. *See* section 6.5.1 for the analytical proposal for identifying restrictions by object.
1491. *See* Bennet and Collins (2010), p. 325.
1492. *Ibid.*, p. 326.
1493. *See* Bennet and Collins (2010), p. 327: 'Correspondingly, the difference in approach between economists and lawyers appears to arise due to different uses of language. When lawyers and judges talk about uncertainty being necessary for competition, they are talking about it in the context of the specific facts and circumstances of a case – that is, a reduction in uncertainty having come about through direct communications between competitors. Lawyers are concerned to ensure that clear advice can be given to, and understood by, companies not to engage in reductions in uncertainty via private communications with competitors. However, economists think about reductions in uncertainty in the abstract, being content to assume away any possibility of coordination (tacit or explicit) via the communication mechanism. This is where the difference between lawyers and economists lies.'
1494. *See* section 6.5 below for complex issue of signalling by using public announcements.
1495. *See* already section 3.3.6.c for this principle.
1496. *See* section 3.1.2.

6.3.3 Normative Perspective: What Should Be the Scope of the Object Box?

6.3.3.a *Is the Dispute Between the Case Law and the Horizontal Cooperation Guidelines Justified?*

What becomes apparent when comparing the case law with the Horizontal Cooperation Guidelines is that in the latter the scope of the object box is narrower.[1497] This becomes particularly obvious in *T-Mobile* which concerned the exchange of future production costs. While the CJ's guidance to the relevant national court suggests that it considered the conduct in question as a restriction by object, the guidance in the Horizontal Cooperation Guidelines suggests that this would be regarded as a restriction by effects as it did not concern future prices or quantities. Furthermore, the more recent *Banana* cases suggest that there may be even more scope for other types of future intentions (i.e., other than price, quantities or production costs).

On the positive side, the narrower scope of the Horizontal Cooperation Guidelines addresses the criticism of a checklist approach that is often raised by economists. It puts a stronger emphasis on the economic analysis of information exchanges.[1498] It focuses on those competitive variables that are most harmful for the competitive process (price and quantities) and condemns other variables of competition only after the in-depth scrutiny of an effect-based analysis.

On the negative side though, this friction reduces legal certainty and may undermine the very aim of the Horizontal Cooperation Guidelines. If the EU Courts are willing to classify a wider scope of information exchanges about future intentions as a restriction by object, the Commission should not hesitate to reflect this willingness in its guidance in the Horizontal Cooperation Guidelines. The Commission could even try to pursue cases that would test the limits of the EU Courts' willingness. A case that would involve the exchange of future intentions but that would not be classified by the EU Courts as a restriction by object would be an excellent way to clarify the law.

However, the Horizontal Cooperation Guidelines do technically not confine the Commission to only classify those information exchanges as restrictions by object that concern the exchange of future intentions of prices or quantities. The Guidelines merely state that in these two cases it is 'particularly likely' that this will lead to a collusive outcome.[1499] They continue to provide in the same paragraph that it is less likely that exchanges concerning future intentions (without only referring to prices and quantities) are made for pro-competitive reason. Thus, an alternative reading of the Horizontal Cooperation Guidelines is that the Commission wants to focus its resources on those cases that concern the exchange of future prices and quantities. After all, those cases are normally the most harmful to consumers. However, exchanges of other types of future intentions may well be pursued as by object cases if they lack plausible pro-competitive efficiencies (such as *T-Mobile*). Thus, a more advantageous reading of

1497. *See* Robertson (2013), p. 486.
1498. *Ibid.*, p. 486.
1499. *See* Horizontal Cooperation Guidelines, para. 73.

the Horizontal Cooperation Guidelines is that the statement about the scope of the object box is merely an expression of enforcement priorities.

6.3.3.b *Is the Exclusion of the Exchange of Disaggregated Data from the Object Box Justified?*

There is another divergent approach in the classification, this time between the case law and the economic literature. It concerns the classification of highly disaggregated current information on prices and quantities. The economic literature classifies such exchanges as 'high-risk'.[1500] This would suggest that such types of information exchange should be classified as a restriction by object which is by definition reserved for the most severe restrictions of competition. The case law and decisional practice though classifies such exchanges as restrictions by effect.[1501]

There might be a good conceptual reason for this divergence. As pointed out by González, although the exchange of highly disaggregated data on prices or quantities is an effective tool for monitoring, it only helps to *sustain* collusion once a collusive outcome has been already found. Without communication on future intentions, undertakings may not be able to *find* a collusive agreement in the first place.[1502] Although there may be circumstances where even the exchange of past data acts as a focal point that enables undertakings to derive from it future strategies of competitors, these circumstances are exceptional and do not justify the classification as a restriction by object.[1503] The object box is reserved for conduct that in *most cases* according to experience entails anti-competitive effects without the need to consider actual or potential effects on competition.[1504]

Thus, the exchange of highly disaggregated data is merely a facilitative practice that makes collusion easier if the market is characterised by certain structural features. The justification for condemning the exchange of highly disaggregated data does not lie in the fact that it already entails immediate detrimental effects, but in the fact that it *likely* leads to a market situation where even tacit collusion may be sufficient to achieve supra-competitive outcomes. Accordingly, such type of exchanges should be dealt entirely under the effects analysis.[1505]

The independence doctrine as such does not sufficiently explain the distinction between those information exchanges that should be considered as restrictions by object and those that should be considered as restrictions by effect. The test of

1500. *See* section 3.3.6.b.
1501. *See* already section 6.2.2.a.
1502. *See* González (2012), p. 36.
1503. Bennet and Collins mention two situations where past conduct may create a focal point: (1) in markets with price leadership and (2) when the exchange involves the sharing of costs or demand (*see* Bennet and Collins (2010), p. 322; also cited by González (2012), p. 27 for this argument).
1504. *See* already section 4.3.2.b.2 on the importance of experience in the object analysis.
1505. *See* González (2012), p. 38. *See* section 6.5.2 for the more sophisticated analytical proposal on the effects analysis.

'reducing uncertainty' as such is problematic because almost any information exchange reduces uncertainty.[1506] One could also argue that even the exchange of highly disaggregated information could fall within its scope. However, only the exchange of future intentions relates to the reduction of uncertainties that the CJ referred to in the independence doctrine. To be told how an undertaking will behave in the future (exchange of future intentions) is something different than to predict future behaviour based on interpreting past behaviour (exchange of past conduct). In the latter case, an additional 'act of prediction' on the side of the interpreting undertaking is required to predict future conduct. In the former case, such act of predication has been substituted by the exchange (of future intentions) itself. Consequently, only the exchange of future intentions has the severe effect on the reduction (or even elimination) of uncertainties the CJ referred to in the independence doctrine.

It is also interesting to draw a comparison between the mere exchange of future intentions and a full-blown cartel. A full-blown cartel not just entails communication about future intentions but also effective monitoring (such as the information exchange of highly disaggregated current data) and effective punishment mechanisms (targeted punishments of cheaters).[1507] Since the exchange of future intentions as such *does* fall within the object box, while effective monitoring mechanism as such *does not* (past conduct), one could argue that at the heart of condemning cartels is the former aspect, not the latter. Put differently, at the heart of a cartel is the legal notion of a 'concertation'. It is not the success of effective cartels that is condemned. Instead, any attempt to engage in a concertation that lacks any plausible efficiencies (such as the exchange of future intensions on particularly prices and quantities) is sufficient for an infringement of Art. 101 TFEU. It is not surprising that the exchange of future intentions has been descripted as an 'underdeveloped cartel'.[1508]

6.4 PUBLIC ANNOUNCEMENTS CASES

This section discusses unilateral public announcements of undertakings. Before discussing the case law (*see* section 6.4.2) this section lays down the analytical economic framework for understanding the potential benefits and concern of public announcements (*see* section 6.4.1). This section identifies those features of public announcements that are seen as most problematic (*see* section 6.4.3) and argues that even public announcement can be classified as restrictions by object (*see* section 6.4.4).

1506. *See* Niels, Jenkins and Kavanagh (2016), para. 5.30.
1507. *Ibid.*, para. 5.07.
1508. *See* González (2012), p. 43.

6.4.1 Economic Perspective

6.4.1.a The Pro-competitive Aspect of Public Announcements

Public announcements have an important function for the proper functioning of competitive markets. While some types of information exchange only increase private market transparency, public announcements increase public market transparency because they provide information that is accessible to all market players including customers and potential competitors.[1509] The economic literature argues that in general public transparency intensifies competition, while private information exchange is likely to restrict it.[1510]

The Commission emphasises on various occasions that public announcements are generally beneficial. For instance, in its Horizontal Cooperation Guidelines the Commission explains that unilateral public announcements do 'normally' not constitute concerted practices.[1511] Similarly, in the contribution of the EU to the OECD paper on unilateral announcements the Commission emphasises the positive effects on competition: 'Generally, the disclosure of information to the public at large, for example through a press release, can often be seen as beneficial. Customers with complete knowledge of what is on offer may fully utilize their power of choice. Competition can be maximized.'[1512] Thus, there is consensus that generally public announcements generate efficiencies that make markets work better.

6.4.1.b The Anti-competitive Aspect of Public Announcements

However, public announcements may also facilitate collusion because they relate to *future* intentions of what a firm's policy will be.[1513] Even though the exchange of future intentions is merely cheap talk (i.e., costless, non-binding and non-verifiable communication),[1514] it may be still employed as a powerful signal to communicate the willingness to collude (*inter alia* by announcing a price increase) and test the strategic responses of other firms.[1515] Such signalling is cheap as it avoids the potential loss of sales that would come with an actual price increase.[1516] This is why signalling of future intentions has been descripted as 'unilateral disclosure of information with anticompetitive effects'.[1517]

1509. *See* already section 3.1.2.
1510. *See* Kühn and Vives (1995); OECD (2011), para. 25. The economic literature argues that private market transparency lacks any meaningful efficiency and thus should be treated strictly (*see* Kühn (2001), p. 196; Motta (2004), pp. 153-154 and 156).
1511. *See* Horizontal Cooperation Guidelines, para. 63.
1512. OECD (2012b), p. 183
1513. *See* OECD (2001), p. 27; OECD (2011), para. 29; Jones and Sufrin (2016), p. 698; Niels, Jenkins and Kavanagh (2016), para. 5.36.
1514. *See* Farrell (1987).
1515. *See* OECD (2011), para. 29; das Nair and Mncube (2013).
1516. *See* Nitsche and von Hinten-Reed (2014), p. 19.
1517. *See* OECD (2012a).

The Horizontal Cooperation Guidelines explain that if unilateral price announcements are (mis)used to signal strategic behaviour to competitors, they act as a focal point for collusion. In such cases, public announcements are used to test the strategic responses of competitors to each other's announcements. This might also involve the readjustment of earlier announcements or the non-implementation of announced conduct.[1518] If public announcements are employed as means to coordinate prices with the aim of reducing uncertainty about competitors' future pricing behaviour, they are considered as concerted practices.[1519]

However, collusion via public exchange of information - as opposed to the private exchange of information - is generally more difficult to *achieve* because it is more exposed (i.e., all other market players are able to detect it) and more limited in its scope (i.e., mostly relates to prices). For instance, non-colluding firms will be able to undercut colluding firms and customers will be able to punish colluding firms by switching to non-colluding suppliers. Since any attempt to collude in public is more difficult, public announcements are generally seen as less suspicious.[1520]

It should be also emphasised that the market structure matters for the success of the collusion.[1521] For instance, if the market is highly concentrated collusion is easier to sustain.[1522] Since any attempt to collude via public announcements is more difficult one could argue that it may be wise to focus on those markets which are more prone to collusion because the threshold for tipping the market from a non-collusive equilibrium to a collusive equilibrium is lower.

6.4.2 Case Law and Decisional Practice

6.4.2.a The **Dyestuffs** *Case*

In *Dyestuffs*, the CJ concluded that the price announcements in question were evidence of a concerted practice. It concluded that undertakings 'announced their intentions of making an increase some time in advance, which allowed the undertakings to observe each other's reactions on the different markets, and to adapt themselves accordingly. By means of these advance announcements the various undertakings eliminated all uncertainty between them as to their future conduct and, in doing so, also eliminated a large part of the risk usually inherent in any independent change of conduct on one or several markets. This was all the more the case since these announcements, which led to the fixing of general and equal increases in prices for the markets in dyestuffs, rendered the market transparent as regard the percentage rates of increase'.[1523] In other words, the CJ concluded that the price announcements rendered the market artificially

1518. *See* Horizontal Cooperation Guidelines, para. 63.
1519. *See* already section 4.2.
1520. *See* Rabinovici (2017), p. 150.
1521. *See* already section 3.3.1.d.
1522. *See* OECD (2012a), para. 54 (about the market structure and product characteristics) and 68 (about the issue of collusive price leadership).
1523. Case C-48/69, *Dyestuffs*, paras 100-102.

transparent and thus eliminated 'all' uncertainty about competitors' future pricing policy on the market.

However, the reasoning of the CJ is economically neither convincing nor robust.[1524] Statements, such as the one that price announcements eliminate 'all uncertainty on the market', are quite formalistic. One has to question whether the judgment has much authority in light of the economically more sound, robust and in-depth analysis applied in *Woodpulp II*.[1525] Still, the judgment may be used as an example for the preposition that price announcements *can* indeed constitute concerted practices.

Another way to interpret the judgment is to read the statements in light of its factual context. The case dealt with three price increases. Although the second price increase followed after the public announcements, the third price increase actually occurred after private meetings.[1526] Thus, a holistic appraisal of the facts of the case (including these private meetings) may have induced the CJ to provide such formalistic statements. In that sense, the statements on public announcements carry not much weight if they are understood in abstract. They only make sense if they are understood in the specific context of a suspected concertation: public announcements are merely one of the *means* to execute a concertation.

6.4.2.b The **Woodpulp II** *Case*

In *Woodpulp II*, the CJ came to the opposite conclusion as in *Dyestuffs*.[1527] As mentioned above,[1528] the first hypothesis of the Commission was that the system of quarterly price announcements *in itself* constituted an infringement of Art. 101 TFEU. The CJ disagreed and concluded that 'the communications arise from the price announcements made to users. They constitute in themselves market behaviour which does not lessen each undertaking's uncertainty as to the future attitude of its competitors. At the time when each undertaking engages in such behaviour, it cannot be sure of the future conduct of the others'.[1529] Here, the CJ endorsed the economic consensus that public announcements generally entail significant efficiencies for customers.

The CJ also disagreed with the Commission's second hypothesis that the system of price announcements constituted *evidence* of a concertation at an earlier stage. The CJ found other plausible commercial justifications for the price announcement system. It was a rational response to the long-term and cyclical nature of the market and the desire of suppliers and customers to limit commercial risk.[1530] One should emphasise

1524. *See* already section 5.1.2.b.
1525. The book by Niels, Jenkins and Kavanagh for instance, a standard textbook about economics for competition lawyers, does not even mention *Dyestuffs* in their discussion about price announcements (*see* Niels, Jenkins and Kavanagh (2016), para. 5.36).
1526. Noted by Rabinovici (2017), p. 152.
1527. Ezrachi (2018, pp. 72 and 75) emphasises these opposing conclusions.
1528. *See* section 5.1.2.f.
1529. Cases C-114/85, etc., *Woodpulp II*, para. 64.
1530. *See* Niels, Jenkins and Kavanagh (2016, para. 5.36) for that summary. *See also* Cases C-114/85, etc., *Woodpulp II*, paras 77-78: 'The experts point out that it is in the context of

the fact that these price announcements that were sent out to customers (and only sporadically to the trade press) may have played a role in CJ's substantive conclusion that producers had not deliberately made the market more transparent.[1531] It is likely that the price information was forwarded to the trade press by customers and agents who received the price information in private.[1532] The CJ was reluctant to hold undertakings responsible for conduct of independent actors which they did not control.[1533] Still, the CJ may be open for allegations in future cases where undertakings play a more active role in setting-up a system of price announcements in order to make the market more transparent.[1534]

From an economic perspective, the reasoning of the judgment is economically sound and an appreciated evolution from *Dyestuffs*. In markets with almost perfectly homogeneous goods (such as the one in question) one should expect parallel pricing. Parallel pricing is a feature of homogeneous goods markets and do as such not offer a robust *indicium* for a concertation. However, the situation may have been different, if the undertakings would have not committed to the prices after their announcements.[1535] This was not the case though.[1536]

6.4.2.c *The Container Shipping Commitment Decision*

There is a long history of competition policy in the liner shipping industry. For many years, they have enjoyed special treatment in competition law. This was justified by the large investments necessary for ports and vessels. However, recent competition policy has shifted towards a more hostile treatment. This has led to the repeal of Regulation 4056/86 in 2006 and thus the end of the special treatment.[1537]

The *Container Shipping* commitment decision[1538] is a recent example of price signalling by public announcements. Its sophisticated economic framework makes it the best precedent for lawyers to be used in assessing public announcements. When the Commission opened formal proceedings,[1539] it raised concerns about the regular public announcements of price increase intentions through press releases. In its

those long-term relationships that, after the Second World War, purchasers demanded the introduction of that system of announcements. Since pulp accounts for between 50% and 75% of the cost of paper, those purchasers wished to ascertain as soon as possible the prices which they might be charged in order to estimate their costs and to fix the prices of their own products. [...] The explanation given for the use of a quarterly cycle is that it is the result of a compromise between the paper manufacturers' desire for a degree of foreseeability as regards the price of pulp and the producers' desire not to miss any opportunities to make a profit in the event of a strengthening of the market.'

1531. *See* Van Gerden and Varona (1994), p. 595; Kühn and Vives (1995), p. 87.
1532. *See* Rabinovici (2017), p. 153.
1533. Emphasised by Rabinovici (2017), p. 153.
1534. *See* Jones and Sufrin (2016), p. 699.
1535. *See* section 6.4.3 for the issue of contingent implementation.
1536. *See* Kühn and Vives (1995), p. 86.
1537. *See*, on this background issue, e.g., Møllgaard and Overgaard (2006), pp. 116-118.
1538. Commission decision, *Container Shipping*.
1539. Commission press release on 22 November 2013, 'Antitrust: Commission opens proceedings against container liner shipping companies', IP/13/1144.

commitment decision, the Commission further elaborated that 14 container liner shipping firms have regularly announced their intended future increases of freight prices. These price announcements did not indicate the final prices but only the amount of the price increase, the affected route and the planned date of implementation. The implementation usually took place three to five weeks after the announcement, during which some or all undertakings announced similar intended price increases and same or similar implementation dates. Crucially, some undertakings have also postponed or modified price increases after their announcements.[1540]

The Commission was concerned that these press releases allowed the undertakings concerned to signal future price intentions in order to increase the price level. In its press release the Commission summarised the theory of harm as following: 'Announcing future price increases may signal the intended market conduct of carriers and by reducing the level of uncertainty about their pricing behaviour, decrease their incentives to compete against each other. Because the announcements provide only partial information to customers, and may not be binding on the carriers, customers may not be able to rely on them and therefore carriers may be able to adjust prices without the risk of losing customers.'[1541] The Commission was concerned that the system in place allowed undertakings to 'test' whether competitors are willing to implement a price increase without incurring the risk of losing customers.[1542] An undertaking would first push for a price increase and (i) if there is not enough support by other undertakings, cancel or postpone the price increase; or (ii) if enough undertakings have 'responded' with similar price increases, stick with the price increase.[1543]

The Commission also concluded in its preliminary assessment that the public announcement system in question may have amounted to a restriction by object.[1544] It concluded this on the basis of (i) the content and nature, (ii) the objective and (iii) the economic and legal context of the information exchange. On the first issue, the Commission expressed concerns that the information exchange was able to reduce uncertainty regarding the future conduct of competitors because the public announcements entailed *inter alia* the intended price increases, the intended implementation date and the geographic area.[1545] On the second issue, the Commission concluded that the announcements had only limited value for customers and were merely intended to coordinate future prices.[1546] On the last issue, the Commission concluded that the regularity of the conduct created a climate of mutual trust and thus lost its connection to real market conditions.[1547]

1540. *See* Commission decision, *Container Shipping*, paras 25-29.
1541. *See also* the Commission press release on 7 July 2016, 'Antitrust: Commission accepts commitments by container liner shipping companies on price transparency', IP/16/2446. For the theory of harm, *see* Commission decision, *Container Shipping*, paras 37 et seq.
1542. *See* Commission decision, *Container Shipping*, para. 37.
1543. *Ibid.*, para. 39.
1544. *Ibid.*, paras 48-55.
1545. *Ibid.*, paras 49-51.
1546. *Ibid.*, para. 52.
1547. *Ibid.*, paras 53-54.

The undertakings concerned offered the following commitments, which in the Commission's view were able to increase price transparency for customers, while reducing the likelihood of coordination via public price signalling:

- The undertakings will cease to publish the price increase solely expressed as an amount or percentage of the change.
- The undertakings will announce figures that include at least the five main elements of the total price.
- The undertakings cannot exceed the prices announced for the period of validity once they have announced them (they are free to lower them though).
- The undertakings will not make price announcements more than 31 days before their date of implementation (which is normally the time when customers start booking).

Overall, the commitment decision provides a useful guidance for how to operate price announcements without infringing Art. 101 TFEU. In that sense, it provides legal certainty for undertakings that regularly announce prices: disclose all price information that is relevant for customers to determine the total price; only lower but not increase prices after their announcements; and delay the implementation of announced prices only as long as it makes sense for the customer's predictability of business decisions.

Although the commitment decision adds some clarity to the assessment of public announcements (in light of the limited guidance by the two other cases discussed above), EU Courts still have to produce a case that deals with this more sophisticated economic framework on signalling that underlies the *Container Shipping* commitment decision.[1548] A commitment decision is still on the lowest end of the authoritative scale. It is even behind a 'normal' infringement decision because the Commission does not make a formal finding whether an infringement has occurred. Still, its practical weight is significant.

6.4.3 Descriptive Perspective: Identifying the Problematic Features

6.4.3.a The OECD Paper on Unilateral Announcements

The OECD paper on unilateral announcements provides a useful economic framework on how to assess public announcements.[1549] The OECD paper provides that the assessment of public announcements should focus on whether announcements are constructed as an invitation to collude. The OECD paper suggests that the following four scenarios should raise concerns:[1550]

1548. *See* Rabinovici (2017), p. 156.
1549. *See* OECD (2012a), paras 53-74.
1550. *Ibid.*, para. 62.

(1) *Audience*: if the public announcement contains information that is not intended for customers but for other audience (e.g., reference to specific competitor).[1551]
(2) *Scope*: if the public announcement discloses more information that is necessary for the purpose of the announcement.
(3) *Contingency*: if the public announcement makes the announced conduct contingent on what other market players will do subsequently.
(4) *Threats*: if the public announcement includes threats if competitors do not follow the invitation to collude.

6.4.3.b *The Container Shipping Commitment Decision*

In the *Container Shipping* commitment decision two features of the price announcement system were particularly problematic. The common feature of both these features was that it was questionable whether the price announcements actually helped customers in making a more informed decision. In other words, there may be good reasons to argue that the *audience* of these price announcements were competitors, not customers.[1552]

First, the fact that the information disclosed in the public announcements only contained *parts* of the price information was viewed as problematic. The disclosed information was sufficient enough to enable coordination, but insufficient enough to facilitate the competitive process. If customers do not receive all the information necessary to determine the final price, price announcements do not materialize the efficiencies that normally come with public announcements (such as reduced search costs for customers).[1553] Such incomplete announcements helped competitors to increase their prices relatively (and thus keep the respective relative competitive positions). Relative increases retain the high price level for some customers. Thus, there is an inherent imbalance of benefits when full prices are not announced.[1554]

Conversely, if customers receive the full price information, customers are able to compare offers more easily and thus enhance competition among suppliers. The first two commitments offered by the undertakings confirm the view that full price transparency has the potential to enhance competition.[1555]

Second, the fact (i) that some announced prices were subsequently not executed and (ii) that the time period between the announcement and implementation was in most cases sufficiently long enough so that the undertakings were able to take into account the market reactions before the implementation was also viewed as problematic. It is questionable if and how such 'test the market approach'[1556] actually helped

1551. *See also* OECD (2001), p. 27.
1552. *See* Lunde (2017), p. 10.
1553. *See* Rabinovici (2017), p. 155.
1554. *Ibid.*, p. 155.
1555. *See* Niels, Jenkins and Kavanagh (2016), para. 5.36.
1556. *See* Lunde (2017), p. 10.

customers in making a more informed purchase decision. Some announcements were contingent on other undertakings following the announced price increase. Such 'cheap talk' (without any commitment to implement the announced prices) deprived customers of their benefits that normally come with public announcements.[1557] Thus, the system mainly operated in a way to test the feasibility of price increases without risking losing any customers.[1558] Thus, these two features of the public announcement system served primarily the facilitation of coordination between undertakings rather than customers.

The conclusion in the *Container Shipping* commitment decision can be contrasted with *Woodpulp II* where the CJ concluded that the price announcements were demanded by customers and served them since they were non-contingent. The third and fourth commitments in *Container Shipping* acknowledge that price announcements should primarily benefit customers (predictability and calculability) which require that announced prices are subsequently not abandoned.

6.4.3.c The Literature: Contingent Announcements Are Problematic

The literature essentially views those public announcements as problematic where the implementation of the announcement is made contingent on a sufficient number of competitors following the announced conduct (contingent or non-binding announcements). If undertakings are not committed to execute the announced prices, the public announcement does not materialise efficiencies for *customers*. This is because if undertakings are likely to revise announced prices, the announcement is of no use for customers and their purchase decisions.[1559]

Non-binding public announcements are a cheap means to signal collusive intentions to competitors without incurring any losses. When a firm does backtrack of its intended price increases after the public announcement because competitors have not followed the price increase, no harm is done to the firm's profit.[1560] Conversely, *actual* price increases may entail significant losses of sales to competitors that do not follow the invitation to raise prices and stick with their current prices.[1561]

1557. *See* already section 3.1.2 for these benefits.
1558. *See* Commission decision, *Container Shipping*, para. 37.
1559. *See* Lévêque (2007), p. 355; Bennet and Collins (2010), pp. 334-336; das Nair and Mncube (2013); Wijckmans and Tuytschaever (2015), paras 11.56 and 11.76; Rabinovici (2017), pp. 151 and 154. It should be noted that price announcements do not entail any risk of actually losing any sales to competitors. Conversely, actual price increases may entail significant losses of sales to other competitors that do not follow the invitation to raise prices (*see* OECD (2001), p. 27).
1560. *See* Rabinovici (2017), p. 151.
1561. *See* OECD (2001), p. 27.

6.4.4 Normative Perspective: Classification as a Restriction by Object or Effect?

6.4.4.a Is There Scope for Classification as a Restriction by Object?

In the *Container Shipping* commitment decision, the Commission classified the public announcement system in question as a restriction by object. From a normative perspective one should ask the question whether public announcements should ever be classified as restrictions by object. The question comes down to whether the distinction between public and private public announcements justifies a different classification.

In a nutshell, even public announcements should be classified as restrictions by object. The distinction between public and private exchanges should not be the determining factor for the classification. For both means of collusion the temporal perspective should be decisive for the classification as restrictions by object.[1562] Public announcements should be only classified as restrictions by object if they are used to signal future collusive intentions. This is particularly the case when the implementation of the announcement is contingent or when only parts of the prices are announced.[1563] In both of these situations efficiencies that normally come with vertical market transparency[1564] are not materialised.

Although it is generally unlikely that restrictions by object can be exempted by Art. 101(3) TFEU, it is more likely in case of public exchanges of future intentions. As noted by Wijckmans and Tuytschaever, the Horizontal Cooperation Guidelines provide that the double presumption (i.e., the presumption that the conduct falls within the scope of Art. 101(1) and outside the scope of Art. 101(3) TFEU) only applies to *private* exchanges of future intentions.[1565] This statement expresses a generally more favourable treatment of public exchanges over private exchanges. It should incentivise firms to exchange future intentions in public rather than in private (if they stick to their announcements subsequently).[1566]

6.4.4.b The Role of Circumstantial Evidence

One may wonder though whether a hypothetical infringement decision in *Container Shipping* (instead of the commitment decision) would have survived the judicial scrutiny of EU Courts. There are no indications in the commitment decision that the Commission had actually found any documentary evidence of a concertation. As *Woodpulp II* and *CISAC* have shown, the judicial scrutiny is quite intense when the Commission relies solely on circumstantial evidence. The standard of proof for

1562. *See* already section 6.3.2.d.
1563. *See* Bennet and Collins (2010), p. 335; Wijckmans and Tuytschaever (2015), para. 11.36-37. *see* already section 6.4.3.b.
1564. *See* already section 3.1.2.
1565. *See* Horizontal Cooperation Guidelines, para. 74. This is noted by Wijckmans and Tuytschaever (2015), para. 11.40.
1566. *See* Wijckmans and Tuytschaever (2015), para. 11.41.

circumstantial evidence is extreme high.[1567] It is not excluded that EU Courts would have accepted other plausible explanations provided by the parties for why the public announcements were conducted the way they were.

One may even argue that the strict stance of the EU Courts regarding circumstantial evidence was the reason why the Commission decided to opt for a commitment decision instead of an infringement decision. This would mean that commitment decisions can be used as a powerful tool to tackle the oligopoly problem under Art. 101 TFEU. The Commission should raise concerns and substantiate them sufficiently enough so that undertakings are persuaded to offer commitments in order to escape the uncertainty of appealing a possible infringement decision. In other words, the legal risk management of undertakings may enable the Commission to use Art. 101 TFEU through commitments to overcome the judicial challenges faced in circumstantial evidence cases.

On the other hand, one could also interpret the fact that the parties offered commitments as an admission that the public announcement system in place lacked any meaningful efficiencies. After all, the commitments offered did not eliminate the possibility to announce price in the future. It did merely amend the system in a way that unleashes the full potential of vertical efficiencies for customers.

6.5 THE PROPOSAL FOR A MORE COHERENT ANALYTICAL FRAMEWORK

This section proposes an analytical framework that makes the assessment of pure information exchanges more straightforward. On the one hand, it proposes a more coherent analytical framework for identifying restrictions by object (*see* section 6.5.1). On the other hand, it also proposes to further develop the concept of a facilitative practice to assess pure information exchanges that are restrictive by their effect (*see* section 6.5.2).

6.5.1 The Object Box: A Proposal for Identifying Restrictions by Object

6.5.1.a The Issue

There is a perception in the literature that some of the cases on the effect/object distinction has blurred the line between both concepts, particularly *T-Mobile* as one of the leading cases on the by object classification of pure information exchanges.[1568] These cases have caused confusion regarding the scope and extent of the effects analysis required for the classification of conduct as restriction by object.[1569] The long-lasting struggle of the EU Courts to settle on an abstract legal test has further

1567. *See* already section 5.1.3.b.
1568. *See* already section 4.3.2.a.1.
1569. *See*, e.g., Killick and Jourdan (2014), p. 4.

contributed to that confusion. The language used by the EU Courts in these judgments is often criticised as being too broad, too formalistic and too ambiguous.[1570]

This perceived blurriness of classification exercise creates a variety of problems in the context of pure information exchanges. First, it reduces legal certainty because neither undertakings nor practitioners are able to predict whether a certain type of information exchange will be classified as a restriction by object or effect. The problem is that it is unclear what characteristics of pure information exchanges are decisive for the classification as restriction by object. This runs counter to the very aim of the concept of a restriction by object: to offer legal certainty and predictability of legal consequences if undertakings engage in certain types of pure information exchanges.[1571]

Second, an ambiguous demarcation between restrictions by object and effect also runs counter to another rationale of the concept of a restriction by object: to deter undertakings from entering into conduct that is classified as a restriction by object in the first place.[1572] If undertakings are not able to clearly identify restrictions by object *ex ante*, the deterrence effect will not work. Undertakings will simply not know in advance which types of pure information exchanges they should avoid in light of the presumption of the anti-competitive harm that comes with the classification as a restriction by object.

Third, the perceived blurriness may also have the unintended consequence of creating false positives, which are detrimental for welfare. There is a real danger that less sophisticated competition authorities or national courts that deal with competition law matters less often might not be able to read between the lines of the judgments and identify the common themes in the 'object cases'. They may use the ambiguous abstract test for identifying restrictions by object to over-inclusively classify certain types of information exchanges as restrictions by object. As a result, undertakings might be deterred from engaging in pro-competitive forms of information exchanges simply because they fear over-inclusive competition law scrutiny.

Such blurriness between restrictions by object and effect is certainly not desirable. The analytical framework for identifying pure information exchanges that are restrictive to competition by object should go beyond the subsumption of facts under an abstract legal formula (*see* section 6.5.1.b). Instead, reference to other 'sources' are needed to consistently and robustly classify certain types of information exchanges as restrictions by object. This is why it is proposed that the identification of restrictions by object should follow a two-step analysis which entails: (1) a context analysis (*see* section 6.5.1.c) and (2) an objectified plausibility analysis for claimed efficiencies (*see* section 6.5.1.d).

1570. *See*, e.g., Baño Fos (2015), pp. 164-176.
1571. *See* already section 4.3.1.a.3.
1572. *Ibid.*

6.5.1.b *The Need to Go Beyond an Abstract Legal Formula*

From a legal perspective, it is not obvious which types of pure information exchanges should be classified as a restriction by object. As the case law has shown, EU Courts struggled to settle on an abstract formula. Instead, EU Courts have provided a series of different (often substantially overlapping) formulas. Although these formulas have been recently refined in *Groupement des cartes bancaires*, it would be naïve to think that the struggle is now settled.

Part of the explanation for this long-lasting struggle in the case law is that the precise legal formula should not be the decisive test for the classification as a restriction by object. At best, the discussion about the precise legal formula has merely academic value. At worst though, it exposes a fundamental analytical flaw on how to identify restrictions by objects. This analytical flaw was well hidden in a centralised enforcement system where the EU Courts could afford to put forward different abstract legal formulas because ultimately, they had to decide on the substantive outcome of the case. On a substantive level, the EU Courts were remarkedly consistent.[1573] However, in a decentralized enforcement system of EU competition law, an overly enthusiastic emphasis on an abstract legal formula entails the risk of a too loose application of the concept of a restriction by object by the various actors (such as national competition authorities and national courts).

What conduct 'reveals a sufficient degree of harm to competition'[1574] or is 'by its very nature injurious to the proper functioning of competition'[1575] is not obvious in itself. Instead, it is argued that the abstract legal 'formula' should merely offer a description of the substantive outcome of a more sophisticated test that goes beyond legal considerations (this test is discussed below in section 6.5.1.d). Once the substantive conclusion has been reached that a specific information exchange is classified as a restriction by object, the abstract legal 'formula' merely gives this conclusion a description. The abstract legal 'formula' helps to bind together the various 'object cases' by referring to common language of description. Thus, it has merely a descriptive value, not a substantive one.

6.5.1.c *Step 1: Context Analysis*

6.5.1.c.1 General Analytical Considerations

The first step of identifying restrictions by object refers to a thorough context analysis. Although the context is not 'everything'[1576] it is certainly an important preliminary

1573. As observed by Ibáñez Colomo and Lamadrid de Pablo more generally (*see* Ibáñez Colomo and Lamadrid de Pablo (2016), p. 28) and as shown in section 6.3.2 specifically in the context of pure information exchanges.
1574. Case C-67/13 P, *Groupement des cartes bancaires*, para. 50.
1575. *See* Case C-19/77, *Miller International Schallplatten*, para. 7; Case C-209/07, *Beef Industry Development Society*, para. 17; Case C-8/08, *T-Mobile*, para. 29; Case C-226/11, *Expedia*, para. 36; Case C-32/11, *Allianz Hungária*, para. 36.
1576. For this expression, *see* Murray (2015), p. 48.

(first) step. The idea is that the objective of a conduct cannot be ascertained in vacuum.[1577] Instead, the objective of a conduct has to be understood and interpreted in its specific legal and economic context.

The context analysis tries to identify the 'true nature' of the conduct in question. For instance, a conduct may not seem like a naked cartel at first sight but may resemble at closer examination of the legal and economic context many elements of a cartel. In the early days of category-building there was no need for an in-depth analysis of the context since the anti-competitive nature of those conducts that were classified as a restriction as object was so obvious that no one felt the need to further explain this (such as the classic price-fixing cartels). However, as the underlying factual understanding of the objective of the conduct got more difficult and the anti-competitive nature less obvious (*Groupement des cartes bancaires* concerned a two-sided market), the case law has begun to emphasise the need for a thorough context analysis. As mentioned, the context analysis has only relatively recently gained weight in the case law and has been also highlighted by the literature as an important factor in the by object classification.[1578]

The abstract legal formulas used by the EU Courts use words like 'obvious'[1579] or 'by their very nature'.[1580] Even the literature sometimes describes restrictions by object as something 'instinctively'[1581] bad or as something that 'you know when you see them'.[1582] What seems to be the underlying idea is that the concept of a restriction by object refers to 'something bad' for which there is no need to explain it because its anti-competitive nature is so obvious. Killick and Jourdan clarify that the obviousness of certain conduct as a restriction by object does hold only true for the parties. They argue that if the classification as a restriction by object is not obvious for the parties, it should not be classified as a restriction by object.[1583] Thus, the context analysis should be understood as a tool for enforcers, not for the parties. It helps the enforcer in understanding the commercial context of the conduct from an *ex post* perspective. It aims to reveal the 'true nature' of the conduct in its legal and economic context that is already obvious to the parties when they engage in the conduct. Thus, the context analysis offers little value for the parties. Instead, it helps to put the enforcers (which may not know the industry, common practices in the industry or the wider objective of the conduct) in the shoes of the undertakings.

The case law does not seem to put any limitations on the depth of the context analysis in order to 'understand' the purpose and objective of the conduct. The procedural efficiencies of the concept of a restriction by object relates to the effects analysis, not the context analysis.[1584] This may help to explain why competition

1577. *See* Bailey (2012), p. 582.
1578. *See* already section 4.3.2.b.1.
1579. *See* Cases T-374/94, etc., *European Night Services*, para. 126.
1580. *See* Case C-19/77, *Miller International Schallplatten*, para. 7; Case C-209/07, *Beef Industry Development Society*, para. 17; Case C-8/08, *T-Mobile*, para. 29; Case C-226/11, *Expedia*, para. 36; Case C-32/11, *Allianz Hungária*, para. 36.
1581. For that expression, *see* Brankin (2016), p. 379.
1582. *See* Murray (2015), p. 50.
1583. *See* Killick and Jourdan (2014), pp. 8-9.
1584. This is also the understanding of Peeperkorn (2015), para. 29.

authorities are sometimes well advised to conduct thorough market investigation or other forms of market studies in order to understand a given market. Market investigations are an efficient way to gather insights about the functioning of the market and to understand the challenges faced by the undertakings operating in the market.

However, even an extensive context analysis cannot turn into an effects analysis. If a context analysis comes close to even a light effects analysis, it is a strong indication that the classification as restriction by object is not appropriate. *Groupement des cartes bancaires* is understood as a powerful example where the CJ was dissatisfied with the direction of the analysis.[1585] Since the concept of a restriction by object presumes the existence of anti-competitive effects, it would be contradictory to require their assessment. Instead, the concept of a restriction by object should focus on the plausibility of claimed efficiencies.[1586]

The contextual analysis is mainly a factual analysis.[1587] The main substantive economic analysis is undertaken at the second step. However, the context analysis still requires some economic understanding because it lays down the foundation for the subsequent economic analysis. The CJ itself has provided in *Groupement des cartes bancaires* that *inter alia* the nature of the goods or service affected and the 'real conditions' of the functioning and structure of the market have to be considered when analysing the specific context.[1588] The difference of the economic analysis undertaken at the second step is that the context analysis does not delve into the substantive analysis of economic theory (i.e., consider and evaluate the various theories of harm and their 'mainstreamness' in economic theory). Instead, it lays down the factual foundation on which the economic analysis of the second step can be built on.

6.5.1.c.2 Application to Pure Information Exchanges

The context analysis and its application to pure information exchanges entail two steps. First, the different characteristics of the pure information exchange need to be assessed. This requires an assessment of the inner layer (public availability, commercial sensitivity, level of detail and age of the exchanged information) and outer layer (frequency and public availability of the exchange and market coverage) of information exchanges.[1589]

Second, the nature and the structure of the market need to be assessed. This requires the assessment of *inter alia* the nature of the products concerned (homogeneous or heterogeneous), the functioning of the market (e.g., whether innovation is

1585. Noted by Italianer (2014), p. 14. *See*, e.g., Case C-67/13 P, *Groupement des cartes bancaires*, para. 65: 'Although it is apparent from the judgment under appeal that the General Court took the view that the restrictive object of the measures at issue could be inferred from their wording alone, the fact remains that it did not at any point explain, in the context of its review of the lawfulness of the decision at issue, in what respect that wording could be considered to reveal the existence of a restriction of competition "by object" within the meaning of Article [101(1) TFEU].'
1586. *See* section 6.5.1.d.
1587. *See* Mahtani (2012), pp. 5-6.
1588. *See* Case C-67/13 P, *Groupement des cartes bancaires*, para. 53.
1589. *See* already section 2.2.

one of the main drivers of the competitive process or whether the main competitive factor relates to prices or quantities), the concentration of the market (i.e., whether certain undertakings have some degree of market power) and the nature and concentration of buyers (i.e., countervailing buyers power). This assessment should not be conducted too formalistically because, depending on the specific market in question, some factors may be more important than others. The ultimate aim of this assessment is to identify the most relevant factors that affect the competitive process in the specific market.

This fact-gathering (first step) helps to assess and appraise facts substantively (second step). For instance, it makes a difference for the substantive assessment of the plausibility of efficiencies whether an information exchange takes place in a highly dynamic market, where innovation is for the competitive process, or in a non-dynamic market, where the supplied goods do rarely change. Similarly, it makes a difference for the substantive assessment whether the market is concentrated or not. In less concentrated markets, the scope of a lawful information exchange may be wider than in more concentrated markets. In both *Eudim* and *T-Mobile* the parties had the objective to reduce production costs. However, while in *Eudim* this was done in order to get more leverage against concentrated suppliers, no such justification could be used in *T-Mobile*. Thus, in *Eudim* an even more far-reaching information exchange than in *T-Mobile* was not viewed as anti-competitive.

In essence, the context analysis aims to reveal the 'true' nature of the objective of the pure information exchange in question. It equips competition authorities with the ability to distinguish between arguments made by the undertakings that are meant to 'distract' and those that have commercial and economic 'substance'. For instance, in *Bananas* it could be argued that at first sight the information exchange should be viewed as pro-competitive because it improved the forecast abilities of undertakings and thus *inter alia* prevented shortages of bananas supply on the European markets. However, on closer scrutiny the investigation revealed that the system involved the exchange of pre-pricing information that was a powerful focal point for collusion, even though the undertakings concerned did not exchange actual prices charged to customers. The communication was 'cheap' for the undertakings because it related to their intended conduct and did not involve any immediate losses that actual price increases would have entailed.

Similarly, in the *Container Shipping* commitment decision, the context analysis revealed the lack of vertical efficiencies. The case at first sight might suggest that undertakings engaged in public announcements of prices in order to benefit customers. However, on closer scrutiny these public announcements were subsequently abandoned if not enough undertakings followed the announced price increase. Contingent public announcements hardly benefit customers because they do not offer them the certainty necessary to make investment or purchase decision based on these announcements.

Thus, in both cases a thorough context analysis revealed the anti-competitive objective of the information exchange, which might have been missed by a shallower 'first sight' analysis. These cases also show that the context analysis is not optional for the substantive assessment undertaken in the second step. Instead, the context analysis is a necessary (preliminary) step for assessment of the plausibility of efficiency claims.

6.5.1.d Step 2: Objectified Plausibility Analysis for Claimed Efficiencies

6.5.1.d.1 General Analytical Considerations

In the second step, the plausibility of claimed efficiencies has to be assessed. A hybrid approach between the plausible efficiency theory (Ibáñez Colomo and Lamadrid de Pablo)[1590] and the intended ends theory (Fai Kwok)[1591] should be adopted. This proposed approach can be described as the 'objectified plausibility analysis for claimed efficiencies'. It assesses whether it is comprehensible that the claimed efficiencies are plausibly the ultimate purpose (intended aim) of the conduct. What matters is the ultimate purpose, not possible anti-competitive 'side effects' that are merely a necessary means for its achievement. In other words, the benchmark for the classification should be whether the parties are able to plausibly explain that the ultimate purpose of the conduct is pro-competitive. If so, a classification as a restriction by object is ruled out. Possible anti-competitive 'side effects' to achieve the pro-competitive purpose then need to be assessed under the effects analysis. It may be that these anti-competitive side effects go beyond what is necessary to achieve these efficiencies (principle of proportionality). However, this does not result in the classification of the conduct as a restriction by object.

It is worth emphasising this point again. What matters for the classification as a restriction by object is the plausibility of *efficiencies*. The presumption of anti-competitive effects is merely the result of the lack of plausible efficiencies. Thus, one could argue that the discussion in the literature about the nature and extent of the analysis of the anti-competitive effects is a 'distraction' from the key issue for the classification: the plausibility of efficiencies. While it is true that the economic effects analysis is more intense in case of restrictions by effect than for restrictions by object, this is merely the result of a presumption, not the result of some form of 'lighter' effects analysis. The presumption of anti-competitive effects is merely the consequence of the substantive conclusion that the conduct lacks plausible efficiencies.

The plausibility analysis is more abstract than the context analysis and mainly refers to economic theory and (practical) experience. While the context analysis gives more weight to the individual circumstances of a given case, the plausibility test is *objectified*. It compares the likely net effects on competition of the conduct in question with conduct in the same or in a very similar context (objectified context standard). In other words, the ultimate purpose of the conduct is benchmarked against an objectified context standard that assesses what net effects can be expected from conduct in the same or very similar context according to economic theory and experience. Although

1590. *See* Ibáñez Colomo and Lamadrid de Pablo (2016), particularly section 3.
1591. *See* Fai Kwok (2018). In a similar vein goes the theory proposed by Mahtani that one way to establish the classification as a restriction by object is the reference to its 'objective' (*see* Mahtani (2012), pp. 29-32).

these different directions of both analyses create a certain degree of friction,[1592] the friction is mitigated by the option to individually exempt restrictions by object under Art. 101(3) TFEU and thus put aside the 'prediction' of the objectified context standard. However, efficiency claims under Art. 101(3) TFEU are much more difficult.[1593]

This more abstract plausibility assessment of expected net effects on competition is justified by the idea of procedural efficiency. An effects analysis is time-consuming and requires substantial resources of a competition authority. If most cases would need to be pursued by the resource-intensive effects analysis, anti-competitive conduct would not be sufficiently deterred.[1594] Thus, it is justified that an effects analysis can be avoided (and its anti-competitive effects be presumed) if it is expected that the conduct usually and very likely entails net anti-competitive effects.

The prediction of the objectified context standard has to be economically robust and sound. If the objectified context standard is not well developed (*inter alia* because economic theory is ambiguous, because it involves novel types of restriction or because the complexity of the restriction requires a more nuanced appraisal of the possible effects on competition), an effects analysis is more appropriate. As rightly pointed out by Dnes, the more information gathering on the effects of the conduct is felt necessary, the less appropriate the classification as a restriction by object.[1595] This idea can be described as the principle of cautious or (to adopt a Latin expression) as the principle of *in dubio pro effectu*.[1596] The use of that principle can be justified by the risk of false positives that would come with the classification of such 'greyzone' conduct as a restriction by object. The avoidance of the effects analysis is simply not justified in those situations. Instead, a more nuanced effects analysis is required. However, if sufficient experience is gathered over time on the likely net effect on competition of such conduct (i.e., the establishment of an economically robust objectified context standard), a classification as a restriction by object can be justified based on the procedural efficiency argument.

The plausibility analysis results in a lower standard of proof for the parties claiming the efficiency. Parties merely have to make 'plausible' that their ultimate objective is pro-competitive. They do not have to prove it to a higher standard of proof normally necessary for establishing facts in competition law. As mentioned, the normal standard of proof in antitrust cases is closer to the standard of proof applied in criminal law cases ('beyond any reasonable doubt') than in civil law cases ('balance of probabilities').[1597]

The lower standard of proof can be justified based on two arguments. On the one hand, it can be justified by the rationale of the by object classification: to achieve procedural efficiency. Competition authorities should not waste valuable resources on cases that hardly entail pro-competitive effects.[1598] On the other hand, the lower

1592. Similarly, Mahtani (2012), pp. 18-19 and 26.
1593. *See* already section 4.3.1.c.2.
1594. *See* Bennet and Collins (2010), p. 313; Smith, Ridyard and Petrescu (2015), p. 36.
1595. *See* Dnes (2016), p. 249.
1596. *See* already section 4.3.2.b.1.
1597. *See* section 4.2.3.b.
1598. *See* section 4.3.1.a.3.

standard of proof can be also justified by one factor of the concept of 'effort probatoire': the perception of normality according to which the standard of proof should be higher in situations that deviate more from the judge's prior views on the normality.[1599] This means for the object/effect classification that claims of pro-competitive efficiencies should be proven to a higher standard of proof when the objectified context standard 'predicts' net negative effects for similar conduct. In such situations, efficiency claims must be substantiated under the higher standard of proof used in Art. 101(3) TFEU.

It becomes obvious that the substantive assessment of conduct as a restriction by object is not derived from an abstract legal formula. It is the other way around. What is a 'sufficiently deleterious' or 'obvious' harm cannot be determined on its own without reference to economic theory or experience. Instead, the 'instinctiveness' of certain conduct as a restriction by object can be rationalized by the plausible efficiency test.

6.5.1.d.2 Application to Pure Information Exchanges

The 'objectified plausibility analysis for claimed efficiencies' can be applied to pure information exchanges. A common theme in case law of those pure information exchanges that were classified as restrictions by object was that they concerned the exchange of *future* individualised intentions (except for the *Fatty Acid* decision which is considered an outliner in many regards). In *Tate & Lyle* and the two *Bananas* cases, the exchange of future intentions related to prices or price-related information. In *T-Mobile*, the exchange of future intentions related to production costs. In the *E-Book* commitment decision, the exchange of future intentions related to a commercial strategy to move the market towards a retail model that enabled higher prices. Thus, the temporal perspective was the decisive factor for the demarcation to those pure information exchanges that were classified as restrictive by their effect.[1600] The exchange of future intentions was consistently classified as a restriction by object, while the exchange of past data (even if it was highly disaggregated and relatively recent) was consistently assessed under the effects analysis.

All these by object cases lacked any plausible efficiency which could have justified the exchange of future intentions.[1601] The entire existence of the Horizontal Cooperation Guidelines can be seen as the recognition that cooperation between competitors can generate significant efficiency. However, in these by object cases the exchange was neither part of a broader pro-competitive cooperation (the nature of pure information exchanges), nor did they generate any plausible efficiencies. In *Tate & Lyle*, the unilateral announcement of future prices could have generated significant efficiencies for customers. However, the unilateral announcement was done in private in a meeting with competitors. In *T-Mobile*, one could argue that the exchange of future production prices was necessary in order gain leverage against powerful retailers on the downstream market (i.e., offset market power) similar to the *Eudim* decision.

1599. *See* section 4.2.3.b.3.
1600. *See* already section 6.3.2.d.
1601. *See* section 6.3.2.b.

However, this argument is flawed since the exchange completely eliminated any competition for the procurement of services of dealers which is why it is questionable how this could have made the market more efficient.[1602] In the *E-Book* commitment decision, the exchange essentially aimed to move the industry to a distribution model that enabled higher prices. It was not plausible why one model (agency model) was superior to the other model used in the market (wholesale model). Instead, the commitments ensured that there is a healthy competition between both models. They even ensured that new distribution models could emerge.

It is also clear from the case law that the means of communication do not hinder the classification of exchanges on future intentions as restrictions by object. Even public exchanges were classified as restrictions by object (*see* the *Container Shipping* commitment decision). However, the vast majority of cases on restrictions by object concerns private communication. It is thus fair to say that although private communication about future intentions is more difficult to detect, it raises more easily suspicion about its anti-competitive objective. For instance, if the unilateral announcement of prices by British Sugar in *Tate & Lyle* would have been done in public, customers would have benefited[1603] which could have made the by object classification questionable. In case of public announcements, a more in-depth context analysis is required to identify whether the ultimate purpose is collusion (*inter alia* by identifying whether the announced behaviour is contingent on what other market players do subsequently). Thus, one could argue that the context analysis has more practical importance for public announcement cases than for private exchange cases, simply because the private exchange of future intentions resembles the elements of the typical cartel setting.

The emphasis on the temporal perspective of an information exchange is also consistent with the economic literature. Although game theory suggests that the exchange of future intentions is merely cheap talk and thus has little value for collusion, more recent economic literature recognises the effectiveness of exchanging future intentions to achieve collusion.[1604] It overcomes the equilibrium selection problem by creating a powerful focal point that makes the otherwise necessary trial-and-error approach for signalling collusive intentions redundant. For instance, in *T-Mobile* an actual reduction of standard commission paid to dealers for brokering post-paid mobile subscriptions could have meant that other competitors may not have followed the 'signal to collude' (also because they may not have understood the unilateral reduction as collusive signal), but instead would have stuck with their current commission. This would have resulted in lost sales since some dealers would have had the incentive to sell less in light of the reduced commission. This dilemma was solved by the exchange of future intentions.[1605] Even a one-time exchange was

1602. *See* Mahtani (2012), pp. 23 and 35.
1603. *See* section 3.1.2 on vertical market transparency.
1604. *See* already section 3.3.5.
1605. *See* Loozen (2010), p. 149.

sufficient to take away the uncertainty that an actual unilateral remuneration reduction would have entailed.[1606]

One could also argue that the exchange of future intentions concerns the type of uncertainty the CJ referred to in *Suiker Unie* when it has established the independence doctrine.[1607] Surely, one can derive future conduct of competitors also from *past* data. Economic theory provides for instance that information about costs of competitors enables the better evaluation and predication of firms' future conduct since costs are necessarily the basis for future pricing strategies.[1608] However, the prediction of future conduct on the basis of past data has much higher error costs than if competitors directly communicate how they intend to behave in the future. To be told how an undertaking will behave in the future (exchange of future intentions) is something different than to predict future behaviour based on past behaviour (exchange of past conduct). The precision of prediction has a different quality because it is undertaken directly by the competitor. To use the analogy by Ghezzi and Maggioline, any card game is hopelessly compromised if a player shows one of his cards to his adversaries.[1609] Thus, only the exchange of future intentions has the severe effect on the uncertainties of future market conduct of competitors (the essence of the competitive process) as the CJ seems to refer in *Suiker Unie.* After all, competition is about the future, not the past. Even the exchange of past data is only relevant insofar as it enables undertakings to derive future conduct.

The exchange of future intentions on its own (if they not part of a broader efficiency-enhancing cooperation) only generates benefits in very narrowly defined situations. First, the exchange of future intentions can materialise *vertical* efficiencies for customers if they are done publicly. The *Container Shipping* commitment decision has pointed out though that vertical efficiencies are only generated if the full prices are announced and if the public announcements are non-contingent. Otherwise any claim of plausible vertical efficiencies is questionable. Second, the exchange of future intentions can also materialise *horizontal* efficiencies. However, the scope for efficiencies is much narrower. In the two *Banana* cases one could have argued that the exchange of future pre-pricing information improved the demand and supply forecasts (improvement of allocative efficiencies). However, it is not comprehensible why the exchange of price-related information was necessary to achieve such efficiencies. Other means might have been better suited for such forecast (e.g., market research or other studies that also investigate the supply side).

In both of these efficiency-enhancing situations (vertical and horizontal efficiencies) the underlying principle is the principle of indispensability. The classification as a restriction by object seems to entail the idea that if undertakings aim to generate efficiencies, they should do so by using the least restrictive means. As mentioned, the principle of indispensability is also the underlying idea for the high-risk classification of

1606. *Ibid.*, p. 150.
1607. *See* already section 6.3.3.b.
1608. *See* Niemeyer (1993), p. 154.
1609. *See* Ghezzi and Maggioline (2014), p. 661.

certain types of information exchanges in the economic literature.[1610] For instance, if undertakings aim to materialise vertical efficiencies that come with the exchange of future intentions on prices and production plans, the *public* exchange is the least restrictive means to do so. Thus, the classification of an exchange of future intentions as a restriction by object also entails the condemnation of choosing the more restrictive means to do so. Put differently, the efficiencies claimed by undertakings becomes less credible and less plausible if a means is chosen that is not the least restrictive means available.

6.5.1.d.3 A Concerted Practice That Restricts Competition by Object: What Else!

A thorough analysis of the case law reveals that the concept of a concerted practice and the concept of a restriction by object seem to be intertwined. All those cases that were classified as a restriction by object were also considered as a concerted practice (with the exception of the *Fatty Acid* decision). There seems to be a 'natural connection' between these two conditions of Art. 101(1) TFEU.

At best, an analytical framework that examines both of these conditions separately exposes a rather mechanical application of Art. 101(1) TFEU. At worst though, it would miss certain common themes in the case law which offer valuable guidance for predicting the outcome of future cases. The connectedness between both concepts calls for a more holistic assessment of Art. 101(1) TFEU. Instead of trying to artificially separate the assessment for each condition, one should apply a 'cautiously holistic' approach. The proposed analytical approach is *holistic* because it recognises the intertwinedness between the conduct and restriction related condition of Art. 101(1) TFEU. It tries to prevent an analytical approach that looks at each condition separately without recognising the natural intertwinedness between both concepts. The proposed analytical approach is also *cautious* because it does not aim to undermine the legal structure of Art. 101(1) TFEU. Instead, it provides that if the assessment of one element leans towards a certain direction, this also affects the direction of other elements. It identifies a natural couple that make the substantive appraisal of facts more coherent.

The proposed analytical approach suggests that one should use a linguistically more intuitive language. If a joint conduct of competitors aims to be efficiency-generating, it should be described as a 'cooperation'. The entire existence of the Horizontal *Cooperation* Guidelines is an attempt by the Commission to concretise the possible forms of (efficiency-enhancing) cooperation. Conversely, if the joint conduct between competitors lacks any plausible efficiencies, it should be described as a 'concertation'. This reveals the natural connection between the concept of a concertation and the concept of a restriction by object. It would be hard to imagine a 'concertation' that should be considered under the effects analysis. Per definition a concertation lacks any plausible efficiency and should be classified as a restriction by object.

1610. *See* already section 3.3.6.c.

If an information exchange does not entail plausible efficiencies, it can be excepted that these undertakings are less willing to make their joint conduct more formal (*inter alia* by concluding a legally binding contract). It would be hard to image (considering the significant increase of fines in recent years) that undertakings would be willing to make a cartel-alike joint conduct more formal. Conversely, if they are convinced that their information exchange produces efficiencies (such as the exchange of disaggregated data for benchmarking purposes), it can be expected that undertakings are willing to formalise their joint conduct. Thus, the hypothetical test that assesses the willingness of undertakings to make an information exchange more formal may be already an indication of the plausibility of efficiencies.

One should keep in mind the bigger enforcement picture in order to understand the assessment of pure information exchanges. First, the strict stance of EU Courts on mere parallel conduct forced competition authorities to look for conduct that produces documentary evidence of some form of contact. Information exchanges clearly fulfilled that requirement. Thus, the case law on pure information exchanges should be seen as the logical continuation of the case law on parallel conduct. The same economic theories (collusion among competitors) are applied, although with a different quality of evidence (documentary instead of circumstantial evidence). Second, those pure information exchanges that were considered as restrictions by object seem to resemble some looser form of cartel-alike arrangement. The cases seem to reflect the trend towards less formal and looser forms of cartel-alike conducts which, compared to the usually full-blown cartel, lack more sophisticated detection mechanism. Either the higher cartel fines imposed by the Commission show their deterrence effect or undertakings are just generally more aware of competition law. If undertakings desire to achieve anti-competitive objectives, the case law seem to suggest that they do so (increasingly) in a less obvious and less sophisticated way. The focus on pure information exchanges merely reflects that trend.

6.5.2 The Effect Box: A Proposal to Assess Restrictive Pure Information Exchanges

6.5.2.a The Issue

Those pure information exchanges that concern the exchange of past data and are thus not classified as restrictions by object need to be assessed under the effects analysis. The EU Courts have produced three cases from which one can derive substantive guidance for assessing pure information exchanges (*John Deere*, *Thyssen Stahl* and *Asnef-Equifax*). The decisional practice of the Commission also sheds additional light on situations that are not covered by these three cases.

It is argued that the current analytical framework is underdeveloped. While there is general consensus that the cases follow sound economic thinking, an overarching conceptual link between the cases is missing. The link between economic theories and the legal framework is conceptually underdeveloped. This reduces legal certainty because it diminishes the predictability of the competitive assessment of pure information exchanges of past data.

6.5.2.b *The Need to Further Developed the Concept of a Facilitative Practice*

It is argued that the concept of a facilitative practice[1611] provides a useful analytical framework for those exchanges of past data that have to be assessed under the effects analysis. The concept could be used as the analytical tool that coherently translates economic theories on collusion into the legal framework.

As mentioned, the concept of a facilitative concept has been described by Petit as covering conduct that 'artificially' increases the chances of successful collusion.[1612] The concept aims to cover those practices that try to limit the influence of factors that destabilise collusion (e.g., reduce buying power) or that enhance the influence of factors that strengthen collusion (e.g., make the market more concentrated).[1613] According to game theory facilitative practices can affect the pay-off matrix and thus alter the incentives to collude.[1614]

However, the concept of a facilitative practice has been developed as an umbrella for a wide range of phenomena (such as price leadership, basing point pricing or contingency clauses). The concept lacks the sophistication when it comes to pure information exchanges. Although it provides that one has to distinguish between information exchanges that increase market transparency 'artificially' and those that increase market transparency 'naturally', it fails to offer any meaningful *substantive* guidance. At the moment, the concept of a facilitative practice merely provides a rough conceptual umbrella for collusion theories.

This is why it is argued that the concept of a facilitative practice should be further developed to offer more legal certainty for exchanges of past data. A simple four-step approach is proposed. First, the broader market context and the characteristics of the information exchange need to be analysed, which is similar to the object box (*see* section 6.5.2.c). Second, a robust theory of tacit collusion needs to be established (*see* section 6.5.2.d). Third, pro-competitive efficiencies have to be assessed (*see* section 6.5.2.e). Fourth, these pro-competitive efficiencies have to be then weighted against the anti-competitive collusion concerns in order to come to an overall substantive conclusion whether the specific exchange of past data is restrictive to competitive or not (*see* section 6.5.2.f).

1611. *See* already section 3.3.3 on this concept.
1612. *See* Petit (2013), pp. 30-31. *See also* Grillo (2002), pp. 160-161 and Petersen (2016), p. 22. Similarly, the Horizontal Cooperation Guidelines provide in the context of information exchange that by '*artificially* increasing transparency in the market, the exchange of strategic information can facilitate coordination (that is to say, alignment) of the companies' competitive behaviour and result in restrictive effects on competition'. (emphasis added) (Horizontal Cooperation Guidelines, para. 65)
1613. *See* Peeperkorn (1996), p. 5.
1614. *See* Stroux (2004), p. 27.

6.5.2.c Step 1: Context Analysis

The first step involves the assessment of the specific context in which the pure information exchange takes place. As with the identification of by object restrictions, it is an important preliminary step.

The aim of the context analysis as part of the effects analysis is essentially two-fold. First, it requires the analysis of the characteristics of an information exchange. Part of this analysis has been already done as part of the context analysis of the object box since the identifying of the temporal perspective of the exchange is the decisive factor for the classification as a restriction by object. However, the analysis as part of the effect box is more intense and more detailed because the theory of harm that needs to be established in the second step needs to live up to a higher standard of proof than the (lower) standard used for the plausibility of efficiencies. This more vigorous scrutiny is reflected in the case law and decisional practice. The judgment of the GC *John Deere* for instance, has been appraised by the literature for its intense scrutiny and its sound economic reasoning.[1615] Similarly, in the *CEPI-Cartonboard* decision, the Commission analysed very carefully the subject matter of the exchange. The concerns raised by the Commission were then addressed by further aggregating some of the data exchanged.[1616]

Second, the establishment of a robust theory of harm in the second step requires a thorough market structure analysis as a preliminary step. Particularly the level of concentration and the extent of market barriers play a decisive role in the overall appraisal of the outcome of the case.[1617] In the *Eudim* decision for instance, the Commission concluded that the information exchange did not restrict competition because the downstream market was highly fragmented, and the undertakings' collective market power was significantly constrained by the upstream market which was concentrated. Conversely, in *John Deere* the concentrated structure of the market in which the exchange took place supported the substantive conclusion that the information exchange restricted competition.

The emphasis on structural market factors is perfectly consistent with economic theory. Economic theory provides that certain structural factors facilitate collusion and thus make the reaching and sustaining of collusive outcomes more likely. As mentioned, economic theory provides that collusion is more likely when the market is concentrated, when market barriers are high, when competitors interact frequently and regularly, when the market lacks network effects, when demand is expected to grow, when demand is relatively stable, when buyers do not have buying power, when competitors have structural links, when competitors are relatively symmetrical, when innovation is not an important competing factor and when competitors in one market

1615. *See* Jones and Sufrin (2016), pp. 685-686. *See also* Peeperkorn (1996), pp. 16-17 who notes that it fits well with game theory.
1616. *See* Commission decision, *CEPI-Cartonboard*, paras 16-18.
1617. *See* already section 6.2.2.b.

also compete in other markets.[1618] These factors should be on every checklist to understand and assess the structural risk of collusion in the second step.[1619]

As with the context analysis of the object box, the rationale of the context analysis of the effect box is to separate the factual analysis (first step) from the substantive analysis (second, third and fourth step). While both analyses require each other for a robust assessment of a case, they should be conducted separately. Only the latter analysis ultimately entails a normative value judgment about certain policy choices (such as the weight and extent of the preventive approach in assessing pure information exchanges as discussed below). The first step is mostly a value-neutral fact-gathering exercise that builds the foundation for the subsequent steps.

6.5.2.d Step 2: Building a Robust Theory of (Tacit) Collusion

In the second step, the *anti*-competitive effects of pure information exchanges need to be assessed by employing a counterfactual analysis. What should be crucial are the causal[1620] contribution of the information exchange to the collusion concerns and whether the contribution is sufficient to 'tip' the market towards outcomes that enable tacit collusion. This requires an assessment of the situation before and after the information exchange and assessment of the changed conditions caused by the information exchange (the delta).[1621]

To understand what is meant by 'tipping' the market towards outcomes that enable tacit collusion is crucial. The idea is that only those information exchanges are anti-competitive that causally alter the structural conditions of the market in such a way that tacit collusion become likely so that concertation (explicit collusion) is not even necessary to achieve supra-competitive outcomes. In that sense the underlying idea is a *preventive* approach. Although the existence of structural factors that facilitate collusion does not result in concertation, supra-competitive outcomes can be still achieved by a tacit understanding of the undertakings in the market behaving in certain way. What is then prohibited is not concertation but the likely prospective of tacit collusion. Such approach tries to prevent the legal challenges that enforcers face once the market has tipped towards outcomes that enable tacit collusion.[1622]

In *John Deere* for instance, the information exchange system essentially prevented residual competition by eliminating the 'surprise effect' that is inherent to the competitive process.[1623] The exchange created a system that significantly reduced the uncertainty about the market conduct of other competitors.[1624] The market was already structurally prone to collusion (highly concentrated and high barriers to enter). The exchange was 'artificial' because it tipped the market so that residual competition became unlikely and tacit understanding of supra-competitive outcome was possible.

1618. *See* already section 3.3.1.d.
1619. *See* Smith, Ridyard and Petrescu (2015), p. 34.
1620. *See* Caffarra and Kühn (2006), p. 146.
1621. *See* Wijckmans and Tuytschaever (2015), para. 11.61.
1622. *See* already section 5.1 on the challenges of tackling mere parallel conduct.
1623. *See* Capobianco (2004), p. 1252.
1624. Case T-35/92, *John Deere*, para. 81.

The GC did not condemn the exchange because undertakings concerted, but because the exchange causally enabled tacit collusion (so that it was not necessary to concert explicitly in order to achieve supra-competitive outcomes).[1625]

There are two ways in which pure information exchanges can facilitate collusion. On the one hand, it can facilitate the process of *finding* a collusive outcome.[1626] On the other hand, it can facilitate the process of *sustaining* collusion.[1627] This difference is crucial for building a robust theory harm that is well founded in economic theory and deals with both ways of facilitation.

A pure information exchange should be only viewed as restrictive to competition if one is able to demonstrate how the exchange makes the finding *and* sustainment of collusive outcomes easier. In other words, both elements are cumulative, not alternative conditions. Only if both ways of facilitation are demonstrated the theory of harm is sufficiently robust in economic terms. This is because economic theory provides that only if all four conditions of collusion are fulfilled, collusive outcomes can be achieved. Conversely, if only one condition is not fulfilled the collusive outcome cannot be sustained.

Regarding the facilitation of *finding* a collusive outcome, pure information exchanges about past data can offer a powerful focal point for overcoming the equilibrium selection problem. Such exchange can narrow down the options of a possible collusive outcome. Particularly in markets with homogeneous goods such exchange may be sufficient to tip the market towards tacit collusion.[1628] Similarly, in concentrated markets (where undertakings have an increased ability to correctly anticipate actions of their competitors because of the simplification of economic calculations caused by the low number of market players)[1629] the exchange of past data may be sufficient to tip the market. Economic theory also provides that the exchange of cost data may help to overcome the equilibrium selection problem. This is because

1625. *See* Lévêque (2007), pp. 233-234.
1626. *See* the first condition for collusion as explained in section 3.3.1.c.
1627. *See* the second, third and fourth conditions for collusion as explained in section 3.3.1.c.
1628. Horizontal Merger Guidelines, para. 45; Horizontal Cooperation Guidelines, para. 82. *See also* Stroux (2004), pp. 24-25; Whish (2006), p. 22.
1629. *See* Ray Pfeiffer (1974), p. 114. *See also* the description by the OECD (2012a, paras 21-23): 'In oligopolistic markets, firms tend to be interdependent in their pricing and output decisions so that the actions of each firm impact on, and result in, a counter response from the other firms. In such circumstances, oligopolistic firms may take their rivals' actions into account and co-ordinate their actions as if they were a cartel, but without an explicit agreement. [...] In contrast to explicit collusion, in a tacitly collusive context, the non-competitive outcome is achieved by each participant deciding on its own profit maximizing strategy independently of its competitors. [...] No profit-maximising firm wants to make zero profits forever and each firm knows that it could earn supra-competitive profits by collectively charging a non-competitive price. The indefinitely repeated interaction makes the threat of punishment credible so that each firm knows that any deviation from the non-competitive equilibrium would trigger a price war pushing prices towards the competitive equilibrium. Therefore, such oligopolistic interaction renders individual strategies conducive to an equilibrium at noncompetitive prices/output rational, without actually communicating or agreeing explicitly.'

costs are necessarily the basis for future pricing strategies and therefore increase the quality of the prediction of how competitors will behave in the future.[1630]

However, the exchange of past data is not as useful as the exchange of future intentions. As explained, if competitors directly tell other competitors how they will behave in the future, the collusive outcome is found very easily compared to the situation where competitors have to predict competitors' future conduct on the basis of past information.[1631] Thus, the effects analysis has to be conducted carefully in a way to not overenthusiastically conclude that an information exchange of past data facilitates the finding of a collusive outcome. It requires a more holistic assessment of all the relevant market factors than it is necessary for the object box. *John Deere* for instance provides a useful example of such holistic assessment in which almost all market factors facilitated collusion and thus made tacit collusion very likely: the market was concentrated, market barriers were high, products were homogeneous and buyers had little buying power. Conversely, the fragmented nature of the market in *Asnef-Equifax* was one of the reasons why the CJ concluded that the information exchange did not restrict competition.

Regarding the facilitation of *sustaining* a collusive outcome a pure information exchange can increase the internal and external stability of collusion. First, a pure information exchange increases the *internal* stability of collusion when it enables undertakings to monitor each other and detect deviators. The most relevant scenario is the exchange of highly disaggregated (individualised) information that allows the identification of the individual market conduct of competitors. If competitors know exactly how other competitors have behaved in the past, their punishment mechanism is more targeted and thus more effective.[1632] Tacit collusion is easier to sustain if the punishment mechanism is credible enough to deter competitors from deviating in the first place.[1633]

This theory of harm focuses mainly on the following characteristics of pure information exchanges: the age of the information, the level of disaggregation and the frequency of the exchange. The more recent and more disaggregated the subject matter of the exchanged information and the more frequently the exchange takes place, the better the monitoring and thus the more effective the punishment mechanism. In *John Deere* for instance, the information exchange fulfilled those criteria. The sales data was

1630. *See* Niemeyer (1993), p. 154.
1631. *See* section 6.5.1.d.2.
1632. *See* Kühn and Vives (1995), p. 77; Kühn (2001), pp. 173 and 187-188; OECD (2001), p. 24; Ivaldi et al. (2003), pp. 22-26; Møllgaard and Overgaard (2006), pp. 106-108; Vives (2006a), p. 89; Bennet and Collins (2010), p. 322; OECD (2011), p. 11 (bullet point 2 in para. 16); Wagner-von Papp (2012), pp. 10-11; Nitsche and von Hinten-Reed (2014), pp. 25-26. *See also* Wagner-von Papp (2007), pp. 265-266 and 267-268 who suggest that the identification of individual competitors is in any case possible with just two firms in the markets, but may also be possible when there are more players if there are other items of information available that enable the identification (such as press announcements with individual data).
1633. *See* Wagner-von Papp (2007), pp. 267-269. *See also* Motta (2004), pp. 139-140 and 151; das Nair and Mncube (2013); Nitsche and von Hinten-Reed (2014), p. 27. However, even long reaction lags and infrequent communication may be sufficient to sustain collusion is some markets (*see* Vives (2006a), p. 92).

recently recent,[1634] the information enabled the identification of individual sales[1635]and the exchange took place regularly.[1636] Similarly, in *Wirtschaftsvereinigung Stahl*, the information exchanged was individualised,[1637] fairly recent[1638] and the exchange took place quite frequently.[1639] Thus, these three characteristics have a particular importance for establishing a theory of harm based on the facilitation of the internal stability of collusion (monitoring and punishment).

Second, a pure information exchange can also increase the *external* stability of collusion when it enables undertakings to better identify possible opportunities for new market entrants and to better coordinate their responses.[1640] In *John Deere*, for instance, the GC considered the information exchange as a barrier to enter that reduced the competitive pressure from traders from other Member States. Whenever a new trader decided not to join, he did not gain access to important market knowledge. Conversely, when the new trader decided to join, he immediately revealed his commercial strategy to his biggest competitors in the UK. This made it easier for the bigger market players that participated in the exchange to identify and attack new traders and thus increased the external stability of the collusive outcome.[1641]

6.5.2.e Step 3: Efficiencies

Once a robust theory of tacit collusion has been established (step 2), the pro-competitive efficiencies have to be assessed. This assessment is different from the 'objectified plausibility analysis for claimed efficiencies' whose objective it is to determine whether the information exchange in question should be put into the object box. The analysis of the objectified context standard assesses what net effects on competition can be expected from the conduct in the same or very similar context mainly according to economic theory and experience.[1642] Conversely, the analysis of the possible pro-competitive efficiencies is more *concrete* and less objectified. It allows for a more nuanced and thorough appraisal of the facts of the specific case.

Economic theory provides that there are two types of efficiencies for pure information exchanges: those efficiencies that mainly materialize at the level of the suppliers (horizontal market transparency) and those efficiencies that mainly materialize at the level of customers (vertical market transparency).[1643]

While this step does not weigh the importance of the type of efficiencies for the overall competitive assessment (this is done in the fourth step), those pure information exchanges that do (only) involve horizontal benefits need to be more thoroughly

1634. The exchange did not involve future intentions (*see* Kühn (2001), p. 194).
1635. *See* Case T-35/92, *John Deere*, para. 92.
1636. *Ibid.*, para. 81.
1637. *See* Commission decision, *Wirtschaftsvereinigung Stahl*, para. 13.
1638. *Ibid.*, para. 17.
1639. *Ibid.*, para. 17.
1640. *See* Bennet and Collins (2010), p. 323; Wagner-von Papp (2012), p. 10; Wijckmans and Tuytschaever (2015), para. 11.21.
1641. *See* Case T-35/92, *John Deere*, para. 84.
1642. *See* already section 6.5.1.d.
1643. *See* already section 3.1.

analysed than those exchanges that (also) entail vertical benefits. The sheer number of cases that concern private exchanges contrasted against the few cases that concern the exchange of public exchanges (public announcements) is a clear manifestation that efficiencies based on (only) horizontal benefits are more challenging to demonstrate.

However, this is just a general observation and does not rule out that pure information exchanges based on horizontal benefits can indeed materialise substantial efficiencies. In *Eudim* for instance, the information exchange enabled wholesalers to leverage their market power against few suppliers with significant market power. In *Asnef-Equifax*, the CJ recognised the potential of the proposed register to overcome a type of market failure (reduction of the uncertainty of credit risk). There are also those cases with the benchmarking efficiency (*CEPI-Cartonboard*, *Wirtschaftsvereinigung Stahl* and *Thyssen Stahl*). Benchmarking incentivises competitors to improve their internal efficiency, which ultimately improves productive efficiency.[1644] The recognition of such types of efficiency is clearly visible in *CEPI-Cartonboard*. After some exchanges (on consumption and order-inflows) were further aggregated the Commission saw its concerns addressed and thus implicitly recognised the significant efficiency-enhancing potential of pure information exchanges for benchmarking purposes.

6.5.2.f Step 4: Weighting Collusion Concerns Against Efficiencies (and the Importance of Less Restrictive Alternatives)

In the last step, the concerns of tacit collusion (step 2) have to be weighed against the efficiencies (step 3). The substantive outcome decides whether the pure information exchange restricts competition or not.

One could object to this proposed approach that this comes close to US-style rule of reason analysis,[1645] which the GC has explicitly rejected under Art. 101(1) TFEU.[1646] However, the case law on pure information exchanges *implicitly* suggests that the analysis under Art. 101(1) TFEU follows a similar logic. In none of these effect cases Art. 101(3) TFEU has been used. Instead, all these cases have been 'solved' under the Art. 101(1) TFEU analysis, even though efficiencies' considerations played a role in the outcome of the case.

The case law has focused particularly on the level of aggregation of the information exchanged. As explained, once the information has been further aggregated (in *CEPI-Cartonboard* the aggregation of data from at least three undertakings was seen as

1644. *See* OECD (2011), para. 12 (bullet point 4). The use of benchmarking studies has received official recognition by the Commission early on in order to boost the competitiveness of European firms (*see* Commission (1996) and (1997)). Carle and Johnsson note though that these benchmarking communications do not fully consider the anti-competitive side effects of possible collusion concerns (*see* Carle and Johnsson (1998, p. 84). Since they only reflect the underdeveloped economic framework for assessing possible collusion concerns at the time, their today's value for competition law assessment is limited.
1645. For an overview of the discussion about the relevance of the rule of reason for EU competition, *see*, e.g., Geradin, Layne-Farrar and Petit (2012), paras 3.81-3.84; Whish and Bailey (2018), pp. 142-144.
1646. *See* Case T-112/99, *Métropole télévision*, para. 72; Case T-328/03, *O2 Germany*, para. 69.

sufficient to prevent the identification of competitors' conduct),[1647] the information exchange was not seen as restrictive anymore. Thus, the obvious conclusion would be that any exchange of aggregated information fails to entail anti-competitive restrictive effects.

However, this conclusion would not align well with economic theory. Economic theory provides that in fairly concentrated markets tacit collusion can be even achieved through the exchange of *aggregated* information.[1648] The fact that in the case law the aggregation of information was seen as sufficient to tackle collusion concerns is rather a recognition of efficiencies that come with the exchange of aggregated information (as explained particularly the benchmarking efficiency). This suggests that the analytical focus is the *means* chosen to generate efficiencies. In essence, if not one of the less restrictive means is chosen to achieve a given efficiency that is achieved by a pure information exchange, the exchange is viewed as restrictive and contrary to Art. 101(1) TFEU. For instance, to generate the benchmarking efficiency it is not necessary to exchange disaggregated information that enables the identification of market conduct of individual competitors. Instead, the exchange of aggregated information is a less restrictive means to achieve such type of efficiency. Potential collusion concerns in fairly concentrated markets are 'tolerated' if no other less restrictive means are available in order to achieve the benchmarking efficiency.

This proposed analytical approach is an expression of the principle of indispensability. As mentioned, the high-risk classification of certain types of information exchange is based on this idea.[1649] It offers a pragmatic solution for overcoming the inherent tension between the increased risk of collusion caused by increased market transparency and the materialisation of the efficiency. Thus, the proposed approach is economically well founded.

Furthermore, this proposed approach for the effect box also aligns well with the proposed approach for the object box where it is argued that the efficiencies claim by undertakings becomes less credible and less plausible if a more anti-competitive means is chosen over the least restrictive means.[1650] In the *Container Shipping* commitment decision, the possible risk of collusion through the exchange of price intentions was 'tolerated' by the significant vertical efficiencies that could have not been achieved through other less restrictive means. Thus, the proposed approach offers a coherent analytical approach for the object *and* effect box.

Should this proposed analytical approach be described as a rule of reason approach? Probably not. It is not so much the balancing between anti-competitive effects and pro-competitive efficiencies that is paramount in the analysis. It is rather the search for less restrictive means in order to achieve a given efficiency that is central in the analysis. Once the least restrictive means have been chosen, anti-competitive effects are 'tolerated', not weighed against the pursued efficiencies. It is therefore proposed not to refer to the rule of reason analysis in order to avoid confusion (and

1647. *See* Carle and Johnsson (1998), p. 76; Bissocoli (2000), p. 99.
1648. *See* Wagner-von Papp (2007), p. 269.
1649. *See* already section 3.3.6.c.
1650. *See* already section 6.5.1.d.2.

provoke the obvious contradiction with the case law that explicitly rejected such approach under Art. 101(1) TFEU). Instead, the principle of indispensability should be used, which best describes the core of the proposed approach.

CHAPTER 7
Conclusion

This book has analysed the treatment of pure information exchanges between competitors under Art. 101 TFEU, the law on information exchanges which has been often perceived as highly complex and as lacking legal certainty and predictability. This book has clarified the analytical approach in how to assess information exchanges. It has done so by a thorough examination of the relevant case law and decisional practice at the EU level.

First, this book has linked the discussion in the jurisprudential literature with the discussion in the economic literature and thus offers an interdisciplinary analytical approach. It has demonstrated the importance of economic theory for assessing information exchanges in two ways. On the one hand, economic theory lays the theoretical foundation for justifying the object/effect distinction in the first place. Only those information exchanges are regarded as restrictions by *object* that lack any plausible efficiencies as the ultimate purpose. On the other hand, economic literature plays a crucial role in constructing a robust theory of harm for information exchanges that restrict competition by *effect*. The idea is that an information exchange can tip the market in a way that even tacit collusion is sufficient to sustain supra-competitive outcomes (concept of a facilitative practice), even though other less restrictive means would have been available to achieve the efficiency (principle of indispensability).

Second, this book has also demonstrated that information exchanges are the most potent manifestation of collusion theories under Art. 101 TFEU. This has to be understood in light of the strict stance of EU Courts to derive concertation between undertakings for engaging in mere parallel conduct. Particularly in concentrated market, the high degree of interdependency can be always used as a plausible alternative to concentration. The case law on parallel conduct indirectly emphasises the importance of evidentiary issues. While parallel conduct merely constitutes circumstantial evidence of possible concertation, information exchange provides documentary evidence. The EU Courts are more reluctant to derive concertation from mere circumstantial evidence than from documentary evidence. Thus, if economic models are used to condemn undertakings for anti-competitive conduct, they are only relevant once some kinds of contacts (such as information exchanges) can be found.

In conclusion, the issue of information exchange is less complex than commonly perceived. The crucial issue is to identify the common themes in the case law, categorise the different strands of the literature and link the legal with the economic literature. Such holistic view on the issue enables to build a conceptually robust analytical framework for identifying pure information exchanges that restrict competition by object (object box) and for assessing those pure information exchanges that may restrict competition by effect (effect box). This book has developed such an analytical framework and thus added value to the existing literature on information exchanges under Art. 101 TFEU.

Bibliography

Akerlof 'The Market for 'Lemons': Quality Uncertainty and the Market Mechanism' (1970) 89 Quarterly Journal of Economics 488.

Akman 'The Court of Justice's Expedia Ruling Undermines the Economic Approach by Eliminating the 'De Mimimis' Defence in Object Agreements' (2013) Competition Policy Blog, posted on 4 June 2013, available at https://competitionpolicy.wordpress.com/2013/06/04/the-court-of-justices-expedia-ruling-undermines-the-economic-approach-by-eliminating-the-de-mimimis-defence-in-object-agreements/ (accessed on 28 November 2020).

Albors-Llorens 'Horizontal Agreements and Concerted Practices in EC Competition Law: Unlawful and Legitimate Contacts Between competitors' (2006) 51(4) The Antitrust Bulletin 837.

Alese 'The Economic Theory of Non-collusive Oligopoly and the Concept of Concerted Practice under Article 81' (1999) 20(7) European Competition Law Review 379.

Alvin Sng 'The Distinction Between "Object" and "Effect" in EU Competition Law and Concerns after Groupement des Cartes Bancaires (C-67/13P)' (2016) 37(5) European Competition Law Review 179.

Andreangeli 'From Mobile Phones to Cattle: How the Court of Justice Is Reframing the Approach to Article 101 (Formerly 81 EC Treaty) of the EU Treaty' (2011) 34(2) World Competition 215.

Andries and Julien-Malvy 'The CISAC Decision – Creating Competition Between Collecting Societies for Music Rights' (2008) 3 Competition Policy Newsletter 53.

Bailey 'Standard of Proof in EC Merger Proceedings: A Common Law Perspective' (2003) 40 Common Market Law Review 845.

Bailey 'Restrictions of Competition by Object under Article 101 TFEU' (2012) 49 Common Market Law Review 559.

Bailey and John *Bellamy & Child: European Union Law of Competition* (Oxford University Press, 8th edition, 2018) (short citation: Bellamy & Child (2018)).

Baldwin 'The Sisyphean Quest for a Clear Test – on 'By Object' Methodology, Gin & Tonics, and Budapest Bank' (2020) Kluwer Competition Law Blog, posted on 4 May 2020, available at http://competitionlawblog.kluwercompetitionlaw.com/2

020/05/04/the-sisyphean-quest-for-a-clear-test-on-by-object-methodology-gin-tonics-and-budapest-bank/ (accessed on 28 November 2020).

Baño Fos 'The Dogmatic of Article 101 and Information Exchanges' (2015) Doctoral Thesis at the Universidad Autónoma de Madrid.

Bardusco and de Juvigny 'Budapest Bank: New Light Shed on the Notion of Restriction of Competition "By Object"' (2020) 11(3-4) Journal of European Competition Law & Practice 163.

Bennet and Collins 'The Law and Economics of Information Sharing: The Good, the Bad and the Ugly' (2010) 6(2) European Competition Journal 311.

Bergman 'Introduction', in Swedish Competition Authority 'Pros and Cons of Information Sharing' (Lenanders Grafiska, 2006) 11.

Bissocoli 'Trade Associations and Information Exchange under US Antitrust and EC Competition Law' (2000) 23(1) World Competition Law and Economics Review 79.

Black *Conceptual Foundations of Antitrust* (Cambridge University Press, 2005a).

Black 'Communication, Concerted Practices and the Oligopoly Problem' (2005b) 1(2) European Competition Journal 341.

Brankin 'The Substantive Standard Behind the Object/Effect Distinction Post-Cartes Bancaires' (2016) 37(6) European Competition Law Review 376.

Broberg and Jakobsen 'The Concept of Agreement in Article 81 E.C.: On the Manufacturers' Right to Prevent Parallel Trade Within the European Community' (2002) 23(3) European Competition Law Review 127.

Brown Kruse and Schenk 'Location, Cooperation and Communication: An Experimental Examination' (2000) 18(1) International Journal of Industrial Organization 59.

Bruzzone and Capozzi 'Restrictions by Object in the Case Law of the Court of Justice: In Search of a Systematic Approach' (2016), posted on 24 March 2016, available at https://ssrn.com/abstract=2753521 (accessed on 28 November 2020).

Buettner et al. 'Economic Analysis at the European Commission 2012-2013' (2013) 43(4) Review of Industrial Organization 265.

Bushell and Healy 'Expedia: The De Minimis Notice and 'By Object' Restrictions' (2013) 4(3) Journal of European Competition Law & Practice 224.

Caffarra and Kühn 'The Cost of Simplistic Rules for Assessing Information Exchange: The Italian Jet Fuel Decision' in *Swedish Competition Authority 'Pros and Cons of Information Sharing* (Lenanders Grafiska, 2006) 131.

Camesasca and Schmidt 'New EC Horizontal Guidelines: Providing Helpful Guidance in the Highly Diverse and Complex Field of Competitor Cooperation and Information Exchanges' (2011) 2(3) Journal of European Competition Law & Practice 227.

Camesasca, Schmidt and Clancy 'The EC Commission's Draft Horizontal Guidelines: Presumed Guilty when Having a Chat' (2010) 1(5) European Competition Law & Practice 405.

Capobianco 'Information Exchange under EC Competition Law' (2004) 41 Common Market Law Review 1247.

Carle and Johnsson 'Benchmarking and E.C. Competition Law' (1998) 19(2) European Competition Law Review 74.

Carlton, Gertner and Rosenfield 'Communication Among Competitors: Game Theory and Antitrust' (1997) 5 George Mason Law Review 423.

Castillo de la Torre and Gippini Fournier *Evidence, Proof and Judicial Review in EU Competition Law* (Edward Elgar Pub, 2017).

Commission 'Benchmarking the Competitiveness of European Industry' (1996) Office for Official Publications of the European Communities.

Commission 'Benchmarking: Implementation of an Instrument Available to Economic Actors and Public Authorities' (1997) COM(97) 153 final, 16 April 1997.

Commission 'Annex to the Commission Staff Working Paper: Towards More Effective EU Merger Control' (2013) SWD(2013) 239 final, 25 June 2013.

Colangelo and Maggiolino 'Applying Two-Sided Markets Theory: The MasterCard and American Express Decisions' (2018) 14(1) Journal of Competition Law & Economics 115.

Collins 'Of Cattle, Crashes & Cards – Recent Case-Law of the Court of Justice on Restrictions by Object' in Almăşan and Whelan (eds) *The Consistent Application of EU Competition Law: Substantive and Procedural Challenges* (Springer International Publishing, 2017) 43.

Cucu '"Agreements", "Decisions" and "Concerted Practices": Key Concepts in the Analysis of Anticompetitive Agreements' (2013) 3 Challenges of the Knowledge Society 213.

das Nair and Mncube 'The Role of Information Exchange in Facilitating Collusion: Insights From Selected Cases' 181 in Roberts and Moodaliyar (eds) *The Development of Competition Law and Economics in South Africa* (HSRC Press, 2013).

De Mattheis and Giordano 'Payment Cards and Permitted Multilateral Interchange Fees (MIFs): Will the European Commission Harm Consumers and the European Payment Industry?' (2015) 6(2) Journal of European Competition Law & Practice 85.

Dnes 'Object and Effect: What Role for Structured Evidence Rules?' (2016) 11(2) The Competition Law Review 239.

Dunne and Maher 'The "Acceptable" Cartel? Horizontal Agreements Within EU Competition Law: Introduction' (2020) 65(3) The Antitrust Bulletin 335.

Dunne 'Characterizing Hard Core Cartels under Article 101 TFEU' (2020) 65(3) The Antitrust Bulletin 376.

Ezrachi 'Sponge' (2015) 5(1) Journal of Antitrust Enforcement 49.

Ezrachi *EU Competition Law: An Analytical Guide to the Leading Cases* (Hart Publishing, 6th edition, 2018).

Farrell 'Cheap Talk, Coordination, and Entry' (1987) 18(1) The RAND Journal of Economics 34.

Fattori 'The Impact of Groupement des Cartes Bancaires on Competition Law Enforcement' (2015) Antitrust and Regulatory Issues: 2 The Ongoing Debate 22.

Faull, Nikpay and Taylor (eds) *Faull & Nikpay: The EU Law of Competition* (Oxford University Press, 3rd edition, 2014) (short citation: Faull & Nikpay (2014)).

Filippelli *Collective Dominance and Collusion* (Edward Elgar Publishing, 2013).

Flores 'Should Pure Information Exchanges Be Treated as Cartels?' (2017) 13 Centro de Estudios de Derecho de la Competencia 45.

Fonseca and Norman 'Explicit vs. Tacit Collusion – The Impact of Communication in Oligopoly Experiments' (2012) Discussion Paper No 65, Düsseldorf Institute for Competition Economics, August 2012.

Franzosi 'Oligopoly and the Prisoner's Dilemma: Concerted Practices and 'As If' Behaviour' (1988) 9(4) European Competition Law Review 385.

Frazer 'Information Exchange: Don't Slip on the Banana Skin' (2013) Legal Briefing, 1 June 2013, available at http://www.inhouselawyer.co.uk/legal-briefing/information-exchange-dont-slip-on-the-banana-skin/ (accessed on 28 November 2020).

Gassler 'Non-controlling Minority Shareholdings and EU Merger Control' (2018) 41(1) World Competition Law and Economics Review 3.

Gee 'MasterCard: Illegality Confirmed for Multilateral Interchange Fees for Payment Card Transactions' (2012) 3(6) Journal of European Competition Law & Practice 549.

Geradin, Layne-Farrar and Petit *EU Competition Law and Economics* (Oxford University Press, 2012).

Ghezzi and Maggiolino 'Bridging EU Concerted Practice with U.S. Concerted Actions' (2014) 10(3) Journal of Competition Law & Economics 647.

Gilo, Moshe and Spiegel 'Partial Cross Ownership and Tacit Collusion' (2006) 37(1) RAND Journal of Economics 81.

González 'Object Analysis in Information Exchange Among Competitors' (2012) Global Antitrust Review.

González 'Restrictions by Object and the Appreciability Test: The Expedia Case, a Surprising Judgment or a Simple Clarification?' (2013) 34(9) European Competition Law Review 457.

Graham 'Re Thinking the De Minimis Rules' (2013) Competition Law Blog, 17 July, available at http://awa2014.concurrences.com/business-articles-awards/article/re-thinking-the-de-minimis-rules (accessed on 28 November 2020).

Grillo 'Collusion and Facilitating Practices: A New Perspective in Antitrust Analysis' (2002) 14 European Journal of Law and Economics 151.

Havu and Zupani 'Case Comment: Collusion and Online Platforms in Eturas' (2016) 11(2) The Competition Law Review 255.

Heimler 'The Legal Significance of Economic Evidence in Antitrust Cases: Some Comments Based on the Italian Experience', in OECD 'Policy Roundtables: Information Exchanges Between Competitors under Competition Law' (2010) DAF/COMP(2010)37, 11 July 2011, 400.

Henry and van Weert '*Generics (UK) Ltd and Others v. CMA*: Patent Settlement Agreements Unpacked' (2020) 11(7) Journal of European Competition Law & Practice 360.

Fai Kwok 'Re-conceptualizing 'Object' Analysis under Article 101 TFEU: Theoretical and Comparative Perspectives' (2018) 14(3) Journal of Competition Law & Economics 467.

Ibáñez Colomo and Lamadrid de Pablo 'On the Notion of Restriction of Competition: What We Know and What We Don't Know We Know' (2016), posted on 18 October 2016, available at https://ssrn.com/abstract=2849831 (accessed on 28 November 2020).

Ibáñez Colomo 'Legal Tests in EU Competition Law: Taxonomy and Operation' (2019), 10(7) Journal of European Competition Law & Practice 424 (short citation: Ibáñez Colomo (2019a)).

Ibáñez Colomo 'Pay-For-Delay and the Structure of Article 101(1) TFEU: Points of Law Raised in *Lundbeck* and *Paroxetine*' (2019) 10(10) Journal of European Competition Law & Practice 591 (short citation: Ibáñez Colomo (2019b)).

Ibáñez Colomo 'Persistent Myths in Competition Law (III): The "Object Box"' (2019) Chilling Competition, posted on 15 July 2019, available at https://chillingcompetition.com/2019/07/15/persistent-myths-in-competition-law-iii-the-object-box/ (accessed on 28 November 2020) (short citation: Ibáñez Colomo (2019c)).

Ibáñez Colomo 'The Legal Status of Pay-for-Delay Agreements in EU Competition Law: Generics (Paroxetine)' (2020), posted on 16 September 2020, available at https://ssrn.com/abstract=3693746 (accessed on 28 November 2020) (short citation: Ibáñez Colomo (2020a)).

Ibáñez Colomo 'Anticompetitive Effects in EU Competition Law' (2020), posted on 8 June 2020, last revised on 24 October 2020, available at https://ssrn.com/abstract=3599407 (accessed on 28 November 2020) (short citation: Ibáñez Colomo (2020b)).

Ibáñez Colomo 'Vertical Restraints after *Generics* and *Budapest Bank*' (2020), posted on 20 October 2020, available at Ibáñez Colomo, Pablo, Vertical Restraints after Generics and Budapest Bank (31 August 2020). Forthcoming in (2020) 17 Concurrences, Available at SSRN: https://ssrn.com/abstract=3683938 (accessed on 28 November 2020) (short citation: Ibáñez Colomo (2020c)).

Ibáñez Colomo *The Shaping of EU Competition Law* (Cambridge University Press, 1st edition, 2020d) (short citation: Ibáñez Colomo (2020d)).

Italianer 'The Object of Effects' Speech at the CRA Annual Brussels Conference – Economic Developments in Competition Policy (2014), 10 December 2014.

Ivaldi et al. 'The Economics of Tacit Collusion' (2003) Final Report for DG Competition, European Commission, March 2003, available at http://ec.europa.eu/competition/mergers/studies_reports/the_economics_of_tacit_collusion_en.pdf (accessed on 28 November 2020).

Jensen 'The Digital Provide: Information (Technology), Market Performance, and Welfare in the South Indian Fisheries Sectors' (2007) 122(3) The Quarterly Journal of Economics 879.

Joliet 'La notion de pratique concertée et l'arrêt ICI dans une perspective comparative' (1974) 3(4) Cahiers de droit européen 251.

Jones 'Woodpulp: Concerted Practice and/or Conscious Parallelism?' (1993) 14(6) European Competition Law Review 273.

Jones 'Analysis of Agreements under U.S. and EC Antitrust Law – Convergence or Divergence?' (2006) 51(4) The Antitrust Bulletin 691.

Jones 'Left Behind by Modernisation? Restrictions by Object under Article 101(1)' (2010) 6(3) European Competition Journal 649.

Jones 'The Boundaries of an Undertaking in EU Competition Law' (2012) 8(2) European Competition Journal 301.

Jones and Sufrin *EU Competition Law: Text, Cases, and Materials* (Oxford University Press, 6th edition, 2016).

Joshua and Jordan 'Combinations, Concerted Practices and Cartels: Adopting the Concept of Conspiracy in European Community Competition Law' (2004) 24(3) Northwestern Journal of International Law & Business 647.

Käis 'Regulating Information Exchange in EU – No Further Restrictions by Object but Enough Room for Safe Harbours' (2013) 34(7) European Competition Law Review 352.

Killick and Jourdan 'Cartes Bancaires: A Revolution or A Reminder of Old Principles We Should Never Have Forgotten?' (2014) Competition Policy International, December 2014, 1.

Killick 'Patent Settlements as by Object Restrictions: A European Approach, but Is it the Right One?' in Edward, MacLennan and Komninos (eds) *Ian S. Forrester QC LL. D.: A Scot Without Borders, Liber Amicorum. Volume II* (Concurrences Review, 2015) 185.

Killick, Jourdan and Pêcheux 'The *Servier* Judgment: The General Court Annuls the Commission's Market Definition but Confirms the Illegality of Certain Patent Settlement Agreements' (2019) 10(1) Journal of European Competition Law & Practice 25.

King 'The Object box: Law, Policy or Myth?' (2011) 7(2) European Competition Journal 269.

Kühn and Vives 'Information Exchanges Among Firms and Their Impact on Competition' (1995) Office for Official Publications for the European Community, June 1994, revised February 1995.

Kühn 'Fighting Collusion by Regulating Communication Between Firms' (2001) 16(32) Economic Policy 169.

Kühn 'Designing Competition Policy Towards Information Exchanges – Looking Beyond the Possibility Results', in OECD 'Policy Roundtables: Information Exchanges Between Competitors under Competition Law' (2010) DAF/COMP(2010)37, 11 July 2011, 416.

Kyprianides 'Critically Evaluate Treatment of Information Exchange in TFEU Article 101 Cases' (2012) 33(9) European Competition Law Review 406.

Lahtinen and Pierre 'Reverse Payment Settlements in the European Union after the Generics (UK) Judgment – Perplexing Legal Uncertainty' (2020) CoRe Blog, posted on 5 March 2020, available at https://www.lexxion.eu/coreblogpost/reverse-payment-settlements-in-the-european-union-after-the-generics-uk-judgment-perplexing-legal-uncertainty/ (accessed on 28 November 2020).

Lenares 'Economic Foundations of E.U. Legislation on Information Sharing Among Firms' (1997) 18(1) European Competition Law Review 66.

Levenstein and Suslow 'Cartel Bargaining and Monitoring: The Role of Information Sharing' 43, in Swedish Competition Authority 'Pros and Cons of Information Sharing' (2006) Lenanders Grafiska.

Lévêque 'UK Tractors, Paris Luxury Hotels and French Mobile Telephony Operators: Are All Oligopoly Information Exchanges Bad for Competition' (2007) 30(2) World Competition Law and Economics Review 231.

Levy 'EU Merger Control and Non-Controlling Minority Shareholdings: The Case Against Change' (2013) 9(3) European Competition Journal 721.

Loozen 'The Application of a More Economic Approach to Restrictions by Object: No Revolution After All (T-Mobile Netherlands (C-8/08))' (2010) 31(4) European Competition Law Review 146.

MacCulloch 'The "Public" Wrong of Cartels and the Article 101 TFEU "Object Box"' (2020) 65(3) The Antitrust Bulletin 361.

Mahtani 'Thinking Outside the Object Box: An EU and UK Perspective' (2012) 8(1) European Competition Journal 1.

Mandrescu 'Restrictions of Competition by Object and Multi-Sided Platforms – Insights from Budapest Bank' (2020) CoRe Blog, posted on 14 May 2020, available at https://www.lexxion.eu/en/coreblogpost/restrictions-of-competition-by-object-and-multi-sided-platforms-insights-from-budapest-bank/ (accessed on 28 November 2020).

Meyring 'T-Mobile: Further Confusion on Information Exchanges Between Competitors' (2010) 1(1) Journal of European Competition Law & Practice 30.

Møllgaard and Overgaard 'Transparency and Competition Policy' 101, in Swedish Competition Authority 'Pros and Cons of Information Sharing' (2006) Lenanders Grafiska.

Monti *EC Competition Law* (Cambridge University Press, 2007).

Motta Competition *Policy: Theory and Practice* (Cambridge University Press, 2004).

Murray 'In Search of the Obvious: Groupement des Cartes Bancaires and "By Object" Infringements under EU Competition Law' (2015) 36(2) European Competition Law Review 47.

Nagy 'The Distinction Between Anti-competitive Object and Effect after Allianz: The End of Coherence in Competition Analysis?' (2013) 36(4) World Competition 541.

Nagy 'The New Concept of Anti-competitive Object: A Loose Cannon in EU Competition Law' (2015) 36(4) European Competition Law Review 154.

Nagy 'Are Payment Card Systems' Multilateral Interchange Fees Anticompetitive by Object under EU Competition Law?' (2020) Competition Policy International, posted on 2 June 2020, available at https://www.competitionpolicyinternational.com/are-payment-card-systems-multilateral-interchange-fees-anticompetitive-by-object-under-eu-competition-law/ (accessed on 28 November 2020).

Nazzini 'Article 81 EC Between Time Present and Time Past: A Normative Critique of "Restriction of Competition" in EU Law' (2006) 43(2) Common Market Law Review 497.

Nazzini and Nikpay 'Object Restrictions and Two-Sided Markets in EU Competition Law after Cartes Bancaires' (2014) 10(2) Competition Policy International 157.

Neven and Siotis 'Dominance and Market Definition in the Pharmaceutical Industry Following the ECJ Paroxetine Judgment' (2020) 11(3-4) Journal of European Competition Law & Practice 194.

Niels, Jenkins and Kavanagh *Economics for Competition Lawyers* (Oxford University Press, 2nd edition, 2016).

Niemeyer 'Market Information Systems' (1993) 14(4) European Competition Law Review 151.

Nitsche and von Hinten-Reed 'Competitive Impacts of Information Exchange' (2014) Charles River Associates, June 2014.

Obudu *The Boundaries of EC Competition Law* (Oxford University Press, 1st edition, 2006).

Obudu 'Indirect Information Exchange: The Constituent Elements of Hub and Spoke Collusion' (2012) 7(2) European Competition Journal 205.

OECD 'Policy Roundtables: Judicial Enforcement of Competition Law' (1996) OCDE/GD(97)200.

OECD 'Policy Roundtables: Price Transparency' (2001) DAFFE/CLP(2001)22, 11 September 2001.

OECD 'Policy Roundtables: Competition and Regulation in Retail Banking' (2006) DAF/COMP(2006)33, 27 October 2008.

OECD 'Policy Roundtables: Facilitating Practices in Oligopolies' (2007a) DAF/COMP(2008)24, 5 September 2008.

OECD 'Policy Roundtables: Trade Associations' (2007b) DAF/COMP(2007)45, 4 November 2008.

OECD 'Information Exchange Between Competitors under Competition Law' (2011) DAF/COMPLACF(2011)6, 18 July 2011.

OECD 'Unilateral Disclosure of Information with Anticompetitive Effects (e.g. Through Press Announcements)' (2012a) DAF/COMP/WP3(2012)1, 31 August 2012.

OECD 'Policy Roundtables: Unilateral Disclosure of Information with Anticompetitive Effects' (2012b) DAF/COMP(2012)17, 11 October 2012.

Osti 'Information Exchanges in the Obscure Light of Woodpulp' (1994) 15(3) European Competition Law Review 176.

Padilla 'The Elusive Challenge of Assessing Information Sharing Among Competitors under the Competition Laws', in OECD 'Policy Roundtables: Information Exchanges Between Competitors under Competition Law' (2010) DAF/COMP(2010)37, 11 July 2011, 434.

Paha 'The Economics of Competition (Law)' (2013), 8 April 2013, Version 3.0, available at https://www.uni-giessen.de/resolveuid/753da4b3e72a4651874a96f1decb7fc6 (accessed on 28 November 2020).

Paha and de Haas 'Partial Cross Ownership and Explicit Collusion' (2016) Beiträge zur Jahrestagung des Vereins für Sozialpolitik 2016: Demographischer Wandel – Session: Corporate Governance, No A11-V2, available at http://hdl.handle.net/10419/145640 (accessed on 28 November 2020).

Paukste 'Collusive Conduct in Financial Instruments Trading: A Look at the Issues of Dealing via Chatrooms' (2019) CoRe blog, posted on 5 Juni 2019, available at https://www.lexxion.eu/coreblogpost/collusive-conduct-in-financial-instrumen ts-trading-a-look-at-the-issues-of-dealing-via-chatrooms/ (accessed on 28 Nove mber 2020).

Pazzi '*Budapest Bank*: Can a Conduct Be a Restriction by Object and by Effect?' (2020) 4(3) European Competition and Regulatory Law Review 231.

Peeperkorn 'Competition Policy Implications from Game Theory: an Evaluation of the Commission's Policy on Information Exchange' (1996) CEPR/European University Institute Workshop on Recent Developments in the Design and Implementation of Competition Policy, 29 November 1996, available at http://ec.europa.eu/competition/speeches/text/sp1996_057b_en.pdf (accessed on 28 November 2020).

Peeperkorn 'Defining 'By Object' Restrictions' (2015) Concurrences No. 3-2015 40.

Petersen 'Interlocking Directorates in the European Union: An Argument For Their Restrictions' (2016) draft version, available at https://dash.harvard.edu/bitstream/handle/1/23519868/Vidir%20Petersen%20v.2%20-%20Interlocking%20directorates%20-%20final%20version%20for%20DASH.pdf?sequence=3 (accessed on 28 November 2020).

Petit 'The 'Oligopoly Problem' in EU Competition Law' (2013), posted on 6 February 2012, last revised on 18 February 2013, available at http://ssrn.com/abstract=1999829 (accessed on 28 November 2020).

Posner 'Oligopoly and the Antitrust Laws: A Suggested Approach' (1969) 21(6) Stanford Law Review 1562.

Pradelles et al. '"By Object" Restrictions of Competition Revisited: European Court of Justice Endorses Narrow Interpretation' (2014) Latham & Watkins Client Alert, 16 September 2014, Number 1741.

Prewitt and Fails 'Indirect Information Exchanges to Hub-and-Spoke Cartels: Enforcement and Litigation Trends in the United States and Europe' (2015) 1(2) Competition Law & Policy Debate 63.

Quintais 'The Empire Strikes Back: CISAC Beats Commission in General Court' (2013) 8(9) Journal of Intellectual Property Law & Practice 680.

Rabinovici 'Public Exchange of Information After Container Shipping' (2017) 8(3) Journal of European Competition Law & Practice 149.

Ray Pfeiffer 'Uniform Pricing in Concentrated Markets: Is Conscious Parallelism Prohibited by Article 85(1) of the Treaty of Rome' (1974) 7(2) Cornell International Law Journal 113.

Rivas and Van De Walle De Ghelcke 'Concerted Practices and Exchange of Information: An Overview of EU and National Case Law' (2012) e-Competitions No 34913, 9 March 2012, available at http://awa2013.concurrences.com/business-articles-awards/article/concerted-practices-and-exchange (accessed on 28 November 2020).

Rizzuto and Lynch 'Public Exchange of Information After Container Shipping' (2020) 4(2) European Competition and Regulatory Law Review 150.

Robertson 'A Counterfactual on Information Sharing: The Commission's Horizontal Guidelines 2011 Applied to the Leading Cases' (2013) 36(4) World Competition 459.

Rusu 'Eturas: Of Concerted Practices, Tacit Approval, and the Presumption of Innocence' (2016) 7(6) Journal of European Competition Law & Practice 396.

Schelling *The Strategy of Conflict* (Harvard University Press, 1960).

Seitz 'One Step in the Right Direction – The New Horizontal Guidelines and the Restated Block Exemption Regulations' (2011) 2(5) Journal of European Competition Law & Practice 452.

Selten 'A Simple Model of Imperfect Competition, Where Four Are Few and Six Are Many' (1973) 2 International Journal of Game Theory 141.

Sibony and Barbier de la Serre 'Charge de la preuve et théorie du contrôle en droit communautaire de la concurrence: pour un changement de perspective' (2007) 43(2) Revue trimestrielle de droit européen 205.

Ska, Werner and Paul 'Pay-for-Delay Agreements: Why the EU Should Judge Them by Their Effects' (2017) 8(7) Journal of European Competition Law & Practice 437.

Smith, Ridyark and Petrescu 'Price Announcements and Competition Law: An Economic Perspective' (2015) 1(2) Competition Law & Policy Debate 33.

Snyder 'A Dynamic Theory of Countervailing Power' (1996) 27(4) The RAND Journal of Economics 747.

Soames 'An Analysis of the Principles of Concerted Practice and Collective Dominance: A Distinction Without a Difference?' (1996) 17(1) European Competition Law Review 24.

Stigler 'The Economics of Information' (1961) 69(3) The Journal of Political Economy 213.

Stroux 'Is EC Oligopoly Control Outgrowing Its Infancy?' (2000) 23(1) World Competition Law and Economics Review 3.

Stroux *US and EC Oligopoly Control* (Kluwer Law International, 2004).

van der Vijver and Vollering 'Understanding Appreciability: The European Court of Justice Reviews Its Journey in Expedia' (2013) 50(4) Common Market Law Review 1133.

Van Gerven and Navarro Varona 'The Wood Pulp Case and the Future of Concerted Practice' (1994) 31(3) Common Market Law Review 575.

Vaughan et al. *EU Competition Law: General Principles* (Oxford University Press, 2006).

Vives *Oligopoly Pricing: Old Ideas and New Tools* (MIT Press, 1999).

Vives 'Information Sharing: Economics and Antitrust' 83, in Swedish Competition Authority 'Pros and Cons of Information Sharing' (2006a) Lenanders Grafiska.

Vives 'Information Sharing Among Firms' (2006b) Occasional Paper no. 07/3, October 2006, IESE Business School – University of Navarra, available at http://blog.iese.edu/xvives/files/2013/11/2007-Palgrave-info-sharing.pdf (accessed on 28 November 2020).

Wagner-von Papp '"Who Isn't That Can Inform Me?" – the Exchange of Identifying and Non-identifying Information' (2007) 28(4) European Competition Law Review 264.

Wagner-von Papp 'Information Exchange Agreements' (2012), posted on 4 March 2012, last revised on 8 October 2013, available at http://ssrn.com/abstract=2015674 (accessed on 28 November 2020).

Werden 'Economic Evidence on the Existence of Collusion: Reconciling Antitrust Law with Oligopoly Theory' (2004) 71(3) Antitrust Law Journal 719.

Whelan 'CISAC: How Difficult it Is to Prove a Concerted Practice' (2013) 4(6) Journal of European Competition Law & Practice 486.

Whish and Bailey *Competition Law* (Oxford University Press, 9th edition, 2018).

Whish 'Information Agreements' 19, in Swedish Competition Authority 'Pros and Cons of Information Sharing' (2006) Lenanders Grafiska.

Wijckmans and Tuytschaever *Horizontal Agreements and Cartels in EU Competition Law* (Oxford University Press, 2015).

Zampa and Carli 'Information Exchanges, Concerted Practices by Object and Financial/Commodity Trading' (2015) 1(2) Competition Law & Policy Debate 73.

Zelger '"By Object" Restrictions Pursuant to Article 101(1) TFEU: A Clear Matter or a Mess, and a Critical Analysis of the Court's Judgement in Expedia?' (2017) 13(2-3) European Competition Journal 356.

Table of Cases

Judgements of the CJ

Judgement of the CJ from 11 July 1985, Case C-42/84, *Remia and others v Commission (Remia)*, EU:C:1985:327, 84

Judgement of the CJ from 17 September 1985, Cases C-25/84, etc., *Ford v Commission (Ford)*, EU:C:1985:340, 56

Judgement of the CJ from 28 January 1986, Case C-161/84, *Pronuptia de Paris v Pronuptia de Paris Irmgard Schillgallis (Pronuptia)*, EU:C:1986:41, 84

Judgement of the CJ from 27 September 1988, Cases C-89/85, etc., *Ahlström Osakeyhtiö and others v Commission (Woodpulp I)*, EU:C:1988:447, 118

Judgement of the CJ from 13 July 1989, Case C-395/87, *Ministère public v Jean-Louis Tournier (Tournier)*, EU:C:1989:319, 113

Judgement of the CJ from 13 July 1989, Cases C-110/88, etc., *Lucazeau and others v SACEM and others (Lucazeau)*, EU:C:1989:326, 113

Judgement of the CJ from 11 January 1990, Case C-277/87, *Sandoz Prodotti Farmaceutici v Commission (Sandoz)*, EU:C:1989:363, 56

Judgement of the CJ from 28 February 1991, Case C-234/89, *Delimitis v Henninger Bräu (Delimitis)*, EU:C:1991:91, 86

Judgement of the CJ from 31 March 1993, Cases C-114/85, etc., *Ahlström Osakeyhtiö and others v Commission (Woodpulp II)*, EU:C:1993:120, 58, 59, 68, 75, 78, 118, 119, 120, 121, 209,

Judgement of the CJ from 15 December 1994, Case C-250/92, *Gøttrup-Klim and others v Dansk Landbrugs Grovvareselskab (Gøttrup-Klim)*, EU:C:1994:413, 84

Judgement of the CJ from 28 May 1998, Case C-7/95 P, *John Deere v Commission (John Deere)*, EU:C:1998:256, 162

Judgement of the CJ from 28 May 1998, Case C-8/95 P, *New Holland Ford v Commission (New Holland Ford)*, EU:C:1998:257, 162

Judgement of the CJ from 8 July 1999, Case C-49/92 P, *Commission v Anic Partecipazioni (Anic)*, EU:C:1999:356, 56, 57, 58, 64, 65, 66, 69, 74, 110

Judgement of the CJ from 8 July 1999, Case C-199/92 P, *Hüls v Commission (Hüls)*, EU:C:1999:358, 56, 58, 64, 65, 66

Judgement of the CJ from 16 November 2000, Case C-291/98 P, *Sarrió v Commission (Sarrió)*, EU:C:2000:631, 78

Judgement of the CJ from 19 February 2002, Case C-309/99, *Wouters and others v Algemene Raad van de Nederlandse Orde van Advocaten (Wouters)*, EU:C:2002:98, 104

Judgement of the CJ from 2 October 2002, Case C-194/99 P, *Thyssen Stahl v Commission (Thyssen Stahl)*, EU:C:2003:527, 163

Judgement of the CJ from 29 April 2004, Case C-359/01 P, *British Sugar v Commission (British Sugar)*, EU:C:2004:255, 186

Judgement of the CJ from 7 January 2004, Case C-204/00, etc., *Aalborg Portland and others v Commission (Aalborg)*, EU:C:2004:6, 61, 73, 74

Judgement of the CJ from 21 September 2006, Case C-105/04 P, *Nederlandse Federatieve Vereniging voor de Groothandel op Elektrotechnisch Gebied v Commission (FEG)*, EU:C:2006:592, 74, 75

Judgement of the CJ from 23 November 2006, Case C-238/05, *Asnef-Equifax v Ausbanc (Asnef-Equifax)*, EU:C:2006:734, 172, 173

Appeals Currently Pending Before the CJ

Judgements of the GC

Opinions of the AG

Decisions and Case Notices of the Commission

Table of Legislation, Guidelines and Treaties

Treaties

EU Legislation

categories of research and development agreements ('R&D-BER'), OJ [2010] L 335/36, 54, 130, 135, 178

Commission Regulation (EU) No 1218/2010 of 14 December 2010 on the application of Article 101(3) of the Treaty on the Functioning of the European Union to certain categories of specialisation agreements ('Specialisation BER'), OJ [2010] L 335/43, 54, 135, 178

Commission Regulation (EU) No 316/2014 of 21 March 2014 on the application of Article 101(3) of the Treaty on the Functioning of the European Union to categories of technology transfer agreements ('TT-BER'), OJ [2014] L 93/17, 54, 142-143, 147

Commission Guidelines and Notices (Soft Law)

Notice concerning Agreements, Decisions and Concerted Practice in the field of Co-operation between Enterprises ('1968 Notice'), OJ [1968] C 75/3, 151-153

Commission Notice on the definition of relevant market for the purposes of Community competition law ('Relevant Market Notice'), OJ [1997] C 372/5

Guidelines on the applicability of Article 81 of the EC Treaty to horizontal cooperation agreements ('2001 Horizontal Cooperation Guidelines'), OJ [2001] C 3/2, 153

Guidelines on the application of Article 81(3) of the Treaty ('Art 101(3) Guidelines'), OJ [2004] C 101/97, 54, 87, 88, 91, 94, 101

Guidelines on the assessment of horizontal mergers under the Council Regulation on the control of concentrations between undertakings ('Horizontal Merger Guidelines'), OJ [2004] C 31/5, 25, 26, 27, 28, 29, 30, 39, 129, 152, 232

Guidelines on the application of Article 81 of the EC Treaty to maritime transport services ('2008 Maritime Guidelines'), OJ [2008] C 245/2, 122, 153-154

Guidelines on Vertical Restraints ('Vertical Guidelines'), OJ [2010] C 130/1, 7, 10, 54, 83, 91, 134-142, 145-146

Guidelines on the applicability of Article 101 of the Treaty on the Functioning of the European Union to horizontal co-operation agreements ('Horizontal Cooperation Guidelines'), OJ [2011] C 11/1

Notice on agreements of minor importance which do not appreciably restrict competition under Article 101(1) of the Treaty on the Functioning of the European Union ('De Minimis Notice'), OJ [2014] C 291/1, 88-90, 179

Guidelines on the application of Article 101 of the Treaty on the Functioning of the European Union to technology transfer agreements ('TT-Guidelines'), OJ [2014] C 89/3, 142-146

Guidance on restrictions of competition 'by object' for the purpose of defining which agreements may benefit from the De Minimis Notice ('By Object Guidance'), SWD(2014) 198 final, 88, 91, 93, 99

Commission's Press Releases

Press release of the Commission on 22 November 2013, IP/13/1144, 'Antitrust: Commission Opens Proceedings Against Container Liner Shipping Companies', available at http://europa.eu/rapid/press-release_IP-13-1144_en.htm (accessed on 23 July 2019), 210

Press release of the Commission on 7 July 2016, IP/16/2446, 'Antitrust: Commission Accepts Commitments by Container Liner Shipping Companies on Price Transparency', available at http://europa.eu/rapid/press-release_IP-16-2446_en.htm (accessed on 23 July 2019), 211

Press release of the Commission on 13 December 2016, MEX/16/4369, 'Antitrust: The Insurance Block Exemption Regulation Expires on 31 March 2017', available at http://europa.eu/rapid/press-release_MEX-16-4369_en.htm (accessed on 23 July 2019), 17

Press release of the Commission on 16 May 2019, IP/19/2568, 'Antitrust: Commission Fines Barclays, RBS, Citigroup, JPMorgan and MUFG €1.07 Billion for Participating in Foreign Exchange Spot Trading Cartel', available at http://europa.eu/rapid/press-release_IP-19-2568_en.htm (accessed on 23 July 2019), 197

Index

O

P

R

INTERNATIONAL COMPETITION LAW SERIES

1. Ignacio De Leon, *Latin American Competition Law and Policy: A Policy in Search of Identity*, 2001 (ISBN 90-411-1542-0).
2. Wim Dejonghe & Wouter Van de Voorde (eds), *M & A in Belgium*, 2001 (ISBN 90-411-1594-3).
3. Yang-Ching Chao, Gee San, Changfa Lo & Jiming Ho (eds), *International and Comparative Competition Law and Policies*, 2001 (ISBN 90-411-1643-5).
4. Martin Mendelsohn & Stephen Rose, *Guide to the EC Block Exemption for Vertical Agreements*, 2002 (ISBN 90-411-9813-X).
5. Clifford A. Jones & Mitsuo Matsushita (eds), *Competition Policy in the Global Trading System: Perspectives from the EU, Japan and the USA*, 2002 (ISBN 90-411-1758-X).
6. Christian Koenig, Andreas Bartosch, Jens-Daniel Braun & Marion Romes (eds), *EC Competition and Telecommunications Law.* Second Edition, 2009 (ISBN 978-90-411-2564-4).
7. Jürgen Basedow (ed.), *Limits and Control of Competition with a View to International Harmonization*, 2002 (ISBN 90-411-1967-1).
8. Maureen Brunt, Economic Essays on Australian and New Zealand Competition Law, 2003 (ISBN 90-411-1991-4).
9. Ky P. Ewing, Jr., *Competition Rules for the 21st Century: Principles from America's Experience*, Second Edition, 2006 (ISBN 90-411-2477-2).
10. Joseph Wilson, *Globalization and the Limits of National Merger Control Laws*, 2003 (ISBN 90-411-1996-5).
11. Peter Verloop & Valérie Landes (eds), *Merger Control in Europe: EU, Member States and Accession States*, Fourth Edition, 2003 (ISBN 90-411-2056-4).
12. Themistoklis K. Giannakopoulos, *Safeguarding Companies' Rights in Competition and Anti-dumping/Anti-subsidies Proceedings*, Second Edition, 2011 (ISBN 978-90-411-3404-2).
13. Marjorie Holmes & Lesley Davey (eds), *A Practical Guide to National Competition Rules across Europe*, Second Edition, 2007 (ISBN 978-90- 411-2607-8).
14. Sigrid Stroux, *US and EU Oligopoly Control*, 2004 (ISBN 90-411-2296-6).
15. Tzong-Leh Hwang and Chiyuan Chen (eds), *The Future Development of Competition Framework*, 2004 (ISBN 90-411-2305-9).

16. Phedon Nicolaides, Mihalis Kekelekis and Maria Kleis, *State Aid Policy in the European Community: Principles and Practice*, Second Edition, 2008 (ISBN 978-90-411-2754-9).
17. Doris Hildebrand, *Economic Analyses of Vertical Agreements: A Self- Assessment*, 2005 (ISBN 90-411-2328-8).
18. Frauke Henning-Bodewig, *Unfair Competition Law: European Union and Member States*, 2005 (ISBN 90-411-2329-6).
19. Duarte Brito & Margarida Catalão-Lopes, *Mergers and Acquisitions: The Industrial Organization Perspective*, 2006 (ISBN 90-411-2451-9).
20. Nikos Th. Nikolinakos, *EU Competition Law and Regulation in the Converging Telecommunications, Media and IT Sectors*, 2006 (ISBN 90-411- 2469-1).
21. Mihalis Kekelekis, *The EC Merger Control Regulation: Rights of Defence. A Critical Analysis of DG COMP Practice and Community Courts' Jurisprudence*, 2006 (ISBN 90-411-2553-1).
22. Mark R. Joelson, *An International Antitrust Primer: A Guide to the Operation of United States, European Union and Other Key Competition Laws in the Global Economy*, Third Edition, 2006 (ISBN 90-411-2468-3).
23. Themistoklis K. Giannakopoulos, *A Concise Guide to the EU Anti-dumping/ Anti-subsidies Procedures*, 2006 (ISBN 90-411-2464-0).
24. George Cumming, Brad Spitz & Ruth Janal, *Civil Procedure Used for Enforcement of EC Competition Law by the English, French and German Civil Courts*, 2007 (ISBN 978-90-411-2471-5).
25. Jürgen Basedow (ed.), *Private Enforcement of EC Competition Law*, 2007 (ISBN 978-90-411-2613-9).
26. Jung Wook Cho, *Innovation and Competition in the Digital Network Economy: A Legal and Economic Assessment on Multi-tying Practices and Network Effects*, 2007 (ISBN 978-90-411-2574-3).
27. Akira Inoue, *Japanese Antitrust Law Manual: Law, Cases and Interpretation of the Japanese Antimonopoly Act*, 2007 (ISBN 978-90-411-2627-6).
28. René Barents, *Directory of EC Case Law on Competition*, 2007 (ISBN 978-90-411-2656-6).
29. Paul F. Nemitz (ed.), *The Effective Application of EU State Aid Procedures: The Role of National Law and Practice*, 2007 (ISBN 978-90-411-2657-3).
30. Jurian Langer, *Tying and Bundling as a Leveraging Concern under EC Competition Law*, 2007 (ISBN 978-90-411-2575-0).
31. Abel M. Mateus & Teresa Moreira (eds), *Competition Law and Economics – Advances in Competition Policy and Antitrust Enforcement*, 2007 (ISBN 978-90-411-2632-0).
32. Alberto Santa Maria, *Competition and State Aid: An Analysis of the EC Practice*, 2007 (ISBN 978-90-411-2617-7).
33. Barry J. Rodger (ed.), *Article 234 and Competition Law: An Analysis*, 2007 (ISBN 978-90-411-2605-4).

34. Alla Pozdnakova, *Liner Shipping and EU Competition Law*, 2008 (ISBN 978-90-411-2717-4).
35. Milena Stoyanova, *Competition Problems in Liberalized Telecommunications: Regulatory Solutions to Promote Effective Competition*, 2008 (ISBN 978-90-411-2736-5).
36. *EC State Aid Law/Le Droit des Aides d'Etat dans la CE. Liber Amicorum Francisco Santaolalla Gadea*, 2008 (ISBN 978-90-411-2774-7).
37. René Barents, *Directory of EU Case Law on State Aids*, Third Edition, 2019 (ISBN 978-94-035-1101-6).
38. Ignacio De Leon, *An Institutional Assessment of Antitrust Policy: The Latin American Experience*, 2009 (ISBN 978-90-411-2478-4).
39. Doris Hildebrand, *The Role of Economic Analysis in EU Competition Law: The European School*, Fourth Edition, 2016 (ISBN 978-90-411-6245-8).
40. Eugène Buttigieg, *Competition Law: Safeguarding the Consumer Interest. A Comparative Analysis of US Antitrust Law and EC Competition Law*, 2009 (ISBN 978-90-411-3119-5).
41. Ioannis Lianos & Ioannis Kokkoris (eds), *The Reform of EC Competition Law: New Challenges*, 2010 (ISBN 978-90-411-2692-4).
42. George Cumming & Mirjam Freudenthal, *Civil Procedure in EU Competition Cases before the English and Dutch Courts*, 2010 (ISBN 978-90-411-3192-8).
43. A.E. Rodriguez & Ashok Menon, *The Limits of Competition Policy: The Shortcomings of Antitrust in Developing and Reforming Economies*, 2010 (ISBN 978-90-411-3177-5).
44. Mika Oinonen, *Does EU Merger Control Discriminate against Small Market Companies? Diagnosing the Argument with Conclusions*, 2010 (ISBN 978-90-411-3261-1).
45. Eirik Østerud, *Identifying Exclusionary Abuses by Dominant Undertakings under EU Competition Law: The Spectrum of Tests*, 2010 (ISBN 978-90-411-3271-0).
46. Marco Botta, *Merger Control Regimes in Emerging Economies: A Case Study on Brazil and Argentina*, 2011 (ISBN 978-90-411-3402-8).
47. Jürgen Basedow & Wolfgang Wurmnest (eds), *Structure and Effects in EU Competition Law: Studies on Exclusionary Conduct and State Aid*, 2011 (ISBN 978-90-411-3174-4).
48. George Cumming (ed.), *Merger Decisions and the Rules of Procedure of the European Community Courts*, 2012 (ISBN 978-90-411-3671-8).
49. Eduardo Molan Gaban & Juliana Oliveira Domingues (eds), *Antitrust Law in Brazil: Fighting Cartels*, 2012 (ISBN 978-90-411-3670-1).
50. Giandonato Caggiano, Gabriella Muscolo & Marina Tavassi (eds), *Competition Law and Intellectual Property: A European Perspective*, 2012 (ISBN 978-90-411-3447-9).
51. Ben Van Rompuy, *Economic Efficiency: The Sole Concern of Modern Antitrust Policy? Non-efficiency Considerations under Article 101 TFEU*, 2012 (ISBN 978-90-411-3870-5).

52. Liyang Hou, *Competition Law and Regulation of the EU Electronic Communications Sector: A Comparative Legal Approach*, 2012 (ISBN 978-90-411-4047-0).
53. Barry Rodger, *Landmark Cases in Competition Law: Around the World in Fourteen Stories*, 2012 (ISBN 978-90-411-3843-9).
54. Andreas Scordamaglia-Tousis, *EU Cartel Enforcement: Reconciling Effective Public Enforcement with Fundamental Rights*, 2013 (ISBN 978-90-411-4758-5).
55. Bernardo Cortese (ed.), *EU Competition Law: Between Public and Private Enforcement*, 2014 (ISBN 978-90-411-4677-9).
56. Barry Rodger (ed.), *Competition Law: Comparative Private Enforcement and Collective Redress across the EU*, 2014 (ISBN 978-90-411-4559-8).
57. Nada Ina Pauer, *The Single Economic Entity Doctrine and Corporate Group Responsibility in European Antitrust Law*, 2014 (ISBN 978-90-411-5262-6).
58. Urška Petrovčič, *Competition Law and Standard Essential Patents: A Transatlantic Perspective*, 2014 (ISBN 978-90-411-4960-2).
59. David Telyas, *The Interface between Competition Law, Patents and Technical Standards*, 2014 (ISBN 978-90-411-5418-7).
60. Katerina Maniadaki, *EU Competition Law, Regulation and the Internet: The Case of Net Neutrality*, 2014 (ISBN 978-90-411-4140-8).
61. Horacio Vedia Jerez, *Competition Law Enforcement and Compliance across the World: A Comparative Review*, 2015 (ISBN 978-90-411-5815-4).
62. Kadir Ba, *The Substantive Appraisal of Joint Ventures under the EU Merger Control Regime*, 2015 (ISBN 978-90-411-5816-1).
63. Alberto Santa Maria, *Competition and State Aid: An Analysis of the EU Practice*, Second Edition, 2015 (ISBN 978-90-411-5818-5).
64. Lúcio Tomé Feteira, *The Interplay between European and National Competition Law after Regulation 1/2003: "United (Should) We Stand?"*, 2016 (ISBN 978-90-411-5663-1).
65. Giovanni Pitruzzella & Gabriella Muscolo (eds), *Competition and Patent Law in the Pharmaceutical Sector: An International Perspective*, 2016 (ISBN 978-90-411-5927-4).
66. Małgorzata Cyndecka, *The Market Economy Investor Test in EU State Aid Law: Applicability and Application*, 2016 (ISBN 978-90-411-6102-4).
67. Damiano Canapa, *Trademarks and Brands in Merger Control: An Analysis of the European and Swiss Legal Orders*, 2016 (ISBN 978-90-411-6717-0).
68. Inge Graef, *EU Competition Law, Data Protection and Online Platforms: Data as Essential Facility*, 2016 (ISBN 978-90-411-8324-8).
69. Anders Jessen, *Exclusionary Abuse after the* Post Danmark I *Case: The Role of the Effects-Based Approach under Article 102 TFEU*, 2017 (ISBN 978-90-411-8996-7).
70. Baskaran Balasingham, *The EU Leniency Policy: Reconciling Effectiveness and Fairness*, 2017 (ISBN 978-90-411-8479-5).
71. Eugene Stuart & Iana Roginska-Green, *Sixty Years of EU State Aid Law and Policy: Analysis and Assessment*, 2018 (ISBN 978-90-411-8869-4).

72. Anna Renata Pisarkiewicz, *Margin Squeeze in the Electronic Communications Sector: Critical Analysis of the Decisional Practice and Case Law,* 2018 (ISBN 978-90-411-6246-5).
73. Ploykaew Porananond, *Competition Law in the ASEAN Countries: Regional Law and National Systems,* 2018 (ISBN 978-90-411-9102-1).
74. Corinne Ruechardt, *EU State Aid Control of Infrastructure Funding,* 2018 (ISBN 978-90-411-9099-4).
75. Amalia Athanasiadou, *Patent Settlements in the Pharmaceutical Industry under US Antitrust and EU Competition Law,* 2018 (ISBN 978-94-035-0113-0).
76. Miroslava Marinova, *Fidelity Rebates in Competition Law: Application of the 'As Efficient Competitor' Test,* 2018 (ISBN 978-94-035-0570-1).
77. Gabriella Muscolo & Marina Tavassi, *The Interplay Between Competition Law and Intellectual Property: An International Perspective,* 2019 (ISBN 978-90-411-8687-4).
78. Fevzi Toksoy, Bahadir Balki & Hanna Stakheyeva, *Merger Control in the EU and Turkey: A Comparative Guide,* 2019 (ISBN 978-94-035-0934-1).
79. Paulo Burnier da Silveira & William Evan Kovacic (eds), *Global Competition Enforcement: New Players, New Challenges,* 2019 (ISBN 978-94-035-0283-0).
80. Giovanna Massarotto, *Antitrust Settlements: How a Simple Agreement Can Drive the Economy,* 2019 (ISBN 978-94-035-1133-7).
81. Marc Veenbrink, *Criminal Law Principles and the Enforcement of EU and National Competition Law: A Silent Takeover?,* 2020 (ISBN 978-94-035-1434-5).
82. Ferdinand Wollenschläger, Wolfgang Wurmnest & Thomas M.J. Möllers (eds), *Private Enforcement of European Competition and State Aid Law: Current Challenges and the Way Forward,* 2020 (ISBN 978-94-035-0281-6).
83. Jorge Marcos Ramos, *Firm Dominance in EU Competition Law: The Competitive Process and the Origins of Market Power,* 2020 (ISBN 978-94-035-2030-8).
84. Ingrid Margrethe Halvorsen Barlund, *Leniency in EU Competition Law,* 2020 (ISBN 978-94-035-1722-3).
85. Jan Blockx, Mens Rea *in EU Antitrust Law: When Intentions Matter,* 2020 (ISBN 978-94-035-2353-8).
86. Maria Wasastjerna, *Competition, Data and Privacy in the Digital Economy: Towards a Privacy Dimension in Competition Policy?,* 2020 (ISBN 978-94-035-2220-3).
87. Maria Fernanda Caporale Madi, *Regulating Vertical Agreements: A Comparative Law and Economics Review of the EU and Brazil,* 2020 (ISBN 978-94-035-2650-8).
88. Martin Gassler, *Information Exchange Between Competitors in EU Competition Law,* 2021 (ISBN 978-94-035-3183-0).